English La... rd
Ethnic ...

English Law and Ethnic Minority Customs

Sebastian Poulter

MA, DPhil (Oxon), Solicitor,
Senior Lecturer in Law, University of Southampton

Consulting Editor
Desmond de Silva

One of Her Majesty's Counsel,
Member of the Bar of England and Wales,
Member of the Sierra Leone Bar,
Member of the Bar of The Gambia

London
Butterworths
1986

United Kingdom	Butterworth & Co (Publishers) Ltd, 88 Kingsway, LONDON WC2B 6AB and 61A North Castle Street, EDINBURGH EH2 3LJ
Australia	Butterworths Pty Ltd, SYDNEY, MELBOURNE, BRISBANE, ADELAIDE, PERTH, CANBERRA and HOBART
Canada	Butterworth & Co (Canada) Ltd, TORONTO and VANCOUVER
New Zealand	Butterworths of New Zealand Ltd, WELLINGTON and AUCKLAND
Singapore	Butterworth & Co (Asia) Pte Ltd, SINGAPORE
South Africa	Butterworth Publishers (Pty) Ltd, DURBAN and PRETORIA
USA	Butterworth Legal Publishers, ST PAUL, Minnesota, SEATTLE, Washington, BOSTON, Massachusetts, AUSTIN, Texas and D & S Publishers, CLEARWATER, Florida

Poulter, S.M.
    English law and ethnic minority customs.
    1. Race discrimination—Law and legislation—Great Britain
    I. Title
    344.102'873   KD4095

    ISBN 0 406 18000 8

Phototypeset by Titus Wilson & Son Ltd of Kendal, Cumbria
Printed and bound by Biddles of Guildford

Preface

During the 4th century AD a Berber from North Africa crossed the Mediterranean to live in Milan. His mother later joined him there. Being a pious Christian woman and used to fasting on Saturdays in accordance with the practice of the church in her native city, she was disturbed to discover that this custom was not followed among Christians in Milan. On the other hand, fasting on Saturdays was, she knew, the norm in Rome. She therefore asked her son, who would later become known to the world as Saint Augustine, how the problem should be resolved. He in turn put the question to his guide and mentor Saint Ambrose, the Bishop of Milan. Saint Ambrose counselled that in order to avoid giving or receiving offence one should keep the custom of the church in the place in which one was living at the time. The gist of his advice has subsequently become proverbial, for he suggested that she should do what he himself did, namely not fast on Saturdays in Milan but 'when in Rome, do as the Romans do'.

The issues raised by this well-known saying provide a general framework for much of the legal analysis in this book. Should the ethnic minorities who have come to live here conform to English ways or should they be free to continue to practise their own customs in this country? More specifically, should English law adapt its principles and rules to accommodate foreign customs or should new arrivals bear the burden of any adjustment? Is the political objective to be the 'assimilation' of the minorities into the wider community or is a pattern of cultural pluralism and diversity something to be officially welcomed and encouraged as valuable in its own right?

No doubt in the case of matters of relatively little importance it is prudent for a newcomer to take the smooth path of conformity in order to save embarrassment on either side. However, where any particular custom has a deeper and more fundamental significance for him deference and politeness may well have to give way to a more positive assertion on his part that a moral principle is at stake. To have to forego a traditional or religious practice here may be portrayed as tantamount to the surrender of cultural identity and ultimately to the denial of a human right. While the avoidance of friction is clearly desirable, it can be purchased at too high a price.

Broadly speaking, the premise upon which the analysis of social and legal policy in this book is based is that any satisfactory solution must depend upon finding a proper balance and upon the acceptance of some degree of compromise. Legal recognition must be afforded to many ethnic minority customs on grounds of practicality, commonsense, individual liberty, religious tolerance and the promotion of racial harmony. However, a few restrictions and limitations must equally be imposed, in the interests of public policy, to protect certain core values in English society and to obviate any genuine and reasonable claim by the majority that ethnic minorities are obtaining preferential treatment or special dispensations which cannot be justified by reference to established legal principles. In drawing a suitable dividing line reference may usefully be made to the provisions of those international treaties to which the UK is a contracting party which are designed to protect human rights and fundamental freedoms.

While these considerations underlie the comments made in the book about the soundness of existing legal policy and the scope for possible reform, the bulk of the work is naturally devoted to an analysis of the present law. This is the first study of its kind in its attempt to provide a systematic description of those provisions of English law which tend to impinge upon ethnic minority customs. Hitherto the limited interest which English legal writers have shown in these minorities has mainly been confined either to the legal rules governing immigration to this country and the right to British nationality or to questions of racial discrimination. While these are obviously of major importance the relationship between English law and the cultures of the minorities has tended to be largely overlooked. In seeking to fill this void and to encompass a wide range of customs emanating from many corners of the world and a variety of different religions, it is hardly conceivable that I should have appreciated the nuances of each and every one of them with an equal degree of understanding. However, I have been at pains throughout the book to identify the sources for all the statements I make about the operation of ethnic minority customs so that the reader is immediately aware of the written authority upon which I am relying.

A word should perhaps be said at the outset about the way in which most of the ensuing chapters are organised. Each custom is generally introduced by a description of its mode of operation and its social significance in the context from which it is derived. Then, under the heading 'policy considerations', the custom's application and rationale within an English setting are critically examined, with possible objections and justifications being juxtaposed. Next comes a detailed analysis of the relevant provisions of English law, followed by a brief assessment of the scope for legal reform.

In the writing of this book I have received a considerable amount of help from a great many people, to all of whom I should like to express my gratitude. In particular, I owe a special debt to those friends and colleagues who have been kind enough to read and comment on sections of the book in draft, as well as offer general encouragement, namely Susan Atkins, Gerald Dworkin, Rosa Greaves, David Jackson, Paul Meredith, Fatima Mitchell, Michael Newark and Manmeet Sethi. My greatest debt, however, is to my wife Jane Bonvin whose practical experience at the Bar has enabled her to suggest numerous improvements to the text and save me from several errors. She has also done much to sustain my enthusiasm for the project throughout the long period of its gestation.

The onerous task of transforming a disorganised and barely legible manuscript into an acceptable typescript has been achieved through the patient skills of Beryl Johnstone, Fatima Mitchell and Janet Wright-Green.

I am grateful to the publishers of the *International and Comparative Law Quarterly* and *Family Law* for permission to incorporate a small amount of material which first appeared in their journals in article form.

I have endeavoured to state the law as it stands on 1 December 1985.

Southampton   Sebastian Poulter

Contents

Table of statutes

References in **bold** type indicate where the section of the Act is set out in part or in full.

Table of cases

PARA

CHAPTER 1

Introduction

A. THE ETHNIC MINORITIES

1.01 People have been coming to settle in Britain for centuries. They have come from near and far, individually and in groups, fleeing from political or religious persecution and in search of economic advancement.[1] Their influence on the national identity has been so great that one writer has reached the conclusion that the British are 'clearly among the most ethnically composite of the Europeans'.[2]

Among the many groups of immigrants who entered this country between 1400 and 1900 mention may be made of the arrival of wandering bands of gypsies during the fifteenth century, the importation of African slaves and servants from the sixteenth century onwards, the influx of Huguenot refugees from France during the sixteenth and seventeenth centuries and the re-admission of Jews in the middle of the seventeenth century for the first time since the banishment imposed upon them by Edward I in 1290.

Around the turn of the twentieth century many Jews fled to Britain from pogroms in Eastern Europe and others followed later, their numbers being increased during the 1930s by those who escaped from Nazi persecution in Germany.

Immediately after the 1939-45 War a large number of political refugees and exiles from Eastern Europe settled here. They were followed from 1948 onwards by economic migrants from the colonies and the New Commonwealth.[3] To begin with they came principally from Jamaica and other islands in the West Indies, but there were also smaller contingents from the Indian sub-continent, Cyprus, Malta and Hong Kong (amongst others). In addition, a number of West Africans came to Britain to study. Just before immigration controls were introduced in 1962 the pace of immigration from India and Pakistan began to quicken appreciably and it continued to be very substantial even after the enactment of the Commonwealth Immigrants Act 1962, principally through vouchers and the admission of wives and children and other dependent relatives. The late 1960s and early 1970s saw the arrival of a number of East African Asians, who had either found themselves squeezed out of their jobs through the process of 'Africanisation' in Kenya and Tanzania or else had been forcibly expelled from Uganda. More recently, sizeable numbers of refugees have fled here from Vietnam, Iran and Sri Lanka.

1 For excellent synopses, see V G Kiernan 'Britons Old and New' in C Holmes (ed) *Immigrants and Minorities in British Society* (London, 1978) ch 2; S. Patterson 'Immigrants and Minority Groups in British Society' in S Abbott (ed) *The Prevention of Racial Discrimination in Britain* (OUP 1971) pp 41-53.
2 J Giepel *The Europeans: An Ethnohistorical Survey* (London, 1969) pp 163-4.
3 See generally E J B Rose *Colour and Citizenship* (OUP 1969) Part II.

1.02 Due partly to the absence of an 'ethnic question' in the 1981 census and partly to the inadequacies of all government statistics on immigration[1] no reliable, detailed official figures are available as to the present ethnic composition of the population of this country. The best estimates published by the Office of Population Censuses and Surveys (OPCS) have to be based on voluntary sample surveys of only a small proportion of the population.[2] Amongst these surveys perhaps the most useful is the Labour Force Survey[3] which gave the following statistics for the 'ethnic origins' of the population of Great Britain in 1983:

White	50,774,000
Indian	789,000
West Indian or Guyanese	510,000
Pakistani	353,000
Chinese	105,000
African	92,000
Bangladeshi	83,000
Arab	69,000
Mixed	198,000
Other	110,000
Not stated (but thought to be 'white')	952,000
Total	54,035,000

It will be seen from this table that ethnic origin was being viewed in the survey as having a strong national or racial connotation. While this method of classification reflects the traditional meaning ascribed to the word 'ethnic', it is increasingly being seen as rather too narrow to be really informative. The category 'white' in the table, for instance, fails to draw attention to the presence in this country of a Jewish community of around 385,000[4] or of a Cypriot population (including both Greek and Turkish Cypriots) of roughly 140,000,[5] or the existence of at least 30,000 gypsies,[6] to take just three very obvious examples. Moreover, to describe a person as being of 'Indian' origin gives no indication of his religious or linguistic affiliations, while the words 'African' and 'Arab' may mask important cultural differences between the various peoples they comprise. Hence, the expression 'ethnic minority' is more commonly and usefully employed today to denote a minority that is recognisably distinct in terms of its shared historical experiences and its adherence to certain significant 'cultural' traditions and traits which are different from those of the majority of the population.[7] Within a broad definition of culture may be included a community's religious beliefs, rituals, values, language, customs, manners, family structure and social organisation, as well as its achievements in terms of art and knowledge. Such an approach is particularly apposite in the context of the present work which is devoted to the identification of diverse customs and practices rather than merely being concerned with a person's colour, 'race', or national origin.

1 See Runnymede Trust and Radical Statistics Race Group *Britain's Black Population* (Heinemann, 1980) pp 123-6.
2 See (1982) 28 Population Trends 1 at 3.
3 *OPCS Monitor* LFS 84/2 (1984) Table 5.
4 See *Jewish Yearbook* (1985) p 172.
5 See 'Education For All': Report of the Committee of Inquiry into the Education of Children from Ethnic Minority Groups *(Swann Committee Report)* (1985 Cmnd 9453) p 671.
6 Ibid at p 740. Unfortunately, the need to keep the book to its present length has meant that material on the nomadic lifestyle of the gypsies and the laws affecting their encampments and the education of their children has had to be omitted; on these matters, see generally B Forrester *The Travellers' Handbook* (London, 1985).
7 For a judicial application of the modern approach to the meaning of 'ethnic', see *Mandla v Dowell*

Lee [1983] 2 AC 548 at 554-6, [1983] 1 All ER 1062 at 1065-8 (Lord Fraser), discussed below at para 7.25. See also L Lustgarten *Legal Control of Racial Discrimination* (Macmillan, 1981) pp 76-7.

B. THE DEFINITION OF CUSTOMS

1.03 The word 'custom' is employed in this work in its ordinary, primary sense of a habitual or usual practice or a common way of acting. It thus encompasses not only those practices whose origins and justifications are derived from religious doctrine, but also those rooted in cultural tradition. Furthermore, it is by no means to be understood as being narrowly confined to those usages which have acquired the added force of law, though these are obviously not excluded. The intention is to cast the net broadly and examine the widest possible range of social practices found among the ethnic minorities which are, in one way or another, affected by the provisions of English law.

This inevitably means that there will be a considerable diversity in the nature and quality of the customs considered. At one end of the spectrum there will be mandatory or permissive rules of conduct backed by the force of a foreign law. Indeed what was once merely a practice may not only have hardened into a rule of customary law but may even have recently been superseded by a statutory provision to the same effect. Consideration of these customs is not excluded from the compass of this study simply because in some countries their technical legal status has been changed. Moreover, many Islamic and Jewish practices are examined, even though they are sanctioned by legal systems which are largely written and would thus not usually be designated as being 'customary' in the narrow sense of the word. The important point is that it is the actual behaviour patterns of Muslims, Jews and other minorities which fall to be examined, as much as the abstract rules of law that support or compel them.

Near the centre of the spectrum lie customs which are not regulated or enforced by law in the communities from which they originate. They are conventional practices, usually of long standing, fortified by religious beliefs or social traditions which the community regards as morally binding.

Further along the spectrum can be found practices which even the ethnic minority community as a whole does not believe are obligatory. These customs may perhaps only be followed by the most devout, or those who place a particular interpretation upon religious doctrine, or those of the older generation. Discussion of these customs is also included here provided they are commonly adhered to by a substantial group of people; otherwise every time a custom's validity were to be challenged even by a small number of dissenters or deviants it might have to be disregarded. Sometimes, of course, the fact that a custom is declining or in the final throes of decay may be relevant in deciding what importance an English court should attach to it, but there is no question of eliminating it from consideration at the outset merely because of an alleged flaw in its provenance or a lack of universal adherence and support. Strict compliance with a number of customs may, of course, decline when hitherto regular practitioners come to England and they and their children who are born here are exposed to different cultural patterns and feel a strong pressure to conform with English behaviour. In this regard much may depend upon the level of an individual immigrant's educational achievement. D J Smith has, for instance, drawn a vivid contrast between two broadly different groups of Asians living here:

'The educated group are relatively westernized and tend to be mobile, because they have smaller families, are better off and, speaking English well, do not necessarily need to live among other Asians. The uneducated group are less mobile, because they have larger and more extended families and because, not speaking English, they feel cut off from the host community and need the support of others who speak their own language and share their customs.'[1]

Finally, at the other end of the spectrum lie customs which have been formally banned by a foreign law but are still practised by a substantial section of the community concerned. The fact that these customs have been officially outlawed will, of course, have a strong bearing on the approach of the English courts, but their very persistence means that they cannot be ignored in any systematic treatment.

The adoption of a comprehensive perspective towards ethnic minority customs can be justified not only on grounds of convenience but also by reference to some of the foreign cultures of which they form a part. Islam, for example, does not draw hard and fast distinctions between religious and moral customs, on the one hand, and those that have the force of law on the other. Religion and law are inseparable concepts for Muslims. Their *sharia* or sacred law comprises not only laws enforceable by political authority but also morals, manners and obligations binding on the individual conscience alone. Much the same is true of Judaism. Again, the fact that many African customs may be backed by the force of long-standing tradition rather than religious precept or the power of a law enforcement agency in no way lessens the strength of the duty to comply with them. Hinduism is fashioned as much by local custom and tradition as by religious philosophy and Sikhs do not distinguish clearly between religious and social customs. The simple fact is that most non-Christian peoples do not draw the same sharp distinctions between law, religion and other aspects of social and cultural life as the majority of people generally do in the West. All these threads are subtly interwoven into their daily lives in a fashion deeply unfamiliar to the conventional western mode of thought. For this reason alone it would be artificial to unravel them at the outset with a view to including some and excluding others.

1 *Racial Disadvantage in Britain* (Penguin 1977) p 61.

C. THE RANGE OF ENGLISH LAW

1.04 In considering the relationship between a 'foreign' custom and English law the latter often has to be divided up for purposes of analysis and discussion into two distinct portions. What may, for convenience, be called 'English domestic law' governs matters which are regulated solely within the confines of our own legal system. Broadly speaking, if an event occurs in this country its direct legal consequences will, in the vast majority of cases, be governed exclusively by English domestic law. The second branch of English law which may often be relevant is known as 'private international law' or 'conflict of laws'. It has been described as:

'that part of law which comes into play when the issue before the court affects some fact, event or transaction that is so closely connected with a foreign system of law as to necessitate recourse to that system.'[1]

An obvious example of the application by English courts of a foreign rule of law would be where a marriage, divorce or contract took place abroad. In many instances, in order to determine its validity in the eyes of English law our courts would consider primarily whether it was recognized by the appropriate foreign law. This process of determining which system of law should govern the situation (the 'choice of law' question) is a major aspect of 'conflict of laws.'

Although the crucial factor for determining the appropriate legal system is sometimes the place where the event occurred this is far from being the universal rule. In many instances where personal status and family relations are involved the decisive criterion is the nationality, habitual residence or, most importantly in English law, the domicile of the parties. While discussion of the detailed rules of domicile is outside the compass of the present work,[2] the following principles may be regarded as forming sufficient of the central core of the subject for an understanding of subsequent chapters:

(i)   Every person must be regarded as domiciled in a single place with a separate legal system so that he may be treated as 'connected' to that system for certain purposes. Since Britain does not have a single legal system a person would have to be domiciled in, say, England and Wales or Scotland or Northern Ireland.[3]

(ii) At birth a legitimate child automatically acquires the domicile of its father while an illegitimate child automatically takes its mother's domicile. This 'domicile of origin' is usually retained until the age of 16 at least.[4]

(iii) Anyone over the age of 16 can acquire a domicile of choice which will supplant his domicile of origin. To do this he must take up residence in a country with a separate legal system and intend to remain there permanently or at any rate indefinitely. If he only intends to stay there for a limited purpose or time no fresh domicile will have been acquired. He may well, however, be treated as 'habitually resident' there if he regards the place as his home or base and he has some reasonably durable ties there. While it seems probable that many immigrants who have been accepted for settlement in this country are also domiciled here, there must still be large numbers who intend to return to their countries of origin, either when they have saved enough money to enable them to accomplish certain economic objectives there, or when they retire from work here or when they feel their lives drawing to a close.

(iv) Since 1974 a married woman has been capable of retaining and acquiring her own separate domicile, regardless of the domicile of her husband.[5] If spouses are living together they will, however, normally have the same domicile.

(v)   There is obviously no necessary coincidence between a person's domicile (or permanent home) and his nationality, which will normally have been acquired through birth, descent or registration. Nationality reflects a person's political rather than civil status and involves allegiance to a particular state.

1 Cheshire and North *Private International Law* (10th edn, 1979) p 5.
2 See generally, *Cheshire and North*, ch VII; Dicey and Morris *The Conflict of Laws* (10th edn, 1980) ch 7; Bromley *Family Law* (6th edn, 1981) pp 10-15.
3 In some federal countries a person may be domiciled for some purposes in the country as a whole (e g Australia) and for others in a particular state (e g New South Wales).
4 There is an exception in the case of a legitimate child when its parents separate and the child has a home with its mother and no home with its father. The child will then take its mother's domicile: Domicile and Matrimonial Proceedings Act 1973, s4.
5 Domicile and Matrimonial Proceedings Act 1973, s1.

D. EVIDENCE AND PROOF

1.05 It remains in this introductory chapter to draw attention to those aspects of the law of evidence which relate to the proof of ethnic minority customs. To establish the truth about some of these customs is by no means an easy task for English judges as is well illustrated by the case of *Balraj v Balraj*[1] heard by the Court of Appeal in 1980. An Indian wife, resident in India, was defending a divorce petition brought here by her husband, on the ground that she would suffer grave hardship in terms of the Matrimonial Causes Act 1973, s 5 if the marriage were to be dissolved on the basis of five years' separation. The complexity of the problem facing the President of the Family Division, as the court of first instance, was described by Cumming-Bruce LJ in the following terms:

'The family at the time they were living together were Hindus and belonged to a particular group, to use a non-technical expression, in the Hindu caste system. The social customs of different groups of Hindus, as appears from the judgment of the President, varies (sic) enormously. In order to decide the impact of first, desertion and secondly, judicial divorce upon this particular wife, it became necessary for the court to try to obtain such a grasp first of the objective social circumstances, customs and mores relevant to this family's life in India and secondly, to make an assessment of the personal suffering, handicaps and social deprivations that this particular lady had suffered in the past by reason of her husband's disregard of his matrimonial obligations. Having made that assessment, the court had then to attempt to make a further assessment of the probable impact of judicial divorce upon this particular lady and her life, circumstances and happiness. It really does not need any exaggerated rhetoric to express the appalling difficulty of such a judicial task. A task which can hardly be done with any sure prospect of complete success in a court in England brought up upon the customs and mores of the different communities in England with which the court is familiar. For a judge to try to achieve the insight necessary to grasp the prospect of this lady in the outskirts of Hyderabad and the prospects of the daughter of the family living with the mother in Hyderabad calls for the exercise of perhaps greater insight than any English judge should be required to try to exercise'.[2]

In the normal way, as is the case generally with English customs and usages, ethnic minority or foreign customs have to be proved as facts and this will probably most easily be achieved by direct evidence in the form of oral testimony from witnesses who depose either to personal knowledge of the existence of the custom in question or to particular instances of its exercise.[3] There is no need for such a person to be an 'expert'.[4] Although a court cannot usually treat a fact as sufficiently proved merely by reference to evidence accepted in a previous case, this rule does not apply to the proof of custom. The common law has long been prepared to recognise that a time must come when a custom has already been proved on a sufficient number of occasions for it to be otiose to insist that it be proved yet again.[5] In these circumstances the courts will be prepared to take judicial notice of the custom and dispense with any further proof,[6] but not otherwise.[7]

1 (1981) 11 Fam Law 110.
2 At 110-11.
3 See generally *Cross on Evidence* (6th edn, 1985) p 640; *Phipson on Evidence* (13th edn, 1982), para 27-45.
4 *Phipson, ibid*; cf the view expressed by Megaw LJ in *Singh v Singh* [1971] P 226 at 234 [1971] 2 All ER 828 at 833-4.
5 See e g *Brandao v Barnett* (1846) 12 Cl & Fin 787; *In Re Matthews, ex Powell* (1875) LR 1 Ch D 501; *George v Davies* [1911] 2 KB 445.
6 *Cross*, p 66.

7 See, e g *Khan v Khan* [1980] 1 All ER 497, [1980] 1 WLR 355 discussed below at para 5.37.

1.06 A distinction needs to be drawn between a custom not having the force of law, on the one hand, and a rule of customary law, on the other. This is because special rules are applicable to the proof of foreign law as such and these will come into play as soon as a party alleges that he is not so much relying on the existence of a custom as upon the fact that the custom actually has the force of law in a foreign country.

Whereas a rule of foreign law is, like a custom, a question of fact (at least in some senses) and one to be proved by appropriate evidence,[1] here the evidence is usually required to be provided in the form of testimony by an expert witness. Following doubts as to which persons possessed sufficient attributes to be acknowledged as 'experts',[2] the Civil Evidence Act 1972, s 4(1) now provides that a person suitably qualified on account of knowledge or experience is competent to give evidence of foreign law in civil proceedings here, irrespective of whether he has acted or is qualified to act as a legal practitioner in the country in question.

Where the evidence of the expert is uncontradicted by other expert testimony it has been said that the English court should be slow to reject it, though it is by no means conclusive.[3] Where two or more experts give conflicting evidence the court may itself refer to any relevant statutes, cases and authorities and the judge must ultimately resolve the matter himself.[4] However, it is not acceptable for a party merely to refer an English judge to what he alleges are the relevant foreign authorities on the question since the judge has no means of appraising them in the absence of guidance from an expert witness.[5] While it is possible for expert evidence to be given exceptionally by means of an affidavit, the normal course is for it to be given orally.

Only in a few instances will it be possible for an English court to take judicial notice of foreign law. One example is where the rule of foreign law is so notorious as to be common knowledge, for instance that roulette is legal in Monte Carlo.[6] However, the Civil Evidence Act 1972, s4(2) now facilitates proof by permitting the reception as evidence of foreign law of any previous determination by an English court of the point in question, provided it is reported in citable form and notice of an intention to rely upon it has been given to the other party to the proceedings. The foreign law is then taken as being in accordance with the determination unless the contrary is proved.

1 See generally *Dicey and Morris* pp 1206-16; *Cheshire and North* pp 125-30.
2 See *Cross*, pp 630-3.
3 *Sharif v Azad* [1967] 1 QB 605 at 616.
4 *Cross* p 636; *Dicey and Morris*, P 1213; *Parkasho v Singh* [1968] P 233, [1967] 1 All ER 737.
5 See *Dicey and Morris* p 1209; *Cheshire and North* p 126.
6 *Saxby v Fulton* [1909] 2 KB 208.

CHAPTER 2

Marriage

INTRODUCTION

2.01 All societies have sets of rules regulating entry into marriage. These tend to concentrate on such matters as which persons may marry, whom they may marry, who has to agree to the marriage, what ceremonies must take place and what formalities must be complied with.

Where it is a foreign marriage which falls to be adjudicated upon by the English courts the conflict of law rules lay down two general principles. First, the *formal* validity of the marriage is determined by the law of the place of celebration (*lex loci celebrationis*); second, the question of a party's capacity to marry (or the *essential* validity of the marriage) is assessed by reference to the law of his or her ante-nuptial domicile (*lex domicilii*).[1] In the vast majority of cases these rules can be applied mechanically in order to determine whether a foreign marriage is entitled to be recognized as valid for the purposes of English law. However, certain foreign marriage customs may be so markedly different from those followed in England as to give rise to doubts as to whether the normal approach should apply. In addition problems may arise where a foreign marriage custom is practised in this country and is felt to be in danger of conflicting with English norms or laws. It should be borne in mind that since in England (as elsewhere) marriage gives rise to a distinct legal status, English law may only be prepared to accord that status to a foreign union if it displays a clear resemblance to the English conception of marriage.

A variety of marriage-related topics will be dealt with in this chapter, with the principal exception of polygamy which is given separate and extended treatment in ch 3 below. Cohabitation outside marriage and extended families are dealt with in ch 4 below.

1 See *Dicey and Morris* pp 261, 285. For the rival theory that capacity to marry may be governed by the law of the intended matrimonial home, see *Cheshire and North* pp 330-41.

A. MARRIAGES WITHIN PROHIBITED DEGREES

2.02 All known societies place prohibitions on marriages between certain close relatives. However, while some impose a wide band of restrictions others operate a considerably more permissive system. At all events it is not uncommon to find that the details of the prohibitions differ from one community to the next. Both religious beliefs and traditional customs have contributed to this diversity.[1]

Marriages between persons related in the first degree (ie parent and child or brother and sister) seem to have been countenanced only very rarely. The best known examples of marriages between siblings are probably those of the Pharaohs and Ptolemies in Egypt, the Kings of Hawaii and the Incas of Peru.[2] Since such marriages were generally only permitted for the aristocratic élite it has been argued that this special privilege served to mark the distinctive pre-eminence of the rulers of these communities.[3] There are no well-known practitioners of such a custom today. On the other hand, marriages between a half-brother and a half-sister are permissible under the customary laws of certain African tribes such as the Ekoi (Yako) of Nigeria.[4]

Marriages between uncle and niece do not fall within the list of prohibitions found in the Levitical code and are therefore recognised in Jewish law.[5] Although the same stance has been adopted in some of the Lutheran churches, the Anglican and Calvinist churches have taken the opposite line and outlaw such marriages. The Roman Catholic church forbids marriages between all lineal ascendants and descendants and between collaterals to the third degree including uncles, aunts and second cousins. However, dispensations can be granted by the appropriate ecclesiastical authorities in all cases except marriages between brothers and sisters and between ascendants and descendants in contiguous generations since these are regarded as being prohibited by divine law. Uncle-niece marriages are also recognised in some systems of African customary law.[6]

Marriages between first cousins, as well as being generally permissible in Europe,[7] are especially favoured not only in many African societies and among various Arab tribes but also on the Indian sub-continent, as a method of keeping a lineage together and cementing valuable group relationships.[8]

1 For some idea of the variety, see generally Westermarck *The History of Human Marriage* (2nd edn, London 1948) ch XIV.
2 See Mair *Marriage* (Penguin, 1971) p 27; *Westermarck* pp 290-4.
3 Beattie *Other Cultures* (London, 1964) p 126.
4 Obi *Modern Family Law in Southern Nigeria* (Sweet & Maxwell, 1966) p 168.
5 See Lev 18:12-14 in terms of which aunt-nephew marriages are, however, forbidden.
6 See Allott *The Limits of Law* (Butterworths 1980) p 123; Kasunmu and Salacuse *Nigerian Family Law* (Butterworths 1966) p 80.
7 *Westermarck* p 296.
8 *Mair* pp 24-7, ch 3; Radcliffe-Brown and Fortes (eds) *African Systems of Kinship and Marriage* (OUP 1950) pp 53-5, 60-1, 66; Pearl *A Textbook on Muslim Law* (London 1979) p 48; *Beattie* pp 128-9. The commonest type of 'preferential marriage' in Africa is 'cross-cousin' marriage, i e with mother's brother's daughter or father's sister's daughter.

2.03 Turning from relationships of consanguinity to those of affinity, since Christian doctrine treated husband and wife as one flesh it was logical for canon law to impose a ban on marriages between a wide range of persons related to one another by marriage.[1] Thus a widower was prevented from marrying his deceased wife's sister and a widow from marrying her deceased husband's brother. However, the Lutheran church took the opposite viewpoint and allowed such marriages[2] and in many African societies these two types of marriage have traditionally been seen as particularly desirable.[3] The former possessed the merit of providing a sympathetic female substitute who might be expected to look after any of her deceased sister's children with special care. It also ensured that any bridewealth[4] paid for the first wife would not be wasted if she died prematurely, since her younger sister could then step into her shoes without the husband or his family being called upon to make a further substantial payment. Marriages to a deceased husband's brother were also commonly connected with the payment of bridewealth. If the husband died prematurely, and particularly in those cases where his wife had not yet borne him any children, the bridewealth would not have been fully productive in adding more members to the husband's lineage. It was therefore desirable for one of his younger brothers to take over the responsibility for the widow with a view to fathering children in the name of the deceased.[5] A similar practice known as the 'levirate' was recognised in Jewish law.[6] Both these customs reflect the widespread notion of marriage as an alliance between two groups or lineages in terms of which one member of the basic unit (the lineage) may replace another.

1 Jackson, *The Formation and Annulment of Marriage* (Butterworths, 2nd edn, 1969) pp 10, 21.
2 See *Brook v Brook* (1861) 9 HLC 193.
3 *Radcliffe-Brown and Fortes* pp 64-5; Poulter *Family Law and Litigation in Basotho Society* (Oxford 1976) pp 157-60, 260-4; Morris 'Marriage Law in Uganda' in Anderson (ed) *Family Law in Asia and Africa* (London, 1968) pp 35-6.
4 Bridewealth is discussed at para 2.35 below.
5 See *Beattie* pp 119-20.
6 See Deut 25:5-6; H Schneid (ed) *Marriage* (Jerusalem, 1973) pp 49-52.

2.04 In certain societies the prohibited marriage relationships extend well beyond various degrees of consanguinity and affinity to an even wider circle of people. In Muslim law, for instance, a 'foster' relationship creates an impediment. This distinctive Islamic prohibition arises whenever a mother has given milk not only to her own child but also to another's child.[1] The two children are thus barred from intermarrying as would be a male child and its 'foster' mother. A Muslim woman is barred from marrying a non-Muslim husband.[2] Jewish law prohibits a Jew from marrying a Gentile[3] and in the past Hindus were generally prohibited from marrying outside their caste.[4]

1 *Pearl* p 48.
2 Ibid pp 49-50.
3. Elon (ed) *The Principles of Jewish Law* (Jerusalem, 1975) pp 376-7.
4. See Minattur (ed) *The Indian Legal System* (Oceana, 1978) p 641; *Chetti v Chetti* [1909] P 67. The law was changed by the Hindu Marriage Act 1955, ss 5, 29.

Policy considerations

2.05 With the decline in the importance attached to religious doctrine in England the principal objections to allowing marriages with close relatives would appear to rest on moral, genetic and social grounds. In the case of consanguinity it can be argued both that such marriages are offensive in running contrary to the natural order and that they are liable to result in any offspring inheriting undesirable genetic characteristics. To some extent these two arguments coincide and would both probably be expressed more vehemently the closer the relationship in question. Relationships based on affinity would only appear to be objectionable on social grounds in situations where they are likely to disturb normal family life as, for example, where following a divorce a man marries his step-daughter after she has spent her childhood in his household.

Foreign systems which impose wider restrictions than those obtaining under English law may be challenged on the ground that they are unnecessarily restrictive and deprive their subjects of a freedom of choice to which they are entitled in such an important sphere of life. Thus, to take three examples the traditional Hindu prohibition on marriages outside one's caste may be perceived as an undue interference with individual liberty, as may the discriminatory restriction imposed upon Muslim women and the general bar in Jewish law on Jews marrying non-Jews.

English domestic law

2.06 So far as marriages in England are concerned, the law has undergone a progressive process of liberalisation in the bars of affinity over the past 80 years, while retaining the traditional degrees of consanguinity which had become firmly established by the time of the Reformation.[1]

Those persons whom a man may not marry because of the close blood relationship are his grandmother, mother, daughter, granddaughter, sister, aunt and niece.[2] Before the present century there were sweeping bars of affinity derived from canon law and extending *pari passu* to virtually all the relationships which were affected by the bars of consanguinity.[3] Many of these became particularly irksome following the Marriage Act 1835 (Lord Lyndhurst's Act), which rendered future marriages within the prohibited degrees void ab initio rather than merely voidable, as had been the position previously. Eventually after a long campaign and bitter controversy[4] the law was reformed in 1907 by allowing a man to marry his deceased wife's sister[5] and in 1921 a woman was allowed to marry her deceased husband's brother.[6] Ten years later the principle behind these two changes was extended to eight other prohibited degrees of affinity[7] and finally in 1960 the prohibitions of affinity were further relaxed by allowing the foregoing reforms to apply not only to those who had lost their spouses through death but also to those whose marriages had been terminated by divorce or annulment and even though their former spouse was still alive.[8] As a result the principal bars of affinity today serve to prevent a man from marrying his daughter-in-law, his step-daughter, his mother-in-law and his step-mother.

Finally, adoption creates a bar between the adopted child and its adoptive parents.[9] The adopted child also retains all the bars of consanguinity and affinity derived from its natal family,[10] but is not barred from marrying blood relatives of its adoptive parents nor its adopted siblings. No new prohibited degrees are created by the fact that a child has been fostered.

1 The prohibited degrees were laid down in 1563 by Archbishop Parker and were adopted in 1603 in the 99th Canon and set out in the Book of Common Prayer.
2 Marriage Act 1949, s1 and First Schedule.
3 See *Jackson* pp 21-3.
4 See *Radcliffe-Brown and Fortes* pp 62-3; *R v Dibdin* [1910] P 57.
5 Deceased Wife's Sister's Marriage Act 1907.
6 Deceased Brother's Widow's Marriage Act 1921.
7 Marriage (Prohibited Degrees of Relationship) Act 1931.
8 Marriage (Enabling) Act 1960.
9 Marriage Act 1949, Sch 1 as amended by the Children Act 1975, Sch 1, para 4 and Sch 3, para 8.
10 Children Act 1975, Sch 1, paras 3 and 7.

English conflicts law

2.07 This somewhat complex branch of the law is best described by reference to three separate situations.[1]

1 See generally *Dicey and Morris* pp 285-97.

1 Marriages in England by foreign domiciliaries

2.08 A marriage contracted in England in violation of the prohibited degrees appears to be void not only in the case of those domiciled in England but also where both spouses are domiciled in a country whose law permits such marriages. Although this rule is an exception to the general principle that capacity to marry is governed by the *lex domicilii* and there is no precedent in point, this seems to be the view of the most authoritative writers.[1]

The *lex domicilii* does govern the position, however, where its prohibitions are more extensive than those of English law. Thus if two cousins marry in England in defiance of their *lex domicilii* which forbids such marriages, the marriage will be void.[2] To this rule there appear to be two exceptions.

First, where one of the parties has an English domicile and the other a *lex domicilii* which is more restrictive, the marriage will be valid because of the primacy accorded to the English rules.[3] This exception, which is based on the case of *Sottomayor v De Barros (No 2)*, has been criticised by some commentators as anomalous and chauvinistic,[4] but it has been stoutly defended by others, either on broad grounds of public policy,[5] or as a reflection of the need to apply English law as the *lex fori* where one of the parties is domiciled here and the marriage is celebrated in this country.[6]

The second exception, which seems far easier to justify on grounds of public policy, arises where the foreign *lex domicilii* is not only more restrictive than English law but 'penal' (i e discriminatory). As a result, it will be ignored by the English courts. Thus if prior to 1955 two Hindus domiciled in India but from different castes had married in England in contravention of their *lex domicilii* the marriage would probably be treated as valid here.[7] The same approach would probably be adopted towards a marriage here between a Muslim woman and a non Muslim man, i e the marriage would be recognised as fully valid in English law, despite any rule in her *lex domicilii* to the contrary.

1 See *Dicey and Morris* pp 299-300; *Cheshire and North* p 343.
2 *Sottomayor v De Barros (No 1)* (1877) 3 PD 1.
3 *Sottomayor v De Barros (No 2)* (1879) 5 PD 94; *Chetti v Chetti* [1909] P 67.
4 See *Dicey and Morris* pp 286, 302; *Cheshire and North* pp 341-2; Law Com Working Paper No 89: Private International Law: Choice of Law Rules in Marriage (1985) para 3.17.
5 Kahn-Freund 'Reflections on Public Policy in the English Conflict of Laws' (1953) 39 Transact Grotius Soc 39 at 54-9.
6 D Jackson *The 'Conflicts' Process* (Oceana, 1975) pp 335-8, 342-3.
7 *Dicey and Morris* pp 303-4.

2 Marriages abroad by English domiciliaries

2.09 A foreign marriage in violation of the English prohibitions will be void if one or both of the spouses possessed an English domicile, even if it is valid by the *lex loci celebrationis*[1] or the *lex domicilii* of one of the spouses.[2] This predictable rule prevents a person domiciled here from making an excursion abroad for the express purpose of achieving what he or she cannot accomplish in England. Thus in 1860 the House of Lords ruled in *Brook v Brook*[3] that a Lutheran marriage in Denmark was void because the couple were a man and his deceased wife's sister and both parties were domiciled in England. They had expressly gone to Denmark for the wedding because the laws of that country did not prohibit such marriages.

1 *Brook v Brook* (1861) 9 HLCas 193; *Re De Wilton, De Wilton v Montefiore* [1900] 2 Ch 481.
2 *Mette v Mette* (1859) 1 Sw & Tr 416; *Re Paine, Re Williams, Griffith v Waterhouse* [1940] Ch 46.
3 (1861) 9 HLCas 193.

3 Marriages abroad by foreign domiciliaries

2.10 In accordance with the general principle that capacity is governed by the parties' *lex domicilii*, such foreign marriages are recognised as valid by English law if they conform with the *lex domicilii*, even if they violate the prohibited degrees laid down in English law. Thus in *Re Bozzelli's Settlement Husey-Hunt v Bozzelli*[1] a marriage contracted in Italy in 1880 between a widow and her deceased husband's brother, both of whom were domiciled there, was recognised as valid by the English courts. However, it used to be argued during the last century by some academic writers (notably Story)[2] that there was an exception to the general rule in the case of marriages deemed incestuous by the 'laws of all Christian countries'.[3]

The correctness of this view came up for consideration in 1965 in *Cheni v Cheni*.[4] The couple, an uncle and his niece, were validly married by Sephardic Jewish rites in Egypt, the country of their domicile. Some 30 years later they came to England and acquired a domicile of choice here. The validity of their marriage for purposes of English law arose as a preliminary issue when the wife petitioned for a divorce on the ground of her husband's cruelty. Sir Jocelyn Simon P traced the development of judicial attitudes towards Story's exception, showing how it had been referred to with approval in a number of nineteenth century cases. Story had dealt with incest and polygamy together and the same revulsion the Victorian judges expressed towards polygamy[5] was manifested against incestuous marriages. Since, however, there was not a single case in which Story's alleged exception had actually been applied, Simon P took the robust view that it did not represent the law. He therefore repudiated it and upheld the validity of the Egyptian marriage. In its place he put forward an alternative approach in terms of which an English court might refuse recognition where the result might otherwise be unconscionable in terms of English public policy. He indicated that he was influenced in this connection more by our own domestic rules governing the crime of incest (which do not include the uncle-niece relationship) than by attempting to discover what the legal position was in the majority of other countries. The true test, he declared, was

'whether the marriage is so offensive to the conscience of the English court that it should refuse to recognise and give effect to the proper foreign law. In deciding that question the court will seek to exercise common sense, good manners and a reasonable tolerance. In my view it would be altogether too queasy a judicial conscience which would recoil from a marriage acceptable to many peoples of deep religious convictions, lofty ethical standards and high civilisation.'[6]

He also took into account the circumstances of the particular case in which the validity of the marriage had never been called into question during the 35 years of its existence and of which there had been born a child who was legitimate in any event in the eyes of English law because this was his status according to Egyptian law.[7]

In view of this decision it seems clear that uncle-niece marriages contracted abroad in conformity with the parties' *lex domicilii* will invariably be recognised as valid in England. No greater genetic risks are involved in aunt-nephew marriages and since the criminal law of incest does not apply to such relationships the question arises whether a future English court would afford them equal treatment. The reason they are not permitted by Jewish law is because they are considered to reverse the natural order of authority,[8] but whether such a patriarchal justification would carry sufficient weight today to deny them recognition here must surely be extremely doubtful.[9] Recognition should also be forthcoming in the case of a marriage between a man and his step-daughter. The relationship is again not within the incest prohibitions laid down by the criminal law[10] and such couples are now entitled to marry in Australia, Sweden and West Germany, to mention just three examples.[11] Indeed such marriages may also be contracted in England, albeit through the cumbrous and expensive process of a private and personal Act of Parliament.[12]

Greater difficulties might perhaps be encountered if an English court were to be asked to recognise a marriage between a half-brother and a half-sister, assuming that the marriage was recognised as valid by the parties' *lex domicilii*. This type of relationship does fall within the criminal law of incest,[13] and Dicey and Morris express the view that such a marriage would for most purposes be refused recognition in England on grounds of public policy.[14] The proportion of genes which the couple would have in common is, nevertheless, exactly the same as in an uncle-niece marriage[15] and presumably in many cases the genetic aspect could hardly cause an English court much anxiety since the couple would often already have had their children by the time proceedings were instituted. Moreover, there is a certain inconsistency in refusing recognition to such marriages once they have been contracted abroad and yet freely allowing marriages between adoptive siblings who have spent their entire childhood together to be contracted in this country. It is also worth bearing in mind that marriages between a half-brother and a half-sister can now be lawfully entered into in Sweden, provided the dispensation of the King in Council is first obtained.[16]

It is submitted that in all these cases the test propounded above by Simon P remains an appropriate one for the courts to apply, reflecting the need to balance any feeling of repugnancy derived from an English scale of values against a willingness to tolerate diversity, especially where it can be demonstrated that other civilised societies recognise the type of marriage in question. In modern conditions the Christian doctrine propounded with such vigour in the Victorian cases should have little or no place. Instead the English court should not only assess the type of marriage in question in general terms, but also bear in mind the characteristics of the particular marriage and the purposes for which recognition is sought and what its other effects might be. For example, if the couple, as in *Cheni*, had lived for a long period in a country which recognised the marriage, had grown-up children and had subsequently come to England there might well be circumstances in which recognition was appropriate. Examples might include claims for financial support, succession rights and compensation for a fatal accident. Were an English judge to express an uncompromising feeling of revulsion in a case where justice required the grant of the relief or adjudication sought this might well be to sacrifice practical assistance for the sake of an outmoded sense of outrage. Much depends upon the nature of the question presented to the court,[17] for it is the application of the foreign law to the facts of a particular case in England which is at issue, not the desirability of the foreign rule itself. Moreover, the strength of any public policy argument raised against recognition needs to be related to the intensity of the link which connects the facts of the case with this country.[18]

1 [1902] 1 Ch 751.
2 See e g his *Conflict of Laws* (8th edn, 1883) para 113.
3 See *Dicey and Morris* p 288.
4 [1965] P 85, [1962] 3 All ER 873.
5 See para 3.04 below.
6 At 99.
7 See *Re Bischoffsheim* [1948] Ch 79.
8 See *Cheni v Cheni* [1965] P 85 at 92.
9 Such marriages may now be lawfully contracted in Australia — see Family Law Act 1975, s 51(3).
10 Sexual Offences Act 1956, ss 10 and 11.
11 In France the prohibition on such marriages may be lifted by the President for 'grave cause': Civil Code Book I, art 164.
12 See e g the Edward Berry and Doris Eilleen Ward Marriage (Enabling) Act 1980.

13 Sexual Offences Act 1956, ss 10(2) and 11(2).
14 At p 289. Cf the less positive statement at p 87 that the English courts 'might' refuse to recognise such a marriage.
15 See *The Marriage Law of Scotland* (Kilbrandon Report; 1969 Cmnd 4011) p 16.
16 See Baxter 'Recent Developments in Scandinavian Family Law' (1977) 26 ICLQ 150 at 158.
17 See *Dicey and Morris* p 84.
18 See Kahn-Freund 'Reflections on Public Policy in the English Conflict of Laws' (1953) 39 Transact Grotius Soc 39 at 58.

The scope for reform

2.11   There would appear to be room for three types of reform to be considered. The first possibility would be to introduce greater flexibility with regard to the bars of consanguinity in domestic English law by making only a limited number of prohibitions absolute and others subject to legal restrictions. Thus a court might perhaps be authorised to grant leave to marry in the case of uncle-niece and aunt-nephew relationships where the genetic risks had been investigated and found to be low and where there were no social objections. It might be thought particularly appropriate to give the necessary permission where the couple belonged to a community whose religion or customs authorised such marriages. Equally there might be a case for limiting the total freedom of cousins to marry by insisting that they must at least have received some prior genetic counselling.

In recent years evidence has been emerging about the dangers of some cousin marriages among Asians in England.[1] According to a survey in Bradford[2] Asian children there suffer from a far higher degree of physical and mental handicap than non-Asian children. One explanation advanced for this phenomenon is that marriages between cousins, which are common in the Asian community, allow recessive genes to become operative. While in normal circumstances the risks of this occurring might not be particularly great,[3] it would appear that there is a pool of unhealthy genes in this particular community and their harmfulness is being enhanced by the custom of cousin marriage.

A legal ban upon cousin marriages would hardly seem appropriate in view of the fact that the danger comes not from the nature of the relationship but from the possession of hereditary defects by the two individuals concerned. However, compulsory genetic counselling, although initially likely to be unpopular, might help to solve the problem. Admittedly, parties who wish to be married in England have never been legally required to undergo a medical examination in the past and even in France, where this is compulsory, there is no provision for notification of the results to the other party. In its report on the marriage law of Scotland the Kilbrandon Committee supported the principle of a pre-marital medical examination as a responsible step for people to take though it declined to recommend its introduction as a statutory requirement.[4] Even so, if a compulsory medical examination can reduce the risks of children being born with severe handicaps its introduction is surely worthy of serious consideration.

The effectiveness of genetic counselling ultimately depends, of course, on a long-term programme of education and the number of Asian cousin marriages may well decrease in any event as a result of a greater trend towards marrying spouses brought up in this country rather than relatives arriving directly from the Indian subcontinent.[5] Another possible explanation for some of these children's handicaps may be that they are being caused by the medicines and cosmetics used by many pregnant Asian women, certain of which contain heavy metals such as lead, cadmium and mercury. This aspect is considered in a subsequent chapter.[6]

Second, consideration might be given to removing many of the remaining bars of affinity on the ground that there is little to justify their retention in a secular society.[7] A number of private members' bills have been introduced in Parliament in recent years designed to achieve such a reform[8] and in 1984 a committee appointed by the Archbishop of Canterbury reported in favour of a substantial relaxation of current restrictions.[9] The principal difficulty lies in deciding how best to protect step-daughters against undue sexual pressures from step-fathers at a time when the numbers of remarriages following divorce are on the increase. One solution would be to retain the ban on step-parent marriages where the step-child had at any time been treated by the step-parent as a child of his family.[10] Alternatively in such a case a marriage could be authorised only where the step-child had attained the age of 21.[11]

Third, Parliament might perhaps consider reversing the rule that primacy is accorded to English law where one party has an English domicile and the other party a foreign domicile and a marriage takes place in England in violation of the prohibited degrees of the foreign domicile.[12] Provided the rule of the foreign *lex domicilii* is not penal or discriminatory, such a marriage should arguably not be valid but void, in conformity with the general principle that capacity to marry is governed by each spouse's antenuptial domicile.

1 See Arthurton 'Some medical problems of Asian immigrant children' (1977) *Journal of Maternal and Child Health* 316; Lobo *Children of Immigrants to Britain* (London 1978) pp 20-1.
2 Dr Marjorie Penwill 'Handicap in Asian Children in Bradford' (unpublished paper presented to Medical Women's International Association in Birmingham, 1980).
3 See Moore, 'A Defense of First Cousin Marriage' (1961) 10 Cleveland-Marshall Law Review 136.
4 (1969 Cmnd. 4011) paras 42-4.
5 *Lobo* pp 21, 105 and see further para 2.21 below.
6 See para 10.20 below.
7 See Chester and Parry 'Reform of the Prohibitions on Marriage of Related Persons' (1983) 13 Fam Law 237.
8 See, e g Marriage (Enabling) Bills, 1979, 1980 and 1981.
9 'No Just Cause' (London, 1984).
10 See ibid ch 13 (minority report).
11 Ibid chs 10-12 (majority report).
12 Abolition of the rule is proposed in Law Com Working Paper No 89: Private International Law: Choice of Law Rules in Marriage (1985) paras 3.45-3.48.

B. CHILD-MARRIAGES

2.12 Marriages of girls under the age of 16 are not uncommon in many of the countries of Africa, Asia and Latin America. It is very rare for the customary law of an African society to specify a minimum age and since the consent of the couple's parents or guardians will almost invariably be required, it is for them to decide when they consider their children to be ready for marriage.

This is usually at puberty. Under Islamic law there is similarly no fixed minimum age. Girls should not actually be handed over to their husbands before puberty, but their guardians can still contract them in marriage before they reach puberty. In a number of African and Islamic countries, however, statutory reforms have recently been enacted in an attempt to curb child marriages. Criminal penalties have been imposed on those who marry girls under 16 in Pakistan and Bangladesh, or under 18 in India, though any such marriage which is actually contracted is treated as valid.[1] In many states, of course, there has until very recently been no system of compulsory registration of births, hence making it difficult to be sure exactly how old a child is. In Latin America some countries, including Argentina, Colombia, Cuba and El Salvador specify the minimum age for girls as 14, while in Europe the minimum age for girls in Austria is 14 and in Turkey and France 15.[2] In Jewish law boys can marry at 13 and girls at twelve and a half.[3]

In many societies early marriage for girls is associated with a belief that their natural role in life is to be wives and mothers and that they should start on the task as soon as practicable. Once they have reached puberty they are considered to be marriageable. To delay marriage increases the risk of a girl being seduced and giving birth to an illegitimate child, thus bringing shame on her family and considerably reducing her chances of marriage to anyone other than the father of her child. Such attitudes will only begin to change as wider educational and employment opportunities are made available to women and as they achieve greater equality with men throughout the world.

1 *Pearl* pp 43-4. See also Anderson *Law Reform in the Muslim World* (London, 1976) pp 103-4; T Mahmood *Muslim Personal Law* (New Delhi, 1977) pp 51-3. Reform has been complicated by the fact that the Prophet Mohamed himself married one of his wives when she was very young.
2 See generally 'Minimum age at marriage: 20 years of legal reform' (1977) 4 *People* no 3 (International Planned Parenthood Federation fact sheet).
3 Elman (ed) *An Introduction to Jewish Law* (London, 1958) pp 33-4; Elon (ed) *The Principles of Jewish Law* (Jerusalem, 1975) pp 358-9. Marriage of a girl under the age of 17 in Israel is an offence, but the marriage itself remains valid.

Policy considerations

2.13   The two principal objections to very early marriage are first, that it raises considerable doubts as to whether a free and informed consent has been given by the child and second, that the chances of a successful and lasting union may be reduced where the spouses are immature and their personalities have been given insufficient time to develop.

The first objection carries particular weight in Western societies where marriage is meant to be based on individual choice, not only of a partner but also as to whether to marry at all. However, in many other cultures 'love matches' are not regarded as specially desirable and the choice of a spouse is largely left in the hands of parents and relatives.[1] Marriage is treated as the universal norm for a woman and spinsters are virtually unknown.

The second objection is based on English divorce statistics which tend to show that the marriages of teenage brides are more likely to end in divorce than those of women who marry when they are 20 or older.[2] Again, however, their relevance may well be limited to those sections of English society in which the desire for personal fulfilment is a more highly cherished value than family stability. There is no evidence to show that child marriages in other cultures are necessarily less satisfactory than marriages as a whole are in England.

Having said that, it is important to stress the growing concern, worldwide, about the extent to which child marriages reflect the general oppression of women in many societies. This is apparent from the inclusion of the following provision in the Convention on the Elimination of All Forms of Discrimination against Women:

'The betrothal and marriage of a child shall have no legal effect, and all necessary action, including legislation, shall be taken to specify a minimum age for marriage . . . .'[3]

Significantly, however, the Convention contains no definition of the word 'child' and no uniform minimum age for marriage is specified for states parties to comply with, though in 1965 the UN General Assembly recommended 15.

1 See para 2.19 below.
2 See Thornes and Collard *Who Divorces?* (Routledge, 1979) pp 71-80.
3 Art 16(2). The Convention came into force in 1982, but has not been ratified by the UK.

English domestic law

2.14 Prior to the Age of Marriage Act 1929 there was, strictly speaking, no absolutely fixed minimum age for marriages contracted in England. The rule of canon law, which was later adopted by the common law, was that a child acquired capacity to marry on attaining puberty and there was a rebuttable presumption that this stage was reached at the age of 14 for boys and 12 for girls.[1] Marriages entered into before puberty were not void ab initio but could be avoided by either party on reaching puberty.[2]

The 1929 Act changed the law in two important respects. First, it introduced a minimum age of 16 for both boys and girls. Second, any marriage entered into below that age was rendered void ab initio. The provisions of the Act are now to be found in the Marriage Act 1949, s 2 which states:

'A marriage solemnised between persons either of whom is under the age of sixteen shall be void.'

Interestingly, one of the principal reasons which seems to have prompted the initiation of the reform in 1929 was Britain's desire to assist in a campaign to raise the age of marriage overseas.[3] Obviously if such arguments were to sound at all convincing English law needed itself to set a good example. The League of Nations was attempting to prevent trafficking in women and children and early marriages were a device employed by those engaged in this unsavoury business. As the House of Lords Select Committee reported:

'It may be difficult to prove that, in Great Britain, the disparity between the legal age of marriage and the facts of national life impedes the progress of morality. But there is evidence that it does impair the influence of Great Britain in co-operating in the work of the League of Nations for the protection and welfare of children and young people, and does prejudice the nation's effort to grapple with the social problems arising from the early age at which marriages are contracted in India.'[4]

1 Jackson *The Formation and Annulment of Marriage* pp 26, 159.
2 Bromley, *Family Law* (6th edn, 1981) p 32.
3 Cretney *Principles of Family Law* (4th edn, 1984) p 56.
4 74 HL Official Report (5th series) col 259.

English conflicts law

1 Marriages in England by foreign domiciliaries

2.15 A marriage contracted in England in contravention of the minimum age of 16 would appear to be void not only in the case of parties domiciled in England but also where both spouses are domiciled in a country which would recognise the marriage as valid. This seems to be yet another exception to the normal rule of leaving the issue to be determined by the *lex domicilii*.[1] If, however, the parties' *lex domicilii* prescribes a higher minimum age than 16 and the couple marry in England in contravention of their *lex domicilii* the marriage will be void.[2]

1 *Dicey and Morris* pp 299-300.

2 Ibid p 292. The exceptions mentioned in para 2.08 above in connection with prohibited degrees may also apply here.

2 Marriages abroad by English domiciliaries

2.16 A foreign marriage involving a party under the age of 16 would be void if one or both of the spouses possessed an English domicile, even if it was valid by the *lex loci celebrationis* or the *lex domicilii* of one of the spouses.

This emerges clearly from the decision in *Pugh v Pugh*.[1] An Englishman who was domiciled in England married a 15 year-old Hungarian girl in Austria at the end of the 1939-45 War. They subsequently came to live in England and when their relationship deteriorated the wife brought matrimonial proceedings in the English courts. The initial question was whether the couple had ever been validly married in view of the provisions of the 1929 Act. This could only be resolved by determining whether the Act was intended to have extra-territorial effect upon English domiciliaries who married abroad. Pearce J held that this was indeed part of the mischief of the common law which the Act was designed to remedy:[2]

'According to modern thought it is considered socially and morally wrong that persons of an age at which we now believe them to be immature and provide for their education should have the stresses, responsibilities and sexual freedom of marriage and the physical strain of childbirth. Child marriages are by common consent believed to be bad for the participants and bad for the institution of marriage. Acts making carnal knowledge of young girls an offence are an indication of modern views on this subject. The remedy that "the Parliament hath resolved" for this mischief and defect is to make marriages void where *either* of the parties is under sixteen years of age' (italics added).

'To curtail the general words of the Act so that a person can evade its provisions by merely going abroad and entering into a marriage where one of the parties is under sixteen in some country ... where canon law still prevails, and then returning to live in this country after the marriage, seems to me to be encouraging rather than suppressing "subtle inventions and evasions for the continuance of the mischief".'

The marriage was therefore declared void. This would not have been a particularly surprising result had it been the Englishman who was under the age of 16. However, the Act was held to be applicable to cases where it was the foreign domiciliary who was below the minimum age, even though her own *lex domicilii* treated the marriage as valid. This can, of course, still be justified as a valuable protection for English domiciliaries against the risks of an unstable marriage.

1 [1951] P 482, [1951] 2 All ER 680.
2 At 492.

3 Marriages abroad by foreign domiciliaries

2.17 In accordance with principle such marriages do not fall within the ambit of the 1929 Act but will be recognised as valid by English law provided they comply with the *lex domicilii*, even if that law prescribes a minimum age below 16.   Such a situation came before the English courts in *Alhaji Mohamed v Knott*.[1]

An Islamic marriage was contracted in Nigeria between two Nigerian domiciliaries at a time when the bride was only just 13. Three months later the couple arrived in England where the husband was to pursue a course of study. He went for medical treatment of a venereal disease and introduced his young wife to the doctor, indicating that he had already taken her to a clinic to be fitted with a contraceptive appliance. The doctor was sufficiently concerned about the girl's welfare to report the matter to the police who thereupon brought a complaint to a juvenile court that she was in need of care because she was being exposed to moral danger. The court made a 'fit person order' under the Children and Young Persons Act 1963 and admitted her to the care of a local authority. The reasons which prompted the court to conclude that the girl was in moral danger were summed up as follows:

'Here is a girl, aged 13, or possibly less, unable to speak English, living in London with a man twice her age to whom she has been married by Muslim law. He admits having had sexual intercourse with her at a time when according to the medical evidence the development of puberty had almost certainly not begun . . . . He further admits that since the marriage, which took place as recently as January of this year, he has had sexual relations with a prostitute in Nigeria from whom he has contracted venereal disease. In our opinion a continuance of such an association, notwithstanding the marriage, would be repugnant to any decent-minded English man or woman. Our decision reflects that repugnance.'[2]

On appeal this ruling was reversed by the Divisional Court. Lord Parker CJ accepted that it was perfectly possible for a fit person order to be made in respect of a wife who had been validly married on the ground that she was in moral danger. The question was simply whether there was evidence to justify the making of the order in the present case. In a now famous passage his Lordship declared:

'I would never dream of suggesting that a decision by this bench of justices with this very experienced chairman, could ever be termed perverse: but having read that, I am convinced that they have misdirected themselves. When they say that "a continuance of such an association notwithstanding the marriage would be repugnant to any decent-minded English man or woman", they are I think, and can only be, considering the view of an English man or woman in relation to an English girl and our Western way of life. I cannot myself think that decent-minded English men or women, realising the way of life in which this girl was brought up, and this man for that matter, would inevitably say that this is repugnant. It is certainly natural for a girl to marry at that age. They develop sooner, and there is nothing abhorrent in their way of life for a girl of 13 to marry a man of 25 . . . . Granted that this man may be said to be a bad lot, that he has done things in the past which perhaps nobody would approve of, it does not follow from that that this girl, happily married to this man, is under any moral danger by associating and living with him. For my part, as it seems to me, it could only be said that she was in moral danger if one was considering somebody brought up and living in our way of life, and to hold that she is in moral danger in the circumstances of this case can only be arrived at, as it seems to me, by ignoring the way of life in which she was brought up, and her husband was brought up.'[3]

Lord Parker held that the child marriage was entitled to the fullest recognition by the English courts, as indeed were the sexual relations that were a natural corollary. The girl could hardly be said to be exposed to moral danger merely because she carried out her wifely duties. His Lordship raised the question whether any criminal offence would be committed by the husband in having sexual intercourse with his wife while she was under the age of 16 in view of the Sexual Offences Act 1956, s 6(1) which provides:

'It is an offence . . . for a man to have unlawful sexual intercourse with a girl . . . under the age of 16.'

He concluded that no such offence would be committed and suggested that the word 'unlawful' might well be regarded as inappropriate where the parties were recognised as being validly married.[4]

The decision has given rise to a good deal of controversy. It was immediately criticised by Baroness Summerskill in the House of Lords.[5] One writer[6] branded it 'an extreme and disturbing case', while another supported the idea of taking into account the customs and culture of the parties since the question whether the girl was in moral danger clearly involved a value judgement.[7] A third commentator wrote:

'The practical consequences of the findings could be disastrous. The girl did not speak any English; she was quite likely to contract venereal disease from her husband and, eventually, to have children. If the statistics on teenage brides are anything to go by the marriage seemed destined to break down and one can easily imagine the wife as a future deserted uneducated mother incapable of earning a living or bringing up her children and a charge on the state. Lord Parker fully accepted the right of immigrants to continue with their customs but perhaps he would not have been ready to do so had the husband intended to remain in this country.'[8]

This brought forth the retort that it was somewhat presumptuous to assume that teenage African marriages were 'ipso facto destined for breakdown'.[9] While this may have been a valid point to make, events were soon to prove that the Mohameds' marriage at any rate was doomed to failure. The husband subsequently married a second wife in Nigeria and was divorced in England by both of them simultaneously for 'unreasonable behaviour' in 1975.[10]

Yet another commentator suggested that legislative action was required to specify a minimum age below which even the marriages of foreign domiciliaries would not be recognised as valid in England.[11] He stated:

'... there must be limits to English tolerance of foreign customs ... A line must be drawn somewhere. A minimum age ought to be prescribed for recognition purposes. Physical and psychological considerations dictate that this should not be much below the age of puberty .... The ground of non-recognition might then be that a person below this age is incapable of giving true consent to marriage.'[12]

However, there are problems in doing this even if the minimum age were fixed at, say, 13.[13] The parties' status would then fluctuate depending upon which country they were currently living in. Recognition of their marriage in England might even prove beneficial for the child-party, e g for the purposes of maintenance, inheritance, etc. Moreover, it would have to be decided at what stage the process of non-recognition would operate. Should it apply only if at the time the question arose before the English courts the child was still below the age fixed or should it operate retrospectively so that the relevant date would be that of the marriage?[14] In any event account would necessarily have to be taken of the possibility (or probability) of the marriage being ratified once the parties had reached a higher age. On balance it would seem wisest to leave the law as it is and allow the judges to retain a minimal residual discretion to refuse recognition in particularly repugnant cases which are offensive to the conscience of the court, in line with the formula laid down by Simon P in *Cheni v Cheni*.[15]

1 [1969] 1 QB1, [1968] 2 All ER 563.
2 At 15.
3 At 15-16.
4 Cf. *R v Chapman* [1959] 1 QB 100, [1958] 3 All ER 143, on the interpretation of s 19(1) of the 1956 Act.
5 290 HL Official Report (5th series) cols 1321-3.
6 Stone *Family Law* (Macmillan, 1977) p 40.
7 Hoggett *Parents and Children* (Sweet & Maxwell 1977) p 110.
8 Deech 'Immigrants and Family Law' (1973) 123 NLJ 110 at 111.
9 (1973) 123 NLJ 232 (Ramsbottom).

10 See Freeman 'When Marriage Fails' [1978] CLP 109.
11 Karsten 'Child marriages' (1969) 32 MLR 212.
12 At 215-6.
13 This age is suggested by Shyllon 'Immigration and the Criminal Courts' (1971) 34 MLR 135 at 138 on the basis that it is the lowest age for lawful sexual intercourse in purely domestic law terms under the Sexual Offences Act 1956, s 5.
14 Karsten at 216.
15 [1965] P 85 at 99, discussed in para 2.10 above.

The scope for reform

2.18   So far as marriages in England and of English domiciliaries abroad are concerned the minimum age of 16 has recently been endorsed by two official committees[1] and thus seems likely to remain, at any rate for the time being. However, although both committees considered it essential to keep the minimum marriage age in line with the minimum age for consent to sexual intercourse in the criminal law[2] there are distinct flaws in this line of reasoning. The criminal law is designed to prohibit the exploitation of young girls and is usually only enforced strictly where an older man is involved.[3] Probably 16 is about the right age for this purpose.[4] By contrast, specifying a minimum age for marriage in modern circumstances should be seen as a device for preventing unstable marriages. There is clear evidence that the risks are greatest with young brides[5] and it can therefore be argued that it might be sensible to raise the age for marriage to 18 as Denmark, Norway, Sweden and Holland have recently done. There would then be no need to retain the additional requirement of parental consent for those below the legal age of majority.

In Europe there appears to be a growing trend towards enabling courts or government authorities to grant permission, in exceptional circumstances, for individuals to marry below the basic minimum age.[6] If the minimum age for marriage here were to be raised to 18 the possibility of introducing this procedure would seem to merit careful consideration. The wording of the dispensation could follow a formula such as 'where it would be for the welfare and in the best interests of the applicant'. This would enable the dispensing agency (ideally a new-style Family Court) to treat each case on its merits and while doing this give appropriate weight to any argument from an immigrant or ethnic minority applicant that the culture or customs of his or her community looked with favour on earlier marriage. If the final decision were entrusted to a judge this should be sufficient to ensure that no minor entered into a marriage under improper parental or family pressure.

1 See the Latey Committee Report on the Age of Majority (1967 Cmnd. 3342) and the Law Commission Report on the Law of Nullity (Law Com No 33).
2 *Latey Report* p 53; Law Com No 33 p 22.
3 See Honoré *Sex Law* (Duckworth, 1978) p 73; Report of the Home Office Working Party on the Age of Consent (1979) pp 10-11; Wilcox *The Decision to Prosecute* (Butterworths, 1972) p 51.
4 See *Honoré* p 82 where the convenience of having the same age as for the limit of compulsory education is well brought out.
5 See J Eekelaar, *Family Law and Social Policy* (2nd edn, 1984) pp 34-8.
6 See 'Minimum age at marriage: 20 years of legal reform'. (1977) 4 People no. 3.

C. FORCED MARRIAGES AND ARRANGED MARRIAGES

2.19   Lawrence Stone has put forward the proposition that in terms of match-making there are only four basic options available.[1] The first is that the choice of marriage partner is made 'entirely by parents, kin, and family friends without the advice or consent of the bride or groom'. This may be regarded as a 'forced marriage' since the couple themselves have no voice in the matter and are simply bound to follow the dictates of others. Their consent is neither sought nor given; their wishes and desires count for nothing. Such marriages are still recognised as valid in some countries, but there have been a large number of attempts to curb them. Writing of customary marriages in Africa in 1970 Morris has stated:

'. . . the coercion of women by their customary law guardians into marriages against their wishes are by no means things of the past. A woman forced against her will to marry would doubtless obtain redress from a court of law, which would declare, in the interests of natural justice, that such a marriage was invalid, but recourse to the courts in such cases would be unlikely, nor is it easy, in African any more than other societies, to distinguish between parental force and persuasion in such matters.'[2]

Efforts have also been made to restrict forced marriages in the Muslim world by means of statutory reforms. However, it is still the position under Hanafi law applicable to the Indian subcontinent, for example, that marriages contracted under duress are valid and it is perfectly lawful for a guardian to contract such a marriage on behalf of his minor ward, though the marriage is voidable on the ward's attainment of puberty, provided there has been no affirmation by voluntary consummation.[3] Pearl writes:

'Although the rights of the Muslim woman are subordinate to the man, they are certainly not insignificant either in quantity or . . . in extent. In practice, however, both the usage of pre-Islamic Arabia as well as the customs of the communities conquered by Islam have proved stronger than the laws of Islam. This is as true on the [Indian] subcontinent as it is elsewhere in the Muslim world. Women can rarely take full advantage of the rights given them by the personal law. Marriage is arranged by the father or other male guardian, and the girl will find it difficult – indeed in most cases impossible – to refuse the express wish of the guardian.'[4]

The multilateral Convention on Consent to Marriage[5] which came into force in 1964, provides in art 1(1) that:

'No marriage shall be legally entered into without the full and free consent of both parties, such consent to be expressed by them in person after due publicity and in the presence of the authority competent to solemnise the marriage and of witnesses, as prescribed by law.'

This treaty has been ratified by some 30 states, but of these fewer than ten are in Africa or Asia where forced marriages are most widespread.[6]

Stone's second option occurs where, while the choice of partner is still made by the parents or kin, the parties themselves are:

'granted a right of veto to be exercised on the basis of one or two formal interviews which take place after the two sets of parents and kin have agreed on the match. It is a right which can only be exercised once or twice . . . The principle that underlies this concession is that mutual compatibility is desirable to hold a marriage together, and that this will slowly develop between any couple who do not exhibit an immediate antipathy towards each other on first sight.'[7]

This type of process approximates very closely to the 'arranged marriage' so common among people from the Indian subcontinent, whether they are Muslims, Sikhs or Hindus.[8] Such marriages are perceived more as a compact between two families than as simply the union of two individuals and they are firmly rooted both in religious belief and in cultural tradition. Since the families are so closely involved in the inception of a marriage they have a substantial stake in its success and use their best endeavours to ensure that it remains intact and that future differences between the couple are reconciled wherever possible. Divorce rates are generally believed to be low. The tradition of these marriage alliances has grown up in rural communities in South Asia and is closely integrated within their socio-economic context. As Ballard has pointed out:[9]

'The more that property, and particularly land, is the principal source of income and security, the more that families are tight-knit, corporately organised groups which compete with one another for status, and the more that the quality of marriage alliances achieved determines that status, the more probable it is that all important decisions, such as those about marriage, will be regarded as matters of concern for the group as a whole. Throughout the Indian sub-continent, the inheritance of land, property and ascribed occupational status (caste) are of paramount social importance. The family is founded upon joint ownership and co-operative utilisation of resources of this kind, rights in which are transmitted by inheritance to sons only. A family is normally composed of the male descendants of its head, together with their wives, daughters and unmarried sisters. Daughters are given a dowry at marriage (in some senses in lieu of an inheritance) and they should always go to reside in their husbands' households once marriage has taken place. It is taken for granted that all marriages will be the outcome of an arrangement between the two groups concerned.'

Similar circumstances account for similar marriage formation patterns found in many African societies.

Status in the community is accorded particular importance in South Asia:

'... families of all groups are concerned about their honour, *izzat*, and are in constant competition with one another to maintain and advance their relative status. The maintenance of *izzat* requires that family members should conduct themselves honourably and particularly that the women of the family should have an unblemished reputation. *Izzat* can be increased by overshadowing other families by, for instance, the acquisition of more land or, even more importantly by contracting prestigious marriage alliances. In order to maintain its *izzat*, a family must send its daughters in marriage to families of equal status. To enhance its *izzat* it must do better.'[10]

'Arranged marriages' differ from forced marriages in that while the latter are always arranged by the families of the spouses, the former are not normally contracted without the consent of the spouses themselves. Children are socialised to believe that their parents will choose a suitable partner for them and generally they willingly accept both the method of selection and the particular individual proposed.

Stone's third marriage option covers the situation where the choice is made by the parties themselves on the understanding that it will be made from a family of more or less equal financial and status position, with the parents retaining the right of veto. He asserts that in England the shift from arranged marriages to this third option occurred between 1660 and 1800 in response to the rise of individualism. The emphasis moved away from family interest to personal compatibility and greater weight was accorded to the individual pursuit of happiness.[11] Eventually the stage of Stone's fourth option was reached in England during the present century, in terms of which the parties make their own choice of marriage partner and merely inform their parents of what they have decided. Physical attraction and romantic love have become the paramount considerations in making the choice.

1 *The Family, Sex and Marriage in England 1500-1800* (Penguin, 1979) pp 181-2.
2 Phillips and Morris *Marriage Laws in Africa* (OUP, 1971) p 49.
3 *Pearl* pp 44-6; *Anderson* pp 103-5. In classical Muslim law the 'option of puberty' is even more restricted and is available only if the guardian was someone other than the ward's father or grandfather.

4 'The legal rights of Muslim women in India, Pakistan and Bangladesh' [1976] *New Community* 68 at 69-70.
5 See 1970 Cmnd 4538.
6 The following African and Asian countries have ratified the Convention: Benin, Guinea, Mali, Niger, Philippines, Tunisia and Upper Volta.
7 At pp 181-2.
8 Arranged marriages of this kind are also the norm for, e g Greek Cypriots – see Constantinides 'The Greek Cypriots: Factors in the Maintenance of Ethnic Identity' in Watson (ed) *Between Two Cultures* pp 294-5.
9 'Arranged marriages in the British context' [1978] New Community 181 at 183.
10 *Ballard* p 184.
11 For the way in which this happened and the changes in sociological conditions which were necessary, see *Stone* pp 182 ff.

Policy considerations

2.20 A forced marriage in which a party has no voice and no power of veto can be portrayed as repugnant to Western ideas of justice and humane treatment. A marriage involves a close and intimate relationship and one can argue strongly that no-one should be forced into such a commitment against his or her will. To impose such a relationship is to degrade human individuality and violate a personal freedom which is highly cherished in the value system of the majority of English people. Most marriages carry as a natural concomitant the obligation of sexual intercourse. Since English law regards sexual intercourse outside marriage as a crime when it takes place by force against the wishes of either party, it would hardly be logical to approve such conduct through the mechanism of marriage. A further argument might be that such marriages could be especially prone to breakdown on grounds of resentment and incompatibility.[1]

Arranged marriages taken to the stage of compulsion are naturally open to the same objections. However, arranged marriages would normally appear to operate through the tacit consent of the parties and therefore require separate consideration. In the societies in which they occur it is well understood that the parents will propose as a spouse someone whom they regard as suitable on the basis of inquiries they have made. Since they have a strong interest in the success of the marriage and in their children's happiness and since they possess greater experience they are often considered by their children to be acting in their best interests. The practice conforms with their religious beliefs and their cultural traditions and is thus entitled to general respect. Compliance is, therefore, usually forthcoming.

In Western society since marriage is based on ideas of love, affection and compatibility it is felt that some degree of personal involvement, knowledge and intimacy should precede the wedding. Periods of courtship and engagement are designed to test the strength and reliability of the couple's attachment to one another. None of this is available in the case of an arranged marriage. Usually only a very few meetings between the couple (if any) take place before the marriage and these are in rather formal circumstances. There is little opportunity for the couple to get to know one another in any meaningful sense.

In practice, of course, arranged marriages tend to work out just as well (if not better) in South Asia as 'love match' marriages do in English society. Expectations of individual happiness are not pitched unrealistically high and a good working partnership coupled with a certain amount of affection develops over the years. This is particularly true where the couple's leisure activities are segregated and they each have many outside interests and companions.[2] Pressure does not concentrate unduly on the personal relationship of the couple as an isolated pair.[3]

1 For a graphic account of such a marriage, see Sharan-Jeet Shan, *In My Own Name* (London, 1985).
2 See *Stone* p 82.
3 See P Jeffery *Migrants and Refugees* (Cambridge, 1976) pp 30-1.

2.21 So far as arranged marriages between Asians in England are concerned there are further considerations to take into account. Asian children who have spent a large part of their upbringing here and attended schools alongside white children may find themselves caught in a clash of cultures and have difficulty in resolving the conflict between them.[1] They may view with envy the freedom of choice accorded to their English contemporaries and become less willing to accept tacitly their parents' choice without full discussion. Their attitudes are, perhaps predictably, rather ambivalent towards the whole subject. According to a survey conducted in 1975 two-thirds of a large sample of young Asians thought arranged marriages still worked very well in the Asian community here and should be continued, while exactly the same proportion considered that young people would come to rebel against them.[2]

It is also important to bear in mind that Asian couples are less likely to live in the traditional form of extended family in this country[3] and that the personal relationship between the spouses themselves may therefore become far more crucial than it ever was in the past. They will also probably tend to be older when they marry here and hence likely to be more capable of making a mature choice of partner themselves than their predecessors were.

One observer has reported that 'nowadays the arranged marriage is usually with the [express] consent of both parties, the boy and the girl',[4] while another has written that '. . . the *final* decision rests with the boy and the girl, and not with the parents as used to be the case'.[5] However, these statements must be set against a recent study in Leeds which concluded that while young Sikhs there expected to have some say in the matter of choice, a few had none at all.[6] This was either because the marriage was rushed through after a confrontation with their parents or because it had been arranged informally many years before or because they had been socialised to accept the traditional way of doing things. 'Most saw photographs and were given details of the attributes of prospective spouses and were asked if they wanted negotiations to proceed. Sometimes they were given a choice. They then usually met the one that they had picked out, but normally only in the context of a formal meeting between the families, perhaps spending a few minutes alone together'.[7]

Clearly each family will handle the matter in a slightly different way depending on the circumstances. No doubt liberal parents allow their children greater flexibility than those who are more conservative. At one end of the spectrum parents may seek the express agreement of their child to a particular match and afford as much opportunity for a careful decision as possible. At the other end, in rare cases, parents may try to impose a compulsory marriage and refuse all discussion of alternatives. Such a course can have serious consequences such as sons and daughters leaving home and cutting themselves off from their families completely.[8] Even cases of suicide are not unknown.[9] Ballard reports that there is increasing pressure for the system to become more flexible:

'In Britain, as well as in the sub-continent, young Asians are now asking for, and often getting, the chance to meet one another properly, or at least to talk at length over the telephone before the engagement takes place. Most of them are now able to veto a proposed match, but many would like to be able to choose from a number of prospective spouses. Many find the rules about the caste and clan into which one may or may not marry unreasonable, and the majority strongly object to marriage with a boy or girl who has just been brought over from the sub-continent.'[10]

The merits of arranging marriages between someone brought up here and someone brought up in South Asia seem to be the subject of controversy.[11] While the practice is generally resented by the children themselves it is supported by their parents on the grounds that there is insufficient choice available here.[12] Their children, however, point to the likely difference in background, outlook and education as well as the lack of opportunity to meet beforehand, and while some boys may prefer an unsophisticated girl from the sub-continent to one educated here, Asian girls in particular will tend to resist being sent back to the subcontinent to get married.

1 See *Between Two Cultures* (Commission for Racial Equality, 1976) pp 25-31.
2 Ibid pp 27, 30.
3 See further below at para 4.02.
4 See *Between Two Cultures* p 26.
5 Hiro *Black British, White British* (Penguin, 1973) p 171. A similar view is expressed by James *Sikh Children in Britain* (London, 1974) p 86.
6 *Ballard* p 186. See also Taylor *The Half-Way Generation* (NFER, 1976) ch 13 (based on a study in Newcastle); D G Bowen (ed), *Hinduism in England* (Bradford, 1981) pp 105-6.
7 *Ballard* p 186.
8 See *Between Two Cultures* pp 62-73; *Multi-Racial Britain: The Social Services Response* (Commission for Racial Equality, 1978) p 22.
9 See S Crishna *Girls of Asian Origin in Britain* (London, 1975) p 37; *Bowen* p 106.
10 'Conflict, continuity and change: Second-generation South Asians' in Saifullah Khan (ed) *Minority Families in Britain* (Macmillan, 1979) p 125.
11 See *Between Two Cultures* pp 25-9; Ballard [1978] *New Community* at 188, 195; *Crishna* pp 22-3; A Helweg *Sikhs in England* (OUP 1979) pp 32, 85.
12 The impact of the immigration rules upon arranged marriages is beyond the scope of this book; see generally, Macdonald *Immigration Law and Practice in the United Kingdom* (Butterworths, 1983) pp 209-22; Evans *Immigration Law* (2nd edn, 1983) pp 129-42; HC 169 of 1982-3 as amended by H C 503 of 1984-5.

English domestic law

2.22 The Matrimonial Causes Act 1973, s 12 provides that a marriage is voidable if either party did not validly consent to it in consequence of duress. This rule governs the marriage in England of persons domiciled here. If duress can be established the party acting under compulsion is entitled to obtain an annulment from the court, provided proceedings are instituted within three years of the date of the ceremony and that the statutory bar of 'approbation' does not apply.[1] This bar operates when one party, with knowledge that it is open to him to have the marriage avoided, so conducts himself in relation to the other party as to lead the other party reasonably to believe that he will not seek to do so and it would be unjust to that party to grant the decree.

Exactly what constitutes duress is for the courts to decide[2] and there has recently been a remarkable change of approach on their part. The first reported case to deal with this question in connection with an Asian arranged marriage was *Singh v Singh* in 1971.[3] A Sikh girl of 17 went through a ceremony of marriage in a register office with a Sikh man aged 21. The marriage had been arranged by her parents and she had not seen her future husband until shortly before the ceremony. She did not even know his name. She had been told in advance that he was educated and handsome, but when she met him at the register office she quickly formed the opinion that he possessed neither of these qualities.

Immediately after the ceremony she returned home with her parents and refused either to go through the planned religious service in a Sikh temple a week later or to consummate the marriage. In her petition for nullity her main ground was that she had not consented to the marriage but had been induced to enter into it through duress and coercion exercised upon her by her parents. She had felt bound to obey the traditional customs of her people and follow her parents' wishes.

In rejecting her petition the Court of Appeal placed great reliance on the following statement of Simon P in *Szechter v Szechter*:[4]

'It is, in my view, insufficient to invalidate an otherwise good marriage that a party has entered into it in order to escape from a disagreeable situation, such as penury or social degradation. In order for the impediment of duress to vitiate an otherwise valid marriage, it must, in my judgment, be proved that the will of one of the parties thereto has been overborne by genuine and reasonably[5] held fear caused by threat of immediate danger, for which the party is not himself responsible, to life, limb or liberty, so that the constraint destroys the reality of consent to ordinary wedlock.'[6]

Applying that test there was, of course, no danger to life, limb or liberty. Nor was there any fear on the part of the wife, for as Megaw LJ put it:

'A sense of duty to her parents and a feeling of obligation to adhere to the custom of religion there may be, but of fear not a shred of evidence. Reluctance no doubt; but not fear.'[7]

Davies LJ added:

'She went there [to the register office] readily and willingly, thinking that it was the right thing to do. It seems to me that these circumstances are far removed from a case of duress.'[8]

The judgment of the Court of Appeal attracted considerable criticism,[9] for not only did the Court require actual fear on the part of the petitioner (in total disregard of other evidence of her unwillingness) but it also insisted on narrowing down the acceptable causes of such fear to immediate dangers to life, liberty or limb in a way which was inconsistent with the earlier case of *Scott v Sebright*[10] where fear of social and financial ruin and exposure had been held to be quite sufficient. Despite this, the decision was followed and applied by the Court of Appeal in *Singh v Kaur*[11] in 1981. In that case it was a Sikh husband aged 21, who had been brought up in this country, who was seeking to establish duress. His parents had arranged a marriage for him here with a girl who had come over directly from India. He had protested and had a long series of arguments and quarrels with his parents over the question. In his petition for annulment he claimed that if he had not gone through with the wedding he would have lost his job in the family business of market trading and would have had no income. He had never lived away from home before. The Court, while expressing sympathy for his plight, held that the standard required to establish duress could not and should not be relaxed.

1 Matrimonial Causes Act 1973, s 13.
2 For detailed analyses of the subject see Manchester 'Marriage or Prison: The Case of the Reluctant Bridegroom' (1966) 29 MLR 622; Brown 'The Shotgun Marriage' (1968) 42 Tulane LR 837; Davies 'Duress and Nullity of Marriage' (1972) 88 LQR 549.
3 [1971] P 226, [1971] 2 All ER 828.
4 [1971] P 286, [1970] 3 All ER 905.
5 The view that the test is an objective one is inconsistent with *Scott v Sebright* (1886) 12 PD 21 and now seems to have been discredited – see Law Com Report No 33 'Nullity of Marriage' p 27.

6 At 297-8.
7 At 233.
8 At 235.
9 See, eg Pearl 'Arranged Marriages' [1971] CLJ 206; Deech 'Immigrants and Family Law' (1973) 123 NLJ 110 at 111; Poulter 'The Definition of Marriage in English Law' (1979) 42 MLR 409 at 412-8. Cf also the annulment granted in similar circumstances in 1968 by Park J in the unreported case of *Khusai ja Bi*, referred to by Pearl 'Immigrant Marriages: Some Legal Problems' [1972-3] *New Community* 67 at 72. In *Singh's case* the argument in favour of annulment was strengthened by the fact that the husband's qualities and attributes were misrepresented to the wife by her parents. Where such misrepresentation occurs it must surely undermine a girl's resistance to her marriage to a stranger and contribute to the overpowering of her will.
10 (1886) 12 PD 21.
11 (1981) 11 Fam Law 152.

2.23 If the rule regarding duress were to remain as strict as this, recourse might need to be had in such cases to two other, admittedly rather tenuous, lines of argument on behalf of unwilling parties to a forced marriage. First, it might perhaps be possible to establish that the marriage is voidable for 'undue influence' on the part of a parent or other relatives. The Matrimonial Causes Act 1973, s 12(c) refers to a marriage being voidable for lack of consent 'in consequence of duress . . . or otherwise'. This wording would appear to be wide enough to encompass instances of the exercise of improper pressure, as in the case of other contracts generally. No doubt this would be easiest to establish in a case involving a minor, but young adults are not apparently excluded from the operation of the doctrine.[1] A presumption of undue influence arises from the relationship of parent and child and continues until the child is emancipated from parental control.[2]

Second, on a rare occasion it might be possible for the unwilling party to establish that he or she is actually incapable of consummating the marriage because of invincible repugnance to the idea of having intercourse with the other party. The petitioner may, of course, plead his or her own inability as a ground for having the marriage annulled and this approach to the problem was successful in the unreported county court case of *D v D*[3] in 1982, despite the fact that it had earlier failed in *Singh v Singh*. In *Singh's* case the court stressed the need to show that there was some psychiatric or sexual aversion to intercourse with the other party, rather than mere wilful refusal which is a ground which can only be made use of by the other spouse,[4] and medical evidence will, no doubt, be crucial in this regard.

Recently, however, there have been clear signs that the courts may in future be willing to relax the strictness of the rules governing duress. Little more than a year after its decision in *Singh v Kaur* the Court of Appeal appeared to do a remarkable *volte-face* in the case of *Hirani v Hirani*.[5] Ormrod LJ, who delivered the principal judgment in both cases, ruled that the test to be applied was simply whether the petitioner's will had been so coerced as to vitiate her consent. Relying upon a statement by Lord Scarman in the Privy Council case of *Pao On v Lau Yiu Long*[6] (which was concerned with economic duress in a commercial transaction), Ormrod LJ declared:

'The crucial question in these cases, particularly where a marriage is involved, is whether the threats, pressure, or whatever it is, is such as to destroy the reality of consent and overbears the will of the individual.'[7]

In this case the petitioner, an Indian Hindu girl aged 19, had incurred her parents' wrath by forming an association with a Muslim man. Her parents arranged for her to marry a Hindu man instead, someone neither they nor their daughter had ever met. They applied considerable pressure by threatening her with eviction from the family home if she refused to proceed with the wedding. In the end she went through both a civil ceremony and a religious one some six weeks later. She cried throughout the religious ceremony and was utterly miserable. Subsequently she went to live with her husband, though the marriage was never consummated. Her petition for the marriage to be annulled on the ground of duress was granted, Ormrod LJ remarking:

'It seems to me that this case, on the facts, is a classic case of a young girl, wholly dependent on her parents, being forced into a marriage with a man she has never seen and whom her parents have never seen in order to prevent her (reasonably, from her parents' point of view) continuing in an association with a Muslim which they would regard with abhorrence. But it is as clear a case as one could want of the overbearing of the will of the petitioner and thus invalidating or vitiating her consent.'[8]

1 *Re Pauling's Settlement Trusts Younghusband v Coutts & Co* [1964] Ch 303 at 307.
2 *Bainbrigge v Brown* (1881) 18 ChD 188 at 198; *Lancashire Loans Ltd v Black* [1934] 1 KB 380 at 419.
3 See the note in (1982) 12 Fam Law 101.
4 [1971] P 226 at 232, 235.
5 (1983) 4 FLR 232, discussed by Bradley (1983) 46 MLR 499.
6 [1980] AC 614 at 635.
7 At 234.
8 At 234.

The scope for reform

2.24 This long overdue liberalisation of the law of duress is a most welcome development and it is to be hoped that in future *Hirani's case* will be followed in preference to *Singh v Kaur* which, perhaps significantly, did not receive even a passing reference. However, it seems clear that the underlying basis of the legal recognition of duress in general has still to be worked into a coherent theory and further judicial elaboration of the principles may be expected. The 'overborne will' theory espoused by the Court of Appeal in *Hirani v Hirani* relies on a purely subjective approach and is perhaps rather misleading in its suggestion that a person acting under coercion has no intention of performing the act in question. In the normal case he does intend to perform it, albeit only because of the unpleasant consequences likely to follow if he refuses. His action is far from being totally involuntary. He does actually choose to submit to the pressures placed upon him although he does not desire the consequences. All this was clearly recognised by the House of Lords in *Lynch v DPP for Northern Ireland*,[1] a criminal case in which the accused was charged with murder and sought to rely on terrorist threats as affording a defence based on duress. Lord Simon spoke there of the actor's will being 'deflected not destroyed.'[2] From the fact that there exists a choice as to whether to submit to coercion or not, a leading commentator has sought to argue that the real question posed by duress throughout all branches of the law is not whether, as a matter of *fact*, a person's will has been overborne but rather whether, as a matter of *law*, the threats and pressure placed upon him were sufficient to relieve him from the normal consequences of his actions.[3] This involves a more objective assessment in deciding what types of pressure are legitimate in our society and defining the permissible limits of coercion. These may obviously vary from one activity to another so that, for example, a threat which was sufficient to make a contract voidable might well be insufficient to afford a defence to a serious criminal charge. In relation to marriage certain forms of pressure are almost certainly regarded as acceptable in English society. The very fact of a girl's pregnancy may amount to coercion, whether or not it is coupled with a threat to bring affiliation proceedings against the father, but it is highly unlikely that a man who married in these circumstances could obtain an annulment on the ground of duress. Similarly, one party may induce the other to marry by threatening to discontinue their relationship on any other footing. The other party must either resist the threat and refuse the marriage or accept the normal legal consequences of submission. In each case there is a perfectly reasonable alternative to marriage available.[4]

The dilemma posed by arranged marriages is to distinguish between proper and improper pressures imposed not by the other party to the marriage but by the petitioner's own family and the wider ethnic community. The threatened eviction of a dependent daughter from the family home and her subsequent ostracism by her family and presumably by many members of their community (as in *Hirani*) may be regarded in law as a form of coercion which an Asian girl of 19 cannot fairly be expected to resist. Perhaps an Asian man of 21 should (as in *Singh v Kaur*) be expected to be strong enough to leave his family home and seek financial independence elsewhere rather than submit to a marriage he does not want. In the original case of *Singh v Singh* the 17-year-old petitioner did not really specify the exact nature of the pressures placed upon her, other than by claiming that she felt bound to obey traditional Sikh customs and follow her parents' wishes. No doubt, following *Hirani's case* such detailed pleading will become the norm in future proceedings of this type. Once evidence is provided of a family and cultural background in which a strong reluctance on the part of a petitioner to enter the marriage has been overriden by forces of oppression and domination, the case for annulment should be established more easily. On some occasions Asian fathers have actually threatened their daughters with death if they do not accede to an arranged marriage.[5] However, threats of social ostracism from the extended family can be almost as potent and their strength clearly needs to be properly understood by the English judiciary. In 1980 the Family Court of Australia showed that it had developed just such a sensitivity in the case of *In the Marriage of S.*[6] The court departed from previous Australian precedents (which had followed the earlier English approach) and reached a finding of duress in a case of parental pressure exerted upon a 16-year-old Egyptian girl who had been married in a Coptic Orthodox church there. Watson SJ commented:

'The emphasis on terror or fear in some of the judgments seems unnecessarily limiting. A sense of mental oppression can be generated by causes other than fear or terror. If there are circumstances which taken together lead to the conclusion that because of oppression a particular person has not exercised a voluntary consent to a marriage that consent is vitiated by duress and is not a real consent. This is howsoever the oppression arises and irrespective of the motivation or propriety of any person solely or partially responsible for the oppression.'

The bride in this case, he went on:

'. . . was a victim of family loyalty and concern, below the age of majority and on her evidence unable to initiate advice from outside her family. She went on with the wedding not because of terror but because of love, not because of physical threat to herself but because of concern for her younger sister. She was caught in a psychological prison of family loyalty, parental concern, sibling responsibility, religious commitment and culture that demanded filial obedience. If she had 'no consenting will' it was because these matters were operative . . .'

For our courts to uphold forced marriages under the misapprehension that they are giving effect to the respectable custom of arranged marriages would be a great mistake. It would be contrary to the Universal Declaration of Human Rights, the Convention on Consent to Marriage and the International Covenant on Civil and Political Rights, all of which require the 'free and full consent' of the intended spouses.[7] A small administrative reform which might perhaps help to obviate some of these problems would be for all marriage officers to enquire separately and privately of each of the parties to a marriage, both upon notice of the intended marriage being given and immediately before the wedding, whether they were entering it entirely of their own free will. At present the Registrar merely reminds the couple in a civil ceremony that marriage is a voluntary union and makes no attempt to check that this is in fact the case.

1 [1975] 1 All ER 913 at 918, 926, 934, 938, 945, and 951.
2 At 938.
3 Atiyah [1982] 98 LQR 197; see also [1983] 99 LQR 188 (Tiplady); [1983] 99 LQR 353 (Atiyah).
4 See Ingman and Grant 'Duress in the Law of Marriage' (1984) 14 Fam Law 92 at 94.
5 See, e g *The Guardian* 31 July 1976 which carried a report of such threats actually being implemented.
6 (1980) FLC 90-820, discussed by Bates (1980) 130 NLJ 1035.
7 UDHR art 16(2); Convention on Consent to Marriage, Minimum Age for Marriage and Registration of Marriages, art 1(1); International Covenant, art 23(3). The Convention (1970 Cmnd 4538) was ratified by the UK in 1970 and the Covenant (1977 Cmnd 6702) in 1976.

English conflicts law

2.25 In the absence of a single decisive precedent in this area, Dicey and Morris put forward the tentative rule that no marriage is valid if by the law of either party's domicile one party does not consent to marry the other.[1] The question of consent is treated as analogous to capacity. On this assumption that the *lex domicilii* applies, the position would appear to be as follows.

1 At p 304; cf Cheshire and North p 401.

1. Marriages in England by foreign domiciliaries

2.26 A forced marriage would seem to be valid if it is recognised as valid by the *lex domicilii*. A fortiori an arranged marriage with the tacit consent of the spouses must be valid. If the party who was compelled had an English domicile and the other party a foreign domicile it would appear that the marriage would be voidable for duress through applying English law;[1] on the other hand, were the domiciles to be reversed so that the party compelled had a foreign domicile that law might well apply to the exclusion of English law.[2]

1 As happened in *Hussein v Hussein* [1938] P 159, [1938] 2 All ER 344.
2 See *Dicey and Morris* p 305; *Cheshire and North* p 401.

2. Marriages abroad by English domiciliaries

2.27 If a party who was domiciled here went through a marriage abroad under duress the marriage would be voidable in English law.[1] If the party compelled was domiciled abroad the matter would be governed by his or her *lex domicilii*.

1 *Dicey and Morris* pp 304-5.

3. Marriages abroad by foreign domiciliaries

2.28 If each party's *lex domicilii* permitted forced marriages any such marriage would basically be recognised as valid in England.[1] Probably, however, the

English courts retain a residuary discretion on the basis of public policy to refuse recognition where to do otherwise would offend the conscience of the English court.[2]

1 This view is not, however, accepted by Hartley (1972) 35 MLR 571 at 580. Although the point was not raised in *Alhaji Mohamed v Knott* [1969] 1 QB1, it seems possible that this was a forced marriage under Islamic law. Its validity was not, however, challenged on this ground before the English courts.
2 This exception was recognised in the 7th edition of *Dicey and Morris* (see p 253). Curiously, it has since been omitted in subsequent editions.

D. CEREMONIES AND CONSUMMATION

2.29 Most societies recognise the importance of marriage as a *rite de passage* by providing that it should be accompanied by some distinctive formal ceremony. Sometimes this is based on religion, at others upon tradition. Generally speaking, Christians prefer to marry in a church, Jews in a synagogue, Muslims in a mosque, Hindus and Sikhs in their temples – each in accordance with their own religious rites. Many Africans pay bridewealth. Each community may regard its own marriage formalities as such an important part of its culture that they must prevail even when the wedding takes place in England.

Policy considerations

2.30 In a modern industrial society it is vitally important for the state to have accurate information about which of its members are married and which are not. Such knowledge is often required to determine status for purposes of nationality and allegiance, to assess liability to tax and social security entitlements, to collect statistics and so on. The normal method of acquiring the necessary details for these bureaucratic purposes is through a compulsory system of marriage registration. However, the state may also take the view that it wishes to exercise some supervision over the actual process of getting married, claiming that there is a public interest in providing adequate publicity, checking that the basic requirements for a valid marriage are complied with in terms of capacity and consent, and preventing fraud and abuse. If this approach is adopted some limits need to be placed on the freedom of religious sects and other groups to organise their own marriage ceremonies and some minimum requirements about solemnisation must be laid down.

English domestic law

2.31 Aside from the question of preliminaries to marriage and the requirements of registration, English law specifies quite detailed rules about where marriages may take place, who should conduct the ceremony, at what time of day it may occur and the nature of the celebration. All these provisions regarding solemnisation are contained in the Marriage Acts 1949-1983.[1]

The place of marriage must generally be a register office, a church or chapel of the Church of England or a 'registered building'.[2] A registered building must be a 'separate' building certified under the Places of Worship Registration Act 1855 as a place of meeting for 'religious worship'.[3] This requirement can pose two problems for minority sects and denominations. First, the whole building must be used for worship, whereas many mosques and temples are treated as community centres (where a variety of social activities are carried on) or else they simply constitute rooms in ordinary residential accommodation.[4] Second, questions may possibly arise as to whether certain customary practices amount to religious worship. In *R v Registrar General, ex p Segerdal*[5] it was held that meetings of members of the Church of Scientology did not involve any congregation or assembly for reverence or veneration of God or a supreme being or entity. Man, not God, was at the centre of their teachings and beliefs. Hence their ceremonies did not contain any element of worship and thus their chapel could not be registered under the 1855 Act. If rigidly applied this approach would also have adverse implications for Buddhists. Fortunately, in *Segerdal's case* Lord Denning MR expressly stated that Buddhist temples are properly described as places of meeting for religious worship, despite the fact that mainstream Buddhists do not apparently revere a deity.[6] They must therefore be viewed as an exception and there may perhaps be others.

Marriage ceremonies must generally be conducted in the presence of either an officiating clergyman of the Church of England or a registrar or an 'authorised person' (usually a minister of the religious group concerned).[7] In most instances it is a criminal offence knowingly and wilfully to celebrate a marriage outside the hours of 8 am to 6 pm though a marriage solemnised outside these hours will nevertheless remain valid.[8] Marriages in a register office or registered building must be solemnised with open doors, ie the public must not be excluded if they wish to attend,[9] and the bride and bridegroom must attend in person and exchange their vows using a standard form of words.[10] This last requirement poses problems for many Muslims since a Muslim ceremony of marriage (*nikah*) is capable of being effected merely by an exchange of declarations between representatives of the bridegroom and the bride acting on their behalf.[11] The attendance of the couple themselves is not required. Such a ceremony would not, however, amount to a valid marriage in the eyes of English law if it took place in this country, even if the mosque in which it occurred had been designated a registered building.

From all these regulations concerning solemnisation two select groups are exempt. These are Quakers and 'persons professing the Jewish religion'.[12] Their special privileges go back at least as far as the enactment of Lord Hardwicke's Marriage Act of 1753.[13] Their ceremonies may take place at any hour of the day or night, need not be in any particular building (and may even be celebrated in a private home or garden) and do not require the presence of any state official.[14] They are merely required to follow the usages of the Society of Friends or the usages of the Jews, as the case may be.[15]

1 See generally *Jackson* ch 5; *Cretney* pp 19-34. In view of all these requirements it seems clear that a so-called 'gypsy marriage' constituted merely by elopement and some form of blood-mingling ceremony will not be recognised as valid – see National Insurance Decision No R(5) 4/59; *Cheshire and North* p 316.

2 Marriage Act 1949, ss 12, 15, 26, 41, 45.

3 Marriage Act 1949, s 41(1). For registration under the 1855 Act see paras 8.10-8.13 below.

4 Pearl 'Immigrant marriages: some legal problems' [1973] *New Community* 67 at 68; *Hiro* pp 127, 131, 134; *James* pp 35-6; Iqbal *East Meets West: a background to some Asian faiths* (CRE 1981) pp 93-4.

5 [1970] 2 QB 697.

6 At 707. They do, however, appear to recognise a supreme being.

7 Marriage Act 1949, ss 22, 44(2), 45(1).

8 Marriage Act 1949, s 75(1)(a).

9 Marriage Act 1949, ss 44(2), 45(1).

10 Marriage Act 1949, ss 44(3), 45(1).

11 See Pearl *A Textbook on Muslim Law* p 42.

12 Marriage Act 1949, s 26(1)(c), (d).

13 It seems that even prior to this Act Jewish marriages celebrated in England according to the rites of that religion were recognised as valid here and were governed by Jewish law – see

Henriques *Jewish Marriages and the English Law* (Oxford, 1909) pp 15-21 and the authorities cited there; Bartholomew 'Application of Jewish Law in England' (1961) 3 Univ of Malaya LR 83 at 84-90.
14 Marriage Act 1949, ss 26(1), 35(4), 43(3), 75(1)(a).
15 For details of the forms taken by Quaker and Jewish marriages, see *Jackson* pp 198-202; *Lindo v Belisario* (1795) 1 Hag Con 216. In Jewish law there is no absolute necessity for a rabbi to be present at a wedding. If he is there he does not 'solemnise' the marriage in the manner in which, for example, a Christian minister does; rather he attests the marriage as a witness. In Jewish law a marriage is only valid if two fit and proper witnesses are present at the ceremony. A witness may be 'incompetent' either by being a close relative of one of the parties or by reason of his departure from the normal observances of the Jewish faith. In the early case of *Goldsmid v Bromer* (1798) 1 Hag Con 324 the marriage in question was held invalid because one of the witnesses was a first cousin of the bridegroom while the other had consistently profaned the Sabbath and contravened Jewish dietary rules. Despite the antiquity of this decision the competency of witnesses may still raise difficult issues today. In September 1983 the London Beth Din of the United Synagogues declared that some of the marriages which had taken place at the New London Synagogue in the presence of Rabbi Dr Louis Jacobs were invalid because of his lack of competence as a witness. Almost certainly this alleged disqualification arose out of the Rabbi's controversial views about the manner in which the word of God was revealed to Moses – see *Jewish Chronicle*, 30 September 7 and 14 October 1983.

2.32 Persons of any faith may, of course, decide to be married in a civil ceremony at a register office, perhaps because it can be arranged more quickly and conveniently than a religious wedding or else because there is no appropriate 'registered building' nearby. They may then proceed to a religious service some days or weeks afterwards. The latter ceremony does not supersede the former from a legal point of view and strictly speaking the subsequent religious celebration does not constitute a marriage at all in the eyes of English law.[1] However, it may well have particular significance in terms of the legal rules governing the consummation of marriages since many couples believe they should not have sexual intercourse until they have been through a religious ceremony of marriage.

In *Jodla v Jodla*[2] two Roman Catholic Poles were married in a register office because the wife's visa was about to expire and there was insufficient time to arrange a Catholic wedding. The couple intended to be properly married according to the rites of their church soon afterwards. However, this never happened despite several requests by the wife. Eventually the couple drifted apart. Each of them alleged that the other had wilfully refused to consummate the marriage. Hewson J decided that the wife had a complete defence because she had a reasonable and just cause for refusing intercourse, namely the understanding that there must first be a church wedding. The husband was making it impossible for her to live with him with a clear conscience as his wife. Moreover, by his own refusal to proceed with the church service he was impliedly refusing to have intercourse with his wife and therefore it was he who was wilfully refusing to consummate the marriage. The wife was accordingly granted an annulment of the marriage on this ground.

In *Kaur v Singh*[3] the parties, who were Sikhs, were also married in a register office. It was similarly understood by both them and their families that this would be followed by another ceremony in a Sikh temple in order to comply with their religious beliefs. Sikhs commonly arrange to begin with a register office marriage where, as in this case, one of the parties has come over from the Indian subcontinent.[4] Under the immigration rules fiancés and fiancées intending to marry someone settled here are only admitted for a period of three months in the first instance.[5] The Court found that it was recognised by all concerned in this case that the responsibility for arranging the religious ceremony resided with the husband, but despite repeated reminders from the wife's brothers he did nothing about it. After giving various excuses he eventually declared that he had no intention of arranging the religious ceremony at all. The husband never tried to persuade the wife to have sexual intercourse with him and the marriage was never physically consummated. The wife sought a decree of nullity on the ground of the husband's wilful refusal to consummate the marriage and this was granted by the Court of Appeal which held that since the husband had failed to 'implement' the marriage he had also wilfully failed to consummate it.

In the subsequent case of *Singh v Kaur*[6] on similar facts the husband was the party who was granted the annulment by the Court of Appeal. However, evidence was accepted, contrary to that in *Kaur v Singh*, that the duty to arrange the Sikh ceremony rested with the bride's family. Since they had failed do this because the wife was unwilling to proceed with the marriage following a register office wedding, the marriage was annulled on the petition of the husband. It was unnecessary for the husband to establish that he had expressly asked his wife to come and live with him and that she had refused. Ormrod LJ stressed, however, that the petitioner in this type of case must intend to go through the religious ceremony since otherwise there would be no wilful refusal by the respondent.

Although these three decisions almost amount to creating the novel concept of a 'conditional marriage'[7] they are to be supported as upholding important minority customs in a most sensitive area. To have refused decrees and left the petitioners to seek eventual divorces would have been unwarrantably harsh.

1 See *Thynne v Thynne* [1955] P 272 at 304 per Hodson LJ; *Qureshi v Qureshi* [1972] Fam 173.
2 [1960] 1 All ER 625, [1960] 1 WLR 236.
3 [1972] 1 All ER 292, [1972] 1 WLR 105.
4 See Ballard 'Arranged Marriages in a British context' [1978] New Community 181 at 189.
5 See HC 503 of 1985, para 8.
6 (1979, unreported), noted by Pearl [1979] New Community 274.
7 Cf *Kenward v Kenward* [1951] P 124, [1950] 2 All ER 297 per Denning LJ.

English conflicts law

2.33 Where a foreign domiciliary comes to England and marries in a register office the marriage will be valid if it complies with our formalities, regardless of whether the ceremony was appropriate and sufficient to constitute a valid marriage in terms of his *lex domicilii*. This follows from the basic rule that matters of formal validity of marriage are governed by the *lex loci celebrationis*. Thus in *Papadopoulos v Papadopoulos*[1] a husband who was domiciled in Cyprus was held unable to treat his English register office marriage as void because the ceremony was neither conducted by a Greek Orthodox priest nor solemnised in an Orthodox church as it should have been to comply with his *lex domicilii*.

This process of preferring the *lex loci* to the *lex domicilii* in this connection has been taken a stage further in the sphere of non-recognition of foreign nullity decrees. Such decrees are normally recognised by the English courts provided there is a sufficient basis for jurisdiction (e g domicile or residence). However, in two cases the English courts have held that there is an exception where recognition would be contrary to principles of substantial justice. In *Gray v Formosa*[2] a Maltese court had annulled an English register office marriage of a Maltese husband to an English wife on the grounds that as a Roman Catholic he could only validly marry under Maltese law in a Roman Catholic church. The English Court of Appeal refused to recognise the Maltese decree on public policy grounds, Lord Denning MR declaring that it offended against our ideas of justice.[3] Two years later in *Lepre v Lepre*[4] Sir Jocelyn Simon P reached the same conclusion on very similar facts.

These decisions have come in for considerable academic criticism[5] for violating a well established principle that '. . . if the English courts recognise the jurisdiction of a foreign court to annul a marriage, then the ground on which that marriage was annulled by the foreign court is wholly immaterial'.[6] However, the problem is not an easy one to solve. If, following *Papadopoulos*, our courts will refuse to take cognisance of a vitiating defect of the *lex domicilii* to invalidate an otherwise sound English marriage, why should the mere addition of a foreign decree of nullity alter the position? Either the marriage is valid by English law or it is not. In *Gray v Formosa* Lord Denning MR stated:

'I confess, when I consider the simple principles of justice, I have no doubt what the result of this case should be. Here is an Englishwoman lawfully married in England, as lawfully married as any woman could be. She has borne her husband three children in lawful wedlock. Her husband goes back to Malta and gets the courts of Malta to declare he has never been married to her. And the courts of Malta carry that to its logical conclusion: they hold he is not liable to maintain her or to pay maintenance for the children of the marriage . . . Suppose he comes back to England, as he may do. Is the wife to have no redress against him . . . ? Is he to be at liberty in England to marry another woman with impunity? I do not think that there is any rule of private international law which compels her to submit to such indignity'.[7]

In *Lepre v Lepre* although Sir Jocelyn Simon P began by stating that he approached this aspect of the case with 'some misgiving' he subsequently provided a sound justification for the denial of recognition to the Maltese decrees in both cases, namely that it was

'an intolerable injustice that a system of law should seek to impose extraterritorially, as a condition of the validity of a marriage, that it should take place according to the tenets of a particular faith . . . Just as in *Chetti v Chetti* Sir Gorell Barnes P refused to give effect to an incapacity to marry outside his caste or religion imposed extraterritorially on the husband by the law of his domicile, so, I think, the Court of Appeal discerned in *Gray (orse Formosa) v Formosa* an attempt by Maltese law to impose an analogous incapacity based on creed: they would refuse to recognise the incapacity, so they refused to recognise the domiciliary decree founded upon it.'[8]

Much of the criticism levelled at *Gray v Formosa* essentially employed the axiom that 'hard cases make bad law', pointing out that the Court of Appeal was too concerned to do justice to the wife in the peculiar circumstances of the case at the expense of failing to adhere to principle. However, it has been cogently argued that in the choice of law process the best social policy is often to favour the legal system that upholds the validity of the marriage since nullity can destroy something which the parties assumed to have existed; divorce is the appropriate solution where the relationship has subsequently ceased to be viable.[9] This would ultimately appear to be an area in which there is no really satisfactory solution and there is little to choose between two conflicting approaches, both of which have substantial limitations.

1 [1930] P 55.
2 [1963] P 259.
3 At 269.
4 [1965] P 52.
5 See e g *Cheshire and North* p 316; Carter (1962) 38 BYBIL 497; Lewis (1963) 12 ICLQ 298; Blom-Cooper (1963) 26 MLR 94. See also the contrasting South African case of *De Bono v De Bono* 1948 (2) SA 802 where the validity of the Maltese decree was given full recognition.
6 *Corbett v Corbett* [1957] 1 All ER 621, [1957] 1 WLR 486 at 490 per Barnard J. See also *De Massa v De Massa (1931)* [1939] 2 All ER 150n; *Galene v Galene* [1939] P 237, [1939] 2 All ER 148.

7 At 269.
8 At 64-5.
9 See Hartley 'The Policy Basis of the English Conflict of Laws of Marriage' (1972) 35 MLR 571 at 572.

The scope for reform

2.34   In 1973 a joint working party of the Law Commission and the Registrar General produced a report on the solemnisation of marriage and this was quickly followed by a Law Commission report on the question.[1] Although none of their recommendations have yet been acted upon by Parliament some of them are very pertinent to the issues being discussed here.

One of the key proposals of the working party was that Quakers and Jews should cease to enjoy their present privileges as to the place and time of marriage.[2] This was not because these privileges had been abused in any way but because of the discrimination involved against other sects and denominations.[3] They recommended that the 'registered building' concept be somewhat modified and then applied to all marriages save those in a register office or church or chapel of the Church of England.[4] They provided the following general justification for imposing restrictions on where marriages may take place:

'As we see it, the restriction of facilities to marry to prescribed places has positive advantages. It helps to avoid clandestine and irregular marriages by ensuring that weddings take place in buildings which are known to, and recognised in, the community as places where marriages can lawfully take place, and which are under the control of responsible bodies who will see that the requirements of the law are observed. And it precludes any possibility of setting up commercial 'marriage parlours' which, we think, most people would regard as an undesirable development.'[5]

The modifications proposed to the concept of 'registered buildings' were:
(i)   that it need not be a 'separate' building since this operates unfairly against some of the smaller denominations who may use only part of a building as their place of worship, and might also rule out some larger multi-purpose buildings in city-centres;[6] and
(ii)   that it should be extended to cover the 'curtilage' or land attached to a building so as to allow marriages to take place out of doors in a garden. This would enable Jews to follow their occasional practice of using the gardens of synagogues.[7]

The proposed reform would mean that it would no longer be possible to celebrate Jewish marriages in private houses, hotels or restaurants and that the ceremony would have to take place with 'open doors'. The report explained this by stating:

'We question . . . whether it is still necessary to retain the possibility of these extra-synagogue weddings. In the past it may have been justified on the basis that there were so few synagogues and those few were concentrated in particular areas. If so, in days when travel was more difficult, it may have been unreasonable to expect Jews outside those areas to travel long distances in order to marry. This justification is now of much less weight and is, indeed, weightier in the case of some of the smaller Christian sects and, for example, Moslems and Sikhs, than in the case of the Jews.'[8]

So far as the times for weddings are concerned the working party recommended that the hours of 8 a m to 6 p m be made applicable to Jewish and Quaker weddings in the interests of uniformity, depite the fact that it is not uncommon for Jewish weddings to take place after sunset.[9]

However, when the final report of the Law Commission was published it revealed that the members were unable to reach agreement on these issues.[10] Some felt that the actual place and time of weddings were unimportant so long as the preliminaries were complied with and there was a qualified person present (such as the secretary of the synagogue) when the marriage was solemnised and the marriage was duly registered. Others agreed with the proposals of the working party.

It is submitted that the central problem is that, for purely historical reasons, Jews and Quakers now find themselves in a specially privileged position. In present circumstances, with the growth in the numbers of other faiths, the law should not be seen to be discriminating in favour of certain minority groups and against others. Either all sects and denominations must be afforded the same exemptions as Jews and Quakers (which might be to impose too little state control) or Jews and Quakers must be brought into line with everyone else. The present legal position appears to be a clear, if relatively minor, violation of the terms of the European Convention on Human Rights which provide that men and women should have the right to marry without discrimination on the ground of religion.[11]

One matter on which the Law Commission were able to reach unanimity was that the law should provide sufficient flexibility for there to be wider exceptions than at present to the basic rules governing the time and place of weddings. They agreed that the Registrar General should be empowered to issue a licence authorising a marriage outside the prescribed hours and elsewhere than in a registered building if in all the circumstances the parties could not reasonably be expected to comply with the normal requirements and hardship would be caused unless the dispensation were given.[12] The terms of this proviso are, however, perhaps rather too stringent.

One further recommendation of the working party which did have the support of the Law Commission may be mentioned. As we have seen, where a wedding takes place in a mosque (or a temple) designated as a registered building the parties have to exchange vows in a standard form of words in English.[13] Problems may clearly arise if the couple do not understand the meaning of the words or fail to appreciate that the marriage is monogamous in the eyes of English law. The working party proposed that the celebrant should ensure that the statutory formula for the exchange of vows not only made plain the requirement of monogamy but was also translated for the benefit of any couple who did not have a sufficient grasp of English to understand its meaning otherwise.[14] Such a reform is surely desirable.

1 Law Com No 53: Report on Solemnisation of Marriage in England and Wales.
2 See p 6.
3 At p 47.
4 At pp 42-7.
5 At p 43.
6 At p 45.
7 At pp 45-6.
8 At p 48.
9 At p 54.
10 At p 7.
11 Arts 12 and 14. See also arts 2(1) and 23(2) of the International Covenant on Civil and Political Rights.
12 At p 7.
13 See para 2.31 above.
14 At pp 52-3.

E. BRIDEWEALTH, DOWRY AND DOWER[1]

2.35 Bridewealth, dowry and dower are words used to denote transfers of property upon the occasion of or arising out of marriage. Usually these transfers not only have a symbolic value but also represent significant methods of redistributing material wealth in a particular community. Bridewealth is a term most frequently used to describe payments made by the kin of the groom to the kin of the bride, particularly in Africa. Traditionally the payment was often made in the form of cattle, but today this has been replaced by money in many places. The bridewealth received by the bride's family can be utilised for the marriage of one of her brothers and in any event constitutes public recognition that she has moved from one family to another and in patrilineal societies that her children will belong to the lineage of her husband.

Dowry, by contrast, is an expression best employed to denote a transfer of property to the bride herself by her own parents. Thus strictly it relates not to a transaction between two families designed to create a relationship of affinity but rather to one within the girl's own family. It is paid where daughters are recognised as having rights of inheritance and in a sense represents a payment on account of future prospects. Dowry is mainly confined to certain countries in Europe (especially around the Mediterranean) and to parts of Asia. In practice, although it is given to the wife, it is commonly made available to the husband during the marriage and can be used as part of the family assets for business, farming or investment.

Dower (*mahr*) is a recognised institution in Islamic law and is payable by the husband to his wife as a consequence of the marriage rather than in consideration of it. It may either be payable immediately after the marriage ('prompt' dower) or be 'deferred' until its dissolution through divorce or the husband's death. Similar settlements upon the wife in cases of the husband's death or on divorce (as long as she was not at fault) are provided for, at least in theory, by the Jewish marriage contract or *ketubah*.[2]

1 See generally, *Mair*, ch 4; Goody and Tambiah *Bridewealth and Dowry* (Cambridge, 1973); *Pearl* pp 57-64.
2 It would appear that in the view of most writers and judges the modern Jewish *ketubah* is no more than a ceremonial document and does not give rise to any legal obligation or indebtedness – see Horowitz *The Spirit of Jewish Law* (New York, 1953) p 315; Schecter (1969-70) Journal of Family Law 425; *Wener v Wener* 35 App Div 2d 50 (1974); *Morris v Morris* (1974) 2 WWR 193. Cf. *Stern v Stern* (1979) 5 FLR 2810 (US). For the relevance of a *ketubah* to a husband's obligation to deliver a bill of divorce (*get*) to his wife following a civil divorce, see paras 5.17-5.18 below.

Policy considerations

2.36 The payment of bridewealth in Africa and dower in Islamic countries has come in for some strong criticism, particularly from outside observers. During the colonial period it was common for missionaries and other Europeans in Africa to denigrate the custom of bridewealth as amounting to wife-purchase and slavery and to do their utmost to suppress it.[1] The fact that they were nowhere successful, coupled with the careful explanations and justifications provided in recent years by anthropologists, have tended to reflect not only its integral socio-economic importance in many African societies but also its deep-rooted place in traditional culture. Some of its functions are apparent from this comment by Beattie:

'In patrilineal, exogamous societies, where the bride leaves her natal group and is taken into the quite separate group of her husband . . . bridewealth does have the character of an indemnity. By the marriage the bride's group has lost a working member and a potential child-bearer, and the bridewealth paid for her is a kind of compensation for this loss . . . Also the transfer of goods which bridewealth involves is rarely a one-way process. Often return gifts have to be made by the bride's group, and often these exchanges continue for quite a long time after the marriage has taken place. Thus marriage may imply the initiation of a continuing series of exchanges between the two groups concerned.

Again, the payment does not imply the transfer of *all* rights in the bride to the husband and his kin as it would if the transaction were an outright purchase. Marrying a wife is not like buying a slave . . . Even in patrilineally organised societies some rights usually remain with the wife and her group. The bridewealth may serve as security for his good behaviour as well as for hers. If the wife behaves badly her husband may divorce her and demand the return of his bridewealth. Her parents will normally be reluctant to repay it, especially nowadays when it is often cash and may have been spent; they may accordingly put pressure on their daughter to behave herself so that they will not be called upon to refund it. But also, in many societies if the husband maltreats his wife or fails to support her she may leave him, and if he is found to be at fault his affines may refuse to return the bridewealth, so that he loses both property and wife.'[2]

Thus while the modern commercialisation of bridewealth is generally deplored as a distortion of the original concept, the practice still has its merits. The Christian churches in Africa no longer take such a hostile stand against it, but rather tend to believe that if it buttresses the stability of marriage and provided it is not abused it must at least be allowed to continue because of the strength of African public opinion in its favour.[3]

Similar criticisms have been levelled against the Islamic institution of dower on the basis that it amounts to a sale of the wife and that brides' fathers have been able to make extortionate demands on behalf of their daughters, especially if they have received an expensive education. Limited attempts have been made to curb excessive payments or abolish the practice outright, but without much success.[4] However, dower is basically a vital form of economic protection for divorced wives and widows in societies where they might otherwise be left without suitable financial provision.

On the face of it there seems little reason to oppose the obligation of a bride's family to provide her with a dowry on marriage. However, the custom may become so distorted in practice that it creates a grave social evil, as now appears to be the case in India. The greed of some husbands' families has led them to demand that very large dowries should be provided for their future daughter-in-law (often running to several thousand pounds) and when that is not forthcoming they burn her to death.[5] These monstrous killings have been estimated to be as frequent as at least one every day of the year,[6] though the authorities often unrealistically claim that most of these were cases of suicides or accidents. Long established anti-dowry legislation in India[7] prohibits not only dowries payable to brides themselves but also any payment 'as consideration for the marriage', an expression wide enough to include those sums of money sometimes demanded by the husband's family which in reality constitute a form of 'bridegroom-price'.[8] However, the Act is little known and insufficient effort is made to enforce it.

1 See Phillips and Morris *Marriage Laws in Africa* pp 18-20.
2 *Other Cultures* p 124.
3 See Hastings *Christian Marriage in Africa* (London, 1973) pp 108-10; Shorter *African Culture and the Christian Church* (Chapman, 1973) pp 166-72.
4 See *Anderson* p 131; *Pearl* pp 59-60; Mahmood *Muslim Personal Law*, pp 72-4.
5 Chowdhury, 'Burning of the Brides' (1979) 81 New Internationalist 27.
6 *The Guardian*, 28 July 1980, p 5.

7 Dowry Prohibition Act 1961, s 2.
8 See Derrett *Introduction to Modern Hindu Law* (OUP, 1963) pp 145-6. *Mahr* is, however, expressly excluded from the definition of dowry in the Act – see *Mahmood* p 116.

English conflicts law

2.37 Although no obligation to pay bridewealth, dowry or dower is owed under English domestic law (in the absence of a binding contract to that effect[1]), this does not automatically mean that no liability arising out of the provisions of a foreign law can be recognised by our courts.

Obviously no court would ever make an order for the payment of dowry where the foreign legal system in question actually prohibited such payments (as in the case of the Indian Dowry Prohibition Act), but the institution of dowry is a perfectly lawful one in many countries and it emerges clearly from a case about Greek law that such payments may be enforceable through the English courts in certain circumstances.

In *Phrantzes v Argenti*[2] a Greek girl had married in England. She subsequently claimed in the English courts both a declaration that under Greek law she was entitled to be provided with a dowry by her father (who was also a Greek national and was assumed to be domiciled in Greece), and an inquiry to establish the exact amount due. Lord Parker CJ held that if under Greek law her right were simply to payment of a fixed sum of money or a definite proportion of her father's fortune then the English courts would certainly enforce it. However, it transpired from the evidence that the Greek law on dowries was by no means so straightforward. In reality a daughter's right was to an order 'condemning' her father to instruct a notary public to draw up a dowry contract in accordance with the directions of the court and to enter into that contract with his son-in-law, who might not even be a party to the proceedings. Before such order could be made the Greek court would have to inquire into the extent of the father's fortune as well as that of his daughter. The court would also have to consider the respective social positions of the father and son-in-law in deciding on the appropriate amount of dowry to be paid. Many other questions relating to the type of property which should constitute the dowry would also have to be determined. Lord Parker CJ therefore held that since all these inquiries and decisions necessarily involved the discretion of the Greek domestic courts it would be wrong for an English court to claim jurisdiction in the matter. Further reasons for declining to give the remedies sought were that English law as the *lex fori* did not furnish a suitable cause of action nor did it afford appropriate relief, namely an order 'condemning' someone to enter a contract in a particular form with a person who was not even a party to the proceedings. Simply to order the father to pay a fixed sum would be a travesty of the detailed machinery of Greek law on the matter. The English remedy sought had to 'harmonise with the right according to its nature and extent as fixed by the foreign law'.[3]

A case where this harmony was achieved was *Shahnaz v Rizwan*.[4] The plaintiff claimed payment of £1,400 as the sterling equivalent of the deferred dower specified in an Islamic marriage contract. The couple had married in India and the contract provided for the *mahr* to be payable upon the dissolution of the marriage, which occurred when the husband divorced the plaintiff by *talaq*.[5] Winn J upheld the plaintiff's claim on the ground that it was based on a recognised contractual obligation, enforceable under Islamic law by ordinary civil action (aside from matrimonial proceedings) and that there was no sufficient reason why the same remedy should not be afforded here. However, had the amount of dower not been specified in the marriage contract it may be doubted whether the wife would have been successful in her claim. In Islamic law if no *mahr* sum is specified, the religious courts are entrusted with the task of working out a 'proper' dower on the basis of the *mahr* paid to women of similar social status to the wife, notably her close relatives.[6] English courts might well feel incompetent to make such an assessment.[7]

Presumably similar principles would apply to a claim for bridewealth brought before the English courts. The first requirement would be that the obligation was owed under the relevant foreign law. Thus if the couple were married in England the obligation might not necessarily arise if the relevant African law provided that bridewealth was only payable as part of a customary marriage and not upon the occurrence of a civil or statutory marriage, unless there was a separate agreement to pay.[8] Second, the amount payable would have to be a fixed or easily ascertainable one which did not involve the English court in a process with which it was unfamiliar, as in *Phrantzes v Argenti*. Hence where the bridewealth was payable over a lengthy and undefined period depending upon the economic circumstances of the parties an English court might decline jurisdiction and hold that any decision should be left to the discretion of the relevant African courts.

1 Any such contract would need to be made under seal unless some valuable consideration was given in return for the promise to pay.
2 [1960] 2 QB 19, [1960] 1 All ER 778.
3 At 35.
4 [1965] 1 QB 390, [1964] 2 All ER 993.
5 For *talaq* divorces, see para 5.03 below.
6 See *Pearl* p 61.
7 See *Pearl* p 190. Cf his earlier views that English courts ought to assess the proper dower, 'Muslim Marriages in English Law' [1972A] CLJ 120 at 135, 142.
8 See e g Poulter *Legal Dualism in Lesotho* (Morija, 1979) pp 34-40, 58-60; *Phillips and Morris* pp 192-6.

CHAPTER 3

Polygamy

INTRODUCTION

3.01 Polygamy denotes a system of plural marriage in which at one and the same time a husband may be married to more than one wife or a wife may be married to more than one husband. The latter situation (polyandry) has been permitted in very few societies, the most well-known being located in Tibet and India.[1] The former pattern is far more common and though technically designated polygyny it will be referred to here for convenience simply as polygamy. It is widely practised throughout the continents of Africa and Asia, being sanctioned both by traditional customs and by the doctrines of Islam. A marriage may be said to be 'actually polygamous' where the husband is in fact married to two or more wives, whereas it is 'potentially polygamous' if he is currently married to only one wife, while retaining the right to take further wives at some time in the future.

In most of the societies in which polygamy is recognised a variety of justifications for the practice can be found along the following lines.[2]

First, it increases a man's prospects of having numerous children who can not only contribute to the family's material well-being and prestige but also continue its line and carry on its name through future generations. Hillman elaborates eloquently on this aspect when he writes:

'A large number of offspring is regarded as a matter of socio-economic urgency in an area where subsistence food production depends on the labour force that each family provides for itself, where the average rate of child mortality is very high, where the continuation of the family through male heirs is a grave responsibility ..., where leadership qualities are developed only through the good management of large families, where personal relationships are always regarded as more valuable than the possession of things, and where a large number of well-brought-up children is looked upon as the greatest of human achievements. Where the desire for as many children as possible is paramount, as it is in the family units of almost every African society, the practice of polygamy may be seen as an efficient means of realising socially approved goals and social ideals.'[3]

Second, polygamy creates valuable new alliances between families.[4] Apart from making useful political connections, multiple marriage relationships help to provide security in times of need such as sickness, old age or famine. Few people in the Third World can realistically look to their governments for much state support in such circumstances and the wider the range of relatives a man has the better his protection. Reciprocal assistance patterns thus serve to buttress the contribution expected from one's own children.

Third, a plurality of wives can be useful in the cultivation of crops where the husband has a substantial allocation of land and it is customary for women to work in the fields.[5] The wives and what they produce can also help promote the husband's hospitality to visitors and thus extend his family's influence and prestige.

Fourth, in many societies there seems to be an imbalance in the population leading to a larger number of women of normal marriageable age than men.[6] In the past this may have been caused by losses in hunting and battle.[7] To some extent these considerations still apply, but it also appears that today the high figures in many parts of the world for infant and child mortality brought about by illness and disease contain a greater proportion of boys.[8] In these circumstances polygamy can help to provide almost all women with husbands, which is especially desirable where social norms prescribe childbearing as the pre-eminent feminine role and equally demand that such children should be legitimate rather than illegitimate.[9]

Finally, for Muslims polygamy is expressly authorised by the Koran with the twin provisos that before a man takes a second or subsequent wife he is under a religious duty to consider whether he can accord them equal treatment and that in any event the number of wives may not exceed four.[10]

1 See Prince Peter of Greece and Denmark *A Study of Polyandry* (The Hague, 1963).
2 See generally, Hillman *Polygamy Reconsidered* (New York, 1975); Lemu *Woman in Islam* (Leicester, 1978) pp 27-9; El Saadawi *The Hidden Face of Eve: Women in the Arab World* (London, 1980) p 135; Ellis (ed) *West African Families in Britain* (London, 1978) pp 24, 40-1.
3 At pp 114-5.
4 See Mair *Marriage* (Penguin, 1971) p 152.
5 Mair 'African Marriage and Social Change' in Phillips (ed) *A Survey of African Marriage and Family Life* (OUP, 1953) pp 106, 136, 153.
6 This is, it should be admitted, a matter of considerable debate and controversy among demographers and anthropologists.
7 It is interesting to note that even the ancient Greeks temporarily licensed polygamy after the disastrous Sicilian Expedition of 413 BC in which they suffered huge losses. Both Socrates and Euripides appear to have taken second wives under this law – see Zimmern *The Greek Commonwealth* (5th edn, 1931) p 340.
8 See e g Chandrasekhar *Infant Mortality, Population Growth and Family Planning in India* (London, 1972) p 152.
9 See Beattie *Other Cultures* p 118.
10 *The Koran* (Sale's translation, London, 1801), vol I, p 92; Pearl *A Textbook on Muslim Law* (London, 1979) pp 69-70.

Policy considerations

3.02 In the past, as we shall see, the strongest objection to polygamy has been based on its alleged incompatibility with Christian teaching. However, a number of modern theologians have recently cast doubt on whether there really are any passages in the New Testament which expressly forbid polygamy.[1] It appears that the particular evils repudiated by Jesus were adultery, divorce and remarriage (i e serial monogamy) rather than polygamy itself. No doubt these suggestions are extremely controversial[2] and no firm conclusions on the subject can be reached, but what is noticeable is that the Christian Church itself is earnestly seeking a new and conciliatory way forward in its approach towards polygamy in Africa.[3]

Whatever the reactions of previous generations in Britain may have been towards polygamy, it is clear that with the increasing secularisation of English society in the twentieth century fresh grounds for objecting to polygamy must be found if they are to stand up to serious contemporary examination. The first is that polygamy is alien to English traditions and culture which have long prescribed the monogamous form of marriage.[4] This, of course, carries more weight if it is used to justify a ban on polygamy in this country or among members of the indigenous population than among those with different traditions and practices. Even so the valid point may be made that while polygamy may arguably be appropriate for the socio-economic conditions found in some Third World countries, the structure of English society is so markedly different that polygamy is incapable of conferring the same sorts of benefits here. The second is a belief (almost certainly erroneous) that it is an inevitable consequence of polygamy that wives will be lowly rated and ill-treated. Much of the evidence runs in the opposite direction and suggests that, far from being degraded, African wives in polygamous societies have a generally high social position.[5] Moreover, whereas in a monogamous marriage a husband who is dissatisfied with his wife for some reason (eg because she is barren) must discard her if he is to remarry, polygamous societies afford such wives considerable compassion and protection. Third, it is argued that, whatever the position may be in practice, the very fact that a man may have more than one wife while a wife may only have one husband is a serious violation of the principles of sexual equality. Hardly any societies have simultaneously permitted both polygyny and polyandry and whichever system is in operation it confers upon one spouse alone the exclusive right to take further spouses concurrently with the first and the concomitant capacity to affect fundamentally and unilaterally the family life of the first. Modern English values are offended by the clear sexual inequality involved.

1 See *Hillman* pp 139-40. For a revealing account of the 'underground' Christian tradition in favour of polygamy, see J Cairncross *After Polygamy Was Made A Sin: The Social History of Christian Polygamy* (Routledge, 1974).

2 They are not accepted by Shorter *African Culture and the Christian Church* p 175.

3 See generally *Hillman; Shorter* pp 176-7; Hastings *Christian Marriage in Africa* (SPCK, 1973).

4 It would appear that monogamy was the established system in Western Europe long before the advent of Christianity – see Stone (1961) 24 MLR 501.

5 *Hillman* pp 126-7; Bohannan and Curtin *Africa and Africans* (New York, 1971) pp 105-10; *Ellis* pp 24-5.

English domestic law

3.03 English domestic law has attempted to impose an outright ban on polygamy through the operation of three rules.

First, a person who is a party to a subsisting marriage cannot validly contract a second or subsequent marriage with another person. The second or subsequent marriage would be void ab initio.[1] Such conduct might also invite a charge of bigamy. This offence carries a maximum sentence of seven years' imprisonment, but it is a defence for the accused to show either that he reasonably believed his first marriage had been legally terminated or that his spouse had been absent continually for the previous seven years and that he did not know her to be alive within that time.[2]

Second, it would appear that all marriages validly contracted in England are necessarily monogamous, even though the personal laws of the parties may allow polygamy.[3] Hence a party to a valid potentially polygamous marriage contracted abroad cannot enter a second marriage in England.[4] Equally, any subsequent marriage abroad following upon one contracted here ought logically to be void in the eyes of English law, even though it might be valid by the parties' *lex domicilii*.[5] There is, however, no decided case in England on this latter point and the position must be regarded as uncertain.[6]

Third, in order to contract a valid marriage in England the proper statutory procedure must be adhered to and a lawful ceremony must be performed in accordance with the provisions of the Marriage Act 1949. An informal ceremony appropriate for a polygamous marriage will not be recognised by English law as validly constituting the parties' husband and wife.[7] This appears to be rather more clearly established today than it was in the past, although the authorities are still somewhat inconclusive. In *R v Bham*,[8] the most recent decision, the accused was charged with knowingly and wilfully solemnising a marriage in an unregistered building contrary to the Marriage Act 1949, s 75(2). What the accused had done was to perform a type of Islamic ceremony of marriage in a private house. Such a ceremony is designed to create a potentially polygamous marriage. He was acquitted by the court on the ground that the section only applies to ceremonies in a form known to and recognised by English domestic law as capable of producing a valid marriage. The implication of the decision is that ceremonies which do not even purport to comply with the minimum requirements of the Marriage Act do not qualify as marriages for the purposes of English law.

1 Matrimonial Causes Act 1973, s 11(b).
2 Offences against the Person Act 1861, s 57.
3 See Dicey and Morris *The Conflict of Laws* (10th edn, 1980) pp 308-10, 313-4 and the cases cited there.
4 *Baindail v Baindail* [1946] p 122 [1946] 1 All Er 342.
5 *Dicey and Morris* P 313.
6 The contrary was merely assumed in *Nabi v Heaton* [1981] 1 WLR 1052, but without proper argument on the point.
7 *Dicey and Morris* pp 314-6.
8 [1966] 1 QB 159 [1965] 3 All ER 124, overruling *R v Rahman* [1949] 2 All ER 165. Cf *Re Belshah* (1927) *Times*, 18 January.

English conflicts law

1 Hyde v Hyde

3.04 The natural starting point for any discussion of the attitude of English conflicts law towards polygamy is the decision in 1866 of Sir James Wilde (later Lord Penzance) in *Hyde v Hyde and Woodmansee*.[1] Hyde was born in England. In 1848 at the age of 15 he embraced the Mormon faith and was soon afterwards ordained a priest. Later he set out for Salt Lake City and was married there. The wedding was celebrated by Brigham Young, the president of the Mormon church and governor of the territory of Utah. Since the marriage was contracted in Mormon form it was, of course, potentially polygamous – that being an integral part of Mormon doctrine at the time. Hyde soon became disillusioned with Mormon practices and while working as a missionary in the Sandwich Islands (now Hawaii) he publicly renounced the faith and preached against it. This led to sentences of excommunication from the church and divorce from his wife being pronounced against him in Utah early in 1857 and Mrs Hyde was simultaneously declared free to marry again. The same year he published in New York a highly critical account of what he had seen in Salt Lake City under the title *Mormonism: Its Leaders and Designs*,[2] in which he singled out the Mormon practice of polygamy as particularly objectionable. He then returned to England and eventually became the minister of a dissenting chapel at Derby. He had written to his wife begging her to leave Utah and abandon the Mormon faith, but to no avail for she remained with her relatives and some time later married a man named Woodmansee. Hyde thereupon instituted divorce proceedings in England, relying upon his wife's adultery in living with Woodmansee. As will be seen, this step was necessary since English law would not have recognised the validity of the Mormon divorce. Paradoxically, despite Hyde's total public rejection of the theory and practice of polygamy it was to be this very feature of Mormon doctrine and custom which prevented his petition from succeeding. The Divorce Court took the view that potentially polygamous marriages (such as his) were to be treated in exactly the same way as actually polygamous marriages and it rejected his petition on the ground that the Court possessed no remedial jurisdiction over unions of a polygamous nature. Polygamy and 'marriage as understood in Christendom' were held to be totally different institutions;[3] English law was adapted only to the latter and would be quite unsuitable for application to the former. Lord Penzance stated the position in uncompromising language:

'We have in England no law framed on the scale of polygamy, or adjusted to its requirements. And it may well be doubted whether it would become the tribunals of this country to enforce the duties (even if we knew them) which belong to a system so utterly at variance with the Christian conception of marriage, and so revolting to the ideas we entertain of the social position to be accorded to the weaker sex.'[4]

Although Lord Penzance's judgment is replete with invidious remarks about polygamous societies it is important to emphasise the limits of the actual decision that he reached. These are set out in the final paragraph of his judgment as follows:

'. . . the Court must reject the prayer of this petition, but I may take the occasion of here observing that this decision is confined to that object. This Court does not profess to decide upon the rights of succession or legitimacy which it might be proper to accord to the issue of the polygamous unions, nor upon the rights or obligations in relation to third persons which people living under the sanction of such unions may have created for themselves. All that is intended to be here decided is that as between each other they are not entitled to the remedies, the adjudication, or the relief of the matrimonial law of England.'[5]

It is clear, therefore, that polygamous marriages were by no means being subjected to total non-recognition at the hands of the English courts. Even so the decision obviously did make serious inroads into the general policy of English law in relation to the recognition of foreign marriages. As indicated in the previous chapter,[6] this policy was to leave the formal validity of a foreign marriage to be determined by the law of the place of celebration (*lex loci contractus*)[7] and the question of capacity to the law of the parties' domicile.[8] If both these criteria had been properly complied with the marriage basically qualified for full recognition by the English courts. What Lord Penzance's decision achieved was to place an additional obstacle in the way of the complete recognition of a certain class of marriages (i e those of a polygamous nature), on clear grounds of public policy, despite the fact that the rules of both the *lex loci* and the *lex domicilii* had been adhered to.

The most specific reason given by Lord Penzance for denying relief in cases involving polygamous marriages was that if English matrimonial remedies were to be applied to them 'the Court would be creating conjugal duties, not enforcing them, and furnishing remedies where there was no offence.'[9] In support he provided two illustrations of how he considered such a situation could arise.

First, 'it would be quite unjust and almost absurd to visit a man who, among a polygamous community had married two women, with divorce from the first woman on the ground that, in our view of marriage, his conduct amounted to adultery coupled with bigamy.' However, even if English matrimonial remedies were to be applied to them, polygamists in such a situation as this would surely have committed neither adultery nor bigamy, even according to English law. If, as Lord Penzance assumes, the first marriage of a polygamist would be recognised as basically valid in English law, provided the rules of the *lex loci* and the *lex domicilii* had been adhered to, presumably logic would dictate that the same validity be afforded to the second marriage if the same conditions had been satisfied. How, then, could the first wife conceivably maintain that her husband was committing adultery in cohabiting with his second wife? Adultery means sexual intercourse by a married person outside marriage, not within it. Furthermore, the crime of bigamy would surely only have been committed where the second marriage was void in terms of the *lex domicilii*, not where it was recognised as valid.[10]

Second, Lord Penzance contended that it would not be just or wise to attempt to enforce upon a polygamist the same standard of treatment and consideration towards his wife as was her due in a 'Christian' marriage.[11] However, English law was hardly over-zealous at this time in its protection of wives against violent, debauched, adulterous or despotic husbands.[12] Probably greater protection was afforded by Islamic, Hindu and Burmese Buddhist law at this period.[13] Nor does it seem that there could have been any strong policy reasons why the minimal remedies afforded by the English law should not have been made equally available to a wife who had been married polygamously abroad. The English courts would have possessed no jurisdiction over her marriage in any event unless she was domiciled in this country and that necessarily meant that her husband would have had to possess an English domicile too.[14] This would in turn give some indication of the couple's close connection with this country and hence provide a strong justification for subjecting them to the same standards of marital behaviour as those required of the rest of the community. Moreover, the law applied in all matrimonial causes was English law, which meant that no regard was paid to whether any misconduct complained of by the petitioner constituted grounds for relief in terms of the *lex loci celebrationis*.[14] Thus there was never any question of the court having to embark on the task of setting standards of treatment for a polygamous community where the marriage was de facto monogamous nor should this have proved insurmountable in the rare case of an actually polygamous marriage.

The immediate consequence of the decision was that Hyde found himself a party to a limping marriage. He was divorced so far as the law of Utah was concerned but still married in the eyes of English law. The English courts would not have been prepared to recognise the validity of the divorce pronounced by the Mormon elders. At that period foreign divorces were only accorded recognition if they were granted in the country of the husband's domicile[14] and in the present case Hyde seems clearly to have lost his domicile in Utah by the time the divorce was decreed.[15] This outcome seems particularly harsh for two further reasons quite separate from the inadequate justifications put forward by Lord Penzance for distinguishing between polygamous and 'Christian' marriages. First, the Hydes' marriage was in fact only potentially polygamous[16] and there is no good reason to suppose that any of the general criticisms levelled against polygamy by Lord Penzance were applicable to their particular marriage. Second, if polygamy was indeed as evil as Lord Penzance painted it, surely Hyde should have been enabled to escape any further taint from its cloying iniquities as rapidly as possible since he himself had totally and publicly rejected the practice and had also renounced the Mormon faith many years before. Neither of these factors was considered by the court.[17] One practical reason subsequently advanced judicially for not treating a potentially polygamous but de facto monogamous marriage as on all fours with a 'Christian' marriage was that a husband could always invalidate pending proceedings by taking a second wife. 'Such a situation would be incongruous and shows the undesirability of seeking to alter the principle on the ground of convenience in particular cases'.[18] While there is some small degree of force in this argument it should be remembered that the husband could not take a second wife in England and if he was determined to 'invalidate the proceedings', for instance in order to deny his wife maintenance, he could often achieve this just as effectively by leaving the country without going to the extra trouble of marrying a second time as well.

1 (1866) LR1 P & D 130. Part of the material in this section first appeared as an article by the author in (1976) 25 ICLQ 475.
2 (WP Fetridge & Co, New York, 1857.)
3 For criticisms of the judgment on this score see (1976) 25 ICLQ 475 at 480-6.
4 At 136.
5 At 138.
6 See para 2.01 above.
7 *Dalrymple v Dalrymple* (1811) 2 Hagg Con 54; *Herbert v Herbert* (1819) 2 Hagg Con 263.
8 *Brook v Brook* (1858) 3 Sm & G 481, (1861) 9 HLC at 193; *Mette v Mette* (1859) 1 Sw & Tr 416.
9 At 135.
10 See further para 3.16 below.
11 Lord Penzance's copious references to 'Christian' marriage were, of course, mere religious embellishment. He simply meant English monogamous marriages, which could take place either in church or in a register office without regard to whether the parties were Christians or not.
12 See (1976) 25 ICLQ 475 at 480-4.
13 See Vesey-Fitzgerald 'Mixed Marriages' (1948) CLP 222 at 228; Morris 'The Recognition of Polygamous Marriages in English Law' (1953) 66 Harvard LR at 990.
14 *Warrender v Warrender* (1835) 2 Cl & Fin 488; *Harvey v Farnie* (1881) 6 PD 35.
15 He had surely abandoned any intention of returning to Utah from the Sandwich Islands.
16 For the view that it was not merely de facto monogamous but legally so, on the grounds that Utah was not at the time a state but only a territory and hence subject to US Federal law which prescribed monogamy, see Bartholomew 'Polygamous Marriages' (1952) 15 MLR 35 at 36. The main thrust of Bartholomew criticism of *Hyde* is, however, that the concept of polygamy should have been confined to situations where there was in fact a plurality of wives. For this approach, see also Vesey-Fitzgerald 'Nachimson's and Hyde's Cases' (1931) 47 LQR 253.
17 Lord Penzance did consider (at 136-7) whether the English matrimonial law could properly be applied to the first of a series of polygamous marriages, but he sensibly rejected the idea because of the unrealities and inconsistencies that would arise.
18 *Sowa v Sowa* [1961] P 70 at 84.

3.05 The longer term repercussions of the decision in *Hyde* took over a century to work themselves out.[1] Early on the decision itself was misinterpreted both in the courts and in textbooks and for 50 years the law appeared to take an even harder and more intolerant line than Lord Penzance had actually laid down. In *Re Bethell, Bethell v Hildyard*[2] for instance, it was held that in the eyes of English law a potentially polygamous marriage could not be recognised as a valid marriage at all.[3] Ultimately the true rationale of *Hyde* was restored in a series of cases around the time of the 1939-45 war.[4] With the growth of immigration from the Commonwealth after 1945 the volume of cases started to increase and the English courts found themselves on the horns of a dilemma. On the one hand, *Hyde's case* provided a clear precedent which in principle ought to be followed. On the other, the decision seemed to reflect an outmoded Victorian attitude towards foreign customs and was obviously capable of operating extremely harshly on the individuals concerned. The reaction of the courts during the period 1950 to 1968 was to distinguish *Hyde's case* wherever possible,[5] but when the material facts were indistinguishable to follow that decision, even where the court considered the result to be extremely unjust. Thus in *Sowa v Sowa*[6] a party to a potentially polygamous marriage was denied the right to claim maintenance from her husband on the strength of *Hyde's case*.

What is interesting is that although *Hyde v Hyde* was only decided by a single judge in the Divorce Court, i e in modern terms by the equivalent of a judge sitting alone in the Family Division of the High Court, even the Court of Appeal felt constrained to follow it. Admittedly in the majority of cases it did prove possible to distinguish *Hyde*, but only at the cost of introducing the sorts of fine distinction, absurd artificiality and bogus historical explanation which tend to bring the law into disrepute.[7] By the time the matter was considered by the Law Commission in 1968 the case for reform was clear.

1 For a detailed analysis, see (1976) 25 ICLQ 475 at 491-503.
2 (1888) 38 ChD 220.
3 An attitude of total non-recognition of polygamous marriages is also to be found in *Harvey v Farnie* (1881) 6 PD 35 at 53; *R v Hammersmith Superintendent Registrar of Marriages, ex p Mir-Anwaruddin* [1917] 1 KB 634 at 637: *R v Naguib* [1917] 1 KB 359 at 360 (Avory J); Westlake *Private International Law* (6th edn 1922) pp 68-9 and Morris *Cases in Private International Law* (1st edn 1939) pp 89-90.
4 See *The Sinha Peerage Claim* (1939) 171 Lords' Journals 350, [1946] 1 All ER 348; *Srini Vasan v Srini Vasan* [1946] P 67, [1945] 2 All ER 21; *Baindail v Baindail* [1946] P 122, [1946] 1 All ER 342 in which the validity of foreign polygamous marriages was upheld.
5 See e g *Ohochuku v Ohochuku* [1960] 1 All ER 253, [1960] 1 WLR 183; *Parkasho v Singh* [1968] P 233, [1967] 1 All ER 737; *Ali v Ali* [1968] P 564, [1966] 1 All ER 664.
6 See e g *Sowa v Sowa* [1961] P 70, [1960] 3 All ER 196.
7 See Webb (1960) 23 MLR 327; Furmston (1961) 10 ICLQ 180 at 183; Tolstoy (1968) 17 ICLQ 721.

2 The rule in Hyde *abolished by statute: recognition for purposes of matrimonial relief*

3.06 After circulating a working paper on the subject in 1968[1] the Law Commission finally produced a report in 1971 recommending the outright abolition of the rule in *Hyde's case*.[2] Surprisingly, the recommendation was not unanimous, one member dissenting on the ground that for the English courts to grant matrimonial relief in cases where a marriage was *actually* polygamous 'not only represents a departure from the basic principles of English law concerning the marriage relationship, in its many aspects, but its adoption would face the courts with problems with which they are not designed or equipped to deal.'[3] However, the draft Bill which the Commission had proposed passed quickly through Parliament to become the Matrimonial Proceedings (Polygamous Marriages) Act 1972.[4] Its main provision now re-enacted in the Matrimonial Causes Act 1973, declares that an English court is not precluded from granting matrimonial relief or making a declaration concerning the validity of a marriage by reason only that the marriage was entered into under a law which permitted polygamy, whether in the particular case the husband actually had a plurality of wives or not. The Law Commission justified the reform by arguing that parties to polygamous marriages should be encouraged to conform to English standards of behaviour by having, so far as practicable, the same rights and obligations in marriage as other married people living in England.[5] However, the reform can just as easily be seen as one permitting greater diversity as opposed to one imposing a greater degree of uniformity since increased recognition was being given to an essentially alien custom.

1 Law Com Working Paper No 21.
2 Law Com Report No 42.
3 Report, p 46 (Memorandum of dissent by Sir Neil Lawson QC).
4 See 829 HC Official Reports (5th series) col 924; 321 HL Official Reports (5th series) cols 1208-25, 331 HL Official Reports (5th series), cols 16-21, 1186-1202.
5 Law Com Report No 42, p 22.

3.07 The first reported case on the new law was that of *Onobrauche v Onobrauche*.[1]

The husband had married his first wife in Nigeria by customary rites in 1962. The couple came to England and had five children. In 1972 the husband returned to Nigeria and took a second wife, again in accordance with customary law. Since he had retained his Nigerian domicile throughout this period both marriages were recognised as valid in English law. Though the first wife did not object to the second wife coming to share the house with her, she subsequently petitioned for divorce, relying on the husband's alleged adultery in living with his second wife or, in the alternative, his 'unreasonable behaviour'. Comyn J predictably held that it was 'artificial' to describe the second marriage as adulterous and granted the petition on the basis of the alternative ground. Adultery would only be committed by the husband if he had intercourse with someone who was not his lawful wife.

What would be the legal position in this regard in the event of a valid monogamous marriage being followed by a valid polygamous one? If a Muslim husband marries his first wife in England that marriage will very probably be treated as monogamous in terms of English law, even if it is regarded as potentially polygamous by his *lex domicilii* or personal law. If he then takes a second wife overseas through a polygamous marriage which is regarded as valid by his *lex domicilii* or personal law what would be the attitude of English law? It has already been explained that while logic requires that the second marriage be treated as void in English law there is no clear precedent on the point and a future decision might go the other way.[2] If the validity of the second marriage were in fact to be upheld it would hardly seem possible for the first wife to be granted a divorce for adultery by the English courts in view of the definition of adultery given earlier.[3] More realistically, a decree might be based on 'unreasonable behaviour' within the Matrimonial Causes Act 1973, s 1(2)(b).[4]

1 (1978) 8 Fam Law 107.
2 See para 3.03, above; Law Com Report No 146: Polygamous Marriages (1985), paras 4.10-4.14.
3 See, however, the Privy Council decision in *Drammeh v Drammeh* (1970) 78 Ceylon Law Weekly 55 discussed by North *The Private International Law of Matrimonial Causes in the British Isles and the Republic of Ireland* (North-Holland, 1977) pp 111-2.
4 *North* ibid; *Pearl* [1978] *New Community* 287 at 288; *Bromley* p 59. See also the Indian case of *Itwari v Asghari* (1960) AIR (All) 684.

3.08 In *Quoraishi v Quoraishi*[1] it was held that a Muslim wife may be justified in leaving her husband if he marries a second wife, even if the marriage is valid, and that she will not necessarily be regarded as having deserted him in the eyes of English law. The couple, who were citizens of Bangladesh and doctors by profession, had married in Pakistan and had come to live in England during the 1970s. In the absence of any children of the marriage the husband had asked the wife to accept the idea of his marrying a second wife but she had refused to countenance it. Despite this he later contracted a valid second marriage by proxy with a woman in Bangladesh, which was where he was domiciled. His first wife left him and he then brought his second wife to England. His petition for a divorce from his first wife on the basis of her alleged desertion was dismissed by the Family Division. Butler-Sloss J ruled that the first wife had had good cause for leaving her husband because in acting without her consent he had taken a grave step which seriously imperilled the continuance of their marriage. The Court took account of the fact that the couple had been parties to a de facto monogamous marriage for 15 years, nine of them spent in the UK, before the husband's second marriage and that the wife had made abundantly plain to the husband her repugnancy at the notion of his marrying again. The Court was clearly influenced in reaching this conclusion by the decision of the High Court of Allahabad in the Indian case of *Itwari v Asghari*.[2] There it was held that in modern conditions the onus lay upon a husband who married a second wife against his wife's wishes to establish that this did not involve insult or cruelty to his first wife. In the absence of cogent reasons such insult or cruelty would be presumed to have been caused. This decision tended, therefore, to show that a first wife who left her husband in these circumstances had a just cause for doing so.

Under the Muslim Family Laws Ordinance 1961,[3] which is in force in Pakistan and Bangladesh, a first wife can obtain a divorce if her husband marries a second wife without obtaining written permission to do so from an 'arbitration council'. The husband in *Quoraishi's* case had apparently sought such permission but the arbitration council had declined to act because the husband was outside its jurisdiction. However, the absence of such permission and the fact that permission can only be granted in cases where a second marriage is 'necessary and just' no doubt inclined the English court towards the decision it ultimately reached since, although the matter fell to be decided in accordance with English domestic law, the Court expressly stated that in applying English law:

'the background of the parties and the circumstances of their marriage, including the Muslim law which governed the inception of the marriage, are relevant considerations.'[4]

Both the decision of Butler-Sloss J and her Ladyship's approach to the question were subsequently approved by the Court of Appeal.

1 (1983) 4 FLR 706 (FD); (1985) 15 Fam Law 308 (CA).
2 (1960) AIR (All) 684.
3 S 13, amending the Dissolution of Muslim Marriages Act 1939, s 2.
4 At 710.

3 Recognition for other purposes[1]

3.09 Ever since the *Sinha Peerage Claim*[2] in 1939 it has been clear that polygamous marriages are fully recognised for many purposes quite separate from the issue of the adjudication of matrimonial causes. The current position may be summarised as follows:

(i) A party to a potentially or actually polygamous marriage is barred by his or her status as a spouse from entering into a second or subsequent valid marriage in England.[3] The purported second or subsequent marriage would be void. However, somewhat anomalously, it has been decided that no conviction for bigamy can be sustained in such circumstances on the ground that the foundation of the offence is a prior subsisting monogamous marriage.[4] An alternative charge of perjury could nevertheless be brought if the accused had knowingly and wilfully made a false declaration about his status in giving notice of the second marriage.[5]

(ii) The children of a polygamous marriage will be treated by English law as legitimate for purposes of succession,[6] with the possible exception of the inheritance of entailed interests and, in the case of actually polygamous marriages, titles of honour.[7]

(iii) It seems clear that the surviving wife or wives of a polygamous marriage would be entitled to succeed on intestacy.[8] However, in the case of a plurality of wives, while the deceased's personal chattels would no doubt have to be divided equally between them, it is far from clear whether each surviving wife would obtain a statutory legacy of £40,000 (£85,000 in the absence of issue) or whether the legacy would have to be shared equally between them.[9] On the one hand, it can be argued that if the sum specified in the relevant statutory instrument[10] represents what a surviving spouse is thought to need today in order to provide for her accommodation and other requirements, then she should be entitled to it just like any other wife and not be restricted to a proportionate share.[11] On the other hand, the position of the other beneficiaries has to be considered and their prospects of receiving anything are greatly reduced if each of the wives is entitled to a full statutory legacy.[12]

There is no doubt that the widow of a polygamist is qualified to bring a claim for family provision out of her deceased husband's estate under the Inheritance (Provision for Family and Dependants) Act 1975.[13]

(iv) Parties to a polygamous marriage are entitled to use the Married Women's Property Act 1882, s 17 in order to determine their respective property rights. This was decided in *Chaudhry v Chaudhry*[14] where Dunn J pointed out that:

'. . . any other conclusion would be an affront to common sense, because one would have the highly inconvenient situation that parties to a polygamous marriage could apply for transfers and settlement of property under the Matrimonial Causes Act 1973 but could not apply for their rights to be determined or for sale under s 17 of the 1882 Act.'[15]

They are also entitled to assert occupation rights in the matrimonial home under the Matrimonial Homes Act 1983[16] and claim the transmission of a statutory tenancy under the Rent Act 1977 after the tenant's death.[17] Similarly, they would be entitled to claim as dependants under the Fatal Accidents Acts to the extent of their dependence on the deceased spouse.[18]

(v) A polygamous marriage is recognised for the purpose of obtaining national insurance benefits under social security legislation but only insofar as it is actually monogamous. The Social Security and Family Allowances (Polygamous Marriages) Regulations 1975[19] provide that for the purposes of the Social Security Act 1975 a polygamous marriage shall 'be treated as having the same consequences as a monogamus marriage for any day, but only for any day, throughout which the polygamous marriage is in fact monogamous'.[20]

This is a considerable advance on the position which prevailed in the early 1950s in terms of which a wife who was party to a potentially polygamous marriage was barred from claiming any benefits on the strength of her husband's insurance contributions.[21] This applied to maternity grants, widows' pensions, retirement pensions, etc and clearly caused hardship as well as being most unjust. The major reform came in the Family Allowances and National Insurance Act 1956 which recognised polygamous marriages provided they had 'at all times' in fact been monogamous. However, as the Law Commission pointed out, this did not cover cases where the marriage had once been actually polygamous but was no longer (for example because the first wife had died or been divorced before the parties came to England), nor those situations where the marriage was actually polygamous at the time when social security benefits were sought, although only one wife was physically present in England.[22] While the 1975 Regulations successfully dealt with the former problem the latter has been persistently ignored. Thus a woman who claims a widow's pension will still be barred if her husband has another wife living abroad, despite the compulsory contributions her husband has been making here through the national insurance scheme.[23]

(vi) After some doubts it is now clear that where a marriage is polygamous the husband may claim the married man's higher personal allowance for income tax purposes, provided his wife is living with him or is wholly maintained by him.[24] Only one such allowance is permitted, even if the marriage is actually polygamous.

(vii) Under the Criminal Law Act 1977, s 2(2)(a) a husband and wife cannot be convicted of the offence of conspiracy, though they may both be found guilty of conspiring with a third person. It would appear that this rule, reflecting the common law position, applies equally to parties to a polygamous marriage.[25]

1 See generally *Dicey and Morris* pp 320-8; *Bromley* pp 63-4; *Cheshire and North* pp 307-12.
2 (1939) 171 Lords' Journals 350; [1946] 1 All ER 348.
3 *Baindail v Baindail* [1946] P 122.
4 *R v Sarwan Singh* [1962] 3 All ER 612; *R v Sagoo* [1975] QB 885, [1975] 2 All ER 926.
5 Perjury Act 1911, s 3; *Dicey and Morris*, p 322.
6 See *Bamgbose v Daniel* [1955] AC 107, [1954] 3 All ER 263 (PC).
7 *Sinha Peerage Claim (above)*; Law Com Report No 146, para 3.5.
8 See *Coleman v Shang* [1961] AC 481, [1961] 2 All ER 406 (PC); *Dicey and Morris* pp 324-5; *Bromley* p 64; *Cheshire and North* p 311.
9 See *Dicey and Morris* pp 324-5.
10 Family Provision (Intestate Succession) Order 1981, SI 1981/255.
11 See Samuels, 'The Polygamous Wife: How Far is She Treated as a Wife in English Law?' (1984) JSWL 271 at 276.
12 See *Bromley* p 64.
13 *Re Sehota, Surjit Kaur v Gian Kaur* [1978] 3 All ER 385, [1978] 1 WLR 1506.
14 [1976] Fam 148. An appeal to the Court of Appeal was dismissed without discussion of the point: see [1976] 1 WLR 221.
15 At 690.
16 S 10(2).
17 *Bromley* p 64; Law Com Report No 42 pp 40-1.
18 *Dicey and Morris* p 326; Law Com Report No 42 p 41.
19 SI 1975/561.
20 Reg 2. Similar rules apply under the Child Benefit Act 1975 – see reg 12 of SI 1976/965.
21 For the history and background see Law Com Report No 42 pp 41-4; Pearl 'Social Security and the Ethnic Minorities' [1978] JSWL 24.
22 Law Com Report No 42 p 42.
23 There are slightly more favourable regulations applicable to retirement pensions for women – see *Pearl* p 29.
24 Income and Corporation Taxes Act 1970, s 8(1); *Nabi v Heaton* [1983] 1 WLR 626, CA, reversing a decision of Vinelott J [1981] 1 WLR 1052.
25 See *Bromley* p 61; *Mawji v R* [1957] AC 126, [1957] 1 All ER 385.

4. *Capacity to contract a polygamous marriage*

3.10 Although the Law Commission had made no specific recommendation on the point in their report in 1971, the Matrimonial Proceedings (Polygamous Marriages) Act 1972 included a section which incorporated a new situation into the statutory list of grounds upon which a marriage is void, namely where either party to a polygamous marriage contracted abroad was at the time of the marriage domiciled in England and Wales.[1] This provision which applied to both potentially polygamous marriages and actually polygamous marriages was subsequently incorporated in the Matrimonial Causes Act 1973 as s 11(d). Prior to 1972 the authorities on this matter were in a very confused state. Some writers had, improperly, sought to derive this rule from *Re Bethell*[2] and the same line had been adopted in a majority of the pronouncements on the subject from the bench, albeit mainly in the form of obiter dicta.[3] However the 'codification' of this supposed rule into statute law seems to have occurred without sufficient regard having been paid to the likely consequences. This is because the provision did not merely prevent a white Englishman who is domiciled here from circumventing the ban on contracting polygamous marriages in this country by purporting to do so abroad. It was framed so widely that it appeared to apply equally to immigrants who had come to Britain from countries where capacity to marry is governed by a personal or religious law which permits polygamy. All the indications are that quite a large number of Muslim immigrants, for example, particularly those from the Indian subcontinent, have not been marrying in England but have returned to their countries of origin and there entered into potentially polygamous marriages arranged by their families in accordance with the local and religious law. The return of men to find wives in the Indian subcontinent is partly explained by the comparative shortage of single Asian women living in this country.[4] The apparent effect of the new statutory provision in the case of any such person who had acquired a domicile of choice in England was to render his or her marriage totally void.[5] The adverse practical consequence of the ban for those who unwittingly purported to contract such marriages were wide-ranging,[6] affecting entry to this country,[7] the acquisition of British nationality,[8] the right to be maintained, social security benefits, inheritance[9] and possibly even the legitimacy of any children.[10] Naturally no decrees of judicial separation or divorce could be granted by the English courts. It was possible for a decree of nullity to be granted and the court would then have had power to furnish the woman with any necessary financial provision, but this hardly seemed an appropriate method of ending a relationship of long duration which had in all probability been entered into in good faith.

1 S 4, amending the Nullity Act 1971. For discussion of how the section came to be introduced and the role of the Law Commission, see the correspondence between Hartley and Morris in *The Times*, 6 and 9 September 1975; Law Com Working Paper No 83 (1982) p 17.

2 (1888) 38 Ch D 220; see (1976) 25 ICLQ 475 at 492-4.

3 E g *Re Ullee, Nawab Nazim of Bengal's Infants* (1885) 53 LT 711 at 712 (Chitty J); *Risk v Risk* [1951] P 50 (Barnard J); *Ali v Ali* [1968] P 564 [1966] 1 All ER 664 (Cumming-Bruce J). Cf *Kenward v Kenward* [1951] P 124 at 145 (Denning L J); *Radwan v Radwan (No 2)* [1973] Fam 35, [1972] 3 All ER 1026 (Cumming-Bruce J). There was a similar division of opinion on the question when the Bill was debated in the House of Lords. Lord Hailsham took the view that the new section merely codified existing law, while Lord Simon expressed considerable doubts about this (331 HL Official Reports (5th series) vols 1190-94). In *Morris v Morris* (unreported, but noted by Pearl in [1980] *New Community* 354) Wood J held that a domiciled Englishman had no capacity to contract a potentially polygamous marriage abroad in 1959.

4 See Runnymede Trust and Radical Statistics Race Group *Britain's Black Population* (London, 1980) p. 12.

5 See Hartley 'Polygamy and Social Policy' (1969) 32 MLR 155 at 159.

6 See generally Law Com Working Paper No 83 (1982) pp 38-66.

7 For an example of a 'wife' being denied entry on this ground see *Zahra v Visa Officer, Islamabad* [1979-80] Imm AR 48.

8 Under the British Nationality Act 1948, s 6(2) the wife of a UK citizen had a right to register herself as a UK citizen. In terms of s 6 of the British Nationality Act 1981, although the right of registration has disappeared, wives have to satisfy less stringent conditions than other applicants for naturalisation.

9 Although there would be no right to succession on intestacy as a surviving spouse, a claim could be brought under the Inheritance (Provision for Family and Dependants) Act 1975, ss 1(1)(b), 25(4) since a party to a void marriage comes within the category of persons eligible for family provision.

10 Under the Legitimacy Act 1959, s 2 their children could be treated as legitimate if at the time of the act of intercourse resulting in their birth both or either of the parties reasonably believed the marriage was valid. However, it is still an open question whether a mistake of law can be reasonable – *Hawkins v A-G* [1966] 1 All ER 392 [1966] 1 WLR 978.

3.11 All these conclusions about the likely impact of the Matrimonial Causes Act 1973, s 11(d) were, however, thrown into considerable doubt and confusion in 1982 by the court of Appeal's decision in *Hussain v Hussain*.[1] The husband and wife, who were both Muslims, went through an Islamic ceremony of marriage in Pakistan in 1979 at a time when the husband was domiciled in England and the wife domiciled in Pakistan. Upon the breakdown of the marriage the wife petitioned here for a judicial separation. The husband argued that no such relief could be granted by the English courts because the marriage was void in terms of s 11(d). The Court of Appeal, however, held the marriage to be monogamous in English law and hence outside the ambit of s 11(d). Since, therefore, it was a valid marriage the wife was entitled to the decree she had sought. The reasoning of Ormrod L J in giving the judgment of the Court, was quite unexpected, overturning the assumptions of virtually all those lawyers and administrators who had had to grapple with the question during the previous decade. He held that the language used in the Matrimonial Causes Act 1973, s 11 was 'at least consistent' with the following rather tortuous interpretation. In the case of persons domiciled here there is no capacity to enter an actually polygamous marriage, but this derives not from s 11(d) but from s 11(b) which prohibits a person who is already married from marrying again. This meant that s 11(d) must be designed to prevent someone not already married from entering a potentially polygamous marriage and 'a marriage can only be potentially polygamous if at least one of the spouses has the capacity to marry a second spouse'. Since a Muslim man domiciled here has no capacity to take a second wife by reason of s 11(b) and since a wife is not allowed by Muslim law to have more than one husband the marriage in question could not be regarded as potentially polygamous and hence did not fall within s 11(d).

His Lordship placed considerable reliance on the difference in phrasing of the two sections in the Matrimonial Proceedings (Polygamous Marriages) Act 1972 which have now become the Matrimonial Causes Act 1973, ss 11(d) and 47. Whereas s 47 (dealing with the availability of matrimonial relief) refers to marriages 'entered into under a law which permits polygamy', which strongly suggests a reference to a foreign *lex loci celebrationis*, s 11(d) refers simply to 'a polygamous marriage' (albeit with the proviso that at its inception neither party may actually have an additional spouse). This could plausibly be understood to mean that the test under s 11(d) was one of capacity in terms of the *lex domicilii* rather than of nature and incidents by reference to the *lex loci*. As Ormrod L J explained:

'Had the intention of Parliament been to prevent persons domiciled in England and Wales from entering into marriages under the [Pakistani] Muslim Family Laws Ordinance, or under any other similar laws which "permit polygamy", it would have been easy to say so in so many words.'[2]

In the absence of identical terminology there was no reason why the polygamous quality of the marriage should not be assessed by looking to the specific capacities of the parties as opposed to the general nature of Islamic marriages in terms of the *lex loci*.

One objection to this line of argument is, of course, that Parliament was legislating against a clearly established background of principles in the conflict of laws under which it was left to the *lex loci* to categorise a marriage as polygamous or monogamous in nature, at least at the time it is contracted. Indeed this seems to be the commonsense explanation of the inclusion of the proviso to s 11(d) to the effect that 'a marriage may be polygamous although at its inception neither party has any spouse additional to the other'. The difference in phraseology as between ss 11(d) and 47 seems as likely to have been the product of inept draftsmanship as anything else.

If this novel interpretation were to be consistently followed many of the practical difficulties mentioned earlier would be solved. Indeed, whatever the possible defects in the court's reasoning its motives were admirable. Attention was drawn to our 'increasingly pluralistic society' and to the widespread and profound repercussions on the Muslim community here if the decision had gone the other way. However, the court's approach has resulted in the creation of a fresh anomaly. Its ruling has the effect of differentiating between the sexes for no good reason since if it is the wife who is domiciled in England and the husband who is domiciled abroad (rather than the other way round) the foreign marriage would then indeed be potentially polygamous because the husband's personal law would allow him to take a second wife. Such a marriage would, therefore, be void within the terms of s 11(d).

1 [1983] Fam 26, [1982] 1 All ER 369.
2 At 372.

The scope for reform

3.12   Probably the most fundamental question is whether it should be made possible for a polygamous marriage to be contracted in England. If it is assumed that the bulk of public opinion would find this unacceptable for the white majority (while condoning the rapid increase in serial monogamy), this still leaves open its availability for those minority groups whose religion or personal law permits it.[1] Indeed, Muslim organisations in the UK have for some time been pressing the British government to introduce legislation to allow Muslim family law to be given full force and effect in this country.[2]

It is pertinent to point out that while English law offers only one type of marriage (monogamy) with uniform consequences, many other countries cater for the diversity of their populations by enabling them to choose between a number of different types of marriage. Tanzania, for example, provides not only for both monogamous and polygamous marriages to be contracted there but also for their conversion from one type to another.[3] No doubt it was natural for English law to offer no alternative to monogamy while there were only a handful of inhabitants whose religion or personal law permitted polygamy, but with the substantial influx of immigrants in recent decades (especially from the Muslim world) the matter might perhaps be thought worthy of fresh examination.

1 This facility is advocated by Samuels 'Legal Recognition and Protection of Minority Customs in a Plural Society in England' [1981] AALR 241 at 251.
2 See *Why Muslim Family Law for British Muslims* (Union of Muslim Organisations of UK and Eire, 1983).
3 Law of Marriage Act 1971, discussed by Read [1972] JAL 19.

3.13   An important preliminary question is whether the current ban on Muslims practising polygamy in this country amounts to a denial of freedom of religion and violates the guarantees contained in the European Convention on Human Rights and the International Covenant on Civil and Political Rights. The European Convention, Art 9, for example, states that everyone has the right to freedom of religion and to manifest his religion in practice and that such manifestation shall only be subjected to such limitations as are prescribed by law and are necessary in a democratic society in the interests of public safety, for the protection of public order, health or morals, or for the protection of the rights and freedoms of others. While it might perhaps be arguable that a general prohibition of polygamy is required in England to safeguard the morals of the non-Muslim majority or even the rights of Muslim first wives, it may be easier to justify the restriction on the basis that polygamy, even for Muslims, is not really an integral part of religion. Support for this general line of approach can be found in a number of decisions by the Indian courts following the imposition of a statutory ban on Hindus practising polygamy in Bombay in 1946[1] and in the rest of India in 1955.[2] The tendency of the courts there was to rule that polygamy for Hindus was never a matter of religious obligation, that it was merely permissible under certain conditions and hence was not properly an integral part of Hindu religion.[3] While the Indian Constitution, art 25 guarantees to everyone the right to practise his religion, the Indian Supreme Court has observed in one case that:

'. . . in order that the practices in question should be treated as part of religion they must be regarded by the said religion as its essential and integral part; otherwise even purely secular practices which are not an essential or integral part of religion are apt to be clothed with a religious form and may make a claim for being treated as religious practices. . . .'[4]

Whereas for Hindus marriage is a sacrament, for Muslims it is merely a contract and in *Badruddin v Aisha Begum*[5] it was held that any legislative restriction on the capacity of a Muslim to have more than one wife did not amount to an interference with religious practice under art 25. The Indian Court declared that there was no fundamental right of a Muslim to have up to four wives and having more than one wife could not be said to be part of religion. Certainly there was no religious obligation to have more than one wife.

Even if a person were to claim that he was under a religious duty to practise polygamy there is the authority of the US Supreme Court to support the proposition that no unlawful interference with the constitutional right of Americans to the free exercise of religion is involved in the enactment of a statute making bigamy a crime. In *Reynolds v US*[6] in 1878 the accused, an adherent to the Mormon church, raised just such a defence to a charge of bigamy and was unsuccessful. The Supreme Court ruled that while the First Amendment to the Constitution guaranteeing free exercise of religion deprived the state of all power over opinion and belief, it did not proscribe legislative interference with actions which were in violation of social duties or subversive of good order. Marriage, as a civil contract and one of the foundations of social relations, was an area normally regulated by law and one in which government was necessarily required to deal. To permit a man to excuse his overt act of bigamy on the grounds of his religious beliefs would be to make the professed doctrines of religious belief superior to the criminal law and render each person, in effect, a law unto himself. Government could exist in name only in such circumstances.

A further important consideration is that the European Convention on Human Rights provides that men and women shall have the right to marry without discrimination on the ground of sex[7] and that everyone has the right to respect for his or her private and family life.[8] The first wife of a polygamous husband would be denied these rights if he were to be allowed to marry a second wife here. The International Covenant on Civil and Political Rights contains provisions in similar vein,[9] including art 23(4) which provides:

'States Parties to the present Covenant shall take appropriate steps to ensure equality of rights and responsibilities of spouses as to marriage, during marriage and at its dissolution.'

These human rights provisions would seem to militate strongly against any relaxation of the legal regime of monogamous marriage in this country. The following more limited reforms might, however, be considered worthwhile.

1 Bombay Prevention of Hindu Bigamous Marriages Act 1946.
2 Hindu Marriage Act 1955.
3 See e g *State of Bombay v Narasu Appa* [1952] AIR (Bom.) 85; *Ram Prasad v State of Uttah Pradesh* (1957) AIR (All) 411.
4 *Durgah Committee v Hussain Ali* [1961] AIR (SC) 1402 at 1415.
5 [1957] ALJ 300.
6 98 US 145 (1878).
7 Arts 12 and 14.
8 Art 8.
9 See arts 2, 17, 23.

(i) THE CAPACITY OF AN ENGLISH DOMICILIARY TO CONTRACT A POLYGAMOUS
MARRIAGE ABROAD

3.14   As we have seen, the law on this question is in a somewhat confused state following the decision of the Court of Appeal in *Hussain v Hussain*.[1] According to the reasoning in that case a foreign marriage in polygamous form is valid where the husband is domiciled in England and the wife domiciled abroad but it is void under the Matrimonial Causes Act 1973 s 11(d) where the wife is domiciled in this country and the husband domiciled in a country whose law permits polygamy. Reform is clearly required not only to remove this anomaly but also to place this branch of the law on a more secure foundation in view of doubts as to whether the novel analysis presented in *Hussain v Hussain* would be upheld by the House of Lords in a future case.

Exactly what direction any reform should take was examined by the Law Commission in a Working Paper[2] in 1982, followed by a Report in 1985.[3] Two possible solutions to the problem were canvassed in the Working Paper. One of these and the Law Commission's own preferred option was to amend s 11(d) so that it only operates to prohibit actually polygamous marriages. Hence the first marriage of, for example, a Muslim spouse with an English domicile would be treated as valid in English law, but any subsequent foreign marriages would still be regarded as void. This avenue of reform would certainly solve the vast majority of the practical problems which arise in this field and remove most of the injustice of the present situation. It is the solution achieved in *Hussain's* case but extended to cover instances where the wife is the party domiciled in England. It seems likely to be acceptable both to public opinion and to Parliament.

The other option discussed by the Law Commission and provisionally rejected in the Working Paper was far more radical and considerably harder to justify.[4] This alternative solution would allow a Muslim husband, for example, to return to Pakistan or Bangladesh and marry further wives there, hence giving full recognition in English law to actually polygamous marriages contracted abroad by those qualified to do so in terms of the *lex loci* even if they were domiciled in England. One difficulty here is that to adopt such a policy of liberal tolerance runs counter to the guarantees of sexual equality in marriage found in the European Convention on Human Rights discussed earlier.[5] The European Convention's protection clearly extends to couples who are domiciled in this country since the states parties are bound to secure the human rights listed to everyone 'within their jurisdiction'.[6] On the other hand, one advantage of this alternative solution is that, unlike the one advocated in the Working

Paper, it offers a means of escape from the anomaly of using the artificial concept of domicile as the criterion for distinguishing between those who can and those who cannot enter into an actually polygamous marriage abroad and have it recognised as valid here. Those who are domiciled abroad may contract such marriages and obtain legal recognition here even if they are habitually resident in England and possess British nationality. The distinction based on domicile relies heavily upon the intentions of the parties at the time of the marriage as to how long they plan to make their homes in this country. Inevitably an individual immigrant's intentions about how long he will stay in this country may fluctuate throughout his time here, depending on his circumstances, yet it is these very intentions which hold the key to whether or not he may contract an actually polygamous marriage abroad on any given day. One can well envisage two Pakistani neighbours or even brothers with only marginally differing intentions as to the permanence of their future here who find as a result that they have entirely different capacities vis-à-vis the contracting of a polygamous marriage. If the validity of a marriage is to turn on such an elusive concept as intention in this type of situation it can surely be argued that the law is unacceptably uncertain and incoherent and that such distinctions should be removed in the interests both of the immigrants themselves and officials in the great variety of government departments with whom they have to deal. The number of those from the Indian subcontinent who are still domiciled abroad is far from insignificant since although for all sorts of practical reasons most seem likely to remain in this country for the rest of their lives many of them do sincerely intend to return to their countries of origin to retire and die there.[7] This intention, based partly upon deeply-rooted cultural traditions and religious beliefs about death and burial is, of course, of crucial significance in determining their domicile. The burden of proving that a domicile of origin has been lost is a very heavy one and there is a presumption against the acquisition of a domicile of choice by a person in a country whose religion, manners and customs differ widely from those of his own country.[8] Almost certainly, therefore, many of them are still domiciled in their countries of origin and hence entitled in the eyes of English law to contract valid actually polygamous marriages there.

The Law Commission's Working Paper did not address this line of argument directly, being content to relegate the whole problem of reviewing the law of domicile to a separate law reform exercise.[9] However, in its Working Paper on domicile published in 1985 the Law Commission did not propose any reform that would tend to remove this anomaly.[10]

A further difficulty, however, with the radical solution would lie in determining who would be entitled to take advantage of it. Everyone domiciled in England and Wales might well have to be included, regardless of religious affiliation or cultural background. This would incidentally mean that it would become perfectly possible for a white English man or woman to go abroad and contract a series of polygamous marriages, provided he or she had capacity to do so in terms of the *lex loci*. In some countries they might first have to undergo a religious conversion or formal acceptance into a tribal community, sufficiently onerous tasks to limit the attractiveness of the venture in most cases. Social pressures might well provide a further important disincentive, especially since spouses can already be changed, rather than added to, comparatively easily under existing English law. No doubt this 'loophole' is a deficiency in the radical solution and there would be a few white people who would seek publicity from such an enterprise. However, after the first dramatic revelations of such an occurrence, the general public would probably be no more offended by knowledge of it than they are at present by news that their married friends have mistresses and lovers and that English law often gives legal recognition to the extra-marital relationship as well as to the marital one. This would hardly, therefore, seem to be a consideration that should be decisive in determining the issue.

In any event, when the Law Commission published its final Report on the subject in 1985 it came down firmly in favour of the narrower solution of only recognising the validity of potentially polygamous and not actually polygamous marriages contracted by an English domiciliary abroad.[11]

1 [1983] Fam 26, [1982] 1 All ER 369, discussed in para 3.11 above.
2 Law Com WP No 83: Polygamous Marriages: Capacity to contract a polygamous marriage and the concept of the potentially polygamous marriage.
3 Law Com Report No 146.
4 See Poulter 'Polygamy – New Law Commission Proposals' (1983) 13 Fam Law 72.
5 See para 3.13 above.
6 Art 1.
7 See e g Dahya 'Pakistanis in Britain: Transients or Settlers' (1973) Race 241 at 245-7; Jeffrey P *Migrants and Refugees* (CUP, 1976) pp 144-7; Anwar M *The Myth of Return* (London, 1979) pp. xi, 222.
8 See *Dicey and Morris* p 118; *Qureshi v Qureshi* [1972] Fam 173 at 193.
9 See para 5.35.
10 See Law Com Working Paper No 88: The Law of Domicile (1985). The Commission merely proposed that, subject to evidence to the contrary, a person should be presumed to intend to make his home indefinitely in (and hence be domiciled in) a country in which he had been habitually resident for a continuous period of seven years since reaching the age of 16 (para 5.17).
11 Law Com Report No 146, paras 2.17, 4.8.

(ii) SOLEMNISATION OF BOGUS MARRIAGES IN ENGLAND

3.15 In the absence of any move to introduce polygamy as an alternative type of marriage in England there would seem to be a need to impose stricter controls on the solemnisation in this country of what purport to be valid polygamous marriages but really amount to bogus ceremonies. It will be recalled that in *R v Bham*[1] the accused was acquitted under the Marriage Act 1949 s 75(2) because the Islamic marriage he purported to solemnise was not one recognised by English law. In 1973 the Law Commission drew attention to the growing mischief in this area whereby parties are deceived by charlatans into thinking their marriage is valid and only discover the truth much later. The Commission recommended that it should be made a serious offence to perform or permit to be performed any bogus ceremony of marriage or to issue a certificate in respect of such a ceremony.[2] The prohibition would not, of course, apply to a religious ceremony performed after a recognised civil one. So far no steps have been taken to implement this proposal.

1 [1966] 1 QB 159, [1965] 3 All ER 124.
2 See Report on Solemnisation of Marriage in England and Wales (No. 53), pp 10, 73-4.

(iii) BIGAMY

3.16 The process of reasoning by which the courts are currently excluding from the definition of the crime of bigamy those occasions where the first marriage was a valid polygamous one contracted abroad is totally erroneous. If the first marriage is recognised as valid in English law it must surely be possible for bigamy to be committed if the husband purports to marry a second wife here. The rationale for the present stance was given by the judge in *R v Sarwan Singh*[1] as follows:

'If for the purpose of a prosecution for bigamy a potentially polygamous marriage were recognised then in view of the fact that the offence of bigamy can be committed wherever the second marriage takes place whether in England or any other part of the world, a man who married under a ceremony of polygamy a second wife might in some circumstances be liable to prosecution for bigamy; and I cannot believe that the criminal law and those who framed the statute under which the offence of bigamy was constituted ever contemplated that such a position could properly arise.'[2]

However, this argument is totally misconceived since the reason why the hypothetical facts presented would not amount to bigamy is because the second marriage would be valid, not because the first was polygamous.[3] Although the advisability of retaining bigamy as a crime at all has often been challenged,[4] while it remains on the statute book it should surely not discriminate in favour of polygamists as it does at the moment. The social evils which the crime attempts to combat seem just as likely to be present where the first ceremony was a polygamous one as where it was monogamous.[5]

1 [1962] 3 All ER 612.
2 At 615.
3 See Carter [1974-5] BYBIL 376; Leslie 'Polygamous Marriages and Bigamy' [1972] Juridical Review 113. Significantly the Indian Penal Code 1860 defined a bigamist in this way: 'Whoever having a husband or wife living marries in any case in which such marriage is *void* by reason of its taking place during the life of such husband or wife' (s 494). Cf Smith and Hogan *Criminal Law* (5th edn, 1983) p 658 apparently approving the existing position.
4 See e g Williams 'Language and the Law' (1945) 61 LQR 71 at 76-8.
5 See Morse 'Polygamists and the Crime of Bigamy' (1976) 25 ICLQ 229 at 234-5.

(iv) ACTUALLY POLYGAMOUS MARRIAGES CONTRACTED BY FOREIGN
DOMICILIARIES ABROAD

3.17 In considering what attitude the law should take towards parties to actually polygamous marriages contracted abroad by foreign domiciliaries it is worth bearing in mind how many of the countries in which polygamy is practised today were former British possessions or dependencies and what the legal approach was during the colonial era. As an imperial power it was never official British policy to outlaw polygamy overseas by legislation or make it a criminal offence, but rather merely to view it with a mild disfavour and hope that it would eventually wither away under the pressures of education, Christianity and economic advancement.[1] No reliable statistics are available from which to judge whether such expectations are being fulfilled and the only African countries to legislate the abolition of polygamy since independence have been in Francophone rather than Anglophone Africa.[2] Hindu marriages were, however, made monogamous in India in 1955 and some interesting developments have been taking place in various Islamic states.[3] Polygamy was, of course, forbidden in Turkey under Ataturk and a similar prohibition was introduced in Tunisia in 1956. Other reforms have merely sought to restrict polygamy without imposing an outright ban. In Pakistan and Bangladesh prior written permission to contract a subsequent marriage must be obtained from an arbitration council and in several other countries from a Qadi or religious judge. In Morocco and Iraq the courts are entitled to withhold permission if there is any fear that co-wives will not be treated with equal justice and in Syria if it is proved that the husband cannot afford to maintain two wives.[4] This condition, it will be recalled, is specified in the Koran, but the innovation in these countries was for the assessment to be entrusted to a court rather than left to the husband's own conscience. Significantly President Bourguiba publicly justified Tunisia's policy of total abolition by observing that no man other than a prophet was capable of according his wives equal treatment.

Bearing all these considerations in mind it would appear sensible for English law to take a neutral stance towards actually polygamous marriages contracted abroad by foreign domiciliaries. It is for the foreign state to determine its approach to such marriages being entered into on its soil by its own people. When they come to this country they should surely be afforded equal treatment in every way possible with parties to monogamous marriages. While this is the general legal position a notable example of unequal treatment at present exists in the restricted recognition given to actually polygamous marriages in the social security field. National insurance benefits are not available to any of the wives of such a marriage, despite the mandatory obligation on the husband to contribute to the scheme.[5] Although this seems unduly harsh, a simple solution has not been so easy to find. In 1968 the Law Commission considered a number of proposals and concluded that all of them would either be administratively burdensome or fly in the face of public opinion.[6] Thus to allow all the wives of a polygamist to claim the normal rates of benefit would be to put polygamists in a specially advantageous position, while if they had to divide the benefits appropriate to a single wife between them there would be too little to go round and often the state would have to make up the difference through non-contributory benefits. Again if a polygamist were required to make extra contributions so that all his wives could qualify for full benefits this would necessitate keeping a check on every contributor's marital status and might seem unfair on a man who only had one wife actually living in England.

To the argument that it would be unjust for a deceased polygamist who had paid the normal social security contributions to derive double benefit by leaving two eligible widows Samuels has uttered a fierce and persuasive rejoinder-

'This argument is specious, because one man may have numerous children, be constantly in the care of the national health service, and live for many years in retirement, whereas another may be childless, never miss a day's work through illness, and die before retirement. That is the insurance principle, contribution according to means, benefit according to need. [The second wife] will probably fall on to supplementary benefit anyway, so there may not be much in it financially.'[7]

Pearl has put forward the more limited proposal that benefits should be extended to a wife of an actually polygamous marriage where she is the only wife permanently resident here.[8] This, as he suggests, would certainly seem acceptable to public opinion here, even if Samuels' proposal were not. It would surely also be possible to allow a polygamist with two or more wives permanently resident here to make additional voluntary contributions to enable wives other than the first to receive benefits. Voluntary contributions are already a feature of the national insurance scheme, for instance in the case of those temporarily employed abroad, and the administrative burden should not be unduly onerous. Admittedly the first wife would be in a specially advantageous position but the alternative of treating the husband's compulsory contributions as counting for nothing is surely sufficiently harsh to outweigh this type of objection. It is suggested that this solution would prove generally acceptable to public opinion in England and would also be preferred by polygamous families.

1 See e g Phillips and Morris *Marriage Laws in Africa* (OUP, 1971) pp 11, 86-8. Bigamy charges were confined to situations where at least one of the marriages was contracted by Christian or civil rites: see e g Indian Penal Code 1860, s 494; *Phillips and Morris* pp 149-52; Collingwood *Criminal Law of East and Central Africa* (Sweet & Maxwell, 1967) pp 133-5.
2 E g Ivory Coast, Guinea, Madagascar and the Central African Republic – see *Phillips and Morris* pp 37-9.

3 See Anderson *Law Reform in the Muslim World* pp 61-4, 110-4; *Pearl* 70-5.
4 In each of these five countries a marriage contracted without the necessary permission is nevertheless valid, though criminal liability may be entailed.
5 See e g R(G) 2/7 (1975) where maternity benefit was refused.
6 See Law Com Working Paper No 21 pp 48-51; *Pearl* 'Social Security and the Ethnic Minorities' [1978] JSWL 24, 26-7.
7 'Legal Recognition and Protection of Minority Customs in a Plural Society in England' [1981] AALR 241 at 251.
8 At p 29.

CHAPTER 4

Different family patterns

INTRODUCTION

4.01 The Universal Declaration of Human Rights, adopted by the UN General Assembly in 1948, proclaims in art 16(3) that: 'The family is the natural and fundamental group unit of society and is entitled to protection by society and the State.' However, although the family is clearly a natural human grouping the actual form and structure it takes in different societies is extremely varied, as indeed is the legal protection afforded to it by individual states. While it is impossible to generalise about family types to the extent of ascribing particular characteristics to all families of a given type, it is thought that it may be feasible to identify certain patterns of family structure found among the ethnic minority communities in this country which are sufficiently divergent from those of the white majority to warrant discussion and analysis. It by no means follows, of course, that every family from a given minority community will adhere to the pattern described. Indeed, as will be seen, the influence of the English social and economic environment upon these family structures has in many instances been quite considerable.

Statistically by far the most common type of contemporary white family is a 'nuclear' or 'conjugal' one,[1] comprising a monogamously married couple living together with the children of one or both of them.[2] In some families, of course, the couple are not married to one another, whilst in others there is only one parent looking after the children, but these categories account for only a relatively small minority. The 'nuclear' family differs markedly not only from a family based on polygamy (already discussed in ch 3 above) but also from an 'extended' family in which the lives of parents and children are closely integrated with those of their wider kin, notably in the form of intermeshing economic ties and often common residence as well. This type of extended family is the norm in much of Asia, but it is only found among whites in this country in a very modified form, principally reflected in mutually convenient arrangements with wider kin in respect of such matters as child-minding, household help, care for the elderly and occasional financial assistance.[3]

The standard nuclear family based upon marriage also differs significantly from a family formed out of a union between partners who are not married to one another, whether their relationship is merely a transitory one or the product of stable cohabitation. Such families are typical of certain strata of West Indian society.

1 See e g M Farmer *The Family* (Longman, 1979) p 5; L Rimmer *Families in Focus* (Study Commission on the Family, 1981) pp 61-3; *Values and the Changing Family* (Study Commission on the Family, 1982) pp 9-10.
2 This definition includes adopted children.
3 See e g M Young and P Wilmott *Family and Kinship in East London* (Routledge and Kegan Paul, 1957); R M Moroney *The Family and the State* (Longman, 1976) pp 24-7.

A. ASIAN EXTENDED FAMILIES

4.02   In the Indian subcontinent most people, regardless of their religious tenets, live under an extended or joint family system, usually spanning three generations.[1] Broadly speaking, this means that a common household is shared by a man and his wife together with the families of their married sons, as well as any unmarried sons and daughters. Its essential features are a mutual sharing of all belongings and resources, a common residence (if a large enough house can be found) and an overall authority vested in the eldest male member of the family. The conduct of family affairs in general is regarded as a communal activity. Close contact is also maintained with married daughters and their families as well as with more remote kin.[2]

Hiro has explained how the feeling of belonging to a group larger than their immediate families is deeply ingrained in people from the rural areas in the Indian subcontinent from which most migrants to Britain have come:

'Individualism, as fostered by western culture is almost unknown. Children are not allocated separate rooms in which to live and sleep, and do not, therefore, grow up thinking in highly individualistic terms. Moreover, the nature of work – labouring on the family farm – produces a group, rather than individual, identity. On maturity the male child does not detach himself from the family and start on his own, but remains part of the joint family, loyal and respectful.'[3]

As might be expected, the process of individual family members migrating to Britain (as well as the operation of UK immigration restrictions) has had a considerable impact upon the extended families of those involved. Asian households in this country are more likely to be composed of two generations than of three since there are comparatively few grandparents here, but according to one survey conducted in the mid-1970s as many as one-third of such households were of the extended family type compared with two-thirds of the nuclear type.[4]

Furthermore, a Labour Force Survey conducted in 1981 revealed that some 28% of Asian households contained three or more adults together with one or more children, compared with only 8% of white households.[5]

In England it is often not possible, for financial reasons, for Asians who wish to continue to function as an extended or joint family to purchase or rent a house large enough or of suitable design to accommodate every member of such a family.[6] Some members may, therefore, choose instead to live in a house nearby, if possible in the same immediate neighbourhood, to facilitate daily contact including joint meals. However, while the organisation of joint families tends to be weakened by life in Britain, both on account of housing difficulties and through the necessity to pool the wages and earnings of individual members (as opposed to the sharing of work on the land), it would appear that the system is still strong enough for kinship groups and extended families to constitute the focal point of activity for the majority of Asians here.[7] Moreover, there is clear evidence from social surveys to show that at least a substantial minority of Asians will continue to wish to follow the extended family pattern here in the future.[8]

1 See generally, Hiro *Black British, White British* (Penguin, 1973) pp 151-2; McDermott and Ahsan *The Muslim Guide* (Islamic Foundation, 1980) p 13; Anwar *The Myth of Return* ch 4; Anwar *Between Two Cultures* (CRE, 1981) p 16.
2 For discussion of the Pakistani institution of *biraderi*, a kinship network based principally on patrilineal descent, see Anwar *The Myth of Return* ch 5.
3 At p 151.

4 See Anwar *Between Two Cultures* p 17. Cf Smith *Racial Disadvantage in Britain* (Penguin, 1977) p 48, where the PEP survey gave a figure of one-fifth.
5 See (1983) 13 Social Trends 181. In this survey 'children' referred to those persons under the age of 16, 'adults' to those over 16.
6 For the social policy implications of the failure to make it easier for three generational extended families to live together in the same house, see e g *Moroney* pp 28-9; *Smith* pp 227, 325-6.
7 J Cheetham *Social Work with Immigrants* (Routledge and Kegan Paul, 1972), p 161.
8 See Anwar *Between Two Cultures* pp 18-19.

B. COHABITATION AND MARRIAGE PATTERNS AMONG WEST INDIANS

4.03   The pattern of family life in the Caribbean, at least among the classes who form the bulk of the West Indian community settled in this country, is characterised by a variety of features which are strikingly different from life in a typical Asian joint family or white nuclear family. The most notable of these are an extremely high illegitimacy rate running at around 60%, a matriarchal system of authority in which a large proportion of households have female heads, and commonly a sequence of different conjugal and mating forms linked to a couple's social and economic status within the community and usually involving an extended period of stable cohabitation.[1]

Part of the explanation for the generally rather brittle nature of family relationships in the West Indies, including the low marriage rate, lies far back in the historical experiences of the slave trade and possibly even earlier. Traditional West African patterns of kinship and marriage were severely disrupted when the slaves arrived in the New World. As Patterson has explained, the slave-owners were chiefly interested in the reproduction of an ever increasing labour force:

'On the plantations, slaves were property and could set up no permanent conjugal or family ties. Parents had no rights over their own children; indeed, men might not always know which children they had sired. Slave women were liable to be taken as concubines by planters or their overseers. They were encouraged to breed promiscuously, and to produce further slave property for their owners . . .'[2]

The destruction of kinship ties, as well as the imbalance created between the roles of the two parents, has been described by Clarke in the following terms:

'There was, under slavery, no room for the family as a parent-child group in a home; still less for the development of those stable relationships among a wider circle of kin such as can be maintained only if kinsmen live in permanent contact or are able to travel freely and visit one another. The residential unit in the plantation system was formed by the mother and her children with the responsibility for their maintenance resting with the slave-owner. The father's place in the family was never secure. He had no externally sanctioned authority over it and could at any time be physically removed from it. His role might, indeed, end with procreation . . . It is against this background of the weakness of the father role in the system of family relationships that those of mother and grandmother assume particular importance.'[3]

Some writers have additionally sought to attribute the dominance of this sort of matriarchal family system, as well as the modern pattern of serial cohabitation, to the polygynous and matrilineal structure of the West African tribes from whom the slaves were drawn.[4] However, the limited evidence for this derivation has failed to convince other scholars.[5] Whatever may be the correct historical explanation for the dominant role of the mother in modern West Indian society, its pervasive significance is graphically illustrated by the title of one of the leading works on family life in Jamaica, Edith Clarke's *My Mother Who Fathered Me*.[6]

1 See generally, T S Simey *Welfare and Planning in the West Indies* (London, 1946) pp 79-90; F Henriques *Family and Colour in Jamaica* (London, 1953), especially chs 5 and 6; G Roberts *The Population of Jamaica* (Cambridge, 1957), chs 7 and 8; E Clarke *My Mother who Fathered Me* (London, 1966); C Cumper and S Daley *Family Law in the Commonwealth Caribbean* (Mona, Jamaica, 1979).
2 *Dark Strangers* (London, 1963) pp 222-3.
3 At p 19.
4 Cf *Simey* pp 42-3.
5 One reason why this seems unlikely is that the slaves came from a great variety of African tribes only some of which were matrilineal – see *Henriques* p 103. Compare the classic controversy about the derivation of American negro family patterns between Frazier *The Negro Family in the United States* (Chicago, 1937) and Herskovitz *The Myth of The Negro Past* (New York, 1941).
6 The words come originally from George Lamming's *In The Castle of My Skin* (London, 1953) p 11.

4.04 The current organisation of sexual and conjugal relations in the Caribbean may be analysed as follows. Among the poorer peasant classes men and women tend to progress through various different types of unions.[1] Young people typically begin with casual sexual relations in which they do not cohabit with one another. Children may or may not be conceived as a result, but certainly no particular attempt is made to prevent conception. As Clarke has explained, the birth of a child in such circumstances carries no stigma and indeed possesses considerable advantages:

'Not only is sexual activity regarded as natural: it is unnatural not to have had a child and no woman who has not proved that she can bear one is likely to find a man to be responsible for her since no man is going to propose marriage to such a woman. Maternity is a normal and desirable state and the childless woman is an object of pity, contempt or derision . . . Just as a woman is only considered "really" a woman after she has borne a child, so the proof of a man's maleness is the impregnation of a woman. There is, therefore, no incentive for either men or women to avoid parenthood even in promiscuous relationships: on the contrary, it is the hall-mark of adulthood and normal, healthy living.'[2]

Although the girl's first pregnancy is initially greeted with disapproval by her own mother the two of them are soon reconciled and her mother takes over responsibility for caring for the baby. Subsequent children conceived as a result of other casual affairs are either looked after by their mother or join the first child with their grandmother. Greater care may, however, be taken to avoid further pregnancies from such liaisons in view of the increasing economic burdens involved for both mother and grandmother.

A second stage is reached, and this usually occurs by the time a woman has reached the age of 30, when she will set up a joint household with her current sexual partner and live in a form of stable, 'purposive' or 'faithful' cohabitation with him. They will bring up their children in their own house, while the issue of previous relationships will be dispersed among the children's respective maternal kin. Sometimes this type of cohabitation is entered into after a formal courtship and the parties may intend to live together for all intents and purposes as man and wife, with an official wedding contemplated at some distant time in the future, provided all goes well. Sexual fidelity is then expected and unfaithfulness on either side is seen as a justification for terminating the relationship. Both partners accept an obligation to contribute to the household budget by working to make a success of their joint venture. However, there is obviously no guarantee that it will ultimately ripen into the celebration of a formal marriage and many relationships break down before then. The children may then be allocated to various maternal kin when a new cohabitation arrangement is established with a fresh partner. Other forms of cohabitation may, of course, be less purposeful and stable.

The accomplishment of the third and final stage of formal marriage is something which, if the circumstances are propitious, a peasant woman may expect to achieve during her forties. It is well known that a legal marriage is meant to be a union for life to the exclusion of all others and that a husband is legally responsible for the support of his wife and any children they may have. For these reasons a couple can only aspire to marriage when their economic and social conditions are right.[3] Whereas cohabition is viewed financially as a partnership, marriage is seen as involving a husband in maintaining his wife at a higher status and releasing her from the business of earning her own living. It not only brings economic security for the wife but also greater respectability for the couple who thereby provide an indication of their upward mobility on the social scale. The earlier period of 'purposive' cohabitation, following perhaps a number of experimental liaisons, is rationalised as a necessary trial of compatibility which may help to guarantee the stability of the legal marriage. Marriage, as Clarke put it:

'. . . marks the end of a free association which can be dissolved at any time at the will of either party and also the end of a period during which the woman may find herself left wholly responsible for the maintenance of the children of the union. The shared life and the birth of children give the opportunity for the paternal role to be developed and the marriage at this stage is an indication that this role has been learned and that the father accepts his responsibilities . . . Marriage occurring after a period of cohabitation is, in other words, the affirmation of stability, the seal on a proven conjugal union.'[4]

It is important to stress that there is no guarantee that every peasant in the Caribbean will progress smoothly through each of these forms of union, nor that even when this does occur it is entirely a matter of choice for the persons concerned. Account has to taken of the influences of local social and community forces upon the actions of particular couples. As M G Smith has pointed out:

'. . . as individuals increase in age, social maturity, parental responsibilities and local prominence, they are normally constrained by individual and social conditions to convert their non-domiciliary liaisons into stable consensual cohabitation, and in most peasant communities of Jamaica and Grenada, to convert these 'common-law' unions into marriage during middle or late middle age, marriage being institutionalised as the appropriate mating status for senior members of the community.'[5]

M G Smith has also drawn attention[6] to a marked difference between the general family pattern of these subsistence farmers and those of the non-skilled wage earners who form the rural and urban proletariat in the Caribbean. For the latter family life is a great deal more unstable, with a larger amount of non-purposive cohabitation and less finality when the state of formal marriage is reached. Married couples often separate and revert to new informal unions. In general, relationships appear to be more casual and promiscuous than among the peasantry. By way of contrast, among the wealthier middle and upper classes of West Indian society, as well as among those who are church members, any form of cohabitation is frowned upon and early marriage is the norm.[7] From all this it seems clear that formal marriage is specifically identified in the West Indies with property, social position and, to some extent, religious belief. This association may also be derived from the days of the slave trade when slaves drew what seemed to them to be logical conclusions from the marriages of their masters, whose status and wealth contrasted so dramatically with their own.

1 See *Clarke* pp xxi-xxv (Introduction by M G Smith) and chs 3, 4.
2 At pp 95-6.
3 See *Cumper and Daley* p 93.
4 At p 84.
5 'Introduction' to *Clarke* p xxiii.
6 At pp xxiii-xxiv.
7 *Clarke* pp xxxvi, 27, 80-1, 109.

4.05 The next question for consideration is how far these family patterns have been transplanted from the Caribbean to this country and to what extent they are reflected in the lives of West Indians now resident in Britain.[1] There is strong evidence that their general marriage rate is higher than that in the West Indies, though still low by English standards. For this there are a variety of possible explanations. First, a significant number of West Indian immigrants were skilled workers who identified themselves with the lower middle classes and who therefore regarded early marriage as appropriate to their social position. Second, it would appear that quite large numbers of West Indians here are members of churches which take a rather puritanical view of sexual relations outside marriage (for example, the Seventh Day Adventists, Jehovah's Witnesses, Pentecostalists and other evangelical sects) and it would therefore be natural for them to marry rather than cohabit. Third, despite all the problems encountered in this country many West Indians are able to acquire some degree of economic security earlier than they would have done in the Caribbean and thus may feel that their socio-economic status justifies marriage after a shorter period of cohabitation than would be required there. On the other hand, this improvement in their economic position can often only be sustained if the wife goes out to work and thus her role as a married woman will be different from the 'lady of leisure' she might have expected to become in the West Indies. The egalitarianism and independence involved for the couple here accords more with the English style of marriage and with the West Indian pattern of stable cohabitation.

Despite all these pressures towards early marriage, there is every reason to believe that the general pattern of periods of cohabitation, involving varying degrees of stability, has been retained by the West Indian community here. Indeed it seems quite possible that an initial trend towards early marriage during the 1950's and early 1960's, stimulated partly by the desire among the first group of immigrants to conform as far as possible with social mores in Britain and partly by a feeling of isolation from other kin, has since declined. A growing feeling of confidence seems to have developed among later arrivals, as well as among those who had settled in here but not married, that their indigenous family patterns are worth preserving in this country. With the increasing incidence and social acceptability of cohabitation (usually as a prelude to marriage) among the majority white community from around 1970 onwards[2] this would hardly be surprising. At all events, the proportion of children born to West Indian mothers outside marriage rose from around one third in 1971 to over a half in 1978, compared with only a slight increase to only around 10% for all mothers born in this country.[3] Obviously by no means all illegitimate children are subsequently brought up in one-parent families, but there is some evidence to suggest that considerably more West Indian households have only one parent than other groups. The 1981 Labour Force Survey showed that 12% of West Indian households comprised one-parent families compared with only 2% for 'whites' and 1% for Asians.[4] To some extent the weakness of such a family may be compensated for by the strength of bonds with a wider network of kin, but it is unclear how far traditional support provided by extended families in the Caribbean remains available in this country.[5] The Labour Force Survey in 1981 revealed that 19% of West Indian and Guyanese households were made up of three or more adults together with one or more children, in comparison with figures of 8% for 'whites' and 28% for Asians.[6]

1 See generally, *Patterson* ch 16; Rose *Colour and Citizenship* (OUP, 1969) pp 431-2; *Cheetham* pp 121-140; Foner 'Women, work and migration: Jamaicans in London' [1976] *New Community* 85; K Pryce *Endless Pressure: A study of West Indian Life-styles in Bristol*, (Penguin, 1979).
2 See Rimmer *Families in Focus* (Study Commission on the Family, 1981) pp 16-19.
3 (1981) 11 Social Trends 51.
4 See (1983) 13 Social Trends 181.
5 *Simey* p 84; *Hiro* pp 19-20; *Cheetham* p 129; Oliver 'West Indian Childhood' in Hoyles (ed) *Changing Childhood* (London, 1979) pp 143-4.
6 See (1983) 13 Social Trends 181.

Policy considerations

4.06 The principal concern likely to be expressed about the West Indian pattern of cohabitation as an alternative to legal marriage is that it leads to the birth of illegitimate children who may often be denied the stability of a two-parent family involving the presence of a father who is committed to the support of them and their mother. If in fact the father takes little or no interest in the upbringing of his child the burden will fall primarily on the mother and whereas in the West Indies she might have been able to rely on her mother and other members of her extended family to provide the necessary physical care, emotional warmth and mental stimulation, these demands may well not be so easily met in this country.[1] This in turn may either lead the mother to rely on inferior substitute care here in the form of child-minders while she goes out to work or result in the child being received into the care of a local authority.

On the other hand, while no one would wish to endorse a family system which attached little importance to the stable upbringing of children, there is clearly a grave danger of attributing to the West Indian pattern of cohabitation a pathological character which it does not deserve. Obviously some West Indian fathers may neglect their families, but so do many 'white' fathers, regardless of whether their children are legitimate or illegitimate. Cohabitation appears to have become increasingly popular among the majority community in recent years[2] and quite a sanguine view has been taken of such unions officially, simply on the basis that around 50% of current illegitimate births are being registered jointly by the child's mother and father.[3] Moreover, the rapid growth in the incidence of divorce,[4] annually affecting some 150,000 children under the age of 16,[5] can hardly be a convincing advertisement for the stability of marriage in England today.

1 See Griffiths 'Child-rearing practices in West Indian, Indian and Pakistani communities [1983] New Community 393 at 394.
2 See Brown and Kiernan 'Cohabitation in Great Britain: evidence from the General Household Survey' (1981) 25 Population Trends 4 where it is estimated that by 1979 there were about a third of a million cohabiting women under the age of 50. See also (1985) 15 Social Trends 35-6.
3 See Law Com Report No 118; 'Illegitimacy' (1982) paras 4.4-4.5.
4 For details, see Haskey, 'The Proportion of Marriages Ending in Divorce' (1982) 27 Population Trends 4.
5 See Haskey 'Children of Divorcing Couples' (1983) 31 Population Trends 20.

English law

4.07 There is some evidence to suggest that disputes relating to certain of the matters to be discussed in this chapter, particularly those affecting real and personal property, may tend to be settled out of court within the various ethnic minority communities themselves, through their own social and political organisations and by reference to their own customs and values, rather than the principles of English law.[1] In general terms there is no objection to the use of such informal methods of dispute settlement and procedures involving negotiation, conciliation, mediation and arbitration are usually considered preferable to litigation if they can offer a cheaper, speedier and less divisive outcome while still resolving the problems effectively. In what follows, however, the analysis will be confined to the rules of English law because this would be the system applicable in the vast majority of cases if a dispute were to come to court in this country.[2]

1 See eg R Desai *Indian Immigrants in Britain* (OUP, 1963) ch 3; *Rose* p 470 (referring to the Gujeratis); James *Sikh Children in Britain* p 94.
2 Discussion of the details of, for example, the Muslim law of succession or the Hindu joint family property system are outside the scope of this work.

1 Ownership of property

4.08 Broadly speaking, English law does not establish any special regime for regulating the property rights of family members. This is so even if the persons concerned are married to one another.[1] There is, for example, no system of 'community of property' providing for automatic joint ownership of family assets.[2] This means that the ownership of family property is for the most part determined by the ordinary principles of law which are applicable in disputes between strangers. The consequence of this is that, in the absence of any trust providing otherwise, possessions such as houses, vehicles and bank accounts belong in law to the person in whose name the particular item of property is vested. Hence, where the family home has, for instance, been purchased in the sole name of one person, the only manner in which any other family member such as a blood relation, spouse or cohabitant can claim a proprietary interest in it is by proving the existence of a trust. The mere fact that the purchase was generally understood to be for the common use of the whole family will not, of itself, affect the legal position with regard to its ownership.[3]

The normal method by which a person whose name does not appear on the legal title of the family home attempts to establish an equitable or beneficial interest in the property is by reference to an implied, resulting or constructive trust.[4] The circumstances in which trusts of these types will be held to have been created are not entirely clear because, although there have been numerous decisions on the subject in recent years the courts have by no means always been agreed upon the principles involved.[5] Usually a non-legal owner will be entitled to a beneficial interest in the home if he or she has made a substantial contribution to the costs of acquiring the property, provided it was the common intention of the parties that this contribution should give the non-legal owner a share rather than merely the right to the repayment of a loan. Ascertaining the intention of the parties is far from easy in the absence of a clear agreement and there is some evidence to suggest that typical patterns of house-purchase among the Asian and West Indian communities may make it extremely difficult to distinguish cases in which contributors are participating in a form of joint venture or partnership from those where they are merely lending money with the expectation of occupation.[6]

In recent years it has become obvious that some judges are readier than others to infer or impute a common intention that the contributing non-legal owner should have a beneficial share in the property. The most liberal of all, Lord Denning MR, pursued an unorthodox line of his own and was even prepared to impose a trust in the absence of any implied agreement or common intention. Speaking of constructive and resulting trusts in *Hussey v Palmer*[7] a case involving a dispute between a mother and her son-in-law he declared:

'By whatever name it is described, it is a trust imposed by law whenever justice and good conscience require it. It is a liberal process, founded on large principles of equity, to be applied in cases where the defendant cannot conscientiously keep the property for himself alone, but ought to allow the other to have the property or a share in it . . . It is an equitable remedy by which the court can enable an aggrieved party to obtain restitution.'[8]

One of the most difficult questions has been to identify which types of contribution would qualify a non-legal owner for a share. Substantial direct cash contributions to the purchase price are likely to be sufficient whether they be to the deposit, the balance payable on completion of the purchase,[9] the mortgage repayments[10] or even the legal charges at the time of conveyance. However, the position with regard to indirect contributions is far less clear. A typical situation is where a wife has spent her earnings on paying the household bills while her husband has spent his on paying the mortgage instalments. In *Gissing v Gissing*[11] the tenor of some of the speeches in the House of Lords suggested that to qualify her for a share a wife's contributions to the household budget had in some way to be referable to the purchase of the house in the sense of enabling the husband to keep up the mortgage. Both Lord Pearson and Lord Diplock seemed to require some arrangement or adjustment in the handling of the family's finances which would indicate that there was a definite connection between the wife's contributions and the acquisition of the house.[12] However, the division of opinion of their Lordships in that case left the law uncertain and subsequent decisions in the Court of Appeal have considerably widened the circumstances in which indirect contributions may be taken into account. In *Hazell v Hazell*[13] Lord Denning stated:

'It is sufficient if the contributions made by the wife are such as to relieve the husband of expenditure he would otherwise have had to bear. By so doing the wife helps him indirectly with the mortgage instalments because he has more money in his pocket with which to pay them. It may be that he does not strictly need her help – he may have enough money of his own without it – but, if he accepts it (and thus is enabled to save more of his own money), she becomes entitled to a share.'[14]

So long as the contribution by the non-legal owner is substantial it need not be confined to the expenditure of money but may take the form of unpaid work in the legal owner's business[15] or labour in building[16] or improving the property.[17] Contributions which merely take the form of housekeeping and child-care do not, however, qualify, even though they span many years.[18] Inevitably the detailed quantification of the beneficial share of the non-legal owner is often difficult, but it is likely to bear some relationship to the proportion which the cost or value of the contributions bears to the total value of the property in question.[19]

1 The Married Women's Property Act 1964 (dealing with the limited issue of rights over savings from a housekeeping allowance) is a rare exception to this principle.

2 *Pettitt v Pettitt* [1970] AC 777, [1969] 2 All ER 385, *Gissing v Gissing* [1971] AC 886, [1970] 2 All ER 780.

3 *Burns v Burns* [1984] Ch 317, [1984] 1 All ER 244.

4 Alternatively the trust may be express, but such trusts have to be manifested in writing – see Law of Property Act 1925, s 53(1) (b).

5 See generally Bromley *Family Law* (6th edn, 1981) pp 442-56; Cretney *Principles of Family Law* (4th edn, 1984) pp 639-52; S Parker *Cohabitees* (Barry Rose, 1981) ch VII.

6 See e g R Desai *Indian Immigrants in Britain* ch 3; *Richards v Dove* [1974] 1 All ER 888; *Singh v Singh* (1985) 15 Fam Law 97.

7 [1972] 3 All ER 744, [1972] 1 WLR 1286.

8 At 747.

9 *Singh v Singh* (1985) 15 Fam Law 97.

10 *Williams and Glyn's Bank Ltd v Boland* [1981] AC 487, [1980] 2 All ER 408.

11 [1971] AC 886, [1970] 2 All ER 780.

12 At 903 and 907-10 respectively.

13 [1972] 1 All ER 923, [1972] 1 WLR 301.

14 At 926.

15 *Nixon v Nixon* [1969] 3 All ER 1133, [1969] 1 WLR 1676; *Re Cummins, Cummins v Thompson* [1972] Ch 62, [1971] 3 All ER 782.

16 *Smith v Baker* [1970] 2 All ER 826, [1970] 1 WLR 1160; *Cooke v Head* [1972] 2 All ER 38, [1972] 1 WLR 518.

17 *Eves v Eves* [1975] 3 All ER 768. A claim by a spouse on the basis of improvements is regulated by statute – see Matrimonial Proceedings and Property Act 1970, s 37. cf *Pettitt v Pettitt*.

18 *Burns v Burns* [1984] Ch 317, [1984] 1 All ER 244.

19 See, e g *Gissing v Gissing* [1971] AC 886, [1970] 2 All ER 780; *Cooke v Head* [1972] 2 All ER 38, [1972] 1 WLR 518; *Re Nicholson, Nicholson v Perks* [1974] 2 All ER 386, [1974] 1 WLR 476; *Hazell v Hazell* [1972] 1 All ER 923, [1972] 1 WLR 301.

4.09 Although there is no distinctive property regime for married couples this should not be taken to mean that their marital status will make no difference to the outcome of a case. In *Pettitt v Pettitt*[1] Lord Upjohn set out the general position as follows:

'. . . though the parties are husband and wife these questions of title must be decided by the principles of law applicable to the settlement of claims between those not so related, while making full allowances in view of the relationship.'[2]

The significance of the last part of this statement was made clear in the case of *Richards v Dove*.[3] Two Jamaicans whose separate marriages had broken down came to England during 1960-61. They cohabited here for a period of nearly ten years. When their relationship came to an end the woman, Miss Richards, claimed a beneficial share in the house they had been living in, which had been purchased in the sole name of the man, Mr Dove. Conflicting evidence was given by the parties both as to Miss Richards' contributions and as to the couple's intention at the time of the purchase. The court preferred the version given by Mr Dove. This was to the effect that the purchase was not a joint investment but an independent venture on his part giving him complete freedom of action and that the contributions made by Miss Richards were limited to part of the deposit and payments in respect of food and the gas needed to cook it. He had paid the mortgage, the electricity bills, the rates and other outgoings. Counsel for Miss Richards based her claim to a share in the property upon the following six principles[4] extracted from the Court of Appeal decisions in *Cooke v Head*[5] and *Hazell v Hazell*[6] and broadly accepted by Walton J in the present case:

(i) 'When two parties by their joint efforts acquire property to be used for their joint purposes, the court may impose or impute a constructive or resulting trust so as to give effect to their respective shares in the property.'

The court accepted this principle but held that on the facts of the case the house had not been acquired by the couple's joint efforts. It had been acquired solely through the efforts of Mr Dove, albeit with the help of a loan of £150 by Miss Richards to cover half the deposit. This loan had to be repaid but it did not entitle Miss Richards to any beneficial share in the house (which would have increased over the years with inflation). This finding was somewhat curious in the light of the fact that the bulk of the deposit was paid out of a joint deposit account at a bank into which the couple's joint savings were placed. There should surely have at least been a presumption that the joint removal of money from this 'common purse' should lead to a joint share in its investment, bearing in mind that the house was for their joint use.[7]

(ii) 'The use of the concept of trust in this matter applies to a man and his mistress as much as it does to a husband and wife.'

The court was only prepared to accept this proposition with the following qualification:

'It by no means follows . . . that the application of the same principles will produce identical results in the wife and mistress, because it is impossible to leave out of the picture the fact that as between the husband and wife the husband has certain legal duties in relation to maintaining his wife, whereas between man and mistress the whole relationship is consensual – if you like contractual – with no legal obligation superimposed.'[8]

The significance of this distinction in the present case was that Mr Dove had no responsibility in law to provide Miss Richards with food, gas or accommodation and thus insofar as she was paying for her own food and the gas to cook it she was doing no more than she was legally obliged to do.

(iii) 'The size of the beneficial interest of each party does not depend solely on the monetary contributions each has made towards the house. One can look at the matter broadly.'
(iv) 'The time for determining the respective shares is when the parties separate.'[9]
(v) 'The plaintiff's contributions to the acquisition of the property need not be directly related to the cost of acquiring or maintaining it. It is sufficient if the contributions are substantial and such as to relieve the defendant from expenditure he would otherwise have had to bear.'
(vi) 'It is sufficient if the plaintiff's contributions are, for example, towards general housekeeping expenses.'

Walton J held that while contributions under heads (v) and (vi) might well qualify the party making them for an equitable share in the property this was by no means automatic. The contributions had to be made 'with the aim or object of assisting in the purchase of the property and thus with the aim of acquiring some interest in the property'. In this case they were not. Furthermore, in paying for her own food and the gas to cook it Miss Richards was not relieving Mr Dove from expenditure he would otherwise have had to bear. The same argument could not apply to his own food, but the contribution she made here might not have been substantial enough to qualify.

In general terms *Richards v Dove* appears to represent something of a restraint upon the development of the rights of cohabitants. This no doubt explains the caustic comment of Lord Denning MR soon afterwards in *Eves v Eves*[10] that the former case 'turned on its own special circumstances and is not of any general application'. It remains to be seen which approach will ultimately predominate, though more recent decisions have tended to follow Lord Denning's lead.[11]

Similar problems may be expected in cases where indirect contributions are made within an Asian extended family, for example by a brother of the legal owner who pays only for housekeeping expenses while the legal owner meets the instalments on the mortgage.

1 [1970] AC 777, [1969] 2 All ER 385.
2 At 813. See also *Bernard v Josephs* [1982] Ch 391, [1982] 3 All ER 162 per Griffiths and Kerr LJJ.
3 [1974] 1 All ER 888.
4 At 893 – 4.
5 [1972] 2 All ER 38, [1972] 1 WLR 518.
6 [1972] 2 All ER 923, [1972] 1 WLR 301.
7 See *Jones v Maynard* [1951] Ch 572, [1951] 1 All ER 802; Parry *Cohabitation* (Sweet and Maxwell, 1981) p 39; cf *Re Bishop, National Provincial Bank Ltd v Bishop* [1965] Ch 450.
8 At 894.
9 Subsequent decisions have established that this is not an invariable rule – see e g *Gordon v Douce* [1983] 2 All ER 228, [1983] 1 WLR 563.
10 [1975] 3 All ER 768, [1975] 1 WLR 1338.
11 See, e g *Hall v Hall* (1981) 3 FLR 379; *Gordon v Douce* [1983] 2 All ER 228, [1983] 1 WLR 563.

4.10 Where property is conveyed to purchasers in their joint names they automatically become joint legal owners. This does not, however, solve the question as to the beneficial ownership of the property. If the conveyance also expressly declares the beneficial interests then this will be conclusive in the absence of fraud or a mistake.[1] Normally in such a case the parties will either be beneficial joint tenants or beneficial tenants in common. The principal difference between these two forms of co-ownership relates to what happens when the first tenant dies. In the case of a joint tenancy since both parties are regarded as jointly owning the whole interest the death of the first causes the whole interest to pass to the survivor by operation of law. In the case of a tenancy in common the parties own distinct shares and on death such shares pass in accordance with the deceased's will or the rules of intestacy. Where there is no such declaration in the conveyance there is no presumption that the parties are beneficial joint tenants and regard must be had to their respective contributions as well as their common intention in order to discover their equitable shares.[2]

Property which is owned jointly or in common is automatically subject to a trust for sale, albeit with an implied power to postpone the sale in certain circumstances. The basic rule is that if the parties cannot all agree to postpone the sale then the sale should go ahead and application may be made to the court for an order for sale under the Law of Property Act 1925, s 30.[2] However, the court has a discretion in the matter and it will not order the sale to proceed where it would be inequitable to do so[3] or some purpose of the trust remains to be discharged.[4] A typical example of a situation in which an order for sale might well be refused by the court is where the property in question was purchased as a family home and following the separation of the owners the parent who has care and control of the children does not wish to move house.[5]

In *Dennis v McDonald*[6] parties of Jamaican origin had cohabited here for about 12 years before the mother left the family home because of the father's violence towards her. She went to live in a council house. Six years later she sought an order for the sale of their family home which had been conveyed to the couple in joint names as tenants in common. There were five children of the family. Custody of the two younger children had been granted to the mother, with the three older children remaining with their father. The court refused to order an immediate sale because the property was still required by the father and the older children for the purpose of a family home, one of the primary objects of the original trust. However, the court did make an order that the father should pay the mother an occupation rent since she was a co-owner of the premises who had been involuntarily excluded from enjoying possession of her property through the conduct of the father.

In an Asian extended family the situation might arise where the property was held in the joint names of two brothers, each of whom had a family living in the house. If only one of them wished to sell the court would have to decide whether it was just and reasonable to allow him to do so if it meant rehousing other members of the family against their wishes.

1 *Pettitt v Pettitt* [1970] AC 777 at 813; *Leake v Bruzzi* [1974] 2 All ER 1196, [1974] 1 WLR 1528; *Re John's Assignment Trust, Niven v Niven* [1970] 2 All ER 210, [1970] 1 WLR 955 *Goodman v Gallant* (1985) *Times*, 7 November.
2 *Bernard v Josephs* [1982] Ch 391, [1982] 3 All ER 162.
3 *Jackson v Jackson* [1971] 3 All ER 774, [1971] 1 WLR 1539.
4 *Jones v Challenger* [1961] 1 QB 176, [1960] 1 All ER 785.
5 *Re Evers' Trust, Papps v Evers* [1980] 3 All ER 399, [1980] 1 WLR 1327.
6 [1981] 2 All ER 632, [1981] 1 WLR 810.

2 Occupation of the family home

(i) RIGHTS OF OCCUPATION[1]

4.11 Members of a family may obtain rights to occupy the family home from a variety of sources. Proprietary interests, whether legal or beneficial, will usually confer such an entitlement, as for example where the title is in joint names or where although the title is in the sole name of one family member[2] another has an equitable interest in the property.[3] Occupation rights may also be derived from statute law or from general principles of contract law.

The Matrimonial Homes Act 1983 (an Act which consolidated the Matrimonial Homes Act 1967 and later amendments to it) grants statutory 'rights of occupation' in respect of the matrimonial home to spouses who do not have a legal interest in the property. This means that the non-legal owner has a right, if already in actual occupation, not to be evicted or excluded from the whole or any part of it except with the leave of the court and, if not in occupation, a right to enter and occupy with the leave of the court.[4] The Act gives the courts wide powers to regulate such 'rights of occupation' as well as the occupation rights of the legal owner.[5] The Act does not, however, apply to a dwelling house which has at no time been a matrimonial home of the spouses in question,[6] a restriction which was highlighted by the case of *Syed v Syed*[7]. The parties, a married couple, were of Pakistani origin. After the wedding they had lived here with their in-laws until the wife returned to Pakistan on what was initially intended to be a brief visit. However, in the event her return was delayed for a period of some two years by means of her husband's contrivance and prevarication. During her absence he had purchased a house in his sole name and had been living there with another woman. The wife ultimately returned to this country, accompanied by her mother, with the intention of achieving a reconciliation with her husband and, if that failed, with a view to enforcing her rights against him. Once it became clear that reconciliation was a forlorn prospect she applied for an injunction to allow her to enter and live in the husband's house rather than remain in the room she was having to rent elsewhere. Since, however, it had never been used as their matrimonial home it was held that the 1967 Act had no application. Nor was the court prepared to invoke its own inherent jurisdiction in support of the wife's application in the absence of any legal right on her part in the property. French J held that even if the court had possessed such jurisdiction no injunction should be ordered because the wife possessed sufficient means of her own to pay for reasonable accommodation. A curious feature of the case was that the judge declared himself satisfied that any prospective financial interest she might have in the property as a result of divorce proceedings was adequately protected through the Class F land charge which she had earlier registered against the property. However, such a land charge can only validly be registered against a dwelling house which has been used as the parties' matrimonial home, which this property had not.

The decision in *Syed's case* has been criticised for failing to consider the cultural background of the parties and the fact that in terms of Pakistani law a husband has a duty to provide his wife with accommodation and shelter.[8] On the other hand, it is in line with a similar ruling involving an Indian wife made here some 12 years earlier.[9] However, it seems fair to conclude that the present state of English law is unsatisfactory not only for Asian wives but for all wives in this country. The 1967 Act was designed to improve upon the rights which a wife previously had at common law. In terms of the common law a husband had a duty to provide accommodation for his wife as a part of her right to consortium and her right to be maintained by him.[10] It was because this did not give her a right to occupy a specific house[11] that her rights were strengthened, but the current Act plainly does not go far enough.

1 The discussion which follows is principally concerned with the rights of family members inter se. For the position vis-à-vis third parties, see *Parry* pp 22-34; *Bromley* pp 465-9; *Williams and Glyn's Bank Ltd v Boland* [1981] AC 487, [1980] 2 All ER 408; *Re Sharpe* [1980] 1 All ER 198; *Bristol and West Building Society v Henning* [1985] 2 All ER 606, [1985] 1 WLR 778.
2 *Gurasz v Gurasz* [1970] P 11, [1969] 3 All ER 822.
3 *Bull v Bull* [1955] 1 QB 234, [1955] 1 All ER 253; *Williams and Glyn's Bank Ltd v Boland* above.
4 Matrimonial Homes Act, s 1(1), (9).
5 S 1(2).
6 S 1(8).
7 (1980) 1 FLR 129.
8 Pearl [1980] New Community 147.
9 *Nanda v Nanda* [1968] P 351, [1967] 3 All ER 401.
10 See *National Provincial Bank Ltd v Ainsworth* [1965] AC 1175, [1965] 2 All ER 472; *Gurasz v Gurasz* [1970] P 11, [1969] 3 All ER 822; *Bromley* pp 456-7.
11 See *National Provincial Bank Ltd v Ainsworth* above at 1229, 1245; *Cretney* p 245.

4.12 A family member who has no legal or equitable interest in the family home and who cannot rely upon the Matrimonial Homes Act 1983 may in certain circumstances be able to claim a right of occupation on the strength of a contractual licence. In the leading case of *Tanner v Tanner*[1] a man had purchased a house in his own name in the expectation that it would provide a home for the woman he had been cohabiting with and their twin daughters. He induced her to give up a rent-controlled tenancy elsewhere and move into the house. He also stopped paying maintenance for the children on the ground that he was providing them with free accommodation. The Court of Appeal inferred from these circumstances that the woman had acquired a contractual licence to remain in the house with the children for so long as the twins were of school age and they all reasonably required the accommodation. The licence was held to be specifically enforceable by injunction and thus could not legally be revoked by the owner of the property as soon as the couple's relationship broke down.

One of the problems for the courts in cases such as these is to infer how long such a licence was intended to endure[2] and in another case where a cohabitant was told by the owner of the house that she would be completely secure there in the event of a breakdown of their relationship the court nevertheless held that in the light of all the surrounding circumstances the licence was determinable on 12 months' notice.[3] Consideration for the licence also has to be established. In *Tanner's* case this was provided by the surrender of the woman's rent-controlled tenancy, but other claims have failed for lack of sufficient consideration.[4] A further difficulty with these 'family arrangements' is the danger that a court may find that the parties never intended to create legal relations between them, regarding their agreements as merely social or domestic arrangements.[5] Lord Denning commented in general terms upon this aspect in *Hardwick v Johnson*[6] as follows:

'. . . these family arrangements do have legal consequences; and, time and time again, the courts are called on to determine what is the true legal relationship resulting from them. This is especially the case where one member of the family occupies a house or uses furniture which is afterwards claimed by another member of the family, or when one pays money to another and afterwards says it was a loan and the other says it was a gift, and so forth. In most of these cases the question cannot be solved by looking to the intention of the parties, because the situation which arises is one which they never envisaged and for which they made no provision. So many things are undecided, undiscussed, and unprovided for that the task of the courts is to fill in the blanks. The court has to look at all the circumstances and spell out the legal relationship. The court will pronounce in favour of a tenancy or a licence, a loan or a gift, or a trust, according to which of these legal relationships is most fitting in the situation which has arisen; and will find the terms of that relationship according to what reason and justice require.'[7]

Although this is a rather unorthodox approach in its rejection of a search, albeit perhaps an artificial one, for some common intention or assumption,[8] it does seem to reflect the reality of the operations of the courts in recent years.

1 [1975] 3 All ER 776, [1975] 1 WLR 134.
2 See, e g *Hardwick v Johnson* [1978] 2 All ER 935, [1978] 1 WLR 683.
3 *Chandler v Kerley* [1978] 2 All ER 942, [1978] 1 WLR 693.
4 See, e g *Horrocks v Forray* [1976] 1 All ER 737, [1976] 1 WLR 230.
5 See *Balfour v Balfour* [1919] 2 KB 571; *Horrocks v Forray* above.
6 [1978] 2 All ER 935, [1978] 1 WLR 683.
7 At 938.
8 See, e g *Re Sharpe* [1981] 1 All ER 198 at 201 for a return to the more orthodox line.

(ii) RIGHTS TO PROTECTION

4.13   A family member's rights of occupation may be rendered valueless in a practical sense, from whatever source they may be derived, if he or she is subjected to violence or ill-treatment at the hands of other members of the family. It is, therefore, necessary to consider what forms of protection the law can give in these circumstances.

The most important procedural device available to the courts in this regard is the use of an injunction. An injunction may either be granted to prevent molestation, for example where one partner is pestering or annoying the other, or it may operate to exclude a partner from the family home where his conduct has reached the level of violence or dangerous threats. Today the principal provisions regulating the issue of these injunctions are to be found in the Domestic Violence and Matrimonial Proceedings Act 1976, the Domestic Proceedings and Magistrates' Courts Act 1978 and the Matrimonial Homes Act 1983.[1] Whereas the 1978 Act is confined to affording protection to spouses (and children of their family), the 1976 Act extends such protection to cohabitants provided they fall within the statutory language of 'a man and a woman who are living with each other in the same household as husband and wife'.[2]

This Act enables a spouse or cohabitant to obtain either an injunction against molestation[3] or an order excluding the other partner from the whole or any part of the family home without seeking any other form of relief, such as divorce or damages for assault.

In the leading case of *Davis v Johnson*,[4] which involved a cohabiting couple of West Indian origin, the question arose whether the Act went so far as to empower the courts to exclude by means of an injunction a violent cohabitant from a house of which he was sole or joint legal owner in defiance of his proprietary rights. Both the Court of Appeal and the House of Lords held that this was indeed the legal position. The Act had to be interpreted in this way not only to achieve the objectives of Parliament in affording practical protection to victims of domestic violence but also to give effect to the plain meaning of the language used in the enactment. Although s 1 of the Act did not alter the parties' proprietary rights it did enable the courts to interfere with the enjoyment of those rights by making at least a temporary exclusion order.

How long such an exclusion order should last for is not entirely clear. In *Davis v Johnson* a variety of views were expressed in the House of Lords. Lord Diplock stated that the order could last only so long as there was a danger that if the man was permitted to return he would commit further assaults on the woman and her child.[5] In Viscount Dilhorne's view the purpose of the order was to afford immediate relief and in so far as it excluded a party from property rights in his home 'a county court judge might think it right to make it clear that the injunction is to be of a temporary character to enable both parties to regulate their affairs'.[6] Lord Salmon spoke of the Act as providing 'first aid' rather than 'intensive care' for the victims of 'battering' and affording them a breathing space to find suitable alternative accommodation in safety.[7] 'Much depends on the circumstances of each case, but I find it difficult to believe that it could ever be fair, save in most exceptional circumstances, to keep a man out of his own flat or house for more than a few months.'[8] Lord Scarman's view was that although the period of exclusion would usually be brief it might have to be lengthy in some cases.[9] He contemplated that the county court judge would normally make the exclusion 'until further order', thus enabling either party to apply for its discharge or modification at a suitable time in the future.

In 1978 a Practice Direction was issued by the President of the Family Division specifically relating to injunctions in respect of the matrimonial home. It noted that while the period of the exclusion was a matter for the discretion of the judge in each case, consideration should be given to imposing a time-limit. It went on to indicate that in most cases a fixed period of up to three months was likely to be appropriate in the first instance.[10] That this in no way precludes the use of an injunction as a longer term remedy is clear from the case of *Spencer v Camacho*.[11] There the family home, a council house, was in the joint names of the cohabitants. The courts had already made two exclusion orders against the man, each for a period of three months following his use of violence. Finally, on the third application the Court of Appeal ruled that it was appropriate to make an indefinite exclusion order in the form of an injunction 'until further order' in the hope of remedying the situation and relieving the woman of the need for further applications. On the other hand, where the property is in the sole name of the violent partner it seems unlikely that the court would be willing to keep the owner out of his property by means of an injunction under the Act for more than a period of a few weeks or months at a time.[12]

1 For the application of other possible remedies, see *Parker* ch VII.
2 S 1(2).
3 Including molestation of a child living with the applicants: s 1(1) (b).
4 [1979] AC 264, [1978] 1 All ER 841, CA; [1979] AC 264, [1978] 1 All ER 1132, HL.
5 At 1142.
6 At 1146.
7 At 1151-2.
8 At 1152.
9 At 1157.
10 Practice Note (Family Division: Injunction: Exclusion from Matrimonial Home) [1978] 2 All ER 1056. See also *Hopper v Hopper* [1979] 1 All ER 181, [1978] 1 WLR 1342.
11 (1983) 4 FLR 662. See also *Spindlow v Spindlow* [1979] Fam 52, [1979] 1 All ER 169; *Galan v Galan* [1985] 6 FLR 905.
12 See *Freeman v Collins* (1983) 4 FLR 649.

4.14 Although the title of the 1976 Act would tend to suggest that one precondition of obtaining an exclusion order must be proof of domestic violence, whether actual or apprehended, this does not appear to be the case. Section 1 of the Act makes no reference to violence and an injunction might well be granted if it was required for the security of a woman and her children, as, for example, where she was threatened with eviction.[1] However, following the House of Lords' decision in *Richards v Richards*[2] it is clear that the jurisdiction of the High Court and county courts to make exclusion orders in matrimonial cases is governed exclusively by the Matrimonial Homes legislation. Accordingly in deciding whether or not to make such an order a court must now bear in mind not only the needs of any children but also the conduct of the spouses themselves. The Matrimonial Homes Act 1983, s 1(3) specifically provides:

'On an application for an order under this section the court may make such order as it thinks just and reasonable having regard to the conduct of the spouses in relation to each other and otherwise, to their respective needs and financial resources, to the needs of any children and to all the circumstances of the case . . .'

Prior to this decision the tendency in recent years had been for the courts to concentrate on the practical aspects of meeting the housing needs of members of broken families and in particular providing a home for the children.[3] Since it is usually harder for the woman and her children to find alternative accommodation than for the man it tended to be he who had to move out if the family could not continue to live together peaceably.[4] However, the decision in *Richards* establishes that where the wife and mother gives only the flimsiest of reasons for complaining that she cannot remain in the house with her husband the courts will not exclude him simply because the couple can no longer co-operate with one another. A reasonable ground for her refusal to return to the matrimonial home while he remains there is required. Nor are the courts entitled to accord the interests of any children 'paramount' consideration, although these are obviously a matter of major importance. The same approach seems likely to be adopted in the case of cohabitants since the 1976 Act confers the same jurisdiction upon the county courts in these cases as in cases between the parties to a marriage.[5]

1 *Davis v Johnson* [1978] 1 All ER 1132 at 1145 (per Viscount Dilhorne), 1156 (per Lord Scarman). See also *Spindlow v Spindlow* [1979] Fam 52, [1979] 1 All ER 169.
2 [1984] AC 174, [1983] 2 All ER 807.
3 See, eg *Walker v Walker* [1978] 3 All ER 141, [1978] 1 WLR 533; *Rennick v Rennick* [1978] 1 All ER 817, [1977] 1 WLR 1455.
4 See, eg *Bassett v Bassett* [1975] Fam 76, [1975] 1 All ER 513.

5 See *Lee v Lee* [1984] 5 FLR 243.

4.15 Although the Domestic Violence and Matrimonial Proceedings Act does not empower the courts to exclude members other than spouses or cohabitants from the family home, this does not necessarily mean that there is no procedure for evicting persons such as parents, brothers, in-laws, or grown-up children in appropriate circumstances. In *Pinckney v Pinckney*[1] a wife obtained an exclusion order against her husband's mistress in the exercise of the High Court's inherent[2] jurisdiction to protect the interests of children and of parties to pending litigation (in this instance a divorce). It is thought that on this basis an interlocutory injunction might be obtained by, for example, an Asian wife to obtain the eviction from her home of a member of her husband's extended family who was making life unbearable for her or was having a bad influence on her children, especially if he had committed acts of violence in the home. It would appear that the injunction would have to be ancillary to some proceedings which had already been or were about to be set in motion (such as a petition for divorce or judicial separation, or an application for custody of children, or an action for damages for assault), a burdensome procedural requirement dispensed with in cases brought under the 1976 Act. In view of this it would probably be a desirable reform for the Act to be extended to cover the exclusion of all persons from the family home without the necessity for other proceedings.[3]

1 [1966] 1 All ER 121.
2 The 'inherent' jurisdiction may now be incorporated in the court's statutory jurisdiction under the Supreme Court Act 1981, s 37: see *Richards v Richards* [1983] 2 All ER 807 at 812.
3 See Bottomley *The Cohabitation Guidebook* (London, 1981) p 94.

3 Housing for the homeless

4.16 There is good reason to believe that homelessness afflicts ethnic minorities a great deal more than it does the rest of the population.[1] It is particularly significant, therefore, that a statutory duty has been imposed upon local authorities by the Housing (Homeless Persons) Act 1977 to provide accommodation for those who are homeless or threatened with homelessness.[2] In terms of the extended definition of homelessness employed in the Act, a person is deemed to be homeless, despite the fact that he or she already has accommodation, if it is probable that occupation of it will lead either to violence or to threats of violence from someone living there who is likely to carry out such threats.[3] Under s 4(5) of the Act, where the local authority is satisfied that a person who has applied for accommodation is homeless and has 'a priority need'[4] and has not become homeless intentionally,[5] it has a duty to house that person. Section 1 does not define a person as being homeless exclusively in individualistic terms but includes the situation where he has no right to occupy any accommodation 'together with any other person who normally resides with him as a member of his family or in circumstances in which the housing authority consider it reasonable for that person to reside with him'. The idea behind this terminology is both to prevent the splitting-up of families through homelessness and to encompass a wide range of family relationships within the definition, including cohabiting couples.[6] Among the categories of 'priority need' is the case of a person who has dependent children 'who are residing with him or who might reasonably be expected to reside with him'. This might include children in the voluntary care of a local authority and children temporarily living with relatives or friends as well as step-children and foster-children.

The local authority's duty to secure that accommodation is made available for someone who is homeless is only satisfied if the accommodation offered is available for occupation 'both by him and by any other person who might reasonably be expected to reside with him'.[7] Exactly which persons fall into this category is unclear, although spouses, cohabitants, minor children and elderly grandparents would obviously be included. Whether the category would encompass remoter relatives who would be considered part of an Asian extended family still has to be decided by the courts, but the particular circumstances of the family concerned would obviously be a relevant factor, as would the availability of suitably-sized accommodation within the local authority. In view of Lord Wilberforce's comment in *Din v London Borough of Wandsworth*[8] that the Act was designed 'for the express purpose of bringing families together' there certainly should be no objection in principle to requiring local authorities to respect extended family ties wherever it is feasible to do so. It is certainly reasonable for those who have lived together as an extended family in the recent past to expect to continue to do so.

1 See Smith *Racial Disadvantage in Britain* (Penguin, 1977) p 279.
2 See generally, D Hoath *Homelessness* (Sweet and Maxwell, 1983).
3 Housing (Homeless Persons) Act 1977, s 1(2) (b).
4 This expression is defined in s 2 of the Act.
5 As defined in s 17 of the Act; see generally *Din v London Borough of Wandsworth* [1983] 1 AC 657, [1981] 3 All ER 881; *Islam v London Borough of Hillingdon* [1981] 3 All ER 901.
6 See Housing (Homeless Persons) Act Code of Guidance, para 2.8. Under s 12 of the Act local authorities must have regard to the Code though it has to be interpreted within the framework of the statutory language used – see *R v Waveney DC* [1983] QB 238, [1982] 3 All ER 727.
7 S 16.
8 [1981] 3 All ER 881 at 883.

4 Transmission of tenancies

(i) UNDER THE RENT ACT 1977

4.17 The Rent Act 1977 provides that when either a 'protected' or a 'statutory' tenant[1] dies the tenancy is automatically transferred to the deceased's widow or widower, provided she or he was residing in the property at the time of the death.[2] Where the tenant dies without leaving a surviving spouse, but a person who was 'a member of the original tenant's family' was residing with him at the time of his death (and had been doing so for the period of six months immediately preceding) that person automatically becomes the statutory tenant for as long as he occupies the house as his residence.[3]

There has been much litigation, spanning a period of more than half a century, regarding which persons qualify for inclusion as 'members of the original tenant's family'.[4] These statutory words, the courts have held on numerous occasions, are not being used by the legislature in any technical sense and must be interpreted flexibly and given their 'ordinary and popular meaning'.[5]

The question is, therefore, one of fact in each case that arises.[6] On the basis of previous decisions it may confidently be predicted that the following relatives would definitely be included – children (whether legitimate, illegitimate or adopted);[7] grandchildren;[8] parents; brothers and sisters;[9] and nephews and nieces.[10] The inclusion of grandchildren and nephews and nieces suggests that grandparents and uncles and aunts should also qualify. Children who had been fostered with the deceased from an early age would also probably be included in suitable cases,[11] as would step-children of the deceased.[12] The spouses of the aforementioned individuals would also appear to qualify since in-laws are generally regarded as members of a person's family.[13]

1 A 'protected' tenant is one who holds a contractual lease to which the Rent Act applies; a 'statutory' tenant is one who remains in possession after his contractual lease has ended.
2 Rent Act 1977, Sch 1, para 2 (as substituted by Housing Act 1980, s 76).
3 Ibid para 3. If there is more than one such person the succession has to be decided by agreement between them or in default by a decision of the county court.
4 Prior to 1977 this phrase was to be found in earlier rent legislation dating back to 1920.
5 *Price v Gould* (1930) 143 LT 333; *Brock v Wollams* [1949] 2 KB 388, [1949] 1 All ER 715; *Langdon v Horton* [1951] 1 KB 666, [1951] 1 All ER 60; *Dyson Holdings Ltd v Fox* [1976] QB 503, [1975] 3 All ER 1030; *Carega Properties SA v Sharrat* [1979] 2 All ER 1084, [1979] 1 WLR 928.
6 See Berkovits 'The Family and the Rent Acts: Reflections on Law and Policy' [1981] JSWL 83 at 90-3.
7 *Brock v Wollams* above.
8 *Collier v Stoneman* [1957] 1 All ER 20, [1957] 1 WLR 1108.
9 *Price v Gould* (1930) 143 LT 333.
10 *Jones v Whitehill* [1950] 2 KB 204, [1950] 1 All ER 71.
11 *Brock v Wollams* above.
12 See *Brock v Wollams* above.
13 *Standingford v Probert* [1950] 1 KB 377, [1949] 2 All ER 861; *Jones v Whitehill* above.

4.18 It was recognised as long ago as 1953 that a cohabitant who had lived with the deceased and borne his children could qualify as a 'member of his family',[1] but it was not until 1975 that the Court of Appeal in *Dyson Holdings Ltd v Fox*[2] held that such a woman could be included within the expression in the absence of any children. In the case of *Gammans v Ekins*[3] in 1950 the Court of Appeal had employed avowedly moralistic arguments to deny such recognition to cohabitation. Asquith LJ has summed the matter up as follows:

'To say of two people masquerading, as these two were, as husband and wife – there being no children to complicate the picture – that they were members of the same family, seems to me an abuse of the English language . . .'[4]

By the mid-1970s such judicial sentiments seemed so dated and out of keeping with reality that the decision in *Dyson's case* came as no real surprise.[5] There the Court of Appeal upheld a claim by a woman who had lived with the deceased for more than 20 years. Lord Denning MR explained that they had lived together 'as man and wife' for many years. Bridge LJ pointed out that between 1950 and 1975 there had been a complete revolution in society's attitudes to unmarried partnerships of this kind. Such unions were far commoner than they used to be. The social stigma which once attached to them had almost, if not entirely, disappeared. On the other hand, James LJ declared that not every cohabitant would qualify for inclusion as a member of the deceased's family. Relationships of a 'casual or intermittent character and those bearing indications of impermanence' did not come within the popular conception of a family unit.[6] Bridge LJ himself also referred to the need for an 'appropriate degree of apparent permanence and stability'.[7]

1 *Hawes v Evenden* [1953] 2 All ER 737, [1953] 1 WLR 1169.
2 [1976] QB 503, [1975] 3 All ER 1030.
3 [1950] 2 KB 328, [1950] 2 All ER 140.
4 At 142.
5 See Poulter 'The Death of a Lover' (1976) 126 NLJ 433.
6 [1975] 3 All ER 1030 at 1035.
7 At 1036.

4.19 Despite the mass of decisions on the meaning of 'member of the original tenant's family', it is thought that there still remain a number of difficulties to be resolved by the courts under the 1977 Act.

First, there is the problem of where to draw the line in respect of persons who are relatives of the original tenant by blood. At present it is possible to see the decided cases as drawing the line between nephews and nieces, on the one hand, and cousins on the other. In *Langdon v Horton*[1] two female cousins of the tenant joined her in the property at her request after she had been widowed. They remained with her for nearly 30 years up to her death, but the Court of Appeal held that they did not qualify as members of her family. After expressing approval of the narrow approach adopted in *Gammans v Ekins*, Singleton LJ declared:

'I do not see that it is possible to say that a cousin is a member of another cousin's family merely because she is a cousin. They are members of the same family or stock in the sense that they have the same . . . grandparents; that is all. The mere fact of cousinship does not make every cousin a member of another cousin's family.'[2]

Danckwerts J commented:

'It seems to me that their consanguinity was not the decisive test. They were living together more for reasons of convenience, in which respect this case resembles the case which was referred to by Asquith LJ in *Gammans v Ekins*, when he referred to the case of two old cousins or friends sharing a residence for purposes of convenience.'[3]

It is submitted that this approach is far too restricted and that it is as ripe for reappraisal as *Gammans v Ekins* was in 1975. The man in the street surely would describe a cousin living together with another cousin as a member of that cousin's family. Once it is accepted that 'family' is now being used popularly in a wider sense than merely children (which is perhaps its primary colloquial meaning),[4] then first cousins should certainly be included. On the other hand, it would clearly be difficult to justify the extension of the concept to distant cousins many times removed. However, if attention is focused upon a hypothetical case involving an Asian extended family it is thought that there should be a reasonable chance of persuading a court to recognise at least first cousins, and including those so related by affinity.

1 [1951] 1 KB 666, [1951] 1 All ER 60.
2 At 672.
3 At 673.
4 As in the question 'Do you have a family?'

4.20   The second problem revolves around the degree of stability required for a cohabitant to qualify as a member of the deceased's family. In *Helby v Rafferty*[1] the Court of Appeal denied recognition to a male cohabitant because there had been an insufficiency of permanence and stability in his relationship with the original tenant. Clearly the issue is one of fact and degree in every case, but in this instance the Court's conclusion seemed highly questionable, to say the least. The trial judge, whose reasoning was endorsed by the Court of Appeal, took the view that the couple had not been living together as husband and wife because the woman had not 'adopted the character of a wife', either by having children or by adopting the man's surname as her own, and because she had wanted to retain a certain amount of independence and freedom by not marrying him. While all these facts are clearly relevant to some degree in deciding whether a relationship amounts to a de facto marriage, there appeared to be a number of other factors in the case which when taken together should have led the court to the conclusion that the couple's relationship was sufficiently akin to marriage to make them members of the same family. They had lived together for five years until the tenant died. They had slept in the same bed, shared household and leisure activities and expenses. Their lives had been very closely bound up with one another. When the deceased became ill towards the end of her life the man had nursed her just as a husband would have done. The woman had retained her own name because she was a well-known writer and journalist.

It is submitted that where a couple operate a joint household for a period as long as five years without any sign of instability or impermanence in their relationship and where they share a common life as well as the same bed there should be a very strong presumption in favour of the conclusion that they are living together as husband and wife and hence that one is a member of the other's family for the purposes of the Rent Act. Fortunately, the importance to be attached to the use of a common surname has been considerably reduced by the subsequent decision of the Court of Appeal in *Watson v Lucas*.[2] There Stephenson LJ declared: 'The time has gone by when the courts can hold such a union not to be "familial" simply because the parties to it do not pretend to be married in due form of law'[3] and Sir David Cairns commented: 'It is the relations between the man and the woman that are relevant rather than the appearance that they present to the public'.[4] This case also establishes that a person may be recognised as a member of his or her cohabitant's family despite being married to someone else. There seems no reason whatever why an individual cannot be a member of two (or more) families simultaneously.[5] It also seems important to bear in mind that nowadays wives as well as cohabitants often seek a similar degree of freedom and independence in their family lives as well as a certain level of security. The point is not so much what the law says about such freedom and security upon the breakdown of the relationship (as the Court of Appeal appeared to believe in *Helby v Rafferty*)[6] because this is exactly what distinguishes a formal marriage from a de facto one. Rather it is how couples themselves view the matter and it cannot be regarded in modern times as 'unwifely' to value a degree of independence in practice that wives have not known in previous centuries.

It is still unclear whether sexual relations are required for recognition to be given to claims made by cohabitants. While this might properly be regarded as part of normal married life, account must surely be taken of de facto families where intercourse is impossible on account of disability or old age. On the other hand, the House of Lords have held in *Carega Properties SA v Sharratt*[7] that two adults who live together in a platonic relationship can never establish a 'familiar nexus' by acting, for example, as brother and sister or aunt and nephew. This should not, however, preclude a cohabiting couple from proving that their relationship was a de facto marriage in suitable circumstances.

1 [1978] 3 All ER 1016, [1979] 1 WLR 13.
2 [1980] 3 All ER 647, [1980] 1 WLR 1493.
3 At 653.
4 At 658.
5 See also *Standingford v Probert* [1950] 1 KB 377 at 386.
6 [1978] 3 All ER 1016 at 1023.
7 [1979] 2 All ER 1084, [1979] 1 WLR 928.

(ii) UNDER THE HOUSING ACT 1980
4.21 Following the pattern established for private rented accommodation by the Rent Act, the Housing Act 1980 introduced a similar process of transmission of tenancies in the public sector.[1] Periodic secure council tenancies granted by local authorities are automatically vested in certain circumstances in a successor who, in the absence of a surviving spouse, is 'another member of the tenant's family' who has resided with the tenant throughout the period of 12 months ending with the tenant's death.[2]

Qualification as a 'member of the tenant's family' is specifically regulated by s 50(3) of the Act as follows:

'A person is a member of another's family within the meaning of this Chapter[3] if he is his spouse, parent, grandparent, child, grandchild, brother, sister, uncle, aunt, nephew or niece; treating –
(a) any relationship by marriage as a relationship by blood, any relationship of the half blood as a relationship of the whole blood and the stepchild of any person as his child; and
(b) an illegitimate person as the legitimate child of his mother and reputed father or if they live together as husband and wife.'

No doubt the intention of this section was to remove the element of uncertainty which, as we have seen, has characterised interpretation of the Rent Act and its predecessors. However, it still leaves the meaning to be attributed to 'living together as husband and wife' to the courts and it fails to include first cousins as recommended earlier. Nor does it include co-widows of a polygamist who might well be popularly regarded as members of one another's families.

1 Unlike the Rent Act which allows for two transmissions (sch 1, para 10), there can only be one succession under the 1980 Act (s 30).
2 S 30. Where there is more than one 'member of the tenant's family' the successor is agreed between them or, in default, selected by the council.
3 Chapter 1 of the Act also gives 'members of the tenant's family' the opportunity in certain circumstances to share in his 'right to buy' (s 4), as well as to be included in the mortgage entitlement (s 9).

5 Family provision claims upon death

4.22 The rights of beneficiaries under a will or the intestacy rules are by no means absolute because a broad category of persons may make claims for provision out of the deceased's estate under the Inheritance (Provision for Family and Dependants) Act 1975. Since cohabitants are capable of being included as claimants this Act may enable them to make up for their omission from the intestacy rules. On the other hand, any benefits they may stand to gain from wills made in their favour are liable to be reduced by claims made by the testator's spouse or other relatives.

Whereas a beneficiary under a will or the intestacy rules has an automatic entitlement without the necessity of lodging a claim, an applicant for family provision has to petition the court for the exercise of judicial discretion in his favour. In each case it is a precondition for the making of any order that the court is satisfied that the disposition of the deceased's estate effected by his will or the law relating to intestacy (or a combination of both on a partial intestacy) is not such as to make reasonable financial provision for the applicant.[1]

The following persons are eligible to bring claims – the deceased's surviving spouse, a former spouse who has not remarried, a child of the deceased (including legitimate, adopted and illegitimate children) and anyone who had been treated by the deceased during a marriage as 'a child of the family'.[2] In addition a claim may be brought by any other person who 'immediately before the death of the deceased was being maintained, either wholly or partly by the deceased'.[3] The expression 'being maintained' is defined as arising where the deceased, 'otherwise than for full valuable consideration, was making a substantial contribution in money or money's worth towards the reasonable needs of' the claimant.[4]

Among the persons who could in appropriate circumstances bring a claim as members of this last category are included the deceased's parents, brothers

and sisters, in-laws, uncles and aunts as well as a cohabitant. Often the
principal hurdle such a claimant has to surmount in practice is to show a
substantial dependency upon the deceased, as opposed to an arrangement
whereby both parties shared their resources together and were mutually dependent upon one another or else were independent financially of one another,
albeit perhaps living in the same household.[5] Although the statutory formula
'otherwise than for full valuable consideration' was no doubt chiefly aimed at
barring claims from employees, housekeepers, paying guests and others who
were in a contractual relationship with the deceased, the courts have held that
the expression is not confined to those situations.[6]

Among a large number of factors which the court has to take into account in
deciding whether or not to make an order in favour of the applicant, the most
important would seem to be the applicant's resources and needs (both at the
time of the hearing and in the foreseeable future), the extent to which and the
basis upon which the deceased assumed responsibility for the applicant's
maintenance and the length of time during which he discharged that responsibility, the applicant's conduct towards him, any disability suffered by the
applicant, the size and nature of the estate and the resources and needs of any
other applicants and of the beneficiaries of the estate.[7] However, since the court
is entitled to have regard to any other matter which in the circumstances of the
case the court considers to be relevant the cultural background to the family
ties between an ethnic minority applicant and the deceased could obviously
also be borne in mind. The court has power to make a variety of orders including
the payment of a lump sum or the transfer of property, but the entitlement of
the applicant is limited in all cases except surviving spouses to a reasonable
level of maintenance. This is not restricted to provision of the bare necessities
of life, and certainly extends to the provision of suitable accommodation (such
as a life interest in the house in which the applicant and the deceased have
been living),[8] but equally it does not mean that an applicant is entitled to
whatever he perceives as reasonably desirable for his welfare or benefit.[9]

1 S 2(1).
2 S 1(1) (a) – (d).
3 S 1(1) (e).
4 S 1(3).
5 See, e g *Re Wilkinson, Neale v Newell* [1978] Fam 22, [1978] 1 All ER 221; *Re Beaumont, Martin v
   Midland Bank Trust Co Ltd* [1980] Ch 444, [1980] 1 All ER 266; *Jelley v Iliffe* [1981] Fam 128,
   [1981] 2 All ER 29.
6 *Re Wilkinson* above; *Re Beaumont* above.
7 S 3(1), (4).
8 *Harrington v Gill* (1983) 4 FLR 265.
9 *Re Coventry* [1980] Ch 461, [1979] 3 All ER 815.

6 Welfare benefits

4.23 A variety of statutory provisions in the field of welfare benefits equate a
cohabiting couple with a married couple or treat them as constituting a family.
Significantly, however, the tendency to adopt this approach is most marked
where it will result not in an increase in the availability of benefits but in a
financial saving for the taxpayer.[1] The most notorious example of this practice
is the 'cohabitation rule' in respect of supplementary benefit. This rule provides
for the aggregation of the requirements and resources of an unmarried couple
rather than their treatment as separate individuals, and (save in exceptional
cases) for only one of them to be entitled to receive supplementary benefit.[2]
Whether or not a couple are deemed to be 'living together as husband and

wife'[3] and thus fall within the ambit of the rule is a matter to be determined by the benefit officer of the Department of Health and Social Security in accordance with a number of criteria set out in the Supplementary Benefits Handbook.[4] These include such factors as whether the couple operate a joint household, the length and stability of their relationship, whether they afford financial support to one another, whether they have a sexual relationship, the existence of any children of their union and whether they acknowledge publicly that they are 'married' by the woman using the man's surname. Although these factors have been described judicially as 'admirable signposts',[5] none of them is conclusive proof of the status of the couple one way or the other.[6]

The justification usually put forward in support of the rule is that unmarried partners should not be treated more favourably than a married couple who are barred from claiming the higher rate available to single individuals,[7] but this overlooks one vital consideration. This is that an unmarried couple have no legal duty to maintain one another and therefore the assumption that the one who is paid the benefit is supporting the other is not based on any firm foundation.[8] Certainly there is no legal obligation placed upon the recipient of the benefit to pay any part of it to the other partner.

1 See generally, Pearl 'Cohabitation in English Social Security and Supplementary Benefits Legislation' (1979) 9 Fam Law 232; *Parry* pp 40-53.
2 Supplementary Benefits Act, s 1(2), sch 1, para 3(1), as amended by the Social Security Act 1980, s 6.
3 See the Social Security (Miscellaneous Provisions) Act 1977, s 14(7).
4 (DHSS, 1980).
5 *Crake v Supplementary Benefits Commission; Butterworth v Supplementary Benefits Commission* [1982] 1 All ER 498 at 505 (per Woolf J).
6 See generally 'Living Together as Husband and Wife' (Supplementary Benefits Administration Paper No 5, HMSO, 1976); Rowell 'A Happy Hunting Ground for Lawyers – Aspects of Supplementary Benefit Law' (1982) 12 Fam Law 164.
7 See, e g *Report of the Committee on One-Parent Families* (Finer Committee) (Cmnd 5629 of 1974) para 5.269.
8 See *Parker* pp 39, 43-4.

4.24 A striking illustration of the unfair results which can flow from the imprecision of the rule is to be found in the case of *Amarjit Kaur v Secretary of State for Social Services*[1] in which a Supplementary Benefits Appeal Tribunal held that a 28-year-old Sikh divorcee and a 72-year-old Sikh man were living together as husband and wife. Its ruling was upheld by the High Court on the strength of three facts. First, the parties had shared the same bedroom, though the Court made it very clear that no finding was made that they had ever had sexual relations. Second, the woman had done all the washing and cooking. This seems hardly surprising in view of the fact that these tasks are normally perceived as part of a woman's role not only in the Sikh community but also among the population at large. Evidence was given to the tribunal that the man was a friend of the woman's father and that she viewed him as an uncle. It would therefore be perfectly natural for her to undertake these tasks. Third, the parties split the payment of all household bills on a fifty-fifty basis, an arrangement which hardly seems to indicate that two people are 'living together as husband and wife'. In view of all these factors and in the light of both the disparity in the ages of the parties and the evidence that the Sikh community did not like its women to live alone, it is submitted that the judge was wrong not to overturn the tribunal's decision.

1 (1982) 3 FLR 237.

4.25 Cohabiting couples who are living together as husband and wife are also treated as if they were a married couple for purposes of deciding whether or not they are entitled to Family Income Supplement,[1] a non-contributory invalidity pension,[2] an invalid care allowance,[3] rent rebates and allowances[4] and rate rebates.[5]

Entitlement to widow's benefits provides perhaps the most dramatic contrast in the welfare state's approach to the issue of cohabitation. As one might expect, benefits may not be claimed by a cohabitant on the strength of the national insurance contributions paid by her male partner for the simple reason that the couple were not married to one another. However, once a widow is in receipt of such benefits upon the death of her husband she risks being deprived of them for any period during which 'she and a man to whom she is not married are living together as husband and wife'.[6] Cohabitation is thus recognised when the state wishes to find an excuse for paying out fewer benefits, yet is ignored when this would increase the number of claims.[7]

It is submitted that this is an area in which reform is long overdue. A woman cohabiting with a man should no longer be treated by the state as his wife so as to deny her benefit in her own right. On the other hand, insofar as she is actually being financially supported by the man the extent of this support is a relevant factor to be taken into account in calculating her needs. By approaching the question in this light the financial position of the woman claimant is rightly brought to the fore, the sexual side of the couple's relationship is sensibly relegated to the background, their right to choose a lifestyle outside formal marriage is respected and the state can then justifiably refuse to afford them the welfare benefits and tax allowances which are available to a married couple.

1 Family Income Supplements Act 1970, ss 1(1), 17(1), as amended by Social Security Act 1980, s 7.
2 Social Security Act 1975, s 36, as amended by Social Security (Miscellaneous Provisions) Act 1977, s 22(2); Social Security (Non-Contributory Invalidity Pensions) Regulations 1977.
3 Social Security Act 1975, s 37, as amended by 1977 Act, s 22(2).
4 Housing Finance Act 1972, sch 3, para 2.
5 Local Government Act 1974, ss 11-14.
6 Social Security Act 1975, ss 24(2), 25(3), 26(3), as amended by Social Security (Miscellaneous Provisions) Act 1977, s 22(2).
7 See *Parry* p 52.

7 Maintenance of children

4.26 The obligation of a parent to support his or her child is significantly affected by the child's status in law. Whereas both parents have a duty to maintain their legitimate children,[1] the mother of an illegitimate child can only obtain a court order for the putative father to maintain the child by means of affiliation proceedings brought in the magistrates' courts.[2] These proceedings are surrounded by numerous restrictions and pre-conditions and have severe limitations as a vehicle for providing child support.[3] As a result they are now rarely used in this country.[3] A child of extra-marital cohabitation is automatically illegitimate regardless of the stability of its parents' relationship,[4] but it will be legitimated if they subsequently marry one another.[5]

The liability of a putative father through affiliation proceedings was reflected in the legislation of most of the West Indian islands for many years.[6] In Jamaica, for example, the first law on the subject was enacted in 1869.[7] Some recent West Indian statutes have, however, given all children an equal right to be maintained by both their parents irrespective of whether their parents are married or not.[8] Indeed, Jamaican law has gone much further than this in recognition of the central role of cohabitation there in the pattern of family life. The Maintenance Act 1881, as amended by the Status of Children Act 1976, now provides as follows:

'Every man is hereby required to maintain his own children and also –
(a) every child, whether born in wedlock or not, which his wife may have living at the time of her marriage with him; and also
(b) if he cohabits with any woman, every child which such a woman may have living at the time of the commencement of such cohabitation . . .'[9]

How far it is desirable to make a man legally liable for the support of other people's children in such a broad way seems open to considerable doubt. In Jamaica the legislation appears to have had the effect of discouraging most women from keeping their children by previous men with them when they begin a new relationship, for fear of alienating the man by burdening him with their children's support.[10] The children would normally appear to be placed with their grandmothers or other relatives. No doubt both in the West Indies and in England it is only natural to expect men to be more amenable to paying money for the support of their own children and those they have freely and firmly accepted as members of their family by treating them as such.[11] When eventually, therefore, English law is reformed to place the maintenance of non-marital children on an equal footing with the support of marital children[12] it is submitted that the formula adopted in Jamaican legislation should not be adopted here as well.

1 See e g Guardianship of Minors Act 1971, s 9; Matrimonial Causes Act 1973, ss 23, 24, 27; Domestic Proceedings and Magistrates' Courts Act 1978, ss 1, 2.
2 Affiliation Proceedings Act 1957, as amended by Affiliation Proceedings (Amendment) Act 1972 and Domestic Proceedings and Magistrates' Courts Act 1978. The father cannot bring proceedings against the mother to make her support the child.
3 See Law Com Report No 118: 'Illegitimacy' (1982) paras 3.23-3.25.
4 Except where they are parties to a void marriage and at the time of the child's conception or at the time of the 'marriage' (if later) either or both of the parents reasonably believed the marriage was valid: Legitimacy Act 1976, s 1.
5 Provided the child's father is domiciled in England at the date of the marriage: Legitimacy Act 1976, s 2.
6 For examples of such legislation, see, e g Jamaica: Affiliation Act 1926 as amended by Affiliation (Amendment) Act 1975; Barbados: Affiliation Act 1963 (as amended); Trinidad: Affiliation Act 1939 (as amended).
7 Law 31 of 1869; see Roberts *The Population of Jamaica* p 252.
8 See, e g Trinidad: Status of Children Act 1981, s 3 and Family Law (Guardianship of Minors, Domicile and Maintenance) Act 1981, ss 2, 25; Barbados: Status of Children Act 1979, s 3, Maintenance Act 1981, ss 2, 4 and Family Law Act 1981, s 51.
9 Cap 232, s 2.
10 See *Clarke* pp 91-2.
11 See, e g Trinidad: Matrimonial Proceedings and Property Act 1972, ss 2, 25 and Family Law Act 1981, ss 2, 25.
12 See Law Com Report No 118, Part VI, for the Law Commission's detailed proposals.

8 Parental rights

4.27 Whereas parental rights in respect of a legitimate child are shared equally by its mother and father,[1] in the case of an illegitimate child parental rights are vested exclusively in the mother.[2] Although provisional support was given by the Law Commission in 1979 to the idea of abolishing the status of illegitimacy altogether and giving equal parental rights to a child's mother and father, regardless of whether they were married to one another or not,[3] the Commission ultimately decided in 1982 not to recommend such a change.[4] Just such a reform has, however, been introduced during the past decade into the laws of Jamaica, Barbados and Trinidad.[5] The Jamaican Status of Children Act 1976, s 3, provides, for instance, that the relationship between every person and his father and mother shall be determined irrespective of whether the father and mother are or have been married to each other. Hence both parents have equal rights to the custody of their children regardless of whether the child was born in or out of wedlock. The principal concern expressed in the Report of the English Law Commission about this approach was that it would have the automatic effect of vesting equal parental rights even in irresponsible and 'unmeritorious' fathers, to the possible detriment of the child and contrary to the probable wishes of many mothers.[6] In the absence of any satisfactory way of distinguishing by means of a statutory formula between 'meritorious' and 'unmeritorious' fathers, the Law Commission ultimately concluded that any father who wanted to exercise parental rights should have to apply to the court, as at present. This approach has, however, been strongly criticised for its underlying supposition that most unmarried fathers are social deviants whereas there is clear evidence that large numbers of them are living in stable unions.[7]

On the assumption that, whatever their ethnic origin, parents who are parties to a stable cohabitation might well wish to share their parental rights equally, are there any steps which they can currently take to achieve this? They cannot formally adopt their children because joint adoptions are only available to married couples.[8] They cannot be granted a custodianship order because parents may not apply for such orders.[9] The father of an illegitimate child may apply for 'legal custody' under the Guardianship of Minors Act 1971, s 9,[10] but even an order granting him certain parental rights jointly with the mother ceases to be enforceable if the couple live together for a continuous period of more than six months afterwards.[11] It is not, therefore, of much practical value. Finally, it seems far from clear whether a mere agreement between the parents to share their rights would be of any greater use in view of the Children Act 1975, s 85(2) which provides that a person cannot 'surrender or transfer to another any parental right or duty he has as respects a child.' Possibly this provision is confined to preventing the outright abdication of parental rights and duties (and thus merely reflects the earlier common law position)[12] and is not designed to prohibit the constructive process of sharing them. However, the matter is certainly not free from doubt.[13] In any event no such agreement, even if valid, would be enforced by the courts unless they formed the view that joint custody or a similar order was in the best interests of the child.

If it is assumed that Parliament is not yet ready to equalise the parental rights of married and unmarried fathers, two less far-reaching changes still appear to be desirable. First, legislation should be enacted to uphold the basic legality of parental agreements. Second, provision should be made to enable a court to make an order for the sharing of all parental rights between the parents which will remain effective indefinitely while they are still living together. While the second of these two reforms was advocated in the Report of the Law Commission,[14] the first is only endorsed in so far as any agreement relates to a period when the parents are living apart.[15] This proposal does not go far enough and still requires a stable cohabiting couple to invoke the assistance of the court in order to share joint custody of their children. It should be made possible instead for a couple simply to register with the court a written agreement to this effect, subject to the power of the court in any proceedings to override its terms if they are held not to correspond with the best interests of the child at the time.[16]

1 Guardianship Act 1973, s 1.
2 Children Act 1975, s 85(7).
3 Law Com Working Paper No 74: 'Illegitimacy' paras 3.14-3.22.
4 Law Com Report No 118: 'Illegitimacy' paras 4.14-4.50.
5 Jamaica: Status of Children Act 1976; Barbados: Status of Children Reform Act 1979; Trinidad: Status of Children Act 1981.
6 Ibid paras 4.24-4.34.
7 See Eekelaar, 'Second Thoughts on Illegitimacy Reform' (1985) 15 Fam Law 261.
8 Adoption Act 1976, s 14(1).
9 Children Act 1975, s 33(4).
10 See Guardianship of Minors Act 1971, s 14(1).
11 Domestic Proceedings and Magistrates' Courts Act 1978, s 46.
12 See, e g *Humphreys v Polak* [1901] 2 KB 385; Poulter 'Cohabitation Contracts and Public Policy' (1974) 124 NLJ 1034 at 1036.
13 See *Parker* p 199.
14 Law Com Report No 118 para 7.30.
15 Ibid para 7.47.
16 See *An Accident of Birth* (National Council for One Parent Families, 1980), p 9. This approach was rejected by the Law Commission on the ground that some mothers might be pressured into agreement by fathers: see para 4.39. The agreement would, however, be subject to scrutiny by the court upon application by the mother. See also Law Com Working Paper No 91: Review of Child Law: Guardianship (1985) paras 4.20-4.28.

9 Financial provision on divorce

4.28 Upon the granting of a decree of divorce, nullity or judicial separation or at any time thereafter the courts have wide powers under the Matrimonial Causes Act 1973 to make financial provision and property adjustment orders in favour of either of the parties to the marriage.[1] Section 25 of the Act[2] requires the courts, in deciding how to exercise their powers in this regard, to take into account all the circumstances of each case, including a variety of specified factors such as the parties' needs, resources, obligations and responsibilities. Among the factors listed is 'the duration of the marriage'[3] and in a number of cases the courts have had to decide whether this expression is capable of including a period of cohabitation before the marriage was formally celebrated. The issue has principally arisen in cases where the formal marriage itself only lasted for a comparatively short time and the argument has been put forward on behalf of the husband that this should result in scaling down the normal level of periodical payments ordered in favour of the wife or make it inappropriate for the court to order the payment to her of a substantial lump sum. The counter-argument on behalf of the wife has usually been that the brevity of the marriage is outweighed by a lengthy period of premarital cohabitation.

In *Campbell v Campbell*[4] the wife's argument that three and a half year's cohabitation should count as part of the duration of the marriage, to give a total length of about five and a half years, was rejected by Sir George Baker P in these words:

'It is the ceremony of marriage and the sanctity of marriage which count; rights, duties and obligations begin on the marriage and not before. It is a complete cheapening of the marriage relationship, which I believe, and I am sure many share this belief, is essential to the well-being of our society as we understand it, to suggest that premarital periods, particularly in the circumstances of this case, should, as it were, by a doctrine of relation back of matrimony, be taken as a part of marriage to count in favour of the wife performing, as it is put, 'wifely duties before marriage'.[5]

In *Kokosinski v Kokosinski*[6] the period of premarital cohabitation was some 25 years caused by the need for the couple to wait until the husband's first wife had divorced him in Poland. During this time the 'wife' had borne the 'husband' a child, been faithful, loving and hardworking in the home and had helped to build up the family business. Wood J held that in the interests of justice this could not be ignored in calculating the amount she should receive by way of a lump sum payment, even though the actual marriage only lasted for a few months. However, he took account of all these matters not as forming part of 'the duration of the marriage' but merely as one ingredient in 'all the circumstances of the case' and also within the ambit of another of the matters mentioned in s 25, namely the 'conduct' of the parties. His Lordship was anxious not to do anything which might undermine the institution of marriage, but he did not consider that his decision was really likely to do so.

The Court of Appeal appeared to endorse the approach in both these cases in *Foley v Foley*[7] in 1981. The court held that the periods of marriage and cohabitation are not the same and premarital cohabitation could not be included as part of the duration of the marriage. On the other hand, such cohabitation was one of the other circumstances to which the court had to pay regard and while the weight to be attached to events occurring during it was less than those during the period of the marriage, it was still within the discretion of the court to assess their significance in each individual case. Eveleigh LJ commented:

'Ten years of cohabitation will not necessarily have the same effect as ten years of marriage. During the period of cohabitation the parties were free to come and go as they pleased. This is not so where there is a marriage. In the great majority of cases public opinion would readily recognise a stronger claim founded on years of marriage than on years of cohabitation. On the other hand, in deciding these difficult financial problems there may be cases where the inability of the parties to sanctify and legitimise their relationship calls for a measure of sympathy which will enable the court to take what has happened during the period of cohabitation into account as a very weighty factor. *Kokosinski v Kokosinski* is one such case. *Campbell v Campbell* is certainly not.'[8]

In *Foley v Foley* three years of marriage had been preceded by seven years of cohabitation during which the wife had borne the husband three children and helped renovate and manage an investment property owned by the husband. On the divorce the court awarded her a lump sum of £10,000, a figure upheld by the Court of Appeal. By way of contrast, in *Hayes v Hayes*[9] the wife received a much smaller award in a case where the cohabitation had been very unstable, involving several separations and new liaisons, and where there were no children of the union. The marriage lasted a mere seven weeks after the couple had cohabited on and off over a period of six years. Balcombe J held that the cohabitation was of no relevance and that to consider it as equivalent to a true period of marriage would be 'cynical in the extreme.' Clearly it is the quality and stability of the relationship that is likely to be important and the contributions made by the applicant during this period. It is thought that evidence of the West Indian pattern of premarital cohabitation may well be helpful in appropriate cases in establishing the continuity of the couple's commitment to one another and a common family life together and that a recognition of this fact in divorce awards would not have any general tendency to encourage cohabitation in preference to marriage. It is, after all, only because the couple concerned have ultimately entered into a marriage that financial provision can be ordered in any event. Marriage is encouraged by the fact that such awards are available when it breaks down, whereas the courts possess no comparable adjustive jurisdiction when cohabitants split up.[10]

1 Ss 23 and 24.
2 As substituted by the Matrimonial and Family Proceedings Act 1984, s 3.
3 S 25(1) (d).

4 [1976] Fam 347, [1977] 1 All ER 1.
5 At 6.
6 [1980] Fam 72, [1980] 1 All ER 1106.
7 [1981] Fam 160, [1981] 2 All ER 857.
8 At 861.
9 (1981) 11 Fam Law 208.
10 See eg *Burns v Burns* [1984] Ch 317, [1984] 1 All ER 244.

The scope for reform

4.29 In the course of this chapter a number of legal changes have been suggested involving relatively minor amendments to the Matrimonial Homes Act,[1] the Domestic Violence and Matrimonial Proceedings Act and the Housing Act 1980. In each case the aim would be to give the protection already being afforded to family members a slightly wider ambit than it has at present. The more far-reaching proposal was also made that the 'cohabitation rule', which operates in the field of welfare benefits to restrict the entitlements of claimants, should be abolished. This change can be justified both on the ground of the need to eliminate the anomalies the rule creates and on account of the popular revulsion felt for the way in which it is administered in practice. The state should not be allowed to treat cohabiting couples as spouses whenever this will save taxpayers' money, yet deny them such a status whenever this would require extra benefits to be made available. Suggestions were also made for reforms in the field of parental rights and duties.

The most difficult question which this chapter raises is whether any attempt should be made to ensure greater uniformity in approach either towards cohabit-ants as a class or in defining who are members of a family in the eyes of the law, for there can be little doubt that a number of inconsistencies have grown up as a result of the piecemeal development of the law in both these areas. One further example may be given of this phenomenon. The Leasehold Reform Act 1967 confers upon the tenant of a leasehold house who occupies the house as his residence the right to acquire the freehold (or an extended 50-year lease) of the premises upon fair terms, provided certain conditions are met.[2] At the time when the tenant gives notice to the landlord that he wishes to exercise this right he has to have been occupying the house as his residence for the previous three years or else for periods amounting to three years during the previous ten years.[3] Section 7 enables certain resident members of a deceased tenant's family to add their periods of qualifying residence to that of the deceased for purposes of computing the required period of three years. However, the statutory definition of persons who qualify as members of the family for this purpose does not include either cohabitants or brothers. Yet there is clear evidence that a substantial number of ethnic minority families, particularly Asians, live in precisely the sort of leasehold property to which the Act applies.[4]

While it would clearly be unrealistic to imagine that a simple statutory definition of 'family member' would be appropriate for the great range of enactments where such a concept needs to be employed, it seems desirable that some thought should be given by the Parliamentary draftsmen to achieving a standard formula which might be used in the future unless the context warranted otherwise. Once this was done it could replace earlier definitions whenever this was felt to be appropriate. No doubt the thorniest problem would be to decide how far cohabiting couples should be recognised for this purpose. The statutory recognition afforded to them already in terms of protection under the Domestic Violence Act and their capacity to make financial and property claims on the death of their partners under a number of different Acts[5] seems eminently fair and sensible. Moreover, where legislation extends rights to a whole class of relatives or dependants it seems right that couples who have lived together 'as husband and wife' should normally be included. On the other hand, where such rights are at present exclusively available to those who have married, notably for example, the availability of maintenance during joint lifetimes and property adjustment orders following breakdown, there would appear to be sound policy reasons for the law intervening no further than it has done already.[6] Arguably, for the law to impose a reciprocal duty of support between unmarried partners would be to take such a major step in the direction of equating cohabitation with marriage that a couple's freedom of choice and action would be jeopardised to an unwarrantable degree. The modern trend is away from standardised patterns of family organisation towards a variety of different lifestyles. Couples should remain free, for whatever personal reasons, to choose not to impose such extensive duties upon one another. This is so even in those cases where a child has been born of the relationship and as a result the woman is rendered less capable of supporting herself than she would have been otherwise. The father can already be ordered to support the child in affiliation proceedings and in assessing the amount to be paid the court can take into account the financial needs of its mother.[7] The status of a cohabitant should continue to remain a distinct one, sufficiently different from marriage in terms of legal consequences for those who wish to reject marriage and prostitution, but who do not wish to remain celibate, to be enabled to do so. This has long been the legal position in the West Indies (though there has recently been a change in the law in Barbados)[8] and the current state of English law therefore probably reflects the broad expectations and intentions of West Indians who cohabit here. This does not, however, mean that cohabiting couples should be denied the right to arrange their property and financial affairs by mutual agreement through the ordinary mechanisms of contract and trust law.[9] In recent years the courts have been increasingly prepared to acknowledge their capacity to do this and an extension of the existing position to allow them to agree upon sharing their parental rights subject to the supervision of the courts has already been suggested.[10]

1 S 1.

2 S 1(1) (b), as amended by the Housing Act 1980, sch 21, para 1.

3 S 7(7). Cf the provisions of the Housing Act 1980 in respect of the right to buy council houses – see para 4.21 above.

4 See Smith, *Racial Disadvantage in Britain* pp 228-9.

5 See, e g Inheritance (Provision for Family and Dependants) Act 1975 and Fatal Accidents Act 1976 (as amended by the Administration of Justice Act 1982).

6 For discussion of this question, see generally Freeman and Lyon *Cohabitation Without Marriage* (Gower, 1983) chs 6, 7; Eekelaar and Katz (eds) *Marriage and Cohabitation in Contemporary Societies* (Butterworths, 1980); *Bromley* ch 18; Eekelaar *Family Law and Social Policy* (2nd ed, 1984) ch 8; *Parry* ch 9; Oliver 'The Mistress in Law' (1978) CLP 81; Zuckerman 'Formality and the Family – Reform and Status Quo' (1980) 96 LQR 248.

7 Affiliation Proceedings Act 1957, s 4(3), as amended by the Domestic Proceedings and Magistrates' Courts Act 1978, s 50; *Haroutunian v Jennings* (1980) 1 FLR 62; *Osborn v Sparks* (1982) 3 FLR 90.

8 Under the Barbadian Family Law Act 1981 it appears that maintenance and property alteration orders may be made in favour of a party to a 'union other than marriage', such a union being created by a continuous period of cohabitation lasting at least five years (see ss 39, 50 and 57).

9 See generally Poulter 'Cohabitation Contracts and Public Policy' (1974) 124 NLJ 999, 1034; Dwyer 'Immoral Contracts' (1977) 93 LQR 386.

10 See para 4.27 above.

CHAPTER 5

Divorce

A. GROUNDS AND PROCEDURES

5.01 The availability of divorce naturally varies greatly from one society to another. Rheinstein has rightly identified the principal reason for this variety as residing in the diversity of social factors by which the patterns of each society are determined:

'Among these factors ethical and religious value judgments are as important as, or even more than, objective facts of social, economic, and political development. These value judgments are widely held without conscious reflection or rational deliberation. They may be felt deeply or professed superficially. Upon the living they have been implanted in that process of acculturation which has shaped the civilization of those successive generations by which civilizations have been built and developed.'[1]

In some countries and communities the grounds for divorce are based on the concept of fault or matrimonial offence, while in others they may be more directly tied to the breakdown of the parties' relationship. In some societies divorce is much more easily obtainable than it is in England, whereas in a few there is no provision for divorce whatsoever.[2]

1 *Marriage Stability, Divorce, and the Law* (Chicago, 1972) p 10.
2 No divorce at all is permitted in Argentina, Brazil, Chile, Columbia and Eire.

5.02 It is particularly in those societies where divorce is regulated by traditional or religious custom that there is often a striking contrast with English law. The principal difference lies in the fact that while in the English system a divorce always involves obtaining a decree of dissolution from a competent court of law (even though the procedures leading up to the granting of the decree are predominantly administrative), elsewhere divorce may be obtained extra-judicially.[1] Thus in many African countries customary marriages may be dissolved merely by the agreement of the couple themselves and their respective families.[2] No ground need be established, though obviously some justification is usually put forward by at least one of the parties, and normally efforts to achieve a reconciliation will have been tried and failed. In certain circumstances the whole or part of the bridewealth may have to be returned to complete the dissolution. As Mair has pointed out:

'Many writers have enumerated "grounds for divorce" in African societies, but it should be understood that these are not conditions which must be satisfied before a couple can be released from their obligations. One can only speak of grounds for divorce in that sense where a divorce requires the formal sanction of judicial authorities and the conditions for it are stated in a written law. Otherwise one cannot go beyond recording typical arguments which in different societies have been held to justify a wife in leaving her husband or a husband in driving away his wife.'[3]

Over recent years a number of African countries have attempted to limit the availability of such extra-judicial divorces and have insisted that the dissolution be effected by a court of law.[4] However, the traditional form of divorce is still widespread in many societies throughout the continent.

1 For a useful survey see North *The Private International Law of Matrimonial Causes in the British Isles* (North Holland, 1977) pp 218-22.
2 See Phillips and Morris *Marriage Laws in Africa* (OUP 1971) pp 55, 121, 123.
3 *Marriage* p 182.
4 *Phillips and Morris* p 55.

5.03 Similarly a movement to reform the Islamic law of divorce has been evident in a few jurisdictions with a view to making a judicial decree mandatory[1], but the basic position remains that in most Muslim countries an extra-judicial divorce may be obtained by the husband with the utmost ease. He can repudiate his wife by a unilateral declaration of *talaq* and in classical law this is subject to no external check whatsoever. The only question relates to whether the *talaq* is revocable or irrevocable, the latter being regarded as the least meritorious form.[2] The *talaq* can be either a single or a triple pronouncement, e g 'I divorce you; I divorce you; I divorce you'. In Sunni law it can either be given orally or reduced to writing, while in Shi'ite law it must be pronounced orally in the presence of two witnesses.[3] Significantly, no reason or justification for the divorce need be given, nor does the wife even have to be notified of the *talaq* for it to become effective.

Some Muslim countries have imposed various statutory requirements with a view to fostering greater attempts at reconciliation. A notable example comes from Pakistan where the Muslim Family Laws Ordinance 1961[4] provides that any man who wishes to divorce his wife must, immediately after the pronouncement of *talaq* in any form, give written notice of the *talaq* to the chairman of an administrative council and supply a copy of this notice to his wife. The effect of the notice is to 'freeze' the *talaq* for 90 days during which time an arbitral council is given an opportunity of trying to achieve a reconciliation. It is only after the expiry of the 90 days that the divorce is effective, assuming that no reconciliation has occurred in the meantime. The requirement about giving notice is a mandatory one,[5] but once that step has been taken by the husband there is no obligation upon either party to attend any meetings directed towards a reconciliation and thus the process as a whole really amounts to no more than a formal registration of the divorce.[6] Muslim law also recognises a form of divorce by mutual consent on the initiation of the wife known as *khul*[7]. It usually involves the wife having to forego her dower in return for her release.

1 See Anderson *Law Reform in the Muslim World* (London, 1976) p 126 discussing reforms in Tunisia and Iraq.
2 See generally Pearl *A Textbook on Muslim Law* (London, 1979) pp 89ff.
3 *Pearl* p 92.
4 Discussed in *Pearl* at pp 96–101 and reprinted there at pp 215-20. The Ordinance is also in force, subject to minor modifications, in Bangladesh.
5 If it is not complied with the divorce is ineffective and the husband is liable to a sentence of one year's imprisonment or a fine or both.
6 *Pearl* p 101.
7 *Pearl* pp 102-8.

5.04 In India under Hindu law divorces obtained through the customary process of a simple written agreement between the spouses are still recognised as valid, despite the introduction of judicial divorce by the Hindu Marriage Act in 1955.[1]

1 Derrett *A Critique of Modern Hindu Law* (Bombay, 1970) p 350.

5.05 Jewish Rabbinical law allows a husband to divorce his wife by the mere delivery of a written document or 'bill' known as a *get*.[1] Authority for this simple procedure can be found in the Book of Deuteronomy in the Old Testament.[2] Although the delivery of the *get* has to take place today before a rabbi and two witnesses the process in no way resembles a judicial hearing. The rabbi and the witnesses are present merely to authenticate the bill's delivery, to check that moral grounds exist for the divorce[3] and to ensure that both parties consent and appreciate what is involved. In England most such divorces take place before the London Beth-Din, the 'tribunal' of the Chief Rabbi of the Ashkenazi Orthodox Community.[4] A smaller number of Jewish divorces is granted by the Beth-Din of the Reform Synagogues, while the Union of Liberal and Progressive Synagogues does not give religious divorces at all.[5] The normal practice is for a *get* only to be authenticated by the relevant religious tribunal in England if the couple have first had their marriage dissolved through the ordinary civil procedure.[6]

1 See Horowitz *The Spirit of Jewish Law* (New York, 1953) pp 273-81; Elon (ed) *The Principles of Jewish Law* (Jerusalem, 1975) pp 414-24; Daiches 'Divorce in Jewish Law' (1926) Journal of Comparative Legislation 215; Maidment 'The Legal Effect of Religious Divorces' (1974) 37 MLR 611 and the authorities cited there.
2 See ch 24, v 1.
3 These are listed by Elon at pp 415-9 and by Daiches at p 223.
4 See generally Feldman 'The London Beth-Din' (1929) Juridical Review 1.
5 See B A Kosmin *Divorce in Anglo-Jewry 1970-80* (London, 1982) pp 11-12.
6 See *Leeser v Leeser* (1955) Times, 5 February; *Maidment* at pp 619-21.

5.06 Yet another form of extra-judicial divorce is that granted by the ecclesiastical authorities of the Greek Orthodox Church.[1] In the past such divorces took place among the Greek Cypriot community in England through the auspices of the Archbishop of Thyatira.[2]

1 See *Peters v Peters* (1968) 112 Sol Jo 311.
2 *North* p 220; 816 HC Official Report (5th series) col 1551.

5.07 Divorce purely by mutual consent and without the intervention of a court is also permissible under both the law of Thailand[1] and customary Chinese law applicable in Hong Kong.[2]

1 See *Varanand v Varanand* (1964) 108 Sol Jo 693.
2 See *Lee v Lau* [1967] P 14, [1964] 2 All ER 248.

5.08 In Japan divorce may be obtained not only judicially but also extra-judicially through the mutual agreement of the parties being communicated to the registrar of civil status.[1] The latter type of divorce, though the creature of a modern code, is a modified version of the previous customary procedure and over 90% of divorces are accomplished in this manner.

1 See generally *Rheinstein*, ch 5.

Policy considerations

5.09 There is probably quite widespread public support in England for the view expressed in 1966 by the Law Commission that a good divorce law should seek:

'(i) To buttress, rather than to undermine, the stability of marriage; and
(ii) When, regrettably, a marriage has irretrievably broken down, to enable the empty

legal shell to be destroyed with the maximum fairness, and the minimum bitterness, distress and humiliation.'[1]

When set against these standards there would appear to be a number of possible objections to the types of extra-judicial divorce referred to earlier. First, it may be argued that those systems which provide for divorce merely by mutual consent of the parties not only make divorce so easy that they may well be undermining the stability of marriage in those countries, but also that they may fail to take sufficient account of the possibility that one party's consent (usually that of the wife) may be unfairly obtained through duress. Both these aspects of 'divorce by consent' were considered by the Law Commission in 1966 and they were one reason why this was not felt to be an acceptable mode of dissolution to adopt here.[2] It was also claimed that unless a minimum period of separation were laid down as an additional requirement, marriages which had not broken down irretrievably might too easily be dissolved without sufficient justification.[3] On the other hand, assuming that the consent of both parties is satisfactorily established to be genuine, this approach does have the merit of avoiding the stress and strain of judicial proceedings which may often engender rather than reduce distress, humiliation and bitterness. Moreover, mutual agreement does give some indication that the marriage has indeed broken down irretrievably, a fact which a judicial hearing (unless it is a full and penetrating inquest with all the attendant disadvantages) often cannot conclusively establish. As the Law Commission itself pointed out, 'the parties are likely to be better judges of the viability of their own marriage than a court can hope to be'.[4] A survey of public opinion in this country conducted in 1965 also revealed that some 80% of those interviewed favoured divorce by consent.[5] The vast majority of divorces in England are in any event consensual in the sense that they are undefended.[6] Although it is often alleged that the divorce rates in countries with divorce by consent are higher than elsewhere[7] this is by no means true of all the systems referred to earlier and it is now generally accepted that there is no proof that easier divorce laws necessarily lead to a higher rate of marital breakdown.[8]

1 'Reform of the Grounds of Divorce: The Field of Choice' p 10.
2 Ibid pp 38-42.
3 Ibid p 42.
4 Ibid p 36. The same argument applies with even greater force if the role of the court is reduced to one which is largely administrative in nature.
5 Ibid p 39.
6 In recent years the figure has been well in excess of 95%.
7 'The Field of Choice' p 41.
8 See *Rheinstein* ch 12 and Appendix A; Kahn-Freund 'Divorce Law Reform' (1956)19 MLR 573 at 575-80.

5.10 Turning from divorce by consent to divorce by unilateral repudiation, the *talaq* divorce is open to further criticism. It is clearly discriminatory on the grounds of sex, being available only to the husband. It can be accomplished with the utmost ease and, at least in its classical form, it affords the wife no external protection of her status in terms of an opportunity of pleading her case before an impartial third party. She is not even required to be notified of the dissolution. There is nothing she can do to keep her marriage in being once her husband has determined to repudiate it, even though she may be in no way at fault. In this sense there appears to be a denial of natural justice, though it is important to bear in mind that nothing of the nature of judicial or administrative proceedings is intended in this aspect of classical Islamic law. Although divorce may be relatively easy to obtain under Islamic law this does not necessarily mean that its incidence is generally greater in Islamic societies than elsewhere. While divorce rates in some Muslim countries do tend to be rather high,[1] in others (for example, on the Indian subcontinent) divorce carries a significant social stigma and is comparatively rare.[2]

1 See eg Mair *Marriage*, p 191; Hiro *Black British, White British* (Penguin, 1973) p 153.
2 See eg Jeffrey *Migrants and Refugees* p 11 (referring specifically to Pakistan).

5.11 The Jewish *get* is rather different from a *talaq*. Although formally it can only be implemented by the husband it can equally be insisted upon by the wife where suitable grounds exist. Regardless of who actually instigates the process, both parties must eventually consent to the divorce albeit perhaps under moral pressure from the rabbinical authorities. Moreover, divorce is generally discouraged in Jewish law and the rabbi has a duty to try to effect a reconciliation. The divorce rate among Jews in England appears to be significantly lower than among the English population as a whole.[1]

In weighing up the arguments for and against various systems of divorce the objective of ending marriages 'with the maximum fairness' has recently come to be seen as relating as much to the financial and property aspects of dissolution as to anything else. Therefore the provision that each system makes in this regard, especially for the wife, is of great importance. This subject is dealt with later in this chapter.

1 See *Kosmin* pp 12-20.

English domestic law

5.12 English courts have jurisdiction to hear divorce cases if, and only if, either of the parties to the marriage (whether petitioner or respondent) was domiciled in England on the date when the proceedings were begun or was habitually resident in England throughout the period of one year ending with that date.[1]

The divorce law applicable in the English courts is invariably English law as the *lex fori*.[2] This is now found in the Matrimonial Causes Act 1973 which specifies only one ground for divorce, namely that the marriage has irretrievably broken down.[3] Proof of breakdown is established by showing one or more of the facts set out in s 1(2) as follows:
(a) that the respondent has committed adultery and the petitioner finds it intolerable to live with the respondent;
(b) that the respondent has behaved in such a way that the petitioner cannot reasonably be expected to live with the respondent;
(c) that the respondent has deserted the petitioner for a continuous period of at least two years immediately preceding the presentation of the petition;
(d) that the parties to the marriage have lived apart for a continuous period of at least two years immediately preceding the presentation of the petition and the respondent consents to a decree being granted; or
(e) that the parties to the marriage have lived apart for a continuous period of at least five years immediately preceding the presentation of the petition.
If the court is satisfied on the evidence as to any such fact then, unless it is satisfied on all the evidence that the marriage has not broken down irretrievably, it must normally proceed to grant a decree.[4]

The question naturally arises whether there are any ethnic minority customs which are likely to pose special problems for the courts in determining any of the above facts. The issues that can be raised under (a), (b) and (c) in relation to polygamous marriages have already been discussed in a previous chapter,[5] and need no repetition here.

1 Domicile and Matrimonial Proceedings Act 1973, s 5(2).
2 Dicey and Morris *The Conflict of Laws* (10th edn, 1980) pp 333, 336-7.
3 Matrimonial Causes Act, s 1(1).
4 Matrimonial Causes Act 1973 , s 1 (4). The exception based on s 5 is discussed at para 5.15 below.
5 See paras 3.07-3.08 above.

5.13 In two cases under earlier divorce legislation the English courts have had to consider the relationship between a *get* and the concept of desertion. In *Joseph v Joseph*[1] a Jewish couple were divorced in terms of Jewish law by a *get* obtained at the Beth-Din in London. Although this did not validly dissolve the marriage in the eyes of English law,[2] the wife, who had instigated the process because of the husband's desertion, thought the *get* might be recognised in China, where the couple had previously lived and whither she hoped to return. No doubt it was these unusual facts which prompted the Beth-Din to authenticate the *get* and depart from its normal practice of first insisting that the parties obtain a civil divorce. Subsequently for political reasons the wife decided not to go back to China and instead petitioned for an English divorce on the ground of her husband's desertion during the three years preceding the presentation of the petition. In his defence the husband contended that his desertion had automatically been terminated on the delivery of the *get*. The Court of Appeal agreed, Jenkins L J stating:

'The result seems to me inescapable, that in the present case the wife cannot consistently with the *Get*, given at her own request, maintain that the husband is in desertion. I think her successful request for the *Get* indicated her unwillingness to receive the husband back and amounted to a consent on her part to his continuing to live separate and apart from her.'[3]

This decision was later distinguished in the similar case of *Corbett v Corbett*[4] on the basis that there the *get* was delivered by the husband at his own insistence and against the real wishes of the wife. She had merely given the token agreement required for its issue and was therefore not regarded as having truly consented to the separation. She was thus subsequently entitled to claim that he was still in desertion.

It seems likely that in future these two decisions will principally be of relevance in a case in which a *get* has been obtained abroad without any accompanying civil decree and divorce proceedings are instituted in this country on the basis of desertion. Presumably the delivery of a *get* could also provide cogent evidence of a mental intention to separate for the purposes of the 'living apart' provisions of sub ss 1(2)(d) and (e) of the Matrimonial Causes Act.[5]

1 [1953] 2 All ER 710, [1953] I WLR 1182.
2 See para 5.22 below.
3 At 712.
4 [1957] 1 All ER 621, [1957] 1 WLR 486.
5 See *Santos v Santos* [1972] Fam 247, [1972] 2 All ER 246.

5.14 A further area of possible interaction might concern the extent to which a practice sanctioned by foreign custom might nevertheless amount to 'unreasonable behaviour' within the terms of s 1 (2) (b) of the Act. If, for example, an African, Asian, or Middle-Eastern husband were to claim in his defence to a petition by his wife that a traditional or religious custom upheld his right to beat her as a form of moderate chastisement[1] or to restrain her movement outside the home (including taking employment) or to limit her freedom to have visitors without his permission,[2] what would the attitude of the English courts be? Both domestic violence and physical imprisonment and restraint can be prosecuted as crimes in English law.[3] However, the issue here is not whether the husband could be convicted of an offence but whether he could be divorced by his wife. It was held in *Ash v Ash*[4] that although the test for 'behaviour' was objective since the subsection contained the words 'be *reasonably* expected to live with the respondent', the court in making an overall assessment had to consider the particular parties to the suit together with their individual backgrounds and characteristics. Moreover, although in *Livingstone-Stallard v Livingstone-Stallard*[5] the court considered the question really was:

'would any right-thinking person come to the conclusion that this husband has behaved in such a way that his wife cannot reasonably be expected to live with him, taking into account the whole of the circumstances and characters and personalities of the parties?'[6]

one is still left with the further question as to who is the appropriate 'right-thinking person'. Is he a white Englishman travelling on the Clapham omnibus or is he someone familiar with the customs of the parties in the particular case and thus probably, in origin at any rate, a member of the same ethnic minority community?[7] So far, the matter does not appear to have been raised directly in any reported case, but presumably a balance would have to be struck on grounds of public policy between minimum standards acceptable in this country and customs recognised by the parties themselves. One decision which did take account of a traditional custom was that in *Devi v Gaddu*.[8] The couple, who were Indians and parties to an arranged marriage, lived with the husband's parents. The wife brought a complaint of persistent cruelty against the husband under the Matrimonial Proceedings (Magistrates' Courts) Act 1960 alleging *inter alia* that her mother-in-law had attacked her with a kitchen utensil. Normally it would not be sufficient to rely on conduct by a third party as constituting cruelty by the respondent, but the Divisional Court held that account should be taken of the fact that the wife was living as part of the husband's extended family and that it was not a defence for the husband to claim that his wife had been driven out of the house by his family rather than by himself. On the other hand, in *Khan v Khan*[9] a magistrates' court, no doubt rightly, held an Indian husband to be in desertion after he had told his wife that if she attended a particular wedding she was never to come back to him again. No account was taken of any Indian custom that wives should obey their husbands' wishes on the question of visiting friends and relatives.

1 See, e g Shorter *African Culture and the Christian Church* (London, 1973) p 180; Ellis (ed) *West African Families in Britain* (London, 1978) pp 23, 71.
2 See, e g *Hussein v Hussein* [1938] P 159, [1938] 2 All ER 344; *Anderson* p 115; *Pearl*, p 57; El Saadawi; *The Hidden Face of Eve* (Zed Press, 1980) pp 190, 201 for the law and practice in Muslim countries on this question.
3 See Offences against the Person Act 1861; *R v Jackson* [1891] 1 QB 671; *R v Reid* [1973] 1 QB 299, [1972] 2 All ER 1350.
4 [1972] Fam 135, [1972] 1 All ER 582.
5 [1974] Fam 47, [1974] 2 All ER 766.
6 At 54; approved in *O'Neill v O'Neill* [1975] 3 All ER 289, [1975] 1 WLR 1118.
7 Cf the judgment of Lord Parker C J in *Alhaji Mohamed v Knott* [1969] 1 QB 1, [1968] 2 All ER 563 quoted at para 2.17 above.
8 (1974) 118 Sol Jo 579, (1974) 4 Fam Law 159.
9 [1980] 1 All ER 497, [1980] 1 WLR 355.

5.15 Aside from the question of what has to be established to obtain a divorce in English law it is also necessary to examine what special defences may be raised to a petition. The Matrimonial Causes Act 1973, s 5 enables a respondent successfully to oppose a decree being granted in the case of five years' separation if prospective 'grave financial or other hardship' can be established. However, if the court is to dismiss the petition on this ground it must be satisfied not only that such hardship would result to the respondent if a decree were granted but also that it would in all the circumstances be wrong to dissolve the marriage. In a number of cases involving s 5, Hindu wives have cited by way of 'other hardship' the social and religious attitudes and conventions of their communities in India which, they have alleged, would involve them being ostracised and degraded if they were to be divorced. In *Banik v Banik*[1] the parties had been married in India in 1949. Eight years later they ceased to live together and in 1961 the husband came to England alone. He petitioned for a divorce on the basis of five years' separation and was met with an answer from the wife under s 5, supported by an affidavit from her which stated in part:

'My husband knows and knew when he married me that I was a devout believer in the Hindu religion. A Hindu woman looks to the spiritual aspect of dying as a married woman rather than for any material benefit. A Hindu woman will be destitute as a divorcee. If I am divorced, I will, by virtue of the society in which we live and the social attitudes and conventions existing in it, become a social outcast ... I and the other members of the community in which we live regard the divorce as anathema on religious and moral as well as social grounds. My husband knows the humiliation and degradation I will suffer spiritually and socially if the court grants a decree.'[2]

The Court of Appeal held that this pleading did afford the wife the possibility of making out a case under s 5, but when the evidence came to be examined in detail in *Banik v Banik (No 2)*[3] it was found that although she would have no hope of remarriage she would not be a social outcast but would remain in an unchanged position within her brother's family, where she had been since the separation. Her defence therefore failed. The same result was reached in *Parghi v Parghi*.[4] In this case the parties were well educated, sophisticated Hindus, whereas in *Banik* they were 'lower middle class' and the wife was illiterate. In *Parghi* Latey J held that the wife's belief that marriage was indissoluble was similar to that of many Christians and that the civil decree would not affect her religious beliefs. Drawing a contrast with the attitudes towards divorce of Hindus living in remote, rural parts of India he seemed to imply that in their case a divorce might perhaps amount to grave hardship.[5] However, the subsequent case of *Balraj v Balraj*,[6] in which the wife was admittedly living on the outskirts of Hyderabad, shows just how hard it is likely to be for any Hindu wife to establish a defence under s 5. There the judge found as a fact that among the 'backward Kshatriya community' to which the couple belonged, a divorced wife would be in an anomalous position and certainly at a disadvantage in having no ascertainable status, divorce not being recognised in that community. Moreover, the effect of a divorce on the marriage prospects of the couple's daughter would constitute a hardship both for the daughter and for her mother. Despite this the judge held that, considered objectively, these hardships could not be regarded as 'grave' within the meaning of the section and this decision was affirmed by the Court of Appeal. Even if grave hardship had been established it seems unlikely that an English court would have reached the conclusion that it would be wrong to dissolve the marriage, bearing in mind the fact that the couple had been living apart from one another in different continents for the previous 15 years.

In the earlier case of *Rukat v Rukat*[7] the wife's defence was that, as a Roman Catholic from Sicily, if she were to return there as a divorcee she would be subjected to a hostile atmosphere and she would therefore have to remain in England, separated from her elderly parents, her daughter and her property. The Court of Appeal clearly felt considerable sympathy for her position, but eventually concluded that since she had already been separated from her husband for 25 years and as this must have been known in Sicily and as there was no reason why anyone there should learn about the divorce, the need to destroy the empty shell of the marriage should prevail and the divorce should be granted.

1 [1973] 3 All ER 45, [1973] 1 WLR 860.
2 At 48.
3 (1973) 117 Sol Jo 874.
4 (1973) 117 Sol Jo 582.
5 Generally speaking, however, it would appear to be women from the higher strata of Indian society who would suffer the greatest loss of respectability on divorce – see Derrett 'Divorce at the petition of the wife at Hindu law' (1981) 4 Jewish Law Annual 232 at 246.
6 (1981) 11 Fam Law 110.
7 [1975] Fam 63, [1975] 1 All ER 343.

5.16 If a Jewish spouse were to employ the defence offered by s 5 on the basis that the petitioner was refusing to deliver or receive a *get* (without which remarriage would not be possible under Orthodox Jewish law)[1] there seems every reason to believe that this would constitute grave hardship and lead to the petition being dismissed.[2] The same would apply to a Muslim husband who refused to pronounce a *talaq*. It would surely be wrong to allow the petitioner to obtain a divorce in a manner which would still prevent the respondent from remarrying according to their religious law, when (unlike in the Hindu cases referred to earlier) it was within his power to grant this freedom.

A Jewish woman tied to her ex-husband in this manner is spoken of in Hebrew as an *'aguna'* and her plight has long been recognised.[3] She finds herself in a legal limbo, a party to a 'limping' relationship. While she is divorced in the eyes of the civil law she is still regarded as a married woman in Jewish law. Any children she bears in a second purely civil marriage will be *'mamzerim'* (illegitimate) in the eyes of the Jewish law, as will those children's own descendants. It is a status so anomalous that it prompted one American judge to speak of the ex-husband in the following vein:

'He has reaped the fruits of the secular divorce and has carved out a new life for himself. He refuses to make it possible for the plaintiff to do the same. He has thus condemned her to a dismal future of never being free to remarry. This situation outrages the conscience of this court.'[4]

1 The 'Reform Movement' has discarded the Orthodox law of divorce and its rabbis are willing to perform a marriage ceremony on the strength of a civil divorce – see Schneid (ed) *Marriage* (Jerusalem, 1973) p 76.
2 See Maidment 'The Legal Effect of Religious Divorces' (1974) 37 MLR 611 at 621; Lew 'Jewish Divorces' (1973) 123 NLJ 829 at 830.
3 See generally (1981) 4 Jewish Law Annual, Part I, 'The Wife's Right to Divorce' (a symposium).
4 *B v B* (1978) NYLJ (4 May), quoted by Meislin in (1981) 4 Jewish Law Annual 270.

5.17 Inevitably this raises the further question whether it would be within the jurisdiction and competence of an English court, following the granting of a decree of divorce, to order one of the parties to the proceedings to deliver or receive a *get* or pronounce a *talaq*.[1] In tackling the issue it is worth bearing in mind the fact that a number of objections to such a course of action have been raised in the American courts over a period of many years. In 1932 in *Price v Price*,[2] for example, a Pennsylvania court refused to direct a husband to deliver a *get* on the ground that this would interfere with the 'free exercise of religion' clause of the Constitution. The judge commented: 'The civil tribunals are certainly without authority to order one to follow the practices of his faith. This is a matter dependent entirely upon his conscience or upon his religious belief.'[3] In the more recent Canadian case of *Morris v Morris*[4] the majority of the Manitoba Court of Appeal were swayed by a similar concern to maintain a clear division between matters of religion, on the one hand, and the civil law of marriage and divorce, on the other. In their view civil courts should only be involved in the determination of civil, as opposed to religious rights. However, in a powerful dissenting judgment Chief Justice Freedman rejected the notion that public policy considerations required the ordinary courts to steer clear of any issue that possessed a religious dimension. Significantly, his willingness to order the husband to deliver a *get* was echoed five years later in a judgment of the New York Supreme Court in 1979 in *Stern v Stern*.[5] In that case, as in *Morris*, the wife based her claim upon a *ketouba*[6] in standard form in which the couple had bound themselves to conform with the provisions of the laws of Moses and Israel. The Court ruled that the *ketouba* contract was not one contrary to public policy and its validity could therefore be upheld.[7] In directing its specific performance Judge Held declared:

'The court in granting a civil divorce to the plaintiff would be doing an injustice to her should that be the only relief granted. The wife would then be doomed to being an '*aguna*' for the balance of her life because of the violations of the marriage contract by the husband. To deny her the relief of specific performance of the *ketuba* or marriage contract would be to penalise the plaintiff for the wrongdoings of the defendant husband. There is no question as to the validity of the marriage agreement (*ketuba*) and there is no doubt that the wife may assert her rights thereunder insofar as they are in conformity with, and not contrary to our civil laws. This is a simple agreement between a man and a woman in contemplation of marriage and if not contrary to public policy, should be enforced according to the intent of the parties who made the agreement . . . This court orders the specific performance of the said contract, particularly in view of the policy of our courts to regulate and control the interest of parties to a marriage in the public interest, be it one of a religious or civil nature.'

Although the Court was dealing there with a divorce in which the defendant husband was the 'guilty party' and this accounts for some of the language used in the above passage, it is thought that the principle applied is perfectly capable of extension to the situation where the husband obtains a civil divorce in England on the basis of five years' separation. However, it is worth drawing attention to the fact that in *Stern v Stern* the local Beth-Din had previously ruled that the defendant husband should deliver a *get* and perhaps this will be seen as a *sine qua non* in future cases.

On the question of whether a civil court is trespassing in the religious domain in ordering the delivery of a *get*, the Court in *Stern's* case commented:

'. . . the writing of a *get*, its execution and delivery is not a religious act and although a rabbi is present to supervise and a scribe is utilized, this is only because the average Jewish man is not learned in Jewish law and he needs the rabbi and the scribe just as he needs his lawyer in a civil action.'

In the earlier case of *Koeppel v Koeppel*[8] in 1954 a New York Court had similarly held that the appearance of a husband before a rabbi to effect a *get* pursuant to the terms of his *ketouba* did not involve any interference with religious freedom because:

'complying with his agreement would not compel the defendant to practise any religion, not even the Jewish faith to which he still admits adherence . . . His appearance before the Rabbinate to answer questions and give evidence needed by them to make a decision is not a profession of faith.'[9]

In *Stern's* case the judge emphasised the human rights dimension of the problem in remarking that:

'The United States Supreme Court has stated that the right to marry and raise a family are among the most fundamental civil rights guaranteed to members of a free and democratic society.'

Bearing in mind the provision to the same effect in the European Convention on Human Rights,[10] as well as the provision relating to religious freedom,[11] it seems unlikely that an English court would automatically rule out the possibility of ordering the delivery of a *get* or the pronouncement of a *talaq* as beyond its jurisdictional competence.[12] The constitutional separation between church and state which exercises such a profound influence upon American courts is absent from the English legal scene. It is also worthy of note that the French courts have displayed a fairly consistent tendency in the same direction as the *Stern* decision for a period of more than a century. Ever since the *Darienté* case in 1876 they have broadly taken the view that to deny a wife a *get* is an unjustified interference with her right to remarry in accordance with her religious beliefs and that the actual delivery of the *get* by the husband is a non-religious act of an ordinary civil character.[13]

1 See generally, *Maidment* at 624-6. Whereas an English judicial divorce would probably be regarded as automatically amounting to a *talaq* in the eyes of Sunni law if the husband was the petitioner, Shi'ite law requires an oral repudiation in the presence of two witnesses – see para 5.03 above.
2 (1932) 16 Pa DC 290.
3 Similar views were expressed in *Margulies v Margulies* 42 App Div 2d 517 (1973) and *Pal v Pal* 45 App Div 2d 738 (1974).
4 (1974) 2 WWR 193.
5 (1979) 5 FLR 2810, discussed by Friedell in [1979-80] JFL 525.
6 The nature of a *ketouba* is discussed in para 2.35 above.
7 See also the judgment of the majority of the New York Court of Appeals in *Avitzur v Avitzur* 58 NY 2d 108 (1983).
8 138 NYS 2d 366 (1954).
9 At 373.
10 Art 12.
11 Art 9.
12 Cf Freeman 'Jews and the Law of Divorce in England' (1981) 4 Jewish Law Annual 276 at 283.
13 See Glenn 'Where Heavens Meet: The Compelling of Religious Divorces' (1980) 28 AJCL 1 at 13-16.

5.18 While it therefore seems improbable that an English court has no power to order the delivery or receipt of a *get*, the basis upon which such an order could be made needs to be clarified. Either the court would have to hold the *ketouba* in question to be a binding contract capable of specific performance (as in *Stern's case*) or there would need to have been a prior undertaking given to the court by one of the parties that a *get* would be delivered or received by a specified date. In any event non-compliance with such an order could only ultimately be enforced by a direction for the recalcitrant party to be committed to prison for contempt of court. Just how significant a drawback this is to the making of such orders is well brought out by Glenn on the basis of a detailed review of the position in the United States, Canada, France, Germany, and England:

' . . . measures of incarceration represent the outer limit of secular judicial authority rarely exercised in civil matters even in those jurisdictions accustomed to the broad authority of the contempt power. The finely balanced character of the religious divorce problem, the sanctity of the physical liberty of the person, and the reluctance to punish for non-penal activity, all weigh against measures of incarceration. No one, *sauf erreur*, as yet has been committed by a civil court for refusal to cooperate in religious divorce proceedings, and sanctions of this severity are unlikely to attract general support in the future.'[1]

In some North American cases it has even been doubted whether Jewish law would recognise the validity of a *get* granted under this sort of compulsion,[2] but this may well be incorrect.[3] Certainly in Israel a husband who refuses to deliver a *get*, despite an order from a rabbinical court to do so, can be committed to prison indefinitely.[4]

If it is assumed that imprisonment for contempt will be kept as a remedy of last resort for really exceptional cases, what other solutions to the problem are available under English law? Where the divorce is being obtained by the husband on the basis of two years' separation the wife can, of course, make her consent conditional upon the delivery of the *get* and if the husband subsequently fails to deliver the *get* the civil decree can be rescinded under the Matrimonial Causes Act 1973, s10 (1) provided it has not yet been made absolute.[5] A second possibility is for the civil court to attempt to induce the husband to deliver a *get* by making the financial outcome of the divorce more onerous for him if he fails to do so. Thus in *Brett v Brett*[6] the court's order that the husband pay the the wife a lump sum of £30,000 was coupled with the inducement that if he delivered a *get* within a period of three months from the date of the court order the final instalment of £5,000 due on that date was no longer to become payable. Phillimore L J pointed out that the husband's failure to deliver a *get* would have the effect of preventing the wife from gaining future support from marriage to a second husband, which she was only able to accomplish as an Orthodox Jewess through a religious wedding.[7]

Financial constraints in the guise of fines or damages, payable either on a recurrent or escalating basis during the period of the husband's default or in the form of a lump sum, have been a familiar feature of the orders made during recent years by the American and French courts.[8] In New York the courts have also been prepared to withhold their assistance from an uncooperative partner when matters relating to maintenance or access to children have been at issue following the civil divorce.[9] The difficulty with applying monetary sanctions against a husband who refuses to deliver a *get* is that their efficacy depends first, upon the availability of sufficient assets or other financial resources at his disposal and second, upon the husband's imprisonment being accepted as a suitable weapon of last resort.

In the absence of any reform or re-interpretation of Jewish law to allow the *get* to be pronounced by a rabbi in place of the husband, it would appear that the only other solution would be for English law to insist upon the delivery of a *get* as a condition precedent to a civil divorce decree being made absolute.[10] This would, of course, require legislation. The present practice of the Beth-Din only to authenticate a *get* once the civil dissolution is complete would also require modification so that action on its part could be taken as soon as the decree nisi had been pronounced by the divorce court. In 1984 an amendment to the Matrimonial Causes Act 1973 was proposed in Parliament which would have allowed a spouse to oppose the grant of a decree absolute of divorce on the ground that the other party had failed to remove a barrier to the religious remarriage of the first party.[11] However, the proposed amendment was withdrawn on the understanding that the goverment would give the whole issue serious consideration in the future.[12] The present situation certainly provides unscrupulous spouses with considerable opportunities for blackmail, leading to the possibility of wholly unsatisfactory arrangements being made about financial provision and the upbringing of children as part of the price of a *get* or a *talaq*.

1 Glenn 'Where Heavens Meet: The Compelling of Religious Divorces' (1980) 28 AJCL 1 at 25.
2 See, e g *Margulies v Margulies* 42 App Div 2d 517 (1973); *Morris v Morris* (1974) 2 WWR 193 at 219 (per Matas J).
3 See, e g *Pal v Pal* at 740 (per Martuscello J); *Morris v Morris* above, at 200-1 (per Freedman C J M).
4 Law on Rabbinical Jurisdiction (Marriage and Divorce) 1953.
5 This technique has apparently been used in at least one unreported case: see Freeman (1981) 4 *Jewish Law Annual* 283.
6 [1969] 1 All ER 1007, [1969] 1 WLR 487.
7 At 1015.
8 Glenn at 25-9.
9 Ibid at 29-30.
10 See Jackson (1981) 4 *Jewish Law Annual* 3 at 8.
11 See 61 HC Official Report (6th series) col 926.
12 Ibid cols 930-1.

English conflicts law

5.19 Two questions arise for consideration under this heading. First, is it permissible for a couple, in adhering to their customs, to effect an extra-judicial divorce in this country which will be recognised as valid in English law? Second, in what circumstances will English law recognise a divorce which is obtained abroad and is based on traditional or religious custom?

1 The validity of extra-judicial divorces effected in England

5.20 This is an area in which the law has fluctuated considerably during the course of this century. However, before coming to the modern period it is perhaps worth delving briefly into the uncertainties of the Victorian era. Although until the enactment of the Matrimonial Causes Act 1857 divorce was basically only obtainable by means of a private Act of Parliament, 17 years earlier in *Moss v Smith*[1] the question had arisen whether a *get* delivered in London around 1833 was effective to dissolve a Jewish marriage under English law. Erskine J appeared to believe it could be when he held that 'supposing a Jewish divorce to be capable of effecting a dissolution of the marriage, yet, in the absence of the document of divorce, there was no evidence that any divorce had taken place'.[2] The counter-argument, that divorce could only be obtained by Act of Parliament was placed squarely before him but was apparently rejected.

This isolated and somewhat inconclusive case has given rise to acute controversy. Bartholomew[3] has drawn attention to statements made by the Lord Chancellor in the debates during the passing of the 1857 Act as well as by the Chief Rabbi to the Gorell Commission in 1912,[4] which strongly suggest that Jewish divorces effected here were recognised as perfectly valid right up until 1866 when the Registrar General refused to register them. On the other hand, two experts on Jewish law, Mr H S Q Henriques and Mr D L Alexander both gave evidence to the Gorell Commission to the effect that such divorces were invalid.[5]

1 (1840) 1 Man & Gr 228.
2 At 234.
3 'Application of Jewish Law in England' (1961) 3 Univ of Malaya L R 83 at 103-4.
4 Cmd 6481, vol III p 407.
5 Ibid at pp 414, 416-7.

5.21   The first case on the subject this century, *R v Hammersmith Superintendent Registrar of Marriages, ex p Mir-Anwaruddin,*[1] came before the Court of Appeal during the 1914-18 war. The applicant, an Indian advocate who was seeking a certificate and licence to marry a second wife, alleged that he was a single man on the strength of a divorce from his first wife effected by a *talaq* pronounced in England. He had married his first wife, an Englishwoman, in England but he himself was a Muslim domiciled in India. The superintendent registrar refused to issue the necessary certificate and licence, believing that the applicant's divorce would not be recognised here. The Court of Appeal upheld his refusal, principally on the ground that a monogamous English marriage to an English-woman could only be dissolved in England through the courts, i e in the usual English manner, regardless of the effectiveness of a *talaq* in the eyes of the law of the parties' domicile. The husband's submission to the contrary that the *talaq* should be recognised as valid in English law was dismissed as 'absurd' on the strength of certain remarks made by Lord Brougham in 1835 in *Warrender v Warrender.*[2] Lord Brougham had made great play in that case of the fundamental differences between 'Christian' and 'infidel' marriages[3] and this clearly influen-ced the Court of Appeal in the present case as much as it had Lord Penzance in *Hyde v Hyde* 50 years earlier.[4] During the proceedings before the Divisional Court in the *Hammersmith Marriage Case* Viscount Reading C J had given as an additional reason for rejecting the husband's application that, whereas upon marriage an Englishwoman took on the domicile of her foreign husband:

'she does not acquire his religion or become subject to the laws of his religion except in so far as they are the law of his domicile, and then to that extent only.'[5]

Next in 1926 came the case of *Preger v Preger.*[6] The parties, who were Jewish, had been married in a synagogue in England. The husband later purported to divorce his wife here by delivering her a *get* in the presence of a rabbi. Both parties clearly took the view that while the divorce might be effective under Jewish law it would not be recognised in English law. In subsequent divorce proceedings here Hill J also assumed, without expressly so deciding, that it would not be recognised here. The domicile of the parties was not specifically referred to but was presumably English, since otherwise the court would not even have possessed jurisdiction to hear the proceedings in the first place.

1 [1917] 1 KB 634.
2 (1835) 2 Cl & Fin 488 at 534.
3 At 531. For criticism of this judgment, see (1976) 25 ICLQ 475 at 479 ff.
4 See para 3.04 above.
5 At 642. Indian law, of course, recognises a variety of systems of religious law.
6 (1926) 42 TLR 281.

5.22   The earliest case this century to afford recognition to an extra-judicial divorce performed in this country was *Har-Shefi v Har-Shefi (No 2)*[1] which was decided in the High Court in 1953. A Jewish marriage between an English-woman domiciled in England and an Israeli man domiciled in Israel had taken place in Tel Aviv. The couple later came to England. The marriage broke down and the husband handed the wife a bill of divorcement at the Beth-Din in London. The wife thereupon sought a declaration as to its validity in the eyes of English law. Pearce J upheld its validity on the ground that it complied with the law of the husband's domicile, citing a case in which the Privy Council had recognised the validity of a *get* delivered in Egypt.[2] He was clearly motivated by the desire to avoid a limping marriage.[3]

Har-Shefi differed from the *Hammersmith Marriage Case* in three respects, which no doubt made recognition easier to afford. First, the marriage was not an English one. Second, the husband was not trying to impose an alien system of religious law upon his wife through his utilisation of the Jewish *get*. Third, the divorce was at least effected on the premises of a Rabbinical court, whereas the *talaq* had taken place in a private house. The case also differed, of course, significantly from *Preger* in that the husband was not domiciled here.

A month after *Har-Shefi* was decided the Court of Appeal refused recognition to a *get* in *Joseph v Joseph*.[4] A Jewish couple who had married in a synagogue in Shanghai subsequently became domiciled in England and obtained a divorce by *get* at the Beth-Din in London. The Court treated the divorce as invalid in English law. The same conclusion on this point was reached by Barnard J in *Corbett v Corbett*[5] four years later in respect of a similar *get* delivered in London. In neither case was there any discussion of the issues, nor any reference to *Har-Shefi*, but the obvious distinguishing feature seems to have been the English domicile of the parties rather than the nature of the divorce process. They were therefore consistent with the case of *Preger*.

The next case was *Ratanachai v Ratanachai*[6] in 1960. A Thai student who was on a course here had married an English girl of 17 in a register office following the birth of their child. Six months afterwards the husband returned to Thailand and later sent the wife a document reciting their mutual agreement to divorce, which the wife thereupon signed. She subsequently brought proceedings in the English courts for a declaration that the divorce was valid in English law. The declaration was granted on the grounds that the divorce was valid by the *lex domicilii* (Thai law), the court following the precedent of *Har-Shefi*.

By this time the decision in the *Hammersmith Marriage Case* was beginning to stand out as something of an aberration and in 1962 its authority was seriously undermined as a result of various comments made by the Court of Appeal in *Russ v Russ*.[7] Although the case itself was concerned with a *talaq* pronounced abroad[8] the Court emphasised the importance of the principle that English law should recognise divorces which would be recognised by the courts of the domicile.[9]

The same attitude was quickly reflected two years later in the decision of Scarman J in *Varanand v Varanand*.[10] An Englishwoman and a Siamese prince had married in a register office in London and were divorced here by mutual agreement 14 years later. The divorce was evidenced by a certificate issued by the Thai embassy in London and would have been recognised by the courts of Thailand where the couple were domiciled. Scarman J upheld the validity of the divorce, pointing out that the court's discretion to refuse recognition to a foreign status was one to be most sparingly exercised and should be confined to instances where public policy or principles of natural justice were infringed.

1 [1953] P 220, [1953] 2 All ER 373.
2 *Sasson v Sasson* [1924] AC 1007.
3 [1953] P 220 at 224.
4 [1953] 2 All ER 710, [1953] 1 WLR 1182.
5 [1957] 1 All ER 621, [1957] 1 WLR 486.
6 (1960) Times, 4 June, [1960] CLY 480.
7 [1964] P 315, [1962] 3 All ER 193.
8 The decision is discussed at para 5.25 below.

9 See *Armitage v A-G* [1906] P 135.
10 (1964) 108 SJ 693.

5.23 Finally, in 1971 there came the important case of *Qureshi v Qureshi*[1] in which Simon P declared that the *Hammersmith Marriage Case* and *Russ v Russ* were inconsistent Court of Appeal decisions and that he had to choose between them. He elected to follow the approach in *Russ*. In *Qureshi* the parties, who were Muslims, had married in an English register office. Differences later arose between them, whereupon the husband wrote the wife a letter in this country purporting to divorce her by *talaq*. Being domiciled in, as well as a citizen of, Pakistan he complied with the Muslim Family Laws Ordinance 1961 by sending notification of the *talaq* to the appropriate council chairman, who was the Pakistani High Commissioner in London. Attempts at reconciliation failed and the question arose whether the divorce was valid in English law. Simon P held the *talaq* was entitled to such recognition for the following reasons:[2]

(i)   The *talaq* would in any event be recognised by the country of the husband's domicile and English courts should exercise very sparingly their residual discretion to refuse recognition, on grounds of injustice in a particular case, to divorces recognised by the law of the domicile. The court was obviously concerned to avoid a limping marriage, if that was possible.

(ii) The system of divorce by *talaq* was recognised by the religious law of both spouses.

(iii) By simply returning to Pakistan (which the husband intended to do) he could easily obtain a *talaq* divorce which the English courts would be bound to recognise and there was thus little point in postponing the dissolution of the marriage.

(iv) The wife would probably be better provided for financially if she relied on her claim to 'deferred dower', which became due upon the pronouncement of the *talaq*, than if her husband had to return to Pakistan in order to divorce her. In the latter eventuality he might not return to England and there might be serious difficulties in enforcing any payment due to her.

The decisive importance of the couple's foreign domicile in *Qureshi* (which had also been apparent from some of the earlier cases) was reinforced soon afterwards by the decision of Cumming-Bruce J in *Radwan v Radwan*.[3] Here recognition of a *talaq* pronounced in London was refused because at the relevant time the parties had been domiciled in England.

By the early 1970s the combined effect of the decisions in *Varanand* and *Qureshi* seemed to indicate clearly that extra-judicial divorces of foreign domiciliaries which were accomplished here would be recognised as valid in the eyes of English law, regardless of certain matters which had earlier seemed significant. Thus there was no need for any judicial decree or proceedings, nor for the involvement of any sort of court, nor would recognition be withheld simply because the marriage had been entered into in England or because one party was English.

1 [1972] Fam 173, [1971] 1 All ER 325.
2 At 201.
3 [1973] Fam 24, [1972] 3 All ER 967.

5.24 This position at common law which had been so firmly consolidated by these two cases[1] only survived, however, for about two years before being reversed by statute. The Domicile and Matrimonial Proceedings Act 1973, s

16(1) provided a new rule for extra-judicial divorces occurring after 1 January 1974 and declared that no 'proceeding' in England after that date was to be regarded as validly dissolving a marriage unless it was instituted in an English court of law.

There has been much speculation and debate as to what is meant here by the word 'proceeding'.[2] If it necessarily involves some formal or official act or the participation of some organ of state authority then the paradoxical result would be reached that the more informal the divorce the greater its chance of recognition, since s 16(1) would not govern the situation and recognition would have to be accorded in terms of the position established at common law. This seems hardly likely to have been the intention of Parliament.[3] It is probable, therefore, that 'proceeding' means no more than 'a course of action' or 'a piece of conduct', broad and untechnical definitions to be found in the *Shorter Oxford English Dictionary*. If this is so there is now a complete and outright prohibition of extra-judicial divorces occurring in this country.

1 See also *Chaudhry v Chaudhry* [1975] 3 All ER 687 at 688.
2 See *North* pp 225-30; Jaffey 'Recognition of Extra-judicial Divorces' (1975) 91 LQR 320; *Bromley* Family Law (6th edn, 1981) pp 245-6.
3 *Chaudhary v Chaudhary* [1984] 3 All ER 1017 at 1031, 1035; Jaffey at 320-1.

2 The recognition of extra-judicial divorces obtained abroad

5.25 The earliest case to be reported on this subject appears to be that of *Ganer v Lady Lanesborough*[1] in 1790. The question arose as to whether a marriage between two Jews could be recognised as having been validly dissolved by Jewish rites and customs at Leghorn in Italy so that the parties were free to remarry. An instrument of divorce under the seal of the Leghorn synagogue was produced to the court, but Lord Kenyon held it to be insufficient without evidence as to the position under Italian law. Thereupon the former wife swore that she had been divorced before the rabbi at Leghorn in accordance with Jewish custom and ceremony and this was accepted by the Court of Nisi Prius.

At this time the significance of domicile as a connecting factor in divorce had not yet begun to be appreciated and there was naturally no reference to it in the report. Its decisive importance for the recognition of foreign divorces only became firmly established towards the end of the nineteenth century[2] and proved highly relevant in the first twentieth century case on foreign extra-judicial divorces, *Seni Bhidak v Seni Bhidak*.[3] The couple, a Siamese 'count' and an American-born divorcee, had married in a register office in London. The husband, who had retained his Siamese domicile of origin throughout, later divorced his wife in Bangkok by unilateral declaration having previously deserted her for a period of about nine months. Expert evidence was given that under Siamese law a divorce automatically followed if a husband deserted his wife for three months. Bargrave Deane J held that the suit brought before him by the wife for a judicial separation must fail since the marriage had already been validly dissolved in terms of the *lex domicilii*.

Coming to the period after the 1939-45 war the decisions of the courts in this area were just as liable to be inconsistent with one another as we have seen happened in the case of divorces occurring in England. The judges can broadly be divided into those who concentrated on giving effect to the *lex domicilii* in order to recognise the foreign divorce and those who preferred to apply what they believed to be the underlying principle in the *Hammersmith Marriage Case* in order to justify refusal of such recognition.

In *Maher v Maher*,[4] the first of these cases, a Muslim who was domiciled in

Egypt had married an Englishwoman who was domiciled in England in a register office here. He had subsequently purported to divorce her by *talaq* in Cairo and the divorce was recognised as valid in Egyptian law. Barnard J, however, refused to recognise it as valid in England, relying on the principle he extracted from the *Hammersmith Marriage Case* that 'Christian' or monogamous marriages could not be dissolved by methods appropriate to polygamous unions. 'To hold otherwise would not only be contrary to the law as I understand it', he remarked, 'but would both encourage and sanction the purely temporary union of English women and foreigners professing the Mohammedan religion during their limited residence in this country'.[5]

In the next case, *El-Riyami v El-Riyami*[6] which was decided in 1958, the husband was a Muslim domiciled in Zanzibar and the wife an Englishwoman. He had divorced her by *talaq* in Zanzibar. It was held that the divorce would be recognised here since it was valid by the law of the domicile despite the fact that the couple had married in England. By contrast, three years later in *Soegito v Soegito*[7].a special commissioner for divorce refused recognition to an extra-judicial Javanese divorce despite its validity in Indonesian law, the appropriate *lex domicilii*. The judge found his authority for this in the *Hammersmith Marriage Case*. However, in *Mahbub v Mahbub*[8] decided in 1964, the opposite approach was again adopted. The couple had married in an English register office, the husband being a Muslim domiciled in Pakistan and the wife an Englishwoman. Subsequently the husband divorced his wife by *talaq* pronounced in Pakistan and this was recognised by Wrangham J as validly dissolving the marriage in the eyes of English law because it satisfied the *lex domicilii*.

It should be noted that all these decisions were of judges at first instance and most of their judgments were never fully reported. It was not until later in 1964 that the Court of Appeal at last had an opportunity of pronouncing on the issue in *Russ v Russ*.[9] Although the material facts were almost identical with those in *Maher v Maher* the Court of Appeal expressly overruled that decision and in the process virtually distinguished the *Hammersmith Marriage Case* 'out of existence.'[10] Willmer L J stated:

'I think it must be taken . . . that the real ratio of the majority in the *Hammersmith* case was the absence of any judicial proceeding. If so, the judge [Scarman J at first instance] was, in my view, justified in drawing a distinction between the circumstances of that case and those which existed here. In the *Hammersmith* case the "Talak" pronouncement was made in a private room in London, in the absence of the wife, and there was no suggestion of any judicial proceeding of any kind. In the present case it was pronounced before the appropriate Mohammedan court in Egypt, in the presence of the wife, and the fact of the divorce was duly recorded in the official records of the court. Moreover, the fact of the divorce was judicially recognised in, and formed the basis of, the subsequent proceedings in which [the wife] was awarded maintenance. This fact of judicial recognition by the court of the domicile seems to me to constitute an important element in the present case which was wholly lacking in the *Hammersmith* case'.[11]

The views expressed by the Court of Appeal in *Russ* seemed to mark a decisive step in the recognition of foreign extra-judicial divorces since the judges were particularly concerned to reassert the primacy accorded to the foreign *lex domicilii*.[12] However, the suggestion in the judgment of Willmer L J, quoted above, that recognition might depend on there being some semblance of judicial proceeding or court involvement in the divorce ran counter to some of the earlier first instance decisions. Fortunately, this aspect was not stressed as particularly significant by either Donovan L J or Davies L J nor was it regarded as necessary in the subsequent case of *Lee v Lau*[13] three years later. There a

Chinese marriage had been dissolved in accordance with the law of Hong Kong (where the parties had married and were then domiciled) by means of a written agreement between the parties which had merely been authenticated by the seal of the Sai Kung Rural Committees' Association. Cairns J held that it was entitled to recognition here despite the absence of any judicial or other formal proceedings.

1 (1790) 1 Peake 25.
2 See *Harvey v Farnie* (1882) 8 App Cas 43; *Le Mesurier v Le Mesurier* [1895] AC 517.
3 (1912) Times, 3 December.
4 [1951] P 342, [1951] 2 All ER 37.
5 At 346.
6 (1958) Times, 1 April; [1958] CLY 497.
7 (1961) 105 Sol Jo 725.
8 (1964) 108 Sol Jo 337.
9 [1964] P 315, [1962] 3 All ER 193.
10 See *Dicey and Morris* at p 361.
11 At 325.
12 At 327, 333, 334.
13 [1967] P 14, [1964] 2 All ER 248.

5.26 In 1971 the position established by these decisions at common law was significantly affected by changes introduced in the Recognition of Divorces and Legal Separations Act of that year with a view to extending further the bases of recognition. This Act was also partly designed to implement a draft Convention on the subject adopted by the Hague Conference on Private International Law in 1968, to which Britain was a signatory. Unfortunately, the subtleties of extra-judicial divorce were not fully appreciated either at the Conference[1] or by Parliament and some difficult problems of interpretation have been left to be resolved by the courts.

The first point to be borne in mind is that the common law rules outlined earlier were expressly retained by s 6 of the Act.[2] The position remains, therefore, that extra-judicial divorces obtained in[3] or recognised by[4] the country of both spouses' domicile will be recognised as valid by English law.[5] Since the introduction of separate and independent domiciles for married women by the Domicile and Matrimonial Proceedings Act 1973 divorces obtained in the country of one spouse's domicile and recognised in the other's, as well as divorces obtained in a third country and recognised in the countries of each of the spouses' separate domiciles, will equally be entitled to recognition here.[6]

Second, new grounds for recognition were introduced in s 3 of the 1971 Act in relation to 'overseas divorces'. An overseas divorce is defined in s 2 as one 'obtained by means of judicial or other proceedings' in any country outside the British Isles and 'effective' under the law of that country. Such divorces will be recognised under s 3 if at the date of the institution of the relevant proceedings either spouse was habitually resident in or was a national of the country where the divorce was obtained. These grounds apply even if one or both of the spouses was domiciled in the particular UK jurisdiction in which recognition of the divorce is being sought.

There is clearly a problem here in deciding what actions fall within the expression 'other proceedings' since, if a foreign divorce is obtained without such proceedings, it cannot be recognised on the grounds of habitual residence or nationality. The same uncertainty and controversy arises here as in connection with the meaning of the word 'proceeding' in s 16(1) of the 1973 Act discussed earlier.[7] While it is arguable that 'proceedings' are narrower than 'a proceeding' and that they necessarily connote some element of formality or involvement of an official authority, neither the wording of the Hague Convention itself nor the debates in Parliament preceding the 1971 Act really put that interpretation beyond doubt.[8] If the more commonsense view is taken that 'proceeding' and 'proceedings' are virtually synonymous in this context and if the argument concerning the interpretation of s 16(1) of the 1973 Act put forward earlier is accepted, then even the most informal divorce must surely be entitled to recognition.[9]

1 See J D McClean *Recognition of Family Judgments in the Commonwealth* (Butterworths, 1983) p 75.
2 See generally *North* pp 233-4.
3 *Le Mesurier v Le Mesurier* [1895] AC 517.
4 *Armitage v A-G* [1906] P 135.
5 S 6(2).
6 S 6(3).
7 See para 5.24 above; *North* pp 225-32; *Dicey and Morris* pp 362-4; *Bromley* pp 245-6.
8 *North* pp 226-7.
9 *Bromley* p 246; *Jaffey* at 321. See also *Radwan v Radwan* [1973] Fam 24, [1972] 3 All ER 967 and Polonsky 'Non-Judicial Divorces by English Domiciliaries' (1973) 22 ICLQ 343.

5.27 The question first arose directly for decision in the case of *Quazi v Quazi*.[1] One of the two possible foreign divorces for which recognition was being sought there was a *talaq* which was pronounced in Pakistan and which complied with the Muslim Family Laws Ordinance 1961. Under the Ordinance written notice of the *talaq* must immediately be given to the appropriate administrative council (and a copy supplied to the wife) and this was duly done. Nevertheless the Court of Appeal held that the divorce had not been obtained by means of 'proceedings'. Ormrod LJ in giving the judgment of the Court stated:

'In our judgment, the phrase must be intended to exclude those divorces which depend for their legal efficacy solely on the act or acts of the parties to the marriage or of one of them. In such cases, although certain formalities or procedures have to be complied with, there is nothing which can properly be regarded as "proceedings". We think that, given the apposition of the words "other proceedings" to the word "judicial", "proceedings" here means that the efficacy of the divorce depends in some way on the authority of the state expressed in a formal manner, as provided for by the law of the state. To put it in other words, the state or some official organisation recognised by the state must play some part in the divorce process at least to the extent that, in proper cases, it can prevent the wishes of the parties or one of them, as the case may be, from dissolving the marriage tie as of right.'[2]

The decision of the Court of Appeal to refuse recognition on this ground was promptly reversed by the House of Lords. They held that the *eiusdem generis* rule of construction did not apply to the word 'other' in the phrase 'judicial or other proceedings' so as to require at least quasi-judicial proceedings, because there was no list of two or more expressions from which a common genus could be identified. Moreover, when the policy of the legislation was examined, including the Hague Convention, it was clear that the aim was to recognise divorces which were obtained by proceedings officially recognised as effective by the laws of the foreign countries where they were obtained and thus to avoid limping marriages. Divorces such as the present one were valid in Pakistan and since they were achieved through acts officially recognised by the law of that country as leading to an effective divorce they were entitled to recognition here.

A further problem relates to the fact that under s 2 an overseas divorce must have been 'obtained by means of' judicial or other proceedings. In *Quazi* the House of Lords clearly took the view that a *talaq* divorce in Pakistan is so obtained since the requirement about service of the notice does constitute part of the proceedings and without such service no divorce is obtainable. Lord Diplock stated:

'Without such proceedings the divorce by *talaq* never becomes effective. The proceedings come first, the divorce follows them 90 days after they have been commenced.'[3]

The judgment of Lord Scarman points in the same direction:

' . . . the trial judge was correct in holding that the effective divorce was obtained *by means of* these proceedings; for without them there would have been no effective divorce.'[4]

However, in the earlier case of *R v Registrar General of Births, Deaths and Marriages, ex p Minhas*[5] the Divisional Court had seemed to take a rather different view. In that case the husband, a Pakistani national, had married his wife in Pakistan in 1956. Five years later he came to England. His wife, however, refused to join him here and remained throughout in Pakistan. In 1973 he wrote out a notice of *talaq* and posted a copy of it to his wife in Pakistan. Simultaneously he sent the original of the pronouncement to the chairman of the Salasi Council in Lahore in compliance with the Muslim Family Laws Ordinance 1961. During the ensuing period of 90 days the husband went to Pakistan and appeared before the Council, but no reconciliation was accomplished and he did not revoke the *talaq*. The Council issued him with a certificate of divorce, but this was not authorised by the Ordinance or any other provision of the law of Pakistan and strictly speaking was of no legal effect whatsoever. He then returned to this country and applied for a licence to marry again. This was refused by the superintendent registrar on the ground that he was still married to his first wife in the eyes of English law. He then instituted proceedings for mandamus to compel the Registrar General to authorise the marriage. The question for the court was whether the *talaq* ranked as an 'overseas divorce' in order to qualify for recognition on the basis of the wife's habitual residence in Pakistan or the Pakistani nationality of both spouses. If instead it had taken place in England it would come under a different set of rules. The court reached the conclusion that it was not an 'overseas divorce' because the crucial part of the 'proceedings' (indeed the only event that could be called proceedings by which the divorce was 'obtained') was the actual writing out of the *talaq* which clearly took place in England. The court did not attempt to decide where the service of the notices occurred, merely doubting whether they constituted 'proceedings' at all. As for the husband's attendance before the Council in Pakistan this did not, in the court's view, amount to proceedings by which the divorce was 'obtained'. The divorce was obtained immediately the *talaq* was pronounced; it was merely revocable within the period of 90 days. Hence the upshot of the case was that the divorce was not entitled to recognition as an 'overseas divorce' and the applicant and his wife remained married in the eyes of English law.[6]

The Divisional Court's reasoning seems clearly to have been based on a misapprehension as to when the divorce was effective under the law of Pakistan. That was on the expiry of 90 days from the notice to the chairman of the Council and not upon the pronouncement of the *talaq*.[7] Hence the sending of the notice was a *sine qua non* for obtaining the divorce and should have fallen within the concept of 'proceedings' by which the divorce was 'obtained' under s 2 of the Act. For this reason no reliance was placed upon the decision by the Court of Appeal in the subsequent case of *R v Secretary of State for the Home Department, ex p Fatima*.[8] That case also involved a 'transnational divorce' in which the husband had pronounced the *talaq* in England and then sent the requisite written notices to his wife and the relevant arbitration council in Pakistan. The

Court held that both the pronouncement and the despatch of the notices formed part of the 'proceedings' and that the entirety of the proceedings had to take place abroad for them to amount to an 'overseas divorce' which could be recognised in England. This was apparent from s 3(1) of the Act which refers to 'the institution of the proceedings in the country in which' the divorce was obtained. In this case the divorce was 'obtained' in Pakistan, yet the proceedings began in England with the pronouncement of the *talaq*. Although the decision resulted in a limping marriage, always an unsatisfactory outcome for the individuals concerned, the Court considered it was far from clear that the legislature's policy was to encourage the obtaining of divorces by post by Pakistani nationals resident in England through the *talaq* procedure. The upshot of the decision is, therefore, that Pakistani husbands who wish to divorce their wives by *talaq* must ensure that the pronouncement is made outside the British Isles, either by travelling abroad themselves or possibly by delegating their powers to an agent overseas. However, the viability of this latter procedure has not yet been tested in the courts.[9]

1 [1979] 3 All ER 424, CA; [1980] AC 744, [1979] 3 All ER 897, HL.
2 At 430.
3 At 903.
4 At 918. See also Lord Fraser at 911.
5 [1977] QB 1, [1976] 2 All ER 246, criticised by Poulter 'Talaq Divorces' (1977) 127 NLJ 7, by Canton 'Where is the Lex Loci Divortii' (1976) 25 ICLQ 909 and by Gravells 'Recognition of Extra-judicial Divorces: Theoretical Problems Realised' (1976) 92 LQR 347.
6 Since the divorce was held to have taken place in England and since in all probability the husband was domiciled in England the divorce could not be recognised here: see *Radwan v Radwan* discussed at para 5.23 above.
7 This was pointed out by Lord Fraser in *Quazi v Quazi* (at 910) though there does seem to be some doubt on the question: see Sylvester 'The Islamic Talaq: Problems and Perspectives for the Future' [1980] JSWL 282 at 286-8.
8 [1985] QB 190, [1984] 2 All ER 458.
9 See *Pearl* pp 192-3.

5.28   There has been a serious division of judicial and academic[1] opinion as to whether or not a 'bare *talaq*', i e a simple pronouncement of divorce without notification to the wife or to an arbitral council, qualifies for recognition here as an 'overseas divorce'. Does a purely informal divorce by means of unilateral repudiation without the need for any official involvement fall within the expression 'other proceedings' in s 2? In *Quazi v Quazi* Lord Scarman expressed the following view, albeit in an obiter dictum:

'I construe s 2 as applying to any divorce which has been obtained by means of any proceedings, i e act or acts, officially recognised as leading to divorce in the country where the divorce was obtained, and which itself is recognised by the law of that country as an effective divorce.'[2]

In reliance on this statement Bush J held in *Zaal v Zaal*[3] that a 'bare *talaq*' pronounced in Dubai amounted to a divorce obtained by 'other proceedings' and Taylor J expressed his support for such a view in *R v Immigration Appeal Tribunal, ex p Secretary of State for the Home Department*.[4] By way of contrast, Wood J took the opposite view in three separate cases[5] and in the last of these, *Chaudhary v Chaudhary*,[6] his decision was upheld by the Court of Appeal. There the bare *talaq* had been pronounced in Kashmir where, although the territory forms part of Pakistan, the provisions of the Pakistan Muslim Family Laws Ordinance do not apply. The divorce was denied recognition in the eyes of English law. Cumming Bruce LJ described what the *talaq* in Kashmir involved:

'It is, by religion and tradition, a solemn ceremonial act even though the pronouncement may take place in private as well as in public, and the husband may be alone when he makes the pronouncement three times. . . . Apart from the pronouncement by the husband of the *talaq*, there is no formality, no requirement of any notification to anybody. No institution of the state, legal or administrative, is involved. No religious institution plays any part.'[7]

The Court of Appeal reached the unanimous conclusion that such an informal process did not amount to 'proceedings', emphasising that the inclusion of the words 'judicial or other proceedings' in both the Hague Convention and the 1971 Act clearly signified that not all divorces effective in the countries where they occurred were intended to be entitled to recognition. The words provided a filter and they had to be accorded a restrictive meaning.[8]

This approach does little to prevent limping marriages and if it is correct something of an anomaly is created by the fact that even though for lack of 'proceedings' such informal divorces do not qualify for recognition as 'overseas divorces' under s 3, they can still be recognised under the common law rules preserved by s 6. Thus such divorces obtained outside the British Isles will probably be entitled to recognition here if they were obtained in or recognised by the country of domicile.[9]

1 See *North* pp 229-32; *Dicey and Morris* p 329; *Bromley* pp 245-6; *Pearl* 'Social Security and the Ethnic Minorities' (1978) JSWL 24 at 30; Canton 'Financial Relief after Talaq Divorce' (1983) NLJ 928.
2 At 916. Lord Fraser expressly left the matter open (at 911), while the other members of the House expressed no opinions on the matter.
3 (1983) 4 FLR 284.
4 [1984] 1 All ER 488.
5 *Quazi v Quazi* [1979] 3 All ER 424 CA; [1979] 3 All ER 897, HL; *Sharif v Sharif* (1980) 10 Fam Law 216; *Chaudhary v Chaudhary* [1984] 3 All ER 1017.
6 [1984] 3 All ER 1025.
7 At 1025-6.
8 Reliance was placed in this regard on the judgment of Ormrod LJ in *Quazi v Quazi* [1979] 3 All ER 424.
9 See para 5.26 above. The matter is not entirely free from doubt in view of the reference in s 6(4) of the 1971 Act to the word 'proceedings' - see Smart 'Recognition of Extra-judicial divorces' (1985) 34 ICLQ 392 at 395.

5.29 However, a novel restriction upon the recognition of divorces on the basis of domicile was introduced by s 16(2) of the 1973 Act. This provides that extra-judicial divorces occurring after 1 January 1974 which would otherwise gain recognition on the basis of foreign domicile shall not be recognised here if both parties to the marriage have, throughout the period of one year immediately preceding the institution of the proceeding, been habitually resident in the UK. The purpose of this rule is clearly to prevent couples who have a close connection with this country through residence from circumventing the ordinary judicial procedures and safeguards of English domestic law, especially since the 1973 Act simultaneously gave English divorce courts an enlarged jurisdiction based merely on the habitual residence of one of the parties here for a period of at least one year.[1] Furthermore, s 16(1) of the 1973 Act, which now prevents any extra-judicial divorce occurring within the British Isles from being effective here, would lack teeth if it were open to people who were domiciled abroad but habitually resident here to make a brief trip to a foreign country in order to obtain a divorce, e g if a husband domiciled in Bangladesh flew to Libya for the sole purpose of pronouncing a *talaq* there. However, because of the Hague Convention's acceptance of the link based on nationality s 16(2) is not as inhibiting as it might have been.[2] It contains an exception for divorces obtained by 'proceedings' in a country of which at least one of the parties is a national[3] and thus although Bangladeshi domiciliaries who have been habitually resident here for 12 months cannot be divorced in English eyes by a *talaq* pronounced in Libya they can be so divorced by one pronounced in Bangladesh if either of them holds Bangladeshi nationality. A further problem arises from the fact that s 16(2) only relates to divorces which have been obtained 'by means of a proceeding other than a proceeding instituted in a court of law.'[4] This raises the same difficulties about the meaning of the word 'proceeding'[5] as those mentioned earlier and again points to a commonsense construction of wide dimension. Otherwise the more informal the procedure the less prospect there is that the restrictions imposed by s 16(2) will apply to it, which would surely be the exact opposite of what Parliament intended.

1 S 5(2)(b).
2 See 343 HL Official Report (5th series) cols 319-21; 860 HC Official Report (5th series) cols 1087-8.
3 S 16(2)(c).
4 S 16(2)(b).
5 See *North* pp 235-7.

5.30 A further requirement with extra-judicial 'overseas divorces' is that in order to be recognised as valid here they must, in terms of s 2 of the 1971 Act, be 'effective' under the law of the country where they were obtained. Different countries will naturally tend to have different rules about the basis of recognition of such divorces. For example, whereas under the Pakistan Muslim Family Laws Ordinance a *talaq* pronounced in Pakistan by a husband who is domiciled in England would be treated as effective there (provided the appropriate notices had been served), a bare *talaq* pronounced in India by such a husband would probably not be regarded as effective there because of his English domicile.[1] Moreover, even a *talaq* pronounced in Pakistan by an English domiciliary might not be effective there if the wife had not lived in Pakistan during the marriage, because of the impossibility of finding a public official upon whom the notices required by the Family Laws Ordinance could be validly served.[2] Under the Ordinance the basis of jurisdiction of a union council's chairman to receive such a notice is defined in terms of either the place of residence of the wife at the time of the pronouncement of the *talaq* or the place of the last conjugal residence of the spouses or the place where the husband is permanently residing.[3]

1 See *Noor Jehan Begum v Eugene Tiscenko* (1942) 2 ILR Cal 196; Carroll 'Further Notes on Pakistani and Indian *Talaqs* in English Law' [1981] Jnl of the Indian Law Institute 588.
2 Carroll at 590-2. Giving notice to an official in the Pakistani Embassy in London would not seem to be much help since such notice forms part of the proceedings and these must take place outside the British Isles – see s 2 of the 1971 Act and s 16(1) of the 1973 Act.
3 See further the Pakistani case of *Masood Khan v Chairman, Arbitration Council, Wah* [1982] PLD 532 (Lahore), discussed by Carroll [1983] 99 LQR 515.

5.31 Finally, under the 1971 Act recognition may be refused to a foreign divorce, which would otherwise be entitled to be recognised, on three grounds specified in s 8(2). The first two of these are where the divorce was obtained by one spouse:

'(i) without such steps having been taken for giving notice of the proceedings to the other spouse as, having regard to the nature of the proceedings and all the circumstances, should reasonably have been taken; or
(ii) without the other spouse having been given (for any reason other than lack of notice) such opportunity to take part in the proceedings as, having regard to the matters aforesaid, he should reasonably have been given.'

A divorce by unilateral repudiation would hardly seem to fall within the compass of these provisions.[1] Assuming that the repudiation amounted to 'proceedings' their nature is such that no amount of notice or opportunity to be heard would enable the person repudiated to prevent the divorce. To refuse recognition in such cases would be to apply what are essentially rules of natural justice to proceedings which are in no sense judicial.

The third ground upon which a court may refuse recognition to a divorce is if its recognition 'would manifestly be contrary to public policy'. In *Quazi* the House of Lords held that Wood J, the trial judge, had correctly exercised his discretion in deciding that the Pakistani *talaq* divorce should not be denied recognition on this ground.[2] So far as purely informal divorces are concerned the general view of commentators has been that this residuary statutory power should be very sparingly exercised, as it is at common law.[3] However, this scarcely appears to have been the approach of the judges in recent years. In *Zaal v Zaal*[4] Bush J gave public policy as the basis for his refusal to recognise a bare *talaq* pronounced in Dubai, stating:

'I have come to this conclusion on the restricted ground that what was done, though properly done according to the husband's own customary laws, was done in secrecy so far as the wife was concerned. The first this wife knew of it the deed was done and she was divorced in fact and in law and it was irrevocable and binding according to the law of the husband's state. No opportunity was given to enlist the aid of her or the husband's relatives in repairing the breach. Common justice requires that some notice other than a casual threat ought to be given for so solemn a proceeding. It is this that in this case offends one's sense of justice and jars upon the conscience . . . .'[5]

In this case the wife was an Englishwoman who had retained her English domicile, but she had entered into an Islamic marriage in Dubai knowing the ease with which she could be divorced under Muslim law and most of her married life had been spent within the confines of a Muslim society. Moreover, her husband had provided her with a house in England worth £30,000 following his pronouncement of the *talaq* so that she was reasonably secure financially.

In *Chaudhary v Chaudhary*[6] Wood J declared that the combination of circumstances which a court might need to consider when exercising its discretion under the head of public policy were limitless and went on:

'To those who say that such a wide discretion brings uncertainty into the law, I would reply that in many branches of the family jurisdictions today there is an extremely wide discretion given to the court.'[7]

This, however, loses sight of a major concern in these types of case, namely the need to avoid, wherever possible, creating 'limping' marriages. 'Manifestly . . . contrary to public policy' is a strongly-worded phrase and its application should, it is submitted, be confined to those cases which a reasonable person would describe as 'outrageous'.[8] The Court of Appeal in *Chaudhary* concentrated particularly on the fact that the principal purpose behind the husband's visit to Kashmir for the divorce had been the desire to deprive his wife of her right to claim financial provision in England, the country of their domicile. Fortunately, this loophole in the law has now been closed by Part III of the Matrimonial and Family Proceedings Act 1984.[9]

A more convincing illustration of when the public policy ground should be used is the case of *Viswalingam v Viswalingam*.[10] The marriage in question had apparently been automatically terminated in terms of Malaysian law as a result of the husband's conversion to Islam. The English Court of Appeal considered that this offended against English ideas of substantial justice since the couple had been married for 20 years, the wife knew nothing about the dissolution for over a year after it had happened (and could do nothing about challenging it) and there had been no independent expert evidence regarding the detailed provisions of Muslim law in Malaysia.

1 *Chaudhary v Chaudhary* [1984] 3 All ER 1017 at 1032, 1035; *Dicey and Morris* p 363; *Bromley* p 50; *North* p 240; *Pearl* pp 188-9. Cf *Sharif v Sharif* (1980) 10 Fam Law 216 at 217; *Zaal v Zaal* (1983) 4 FLR 284 at 288-9.
2 At 907, 911 and 918.
3 See *North* pp 240-1; *Pearl* pp 189-90 and see paras 5.22-5.23 above; cf Carroll (1985) 101 LQR 174-5, 178.
4 (1983) 4 FLR 284.
5 At 289.
6 [1984] 3 All ER 1017.
7 At 1025.
8 In *Vervaeke v Smith* [1983] AC 145 at 164, [1982] 2 All ER 144 at 157 Lord Simon stated that the courts should be slow to use the doctrine of public policy in the conflict of laws.
9 Discussed at para 5.40 below.
10 (1980) 1 FLR 15.

The scope for reform

5.32 So far as English domestic law is concerned the current law of divorce has come in for considerable criticism from a variety of quarters. Although when it was introduced in 1971 it was broadly portrayed as a departure from the concept of matrimonial guilt, around two-thirds of all divorces are still obtained on the basis of facts derived from the old 'offences'[1] and the courts are, at any rate in defended cases, required to make important value judgements as to what is acceptable behaviour in marriage.[2] Different judges may naturally have different views on this question, some of which may be out of keeping with the sentiments of public opinion. One way of avoiding these problems and of making the law both simpler and less fault-based would be to follow the Australian example of specifying irretrievable breakdown of marriage as the sole ground for divorce and providing that this can only be established by means of a period of not less than 12 months' separation.[3] The questions raised earlier about what constitutes 'desertion' or 'unreasonable behaviour' would not then arise.

Another issue is whether it should in any circumstances be a defence to a divorce petition for the respondent to establish that this would lead to 'grave hardship'. It certainly runs counter to the philosophy of burying dead marriages and undermines the basic ground of irretrievable breakdown. Since the defence appears to have succeeded in relation to non-financial hardship not once during a period of more than a decade there hardly seems much of a case for retaining it in its present form. On the other hand, there does appear to be a strong case for allowing one party to oppose a divorce on the ground that the other party has failed to remove a barrier to the religious remarriage of the first party.

1 See *Judicial Statistics 1984* p 47.
2 See, e g *Richards v Richards* [1972] 3 All ER 695, [1972] 1 WLR 1073; *O'Neill v O'Neill* [1975] 3 All ER 289, [1975] 1 WLR 1118; *Mason v Mason* (1981) 11 Fam Law 143.
3 Family Law Act 1975, s 48.

5.33 In relation to the question of extra-judicial divorces being accomplished in England by foreign domiciliaries it seems far from clear whether the move to ban them all automatically from the beginning of 1974 was a wise one. Certainly there were some persuasive arguments in favour of the change. From 1971 Parliament had greatly liberalised the English domestic law of divorce and in 1972 it was at last made possible for a person to obtain a divorce here from an actually or potentially polygamous marriage.[1] In 1973 the jurisdiction of the English divorce courts was considerably widened so that virtually anyone with a reasonably close connection with this country could obtain a divorce here.[2] Therefore, the prohibition on future extra-judicial divorces could be justified on the basis that there was little inconvenience for foreign domiciliaries in having to use the English system if they wished to be divorced here. However, it seems probable that there was a further, much more questionable motive in the change, namely that it would provide greater financial protection for divorced wives. As will be seen, English courts have until recently only had jurisdiction to make financial provision and property adjustment orders on divorce if the divorce itself was granted by an English court.[3] Thus refusing to allow extra-judicial divorces was to some degree a device to make up for this deficiency without attacking the core problem and reforming the law governing the availability of financial and property orders.[4] Now that this problem has been solved by the enactment of the Matrimonial and Family Proceedings Act 1984 is there any reason for continuing to ban extra-judicial divorces by foreign domiciliaries in this country? Such divorces would naturally have to comply with the couple's personal or religious law and be fully recognised by their *lex domicilii* and it has to be borne in mind that by refusing to recognise them under the present law limping marriages are inevitably being created.

The process by which an extra-judicial divorce is obtained is, of course, different from the English domestic procedure but not, it is submitted, radically so. In undefended cases English law now permits divorce through what is essentially an administrative process, with the part played by the judge being little more than an empty formality.[5] Divorce by consent and by unilateral repudiation are both authorised, albeit coupled with periods of separation.[6] These periods have been reduced to one of only 12 months in Australia[7] and it seems possible that the same period may soon be incorporated into English divorce law. A peculiar difficulty with consensual divorces is that one party's consent may have been obtained by duress. Even in current English law this problem hardly seems to be solved in relation to the consent needed for the fact of two years' separation merely by requiring the respondent's signature below an affirmative response to a question on the acknowledgment of service[8] and the impression is therefore conveyed that this is not a crucial consideration. Another question is whether divorce through such a process means that it is being made too easily obtainable. However, divorce is now openly acknowledged on all sides to be occurring in England on a massive and unprecedented scale. The current estimate is that around one-third of all marriages will end in divorce.[9] If consensual divorce is recognised by the parties' *lex domicilii* that country must have reached a policy decision on the matter and similarly accepted these sorts of risks. Divorce by consent does possess the advantage of avoiding the stress, embarrassment and humiliation often associated with judicial proceedings and in many cases probably reflects marital breakdown as accurately as a period of separation.

On the other hand, divorce by repudiation, in the Islamic world at any rate, is clearly discriminatory against wives. *Talaqs* are, however, countenanced by the Muslim faith and in so far as any improvement in the status of married women in this regard is concerned one must clearly look principally to the countries concerned for significant reforms.[10] A start has been made in some of them, such as Tunisia, Pakistan and Bangladesh, but it would be presumptuous to imagine that English law can make a real contribution in this direction simply by denying validity to the small numbers of *talaq* divorces which might occur in this country. Even so, to authorise the pronouncement of *talaqs* here would seem to run counter to prevailing attitudes towards sexual equality in marriage and could well involve a violation of the UK's international obligations to respect human rights. The International Covenant on Civil and Political Rights, Art 23(4) provides pertinently as follows:

'States Parties to the present Covenant shall take appropriate steps to ensure equality of rights and responsibilities of spouses as to marriage, during marriage and at its dissolution.'[11]

A further possible argument against permitting a *talaq* to effect a lawful divorce in this country is that it may involve a denial of natural justice. The European Convention on Human Rights, Art 6 declares:

'In the determination of his civil rights and obligations . . . everyone is entitled to a fair and public hearing . . . by an independent and impartial tribunal established by law.'

Since a divorce clearly does affect a wife's 'civil rights' it is at least arguable that whatever view Islamic law may take of the matter, English law should afford her some form of judicial hearing if she wishes it. On the other hand, refusal to authorise *talaqs* in England would not, it is thought, violate the religious freedom of Muslims since there is obviously nothing in Islamic doctrine which actually requires a man to put away his wife in this manner.[12]

A further criticism that has been made of extra-judicial divorces in general is that they are attended by minimal publicity and do not have to be officially registered as a matter of record and that this runs counter to the general policy of requiring publicity and certainty in connection with changes in status.[13] This deficiency is, of course, inconvenient from a bureaucratic point of view, but it hardly seems a sufficient reason on its own to deny them recognition. If they occurred abroad they would normally be accorded legal recognition here and the numbers of people involved would probably be just as great in this category as those divorced here by extra-judicial means. In each case in order to establish status as a divorcee the individual concerned would have to present satisfactory evidence of the divorce. Obviously an official certificate of some description provides the most convincing proof, but as in the case of a foreign marriage other evidence, e g that of witnesses, should be equally acceptable. Alternatively registration of extra-judicial divorces obtained in England could be made compulsory by legislation.

On balance, therefore, there seems a reasonable argument for at least recognising the validity of extra-judicial consensual divorces which take place in England, provided they are so recognised by the countries where the parties are domiciled or of which they are nationals. The only limitation should be, as before, that the courts would have a residuary discretion to refuse recognition which would be exercised very sparingly on grounds of public policy.[14] Such a ground might possibly exist where, for instance, it could clearly be shown that a party's agreement to a consensual divorce was in fact obtained by duress. Normally, however, such a divorce would not be treated as valid by the relevant foreign law and the question of discretion would not arise.

1 Matrimonial Proceedings (Polygamous Marriages) Act 1972 discussed at para 3.06 above.
2 Domicile and Matrimonial Proceedings Act 1973 discussed at para 5.12 above.
3 See para 5.40 below.
4 See particularly the speech of Lord Simon in 1971 in the House of Lords in which he moved the precursor of s 16(1) of the 1973 Act: 316 HL Official Report (5th series) cols 212-6. He himself was not in favour of a clause on these lines and moved it on the instructions of the Lord

Chancellor for purposes of discussion. He expressed a clear preference for extending financial relief as a solution to the problem. See also the other speeches on the amendment motion (cols 216-26), culminating in its withdrawal. See also various statements during debates on the 1973 Act: 850 HC Official Report (5th series) col 1630; 860 HC Official Report (5th series) col 1086; 343 HL Official Report (5th series) col 320.

5 For the misleadingly designated 'special procedure' in which, for 98.5% of divorces, the bulk of the work is done today by the court registrar, see Matrimonial Causes Rules 1977, rr 33(3), 48; Cretney *Principles of Family Law* (4th edn, 1984) pp 181-8.
6 Matrimonial Causes Act 1973, s 1(2)(d) and (e).
7 Family Law Act 1975, s 48.
8 Matrimonial Causes Rules 1977, r 16 and form 6, question 5.
9 Haskey 'The Proportion of Marriages Ending in Divorce' (1982) 27 *Population Trends* p 4.
10 See *Pearl* pp 109-13 for various improvements.
11 See also the 1980 Convention on the Elimination of All Forms of Discrimination against Women, Art 16(1)(c), which is to the same effect.
12 See T Mahmood *Muslim Personal Law* (New Delhi, 1977) p 105.
13 Hartley 'Non-judicial Divorces' (1971) 34 MLR 579 at 582.
14 See *Varanand v Varanand* (1964) 108 Sol Jo 693; *Qureshi v Qureshi* [1972] Fam 173, [1971] 1 All ER 325.

5.34 Whether or not these arguments in connection with divorces in England are accepted, there remains a strong case for reform in relation to the law concerning the recognition of foreign extra-judicial divorces. In the first place the law is very far from being clear in the meaning to be accorded to the word 'proceedings' in s 2 of the 1971 Act, despite the fact that this is central to the whole question of recognition of divorces based on nationality or habitual residence. Second, the Act is inconsistent in requiring the divorce to have been 'obtained' by means of 'proceedings' in the country of nationality or habitual residence, but not where the basis is domicile under s 6. Third, the general policy behind s 2 of broadening the basis for recognition is hampered by s 16(2) of the 1973 Act which unduly restricts recognition based on domicile. Moreover, this section is unlikely to prove particularly efficacious since divorces in the country of nationality are still entitled to recognition and such a country is likely to be as convenient a venue for divorce as any other.

The Law Commission has recently responded to all these criticisms in a constructive fashion.[1] It has recommended both that the law should make it abundantly clear that a bare *talaq* does constitute 'proceedings' and that the requirement that the divorce be obtained by 'judicial or other proceedings' should be extended to divorces accorded recognition on the basis of domicile.[2] In furtherance of its concern to harmonise the treatment of domicile, habitual residence and nationality as equal bases for recognition the Commission also proposed that the domicile of one of the spouses should be a sufficient connecting factor (rather than the domicile of both spouses, as at present) and that a foreign divorce should only be recognised on the basis of domicile if it actually occurred in the country of domicile and not if it was merely recognised by the law of that country and occurred elsewhere.[3] This would involve the abolition of the principle in *Armitage v A-G*.[4] The result would be that a divorce obtained outside the British Isles by judicial or other proceedings would be recognised within the UK if it was effective under the law of the country in which it was obtained and either party to the marriage was habitually resident in, domiciled in, or a national of that country.[5] Once this had been achieved it would be possible to repeal s 16(1) of the 1973 Act as redundant because the only basis upon which an extra-judicial divorce occurring within the UK could possibly be recognised as valid would be in reliance on the principle of *Armitage v A-G*. Since the rule in s 16(2) had only been introduced to buttress s 16(1) it could, in the view of the Commission, sensibly be dispensed with as well.[6]

1 Law Com Report No 137: Private International Law: Recognition of Foreign Nullity Decrees and Related Matters (1984).
2 At para 6.11.
3 At paras 6.21-6.29.
4 [1906] P 135.
5 Law Com No 137, para 6.36.
6 At para 6.30.

B. FINANCIAL AND PROPERTY ASPECTS

5.35 Some of the customary systems examined in the preceding section have, not surprisingly, different rules about the financial and property aspects of divorce.

In traditional Islamic law the basic position is that a former husband only has to pay his ex-wife any deferred dower due to her and additionally provide her with maintenance for a maximum period of three months from the time when the divorce becomes irrevocable.[1] A few states have reformed their laws to provide for a longer period of maintenance; for instance, in India a maintenance order may last until remarriage and in Tunisia a court may order maintenance without restriction.[2]

In Jewish law a divorced wife is not entitled to any maintenance, but she retains the property specified as her marriage settlement in the *ketouba* as well as any dowry given to her by her family at the time of the marriage.[3] The only exception is where she was the guilty party, in which case she may have to forfeit her marriage portion and even, in cases of grave guilt, some of her own possessions.[4]

Under most systems of African customary law a former wife is similarly debarred from claiming maintenance on divorce. Furthermore, where her husband's family had to provide bridewealth on the occasion or as a consequence of the marriage, the whole or part of this may have to be repaid, depending on how long the marriage lasted, how many children were born and who was chiefly at fault in the breakdown.[5]

1 See *Pearl* pp 64-5.
2 See *Pearl* pp 66, 94-5.
3 See Elman *An Introduction to Jewish Law* (London, 1958) pp 35, 42.
4 *Elman* p 42.
5 See Phillips and Morris *Marriage Laws in Africa* p 55.

Policy considerations

5.36 The principal objection to some of these systems is that they do not provide sufficient support and protection for divorced wives and that where these women are intending to remain in this country they may well become a burden on the taxpayer when they might otherwise be the responsibility, at any rate to some extent, of their ex-husbands. However, there has recently been much debate here as to what is the 'fairest' financial solution on divorce in domestic law and there are some who argue that ex-wives should be encouraged to become independent and self-sufficient as soon as possible and that if this is impossible they should be obliged to look to the state for continuing support rather than to their former husbands.[1] It is, however, generally felt that the growing equality of women demands that they obtain a just, if not necessarily a mathematically equal, share of the matrimonial assets on divorce.[2] This does not seem to be guaranteed under most of the customary systems referred to.

1 See, eg Deech 'The Principles of Maintenance' (1977) 7 Fam Law 229. Cf O'Donovan 'An Alternative View' (1978) 8 Fam Law 180.
2 For cogent arguments in favour of an equal division of matrimonial property on divorce see Gray *Re-allocation of Property on Divorce* (Professional Books, 1977).

English domestic law

5.37 The Matrimonial Causes Act 1973, Part II sets out the powers of the English courts with regard to financial provision and property adjustment orders. The central feature of the legislation is that it leaves considerable discretion in the hands of the courts[1] and does not specify fixed proportions either for maintenance or for a division of the capital assets. Under a set of guidelines which were revised by the Matrimonial and Family Proceedings Act 1984 the court has to have regard to all the circumstances of the case including a large number of listed factors such as the parties' resources, earning capacity, obligations and responsibilities. First consideration has to be given to the welfare while a minor of any child of the family who has not attained the age of 18.[2]

There would appear so far to have been only two judicial decisions involving foreign customs that might be relevant here, though neither of these was in fact directly applying Part II of the 1973 Act. It will be recalled that in *Brett v Brett*,[3] which was decided under earlier legislation,[4] the court had to consider the significance of a Jewish husband's conduct in refusing to deliver a *get*. His wife had divorced him on grounds of cruelty after a very short marriage. He was an extremely wealthy man and she had claimed substantial maintenance from him, including payment of a lump sum. Being an Orthodox Jewess she had demanded that he deliver a *get*, without which she would not be free to remarry under Jewish law. This he refused to do and he appeared to be using his refusal as a bargaining counter in the overall financial settlement. The Court of Appeal eventually awarded the wife a lump sum of £30,000 which included an instalment of £5,000 which was only to become payable if the husband had still failed to deliver a *get* within a period of three months from the making of the order. This appears to be a clear example of judicial recognition of a Jewish custom in deciding upon the appropriate financial order to make upon divorce.

In *Khan v Khan*[5] a deserted wife claimed maintenance in the magistrates' court and contended that no account should be taken of her earning capacity since it was 'not Moslem practice for a married woman to go out to earn an income'. On appeal, the Family Division declined an invitation to take judicial notice of such a practice, pointing out the need for there to be evidence in support of it. The decision has been criticised by Pearl as an example of judicial failure to take account of ethnic minority practices,[6] but this would appear to be unjustified. Certainly there is authority for the proposition that for a Muslim woman to work outside the home or domestic sphere is contrary to the cultural tradition of Islam and thus subject to severe criticism,[7] but in the context of modern English industrial society this stance is obviously rather hard to maintain in practice. Although most of their paid work is still done at home (such as knitting, sewing and weaving), many Muslim women do go out to factories and other enterprises, particularly in groups.[8] Moreover, the general trend in many Muslim states is towards affording greater opportunities for women in the field of employment.[9] Pearl has argued that in *Khan* it would have been appropriate for the Court to have heard evidence as to whether this particular wife was under pressure by her family and others not to go out to work, but again this was surely a matter on which the obligation to present the necessary evidence rested squarely on her. The case is, however, still perfectly compatible with the view that in appropriate circumstances a divorce court might well take account of an ethnic minority custom in fixing the level of maintenance to be ordered.

1 This aspect of the case is usually dealt with by the registrar rather than the judge.
2 Matrimonial Causes Act 1973, s 25 as amended by Matrimonial and Family Proceedings Act 1984, s 3.
3 [1969] 1 All ER 1007, discussed at para 5.18 above.
4 Matrimonial Causes Act 1965, s 16.
5 [1980] 1 All ER 497, [1980] 1 WLR 355.
6 [1980] New Community 147.
7 Khan (ed) *Minority Families in Britain* (Macmillan, 1979) pp 38-9; Macdonald and Macdonald 'Women at Work in Britain and the Third World' [1976] New Community 76 at 79, 81.
8 Khan 'Pakistani Women in Britain' [1976] New Community 99 at 108; *Who Minds? A Study of Working Mothers and Childminding in Ethnic Minority Communities* (CRC, 1975), pp 7-8; Smith *Racial Disadvantage in Britain* (Penguin, 1977) p 66 (the PEP Report revealed that 18% of Muslim women between the ages of 16 and 54 were working).
9 See El Saadawi *The Hidden Face of Eve: Women in the Arab World* (London, 1980) ch 19; A Dearden (ed) *Arab Women* (Minority Rights Group Report No 27 1976); R Jahan (ed) *Women in Asia* (Minority Rights Group Report No 45 1980); Papanek 'Purdah in Pakistan: Seclusion and Modern Occupations for Women' (1971) Journal of Marriage and the Family 517.

English conflicts law

5.38 If a foreign divorce is recognised as valid here two different questions can arise on the financial and property side. First, what orders and remedies are available in the English courts through the application of the relevant foreign law? Second, what provision does English law itself afford in such cases?

1 Remedies derived from foreign law

5.39 As explained in ch 2 above, the English courts are prepared to make orders for deferred dower and similar payments, provided the sum due is fixed or easily ascertainable and does not involve the courts in assessments that should properly be left to the relevant foreign tribunals.[1] Examples of deferred dower payments being ordered in England are to be found in the cases of *Shahnaz v Rizwan*[2] and *Qureshi v Qureshi*.[3] In the latter case the contract for deferred dower had been entered into in England pursuant to a wedding solemnised here, yet significantly no question was raised as to whether the contract might itself be void on grounds of public policy as constituting an agreement made in contemplation of divorce and hence prejudicial to the status of marriage.[4] In practical terms the specific rules relating to such dower have a tendency to restrain the breakdown of a marriage rather than encourage it since the dower is normally only payable by the husband upon the declaration of a divorce by *talaq* and only he can accomplish such a divorce. In any event the rules relating to agreements prejudicial to the status of marriage were established at a time when popular values in relation to divorce were very different from those prevailing today and it is thought that it would be quite inappropriate to apply them to contracts for deferred dower.[5]

By statute English courts also have power to enforce automatically certain maintenance orders made in various reciprocating foreign countries provided the orders have been registered here.[6]

1 See para 2.37 above.
2 [1965] 1 QB 390, [1964] 2 All ER 993.
3 [1972] Fam 173 at 200-1.
4 As to which, see Cheshire and Fifoot's *Law of Contract* (10th edn, 1981) pp 349-51.
5 Similar considerations would seem to be relevant in the case of provisions in a *ketouba*: see e g *Stern v Stern* (1979) 5 FLR 2810 discussed at para 5.17 above.
6 Maintenance Orders (Facilities for Enforcement) Act 1920; Maintenance Orders (Reciprocal Enforcement) Act 1972.

2 Provision available under English law

5.40 For a considerable period of time the extensive powers of English courts to make financial provision and property adjustment orders upon divorce were confined to instances where the divorce itself had been granted by an English court. Thus the Matrimonial Causes Act 1973, ss 23 and 24 provided for orders to be made only on the 'granting' of a decree or at any time thereafter. Increasing judicial[1] and academic[2] criticism of this restrictive approach eventually led to proposals from the Law Commission[3] culminating in 1984 in legislative reform.

The Matrimonial and Family Proceedings Act 1984 permits applications to be made here for financial relief following an overseas divorce provided the applicant has not remarried.[4] The leave of the court must, however, first be obtained and the court will not grant such leave unless it considers that there is substantial ground for making the application.[5] This 'filter mechanism' was thought necessary by the Law Commission to rule out undeserving applicants at an early stage such as those who had already achieved a favourable post-divorce settlement of their affairs under a foreign legal system.[6] On the other hand, leave may be granted notwithstanding the fact that there currently exists an order from a foreign court because such an order might be inadequate or not have been complied with or not relate to assets in England. Leave may be granted in certain cases only upon a condition, for example that the applicant undertakes not to enforce any foreign order.

For the jurisdiction of the English courts to be invoked at least one of the spouses must have been either domiciled or habitually resident in this country for at least one year at the date of the application for leave or when the divorce took effect abroad or else have, at the date of application for leave, a beneficial interest in possession in a dwelling house in this country which was at some time during the marriage a matrimonial home of the parties to the marriage.[7]

Before actually making any order for financial relief the court must consider whether in all the circumstances of the case it would be appropriate for such an order to be made.[8] In deciding this question the court must have regard to the following factors which will help to determine whether England is the appropriate venue for the application:[9]
(i)   the connection which the parties to the marriage have with this country, with the country in which the marriage was dissolved and with any other country;
(ii) any financial benefit which the applicant or any child of the family has received, or is likely to receive, in consequence of the divorce by virtue of any agreement or the operation of any foreign law (this would include the deferred dower payable upon the dissolution of a Muslim marriage);
(iii) where a foreign order for financial relief has been made, the amount of the order and whether it has already been or is likely to be complied with;
(iv) whether the applicant had a right to apply for such an order and if she failed to apply the reasons for her omission to do so (in Muslim law a wife

generally has no rights to maintenance for longer than the three-month period of '*idda*' following the divorce[10]);

(v) the availability of property in this country in respect of which an order might be made and the extent to which any order made here is likely to be enforceable abroad; and

(vi) the length of time which has elapsed since the date of the divorce.

If the court is not satisfied that an order would be appropriate it must dismiss the application. However, once the court decides to make an order it possesses the same powers as if the divorce had taken place in this country,[11] save where the sole basis of its jurisdiction is the presence of a former matrimonial home here in which case the court's powers are limited to making a lump sum order up to the value of the respondent's interest in the house or a transfer or settlement of property order or an order for sale in respect of the house.[12] Moreover, in deciding how to exercise its powers the court must consider all the circumstances of the case including all the matters which would be relevant if the application had followed an English divorce.[13]

1 See, e g *Indyka v Indyka* [1969] 1 AC 33 at 38 (Lord Pearce); *Torok v Torok* [1973] 3 All ER 101 at 102 (Ormrod J); *Quazi v Quazi* [1979] 3 All ER 424 at 427 (Ormrod L J); [1979] 3 All ER 897 at 904 (Lord Dilhorne) and 912 (Lord Scarman).

2 See, e g Karsten (1970) 33 MLR 205; Wade (1974) 23 ICLQ 461; Pearl [1974] CLJ 77; Poulter (1977) 127 NLJ 7.

3 Law Com Report No 117: Financial Relief After Foreign Divorce (1982).

4 S 12.

5 S 13.

6 Law Com Report No 117, pp 4-5.

7 S 15. Different jurisdictional criteria apply if the case falls within the Civil Jurisdiction and Judgments Act 1982 Part I.

8 S 16(1).

9 S 16(2).

10 Under Indian statutory law, however, a Muslim divorcee has a right to claim maintenance and the payment of deferred dower does not bar such a claim unless the sum paid is sufficient to take the place of the maintenance which would have been ordered by the courts: see *Bai Tahira v Ali Hussain* [1979] AIR (SC) 362.

11 S 17.

12 S 20.

13 S 18.

CHAPTER 6

Parents and children

INTRODUCTION

6.01 All societies attach considerable importance to the upbringing of children, but their perceptions of what practices are most conducive to the general good (including the welfare of the children themselves) are often strikingly different. This is reflected not only in the allocation of parental rights and duties in the case of a dispute (whether between a mother and a father or between biological parents and foster-parents), but also in the extent to which a parent may lawfully exercise physical control over a child's body, for example through corporal punishment, tattooing, circumcision or similar practices. It is topics such as these which are dealt with in this chapter, while the education of children at school is examined in ch 7 below.

A. CUSTODY

6.02 When a child's parents separate or are divorced the question inevitably arises as to which of them should have custody of that child. Often the most significant concern relates to 'actual custody' or 'care and control' ie the determination as to which parent should have physical care of the child most of the time. However, custody can also have a broader meaning and, while encompassing the right to physical possession, it can extend to parental decisions with regard to other aspects of the child's upbringing, notably in the spheres of education and religion. Custody in this wide sense is now often described by legislation as 'legal custody'.[1]

In some communities there are fixed rules for regulating such matters. This is most apparent in the various schools of Islamic law.[2] In the Hanafi school rigid age limits are prescribed. The mother retains actual custody of her sons up to the age of seven and of her daughters up to the age of nine. Thereafter such custody automatically passes to their father. In the Maliki school the mother only loses actual custody of boys at puberty and of girls at marriage. In Hanbali law, however, the age of seven generally applies in the case of both sons and daughters, while under Ithna Ashari law, which is the law applicable to the majority of Shi'ite Muslims (who are mainly found in Iran, Iraq and India) the age for the transfer of boys is only two. By way of contrast in yet another Islamic school, that of Shafi'i law, the child is entitled to decide which parent he or she wishes to live with as soon as the age of discretion is attained.

In modern times a number of Muslim countries have found these generally rigid age-limits too inflexible and have enacted statutory reforms to enable them to be relaxed in suitable cases.[3] Thus in Egypt and Jordan the Hanafi limits may be extended by a further period of two years if the court considers this would be for the welfare of the child and the Sudan has switched over from the Hanafi rule to that of the Maliki school. The laws of Syria, Tunisia, Iraq and Iran treat the interests of the child as of prime importance and custody may be granted to either parent at the court's discretion in each of these countries. However, the general position in Islamic law is that ultimately guardianship of the child belongs to its father and hence it is he who would have the right to determine its religious upbringing. This explains why Muslim men may marry non-Muslim wives, while Muslim women are forbidden marriage to non-Muslim husbands.[4] Since the Islamic assumption is that children must follow their father's religion a child of the latter type of union would be lost to the Muslim faith.

In many of the patrilineal societies of Africa where bridewealth is paid, one of its main purposes is perceived as that of ensuring that any children born to the wife form part of the husband's lineage. Therefore upon divorce the normal rule under many systems of customary law would be that such children should belong to the husband and his family, although if they were very young they might well be allowed to remain in their mother's care for a short time, e g up to the age of between five and seven.[5] In certain circumstances the mother might be allowed to keep the children permanently, for instance where the children were fathered by someone other than the husband and he had reclaimed the bridewealth upon divorce.[6] Recent reforms in various countries have, however, attempted to establish the principle that the courts should at least pay some attention to the interests of the children themselves in resolving such questions.[7]

1 See, e g Children Act 1975, s 86.
2 See Pearl *A Textbook on Muslim Law* pp 17, 83, 86.
3 See generally Anderson *Law Reform in the Muslim World* pp 141-3, Coulson *Conflicts and Tensions in Islamic Jurisprudence* (Chicago, 1969) pp 109-12.
4 See para 2.04 above.
5 Phillips and Morris *Marriage Laws in Africa* p 126.
6 See, e g Poulter *Family Law and Litigation in Basotho Society* pp 213-8.
7 *Phillips and Morris* p 55.

Policy considerations

6.03 The mode of allocating children to one parent or another according to predetermined and rigid norms seems to imply that children are merely a species of property without individual needs. This view, which was the one which prevailed in the British system of values until comparatively recently, has now given way to one which regards children as young persons in their own right and which seeks to impose considerable limits of the concept of 'parental rights'.[1] Today it is taken for granted here that children need careful and painstaking nurturing if they are both to be good citizens, and perhaps just as importantly, to fulfil themselves and realise their potential to the greatest degree possible. In many societies, however, the expression of such an assumption would be greeted with incredulity. There children are not brought up and developed in this way; rather they grow up by watching and being steadily integrated into the adult activities of their communities from an early age. They are expected to work in the fields or herd livestock or assist in business activities, and their interests are thought to be quite adequately catered for by being incorporated in the wider welfare of the extended family as a whole.[2] Their status in society differs little from that of English children in Tudor times since, as Pinchbeck and Hewitt have explained:

'... the family, not the individual, was the essential unit of social organisation. In such a view, children were no different from the adult members of the family in that they were all conceived as component parts of a far larger unit, the extended family, to whose interest those of the interrelated nuclear families of parents and children were subordinated. The promotion of family ambition, the advancement of family interest, not the realisation of private ambition and the achievement of personal success were seen as the common, all-important social task.'[3]

1 See Pinchbeck and Hewitt *Children in English Society* (Routledge & Kegan Paul, 1969-73) ch XII; Pettit 'Parental Control and Guardianship' in Graveson and Crane (eds) *A Century of Family Law* (London, 1957) ch 4; Hall 'The Waning of Parental Rights' [1972B] CLJ 248.
2 See, e g Hoyles (ed) *Changing Childhood* (Writers and Readers Publishing Cooperative), 1979 pp 57-68, 126-8, 143-6, 154; Parekh (ed) *Colour, Culture and Consciousness* (London, 1974) pp 45, 57; Ellis (ed) *West African Families in Britain* (London, 1978) pp 26, 39, 50-2.
3 *Children in English Society* p 13.

English law

6.04   At common law a father used to have pervasive and exclusive rights over his legitimate minor children.[1] The position of the mother steadily improved during the nineteenth century through the intervention of the legislature, until eventually in 1925 Parliament accorded her parity with her husband in cases which fell to be determined by the courts. The Guardianship of Infants Act of that year proclaimed that courts should henceforth treat the welfare of the child as the most important factor in deciding to whom custody should be awarded and that neither the father nor the mother should from any other point of view be regarded as having a claim superior to the other. This provision is now to be found in the Guardianship of Minors Act 1971, s 1[2] which runs as follows:

'Where in any proceedings before any court . . . the legal custody or upbringing of a minor . . . is in question, the court, in deciding that question, shall regard the welfare of the minor as the first and paramount consideration, and shall not take into consideration whether from any other point of view the claim of the father, in respect of such custody [or] upbringing . . . is superior to that of the mother, or the claim of the mother is superior to that of the father.'

There do not appear to have been any reported cases here yet in which one parent has asserted a right to custody on the explicit basis of a foreign custom. However, the question was raised implicitly in the following three cases in which Muslim fathers claimed a right to supervise their children's religious upbringing through the medium of custody proceedings.[3] Each of them involved a mixed marriage.

1 *R v De Manneville* (1804) 5 East 221; *De Manneville v De Manneville* (1804) 10 Ves 52; *R v Greenhill* (1836) 4 A & E 624; *Re Agar-Ellis, Agar-Ellis v Lascelles* (1883) 24 Ch D 317.
2 As amended by the Guardianship Act 1973, s 9(1), sch 3 and the Domestic Proceedings and Magistrates' Courts Act 1978, s 36(1) (a).
3 See also *Re J* [1973] Fam 106, [1973] 2 All ER 410 in which a Jewish father obtained access to his illegitimate son partly on the basis of the benefits expected from the maintenance of the cultural link between them.

6.05   In *Re O*[1] a Sudanese man and an English woman had married in England and then gone directly to the Sudan. The wife found the conditions there rather hard and returned to England for the birth of each of her two children. Eventually she came back to live here permanently and the husband failed to persuade her to rejoin him in the Sudan. Subsequently, the English courts had to decide which parent should have custody of the son aged six and the daughter aged five. The father, a Muslim, was a successful businessman in Khartoum and wanted to bring up his children as Muslims. The wife was a Christian and held a post as a teacher here; she wanted to bring them up in the Christian faith. Neither child had, however, yet received any religious education. The

Court of Appeal decided that the best solution for the children was for the boy to return to the Sudan with his father and be brought up there and eventually perhaps succeed to the family business, while the daughter remained with her mother here. The Court was aware of the unhappiness likely to be caused by separating the children from one another, but expressed the hope that arrangements would be made for them to meet quite often in the future. A significant factor in the decision appeared to be that the couple originally intended their marriage to be a 'Sudanese' one in the sense that they would bring up their children there.

Ten years later in 1972 a similar judicial concern for children to be brought up with knowledge of the Islamic part of their heritage was manifested in the case of *Jussa v Jussa*.[2] The husband was an Indian Muslim and the wife an English girl. They had married in England and had three children. After the couple separated the children, whose ages ranged from seven to two, went to live with their mother and a dispute as to their custody later came before the Court of Appeal. Both parties appeared to be admirable parents and no criticism was made of either of them. It was held that, although care and control should be vested in the mother because of the youth of the children, their custody should be jointly shared by both parents. Both were capable of co-operating with one another and it was very much in the interests of the children that they should obtain the full benefit of their mixed inheritance. The father should not be denied the opportunity of making a valuable contribution to their upbringing.

A very similar result was subsequently reached in *H v H*.[3] Here an Egyptian Muslim had married an English woman here and there were two children of the marriage, boys of five and one. Following a divorce the county court judge granted both parents joint custody. However, he then proceeded to award care and control of the older boy to the father, so that he could provide him with the appropriate religious and cultural education. This latter aspect of his decision was reversed by the Court of Appeal on the ground that no criticism had been made of the mother and she should therefore have care and control. Ormrod LJ pointed out that by settling in England and marrying an English-woman the father had been faced from the start by the difficulties of a mixed marriage in a foreign country and it would inevitably be difficult for any child to maintain cultural roots which were not those of the people amongst whom he lived. Since the older boy was attending an English school there was no necessity for such a close connection to be maintained with his Arabic and Muslim background that all other factors would have to be overridden. However, by leaving both parents with joint custody the court still enabled the father to play a part in his son's religious and cultural upbringing in line with the earlier decisions.

1 [1962] 2 All ER 10, [1962] 1 WLR 724.
2 [1972] 2 All ER 600, [1972] 1 WLR 881.
3 (1975) 119 Sol Jo 590; (1975) 5 Fam Law 185.

6.06 The willingness of the courts to award sole or joint custody to a parent who wishes to educate a child in the Muslim faith reflects a well-established principle that English law is generally impartial in matters of religious upbring-ing.[1] However, were any particular sect to follow social practices that were felt by the courts not to be conducive to the best interests of children, a parent from that sect might be somewhat less likely to obtain custody in proceedings against someone who was not a member.[2] In the past some judges have evinced a strong aversion to the ways in which Jehovah's Witnesses isolate their children, reject blood transfusions and refuse to participate in festive celebrations.[3] However, recent cases suggest a softer line will be taken in future, especially where other factors are clearly more important and where an undertaking is given by the parent not to involve the child in proselytising and to allow blood transfusions and birthday celebrations in accordance with the wishes of the other parent.[4] At any rate there seems little reason to believe that a traditionalist Muslim mother would be likely to lose custody of her child to a Westernised Muslim father solely because of her degree of social isolation.[5] In *Malik v Malik*[6] the Court of Appeal reversed a decision which had been reached on this sort of basis in a case involving Muslim parents from Pakistan. The trial judge had granted custody of two daughters aged eight and ten to their father because he thought their mother's rather confined and restricted life as a housewife would be less conducive to their welfare. The Court of Appeal drew attention to the cultural patterns of life of Muslim women and concluded that the judge had paid insufficient attention to the practical side of the girls' wellbeing. Continued contact with the father, who was a successful businessman, could be achieved through granting him regular access.

1 *Re Carroll* [1931] 1 KB 317.
2 See, e g *Re B and G* [1985] 6 FLR 134 in which the cult of scientology was described by Latey J as 'corrupt, sinister and dangerous'.
3 *Buckley v Buckley* (1973) 3 Fam Law 106; *T v T* (1974) 4 Fam Law 190. See also *Hewison v Hewison* (1977) 7 Fam Law 207 (Exclusive Brethren – practices designated as 'harsh and restrictive').
4 *Re C* [1978] Fam 105 at 119; *Re H* (1980) 10 Fam Law 248; *Re T* (1981) 2 FLR 239.
5 Cf Bradney 'Religious Questions and Custody Disputes' (1979) 9 Fam Law 139 at 141.
6 C A Transcript No 404/1980 (unreported).

6.07 In a further case, *Adoption Application No 41 of 1975*,[1] an Indian mother successfully asserted a right to custody on the basis of the desirability of her daughter being brought up in the same culture as herself. The child was illegitimate and been placed for adoption soon after it was born. The mother subsequently withdrew the consent she had given to its adoption and the question arose whether her consent should be dispensed with by the courts on the ground that it was being unreasonably withheld. The mother had decided she wanted to keep the child after all and the judge was satisfied that she sincerely believed that such a reunion would ultimately redound to the material and physical welfare of the child. If the proposed adoption by an English couple went ahead the child 'would always be aware of her differences of birth, race and traditions from the adoptive parents and the vast majority of her friends and associates'. His Lordship refused to dispense with the mother's consent and his decision was upheld by the Court of Appeal.

Similar considerations formed the basis of the decision of the court in *Re H*[2] to allow Pakistani parents to remove their infant daughter from the care of a local authority and take her with them on their return to Pakistan. The child had been taken into care because it had been battered by one or both of the parents and the courts had to weigh up the risk of further physical injury if the child was reunited with its parents against the possible psychological harm of growing up here without family ties and in an alien cultural environment. Balcombe J decided to exercise the court's wardship jurisdiction in favour of the parents on the basis that the welfare of the child would be best served by her being returned to her parents on their departure and his decision was upheld by the Court of Appeal.[3]

1 (1975) 5 Fam Law 181.
2 [1978] Fam 65.

3 The decision was subsequently described as 'wise' and 'obviously sensible' by the House of Lords in *A v Liverpool City Council* [1981] 2 All ER 385 at 389, 393 although doubts were expressed as to the jurisdictional grounds on which it was based.

B. FOSTERING

6.08 Children may come to be fostered in England in one of two ways. The first is through the medium of a local authority. This occurs when a child has been taken into care, for instance as a result of court proceedings or because its parents have abandoned it or are temporarily or permanently incapable of providing properly for its upbringing.[1] Here the foster parents are carefully selected by local authority social workers and considerable effort is devoted to matching them with a suitable child.[2] The second method is by means of a direct private placement made by a biological parent with a foster-parent, where the terms of the arrangement are simply a matter of mutual agreement. Usually they will have come into contact with one another through an advertisement and have met only very briefly before the child is placed. Their relationship is determined to a large degree by commercial considerations and reflects the existence of a private 'market' in children.[3]

1 Children and Young Persons Act 1969, s 1; Child Care Act 1980, s 2.
2 Boarding-Out Regulations 1955; Hoggett, *Parents and Children* (2nd edn, 1981), pp 168-9.
3 See generally Holman *Trading in Children: A Study of Private Fostering* (London, 1973).

6.09 A large number of private placements, running into several thousand and perhaps even amounting to the majority of all such arrangements in England, are made by West African students, principally from Nigeria and Ghana.[1] This phenomenon clearly has its roots, at any rate partly, in the customs of the societies from which these couples come.[2] When they arrive in England their primary objective is usually for the husband to obtain an educational qualification which will be of value on their return to West Africa. If they are recently married their first child will commonly be born here rather than delayed until their return since in terms of their culture the birth of a child confers considerable status and prestige. Subsequent children will often also be born here either through a natural desire to enlarge their family or because birth-control techniques are not approved of in their society. A further consideration is the increased chance of survival for babies born in England; the rates of infant and child mortality are still many times higher in West Africa than they are here despite recent improvements in health facilities. In the majority of cases the mother will not be content simply to stay at home and look after the children because this would be to waste the valuable opportunities available in this country. Either the wife will herself seek a qualification or she will take some paid employment in order to provide for the family's immediate or future material needs, especially if the husband's grant is insufficient or if his studies are privately financed. Women in West Africa are brought up to believe they should have a trade or profession and that they should contrive to earn a living even after they have married and had children. They naturally adopt the same attitude while they are in this country.

These parents are prompted to place their children privately with English foster-parents partly on account of difficulties in obtaining suitable day-care facilities and the greater expense and inconvenience of daily child-minders. They do not, of course, qualify for local authority fostering since the requirements for their children being taken into public care have not been met.[3] However, the influence of their cultural background must also be seen as a highly relevant factor. Fostering is common in West Africa, albeit in a rather different form. There children are invariably fostered with relatives, whereas in England they are placed with strangers. Moreover, in West Africa they are fostered at a much older age, whereas in England they are usually placed during the first year of their lives. Furthermore, the underlying purpose is different. In West Africa one of the chief objectives is training, education and a general deepening and broadening of the child's experience of life and social values,[4] whereas in England the primary purpose is to find a substitute parent during a period when the parents themselves are busy with other activities. Nevertheless the fact that fostering is a familiar institution to these students clearly helps to make it an acceptable solution to the problems encountered in trying to meet all the family's needs in England simultaneously.

1 *Holman* pp 31-2.
2 *Holman* pp 167-74; Goody and Groothues 'The West Africans: The Quest for Education' in Watson (ed) *Between Two Cultures: Migrants and Minorities in Britain* (Blackwell, 1977) pp 151 ff; Ellis (ed) *West African Families in Britain* (London, 1978) pp 26-9, 41-2, 52, 64-5, 69-70, ch 5.
3 *Holman* p 172.
4 There would appear to be a marked similarity between the fostering currently practised in West Africa and the 'apprenticing' system common in England in pre-Restoration times – see Aries *Centuries of Childhood* (London, 1962) pp 353-4; *Pinchbeck and Hewitt* pp 25 ff. Later on the English apprentices were grossly maltreated and exploited, but this was not the pattern in the earlier period.

Policy considerations

6.10 A central assumption upon which all the West African parents naturally operate is that whenever they decide to return to Africa their children should automatically accompany them. To return to Nigeria or Ghana without their children would involve shame and scandal and accusations that they had cruelly abandoned them over here. Hence they perceive the physical possession of their children at this juncture as an absolute parental right which cannot be denied them. This, after all, would be the position under the customary law of their tribe and the idea that anyone might be entitled to deprive them of their children against their wishes is quite incomprehensible.[1] However, since the exact length of their studies cannot always be determined in advance (because of the possibilities of having to take full-time employment at various stages to pay the fees or of obtaining additional qualifications or of failing examinations), they are often unable to give the foster-parents a clear indication of when they will wish to remove their children. Alternatively they may be unwilling to do so, believing that if they do specify plainly the very temporary duration of the arrangement (e g for two or three years) the foster-mother will not care for their child as well as if she expected the period to be much longer. The upshot is an open-ended commitment which may well last for many years.[2] As time passes and the child inevitably becomes integrated both into an English school and into the local community some foster-parents may become too attached to the child to allow it to be removed without a struggle. This in turn may lead to 'tug-of-love' disputes in the courts. The idea that parents should have an automatic right to the return of their child is redolent of the concept of the child as a species of property and, as we have seen, this approach is no longer acceptable in modern English society.[3]

In local authority fostering child-care officers are in a position to try to inculcate officially approved attitudes into foster-parents through the close control they exercise over them.[4] A central belief is that while foster-mothers should obviously give plenty of love and affection, they should not try to play the role of a natural mother but rather explain to the child his true origins and why he is currently separated from his natural parents. From this there should develop a clear understanding on both sides of the temporary nature of the commitment and of the overriding bond between the child and its natural parents.[5] A really good foster-mother to a West African child would probably have a constant interest in its parents' studies, always refer to them as 'Mummy and Daddy', talk enthusiastically to the child about its future in West Africa and even carry on a correspondence with its grandparents there.[6]

Many private foster-parents are not, however, imbued with these sorts of attitudes. They regard the child as their own, oppose the establishment of a good relationship between the child and its parents, discourage their visits and generally convey an impression to the child of its parents' inadequacy.[7] They may often genuinely believe that the parents are irresponsible in opting out of caring for the child themselves, but their own insensitive behaviour can only lead to a dangerous crisis of identity for the child later on. In many cases the foster-parents are quite unsuitable to act as such and would almost certainly have been rejected by their local authorities as unfit to look after children in care.[8] Predictably these types of parent live in perpetual terror of having the child removed from them by the natural parents and will often do their utmost to prevent it.

The different perceptions that each side in the transaction has of its proper role can obviously exacerbate conflict in a variety of ways. Among professional social workers it is normally thought extremely important for the biological parents to visit their child during fostering at frequent and regular intervals in order to maintain contact, lessen any feeling of rejection and facilitate its eventual return to them. West African parents generally maintain greater contact with their children than others who foster their children privately,[9] but as already mentioned they are sometimes obstructed by the foster-parents. The differing views of the parties have been graphically described by Biggs:

'The West African mother, visiting the foster home in the same spirit in which she would visit her child in a relative's home, may well bring friends to see her baby, and make an outing of it, but not concern herself over doing anything for the child. She feels she has entrusted this child to the foster mother, and can see no point in interfering with the care he is receiving. She often does not show obvious affection towards her child, which would be quite acceptable in the circumstances at home in Africa, but the foster mother may interpret it as uncaring, heartless behaviour. Also with an African attitude to hospitality, the West African family can see no problem in four or five people instead of two coming to see the child. The foster parents see this as an invasion of their privacy, and a gross presumption on their hospitality. They may well think that their responsibility ends with the care of the child, and although they can accept unwillingly the need of the parents to visit the child, they may only barely tolerate this. The arrival of a party of people to visit a child they are growing to regard as their own, can be a very unwelcome sight.'[10]

Other occurrences during these visits can equally alienate a foster-parent of this possessive type.[11] Following African custom, the parents may give the child a hard ceremonial scrub, or plait their daughter's hair in a distinctive style or try to make the child stand up or walk at a very early age or seek to impose a harsher discipline than is usual in England. The result is often that the foster-mother does her best to discourage future visits and although the parents may at first resent this they may justify their lengthening absences by the thought that they should let the foster-mother carry on with the job for which they are paying her without further disruption. They may take the view that they should place the same amount of confidence in foster-parents as English parents might place in a far-off boarding school, especially if they are given regular reports that their child is happy and well.[12] This can, of course, lead to alienation from the child and rows when the parents subsequently seek to remove him.

The difficulties posed by the 'possessive' foster-mother have been aptly described as follows:

'Sometimes it is the most rewarding relationship they have ever had. Certainly they are conscious of a great investment of their time, money and emotions in the child. They are genuinely concerned for his future, but foresee it as a happier one if it could be spent with them. They often see it as their duty to protect the child from the threat of removal by his natural parents. Gradually, in contrast with the settled life he leads with them, a future with African parents becomes a terrifying prospect to child and foster parents alike. The parents are seen as frightening people with barbaric ways, who may at any moment disrupt the life of the child and the foster parents by claiming his allegiance or even 'kidnapping' him. Very often the whole situation becomes overlaid with racial prejudice. The parents' blackness, unusual social habits, and sometimes alarming manner are much discussed in front of the child, so that he too becomes racially prejudiced, confused and fearful.'[13]

It is quite natural for a black child brought up in this way to identify with his white foster-parents as well as their attitudes and values and aspire to be white himself. This, of course, is bound to lead to acute anxiety and a loss of self-esteem.[14]

1 *Ellis* p 29; *Goody and Groothues* p 160.
2 *Holman* pp 195, 206; *Ellis* p 84.
3 See para 6.03 above.
4 *Holman* pp 265-6.
5 Different considerations, of course, apply in cases of 'long-term' foster-homes, although in practice it is often hard to define the distinction between these and 'indefinite' or 'medium-term' homes – see generally J Rowe 'Fostering in the 1970s' (1977) Adoption and Fostering 15-17.
6 *Ellis*, pp 78-9.
7 *Holman*, pp 78-9; *Ellis* pp 77-8.
8 *Holman* pp 51-5; *Ellis* pp 77, 82-3.
9 *Holman* pp 191-2.
10 In *Ellis* (ed) p 85.
11 Ibid pp 85-7; see also pp 90-1.
12 Ibid p 65.
13 Biggs in *Ellis* (ed) p 88.
14 Milner *Children and Race* (Penguin, 1975) p 146; *Foster Care – A Guide to Practice* (HMSO, 1976) p 43; *Ellis* pp 88-90; Pryce 'Problems in Minority Fostering' [1974] New Community 379 at 384.

English law

6.11 As has already been mentioned, in proceedings relating to the custody or upbringing of a minor the court must treat the welfare of the child as the first and paramount consideration.[1] This principle has been held by the House of Lords to be applicable to disputes between biological parents and foster-parents in just the same way as it operates in disputes between a mother and a father.[2]

1 Guardianship of Minors Act 1971, s 1.
2 *J v C* [1970] AC 668, [1969] 1 All ER 788.

6.12 There have been three reported cases in which West African parents and

English foster-parents have been involved in disputes over the custody of children in private foster care. In the first, *Re O,*[1] the case concerned a Ghanaian girl of nine who had been with her foster-parents since she was three months old. When her natural parents sought to take her back to Ghana with them the foster-parents made her a ward of court and sought care and control. Sir George Baker P held that the girl should remain with her foster-parents and this was later endorsed by the Court of Appeal. The reasons why both courts reached the conclusion that this solution was in the best interests of the child may be summarised as follows:

(i)   The girl herself had expressed a desire to stay in England with the foster-parents. The judge had seen her himself and was convinced that this was a spontaneous reaction on her part and not the result of indoctrination 'unless it was the indoctrination of nine years of loving care'. She was, he stated, '. . . an intelligent, talkative, cheerful, sociable and self-reliant little extrovert', who put his Lordship entirely at his ease.

(ii) The judge was critical of the biological parents. They had 'delegated all their responsibility for nine years and had told untruths about payments and contact with the child in an attempt to persuade the court of their fitness to have her . . . The father had said that he could not go back to Ghana without the child because his family would think that he had sold or pawned her. He would lose face. [He] was incapable of realising that it was fostering over nine years that had caused the trouble and had no real insight into the girl's standards, character and outlook'.

(iii) While the girl might later have to face colour prejudice in England she might equally have problems in Ghana because of her Englishness. 'The girl could well be the butt of children in Accra because she spoke with an English accent and could not speak the language of her parents.'

(iv) There was a distinct risk of disturbing the child's emotional development in moving her. Davies LJ stated: '. . . save for blood and colour she was wholly English. If she were taken away, she might, quite apart from unhappiness and homesickness, suffer both in the long and short view an emotional trauma which might well affect her for life . . . everything pointed to maintaining the status quo. If the child remained, there was no reason to anticipate that anything would go wrong. She would remain in all probability an ordinary English girl, save for her colour. And there were more and more English children in this country who were coloured. But in Ghana, quite apart from the inevitable heartbreak, it was not possible to forecast with any certainty what the future would hold.'

(v)   The foster-parents had been good parents and had lavished loving care and affection on the child. On the other hand, the girl apparently had a real fear of her father.

It is, of course, almost impossible to impugn these sorts of findings especially when so much can turn on the impression the trial judge forms of the parties by actually seeing them in court. However, it is worth mentioning some of the factors which might either have indicated the opposite solution as being in the best interests of the child or which might at any rate help to explain how the 'tug of love' case originated.

First, the foster-parents were not able to have children of their own and at the time the girl was placed with them they were on an adoption society waiting list. Their real wish was to adopt a child and they had tried unsuccessfully to persuade the Ghanaian parents to let them adopt this little girl. Hence the scene was set for conflict from the very beginning. African children are never available for adoption in such circumstances as these and this was not appreciated by the foster-parents. When the girl was two the foster-parents did succeed in adopting two white boys and naturally as she grew up she regarded them as her brothers. This, no doubt, made the foster-parents even more determined to keep the girl throughout her childhood in order to maintain the balance of their family. They even called her by a Christian name of their own making (Tania) rather than the Christian name given to the child by her natural parents (Matilda).

Second, there had obviously been some problems over access by the natural parents. For the first seven years their visits seem to have occurred regularly about six times a year. However, there was clearly some sort of crisis when the child was four. Her parents removed her to London which caused her great distress and she was then returned to her foster-parents. Then five years later she again went to stay with her parents 'somewhat unwillingly'. When the foster-parents came to collect her she was obviously very distressed, having just been told that her parents were going to take her back to Ghana. This coupled with her reported fear of her father strongly suggests the possibility that the foster-parents had done little to make her aware of the importance of her continuing relationship with her parents and of her likely return with them to Ghana.

Third, as Biggs has pointed out:

'When asked in a court case, with whom he would rather live, any child naturally says he would prefer the home he knows to the uncertainty of one which may have been described to him as inadequate, and about which he can only speculate. Especially if there is a possibility of his family returning to Africa, the fears of such a child can be very real: the picture painted in the media, and often reinforced by an ignorant or malicious foster mother, of a wild continent full of fierce animals, snakes, magic and savagery cannot be a reassuring one for a young child. The fact that he might be going to an urban environment with his parents, or to warm, loving and welcoming relatives is not something he can picture and feel enthusiastic about.'[2]

Thus it would seem that the judge paid too much attention to the impression he obtained by seeing the child. Subsequently the practice of doing so in a highly sensitive case was expressly disapproved and it was pointed out that the wishes of children were not of much value at that age.[3]

Fourth, a psychiatrist appointed by the Official Solicitor had advised the High Court of the merits of allowing the girl to return to Ghana, taking the view that the short-term trauma of being separated from her foster-parents would be much less serious than that which she might experience later on if she remained here. There will inevitably be a grave crisis of identity here for such children, while the adjustment process on returning to West Africa will usually prove relatively easy. As Biggs notes:

'. . . it is probable that most children feel immense relief when they go to live in Africa with their parents, even if they have been born in Britain. They recognise that they are just like everyone else. They may never have experienced racial prejudice in Britain, but there is tension in being different and conspicuous, and this tension is often underestimated by foster mothers and social workers . . . [I]t eases any child's anxieties if he is prepared for his journey to Africa by a positive attitude towards his home and culture, and the acceptance from the outset that he will return to it.'[4]

If, on the other hand, they return to West Africa as young adults they may well find to their astonishment that they are unable to adjust to the style of life there and that they are not easily accepted into their extended families. This comes as a deep shock and can lead to despair, breakdown and even suicide.[5]

Fifth, it seems unlikely that the child in *Re O* would have had particular difficulties in West Africa because of her 'Englishness'. One must remember that the majority of West African parents who come to England do so in order to further their education and when they return home they will usually live in an urban environment of considerable sophistication and form part of the élite of their societies. In the major cities there are international schools where the medium is English (which is the official language anyway) and where their children will find many fellow students who have been born abroad.[6] On the other hand, if they spend most of their school years with working class English foster-parents they may possibly not have the same educational aspirations as their parents and may 'under-achieve', though obviously much will depend on the individual circumstances of each case.[7]

1 (1972) Times, 5 December, (1973) 3 Fam Law 40 (Fam Div); (1973) Times, 26 February, (CA); CA Transcript No 86 of 1973.
2 In *Ellis* (ed) p 90.
3 *Re A* (1978) 8 Fam Law 247 discussed at para 6.13 below.
4 In *Ellis* (ed) p 94.
5 *Idem.*
6 Ibid p 93.
7 See *Holman* p 257.

6.13 A similar case involving a Nigerian girl of five occurred at almost the same time as *Re O*. In *Re EO*[1] the child had been placed with English foster-parents during her first year and had remained there ever since. The foster parents were unable to have children of their own and had later adopted a white boy. They had given the Nigerian child excellent care, love and affection and she was naturally well integrated in their home. When the girl was only two her parents had separated and although the father was happy to leave matters as they were the mother wanted to take the child back to Nigeria.

At first instance, after an agonising appraisal of the conflicting factors Latey J decided that on balance the child would be better off in Nigeria because in the long term she would not have the social problems that might face a young black girl in England. However, the Court of Appeal unhesitatingly reversed this decision and ordered that the child remain in the care and control of the foster-parents. Davies LJ stated that since the child had had an English upbringing she was as western in her approach to life as any English girl. In Nigeria she would be in an entirely alien environment. The mother had been unreliable and shown little understanding of the child's needs. The foster parents were fully capable of helping the child to meet any problems that would arise. She was doing well at school and had many friends. If she were taken away after such a length of time she would suffer the most dreadful homesickness which might well result in her developing a permanent emotional scar. Moreover, if she stayed here the mother could still have access to her, whereas if she were returned to Nigeria she would be lost forever to the only parents she had ever known.

Clearly there are far stronger grounds for refusing one parent care and control and the right to take a child back to his or her country of origin when the family is already breaking up and the other parent wishes to remain in England.[2] Here the father was satisfied with the fostering arrangements and had been visiting the child regularly. However, some of the reservations expressed in connection with *Re O* might equally apply to *Re EO*.

Since these two cases were decided by the Court of Appeal in 1973 there have been two further decisions in a similar vein in the High Court. In 1977 in *Re*

B[3] a former African government minister and his barrister wife were refused the return of their children from English foster-parents of modest means. Latey J emphasised that the longer the fostering lasted the more difficult it became to uproot the child from its surroundings. He commented that perhaps embassies, high commissions and other bodies could draw this to the attention of their young nationals here.

In the most recent case, *Re A*,[4] two Nigerian children aged 12 and eight had both been fostered here since they were a few weeks old. Their parents had gone home to Nigeria and sought to have the children returned to them there. The judge found that all the parties were respectable, decent, sincere, well-meaning and well-intentioned. The parents were now prosperous. The foster parents' application to adopt the children was quite rightly rejected by the court as wholly inappropriate, but predictably they were granted custody. The natural parents were given access in England but not staying access in Nigeria (presumably because of a fear that the children would not be returned). The court at least recognised the need for the children to get to know their parents better and learn about Nigeria and its culture so that in the long term they could better decide whether they wished to live there.[5]

In conclusion it is perhaps worth drawing attention to the striking contrast between all these decisions that the children should remain in England and the decision in *Re H*[6] discussed earlier.[7] In that case a Pakistani girl of four who had been battered by her parents and taken into local authority care was returned to her parents on their departure for Pakistan because this was thought to be in her best interests. The crucial consideration was the risk to the child of psychological harm from growing up here without family contacts in an alien cultural environment and this was held even to outweigh the danger of further injuries being inflicted on her by her parents. If that was an appropriate way to approach the long term future of a very young child why, it may be asked, did it not influence the outcome of *Re O* and *Re EO*?

1 (1973) Times, 16 February; (1973) 3 Fam Law 48, CA Transcript No 64 of 1973.
2 See also *Re N* (1973) 3 Fam Law 186 where the father was denied custody of his children in order to take them to Zambia because he was separated from their mother who had decided to stay in England. The mother was given care and control.
3 (1977)Times, 27 January, [1977] CLY 1964.
4 (1978) 8 Fam Law 247.
5 Access by the natural parents was granted in *Re O* (above) but only on occasions and under supervision approved by the Official Solicitor.
6 [1978] Fam 65, [1978] 2 All ER 903.
7 See para 6.07 above.

The scope for reform

6.14 It is a sad commentary on the present situation that one West African parent should be reported as having remarked: 'The unkind foster-mother neglects your child; the kind one steals it.'[1] This statement does, however, draw attention to an area in which the law presently appears to be deficient, namely the legal standards applicable to the control of private fostering.

As we have seen, many private foster-parents not only have a totally erroneous perception of their proper role but would also be regarded by their local authorities as quite unsuitable for the placement of children in public care. This situation is principally accounted for by the fact that the two groups of foster parents are governed by entirely different legal provisions. Those looking after children in the care of local authorities are controlled by the Boarding-

Out of Children Regulations 1955 made pursuant to the Children Act 1948. Private foster parents, by contrast, are regulated by the far less stringent sections of the Children Act 1958, Part I as amended by the Children and Young Persons Act 1969 and the Children Act 1975, and recently consolidated in the Foster Children Act 1980. Despite reforms made by the Children Act 1975,[2] the latter would seem to be open to criticism on a number of counts, including the following[3]

(i) The local authority has no general duty to work for the return of privately fostered children to their natural parents, as it has in relation to children taken into its care.[4] It does not, therefore, have a responsibility for encouraging the maintenance of the child's links with its natural parents and this, as we have seen, is a matter of the greatest importance for the child's future development.

(ii) Those who foster children privately do not have to sign any undertaking as to how the children will be raised and in particular promising to return them to their natural parents, whereas this is compulsory where the children are fostered through a local authority.[5]

(iii) The local authority has no obligation to assist, or even make contact with, the natural parents of privately fostered children. On the other hand, it not only has a duty to keep in touch with the parents of children in its care but also has the power to afford them financial assistance to enable them to receive back their children.

(iv) The local authority has insufficient powers with regard to the removal of a child from an unsuitable foster home. Such a removal can only be effected by means of an order from the juvenile court upon proof of specified grounds.[6] It appears that child-care officers are often reluctant to initiate proceedings unless they feel they have a cast-iron case and will have no difficulty establishing a ground, for instance where they can rely on the fact that the foster-parent has already been disqualified by a previous court order.[7] By contrast, if the child is in care the local authority can remove the child from its foster home without any need to go to court at all.

(v) While it is the duty of a local authority to satisfy itself as to the welfare of privately fostered children in its area, the rules governing its arrangements with regard to visiting these children are far less rigorous than in the case of children in its care. Whereas under the Boarding-Out Regulations children in care must receive a mandatory minimum number of visits each year (depending upon their age),[8] privately fostered children are only required to be visited by local authority officers 'from time to time', and so far as it appears to the authority to be appropriate.[9] Facilities for improving this situation are provided by the Foster Children Act 1980, s 3(2) which empowers the Secretary of State to make regulations requiring visits to private foster children 'on specified occasions or within specified periods of time'. However, so far nothing has been done to implement this provision. The visits obviously need to be properly recorded and the progress of each placement regularly reviewed.

In view of all these deficiencies it is suggested that the legal regulation of private fostering arrangements should be brought into line with that governing children fostered by local authorities as soon as possible.[10]

Ellis makes a key point when she writes:

'It is essential that the placement should proceed in the full knowledge that the fostering arrangement is a temporary one, and that the aim is to reunite the child with his parents as soon as possible. Many placements that begin propitiously, with good will on both sides, end in acrimony because the temporary nature of the placement has been forgotten ... Ideally, at the beginning of the placement there should be a meeting between all parties to draw up a written agreement so that is is clear from the outset what the expectations are . . . and the importance of visiting often and maintaining contact with the child emphasised.'[11]

If at present there are too few social workers to supervise an extension of full local authority regulation to privately fostered children, greater resources should clearly be concentrated on the provision of improved day care facilities, thus significantly reducing the overall need for private fostering.

1 *Ellis* p 74.
2 Ss 95-97.
3 See generally *Holman* pp 216-7, 269-81; *Ellis* pp 97-102.
4 Cf Child Care Act 1980, s 2(3).
5 See Boarding-Out Regulations, reg 20 and sch.
6 Foster Children Act 1980, s 7.
7 *Holman* pp 251-2.
8 See, e g reg 21 (children under five to be visited every six weeks for the first two years).
9 Foster Children Act 1980, s 3(3).
10 *Fostering Black Children* (Community Relations Commission, 1975) p 23.
11 At p 113.

C. DISCIPLINE

6.15 Although there is a natural dearth of hard evidence on the subject, there is a widespread impression that some of the ethnic minority communities, notably those from the West Indies, are used to exercising a more robust form of discipline over their children than is normal in this country.[1] Many West Indian parents appear particularly to favour corporal punishment, adopting roughly the same sort of approach to the correction of their children as parents did in early Victorian England.[2] A responsible West Indian parent does not, therefore, necessarily shrink from imposing quite a violent beating on a wayward child, relying upon the adage 'spare the rod and spoil the child'. Such behaviour would be entirely acceptable and appropriate in the community he or she comes from[3] and the practice is merely continued in England. West Indian parents expect teachers to adopt the same approach at school in this country and regard their failure to do so as a clear sign of weakness.[4]

1 See, e g Findlay *A Study of West Indian Family Life in London* (Zebra Project, 1983) p 6; D Saunders *The West Indians in Britain* (Batsford, 1984) pp 38-9; E J B Rose *Colour and Citizenship* (OUP, 1969) pp 429-30; Cheetham *Social Work with Immigrants* (Routledge, 1972) p 132; Lobo *Children of Immigrants to Britain* p 74. *Ellis* (at pp 49, 115) reports similar findings among West Africans. See also *Multi-Racial Britain: The Social Services Response* (Commission for Racial Equality, 1978) p 16.
2 See, e g *The Education of Ethnic Minority Children* (Community Relations Commission, 1977) p 13.
3 See Clarke *My Mother Who Fathered Me* (London, 1966) pp 156-7, 167-8.
4 See, e g H E R Townsend and E M Brittan *Organization in Multiracial Schools* (NFER, 1972) p 68. This report of a project sponsored by the Department of Education and Science also commented: 'West Indian home discipline was referred to by headteachers as strict, harsh, firm and repressive and was variously described as involving beating, lashing, belting and the strap' *(idem).*

Policy considerations

6.16 Having beaten children cruelly in previous centuries,[1] responsible parents in the white community now take the view that corporal punishment should only be administered in moderation. This would appear to be a reflection not only of an increased concern for the welfare of children but also of a change in society's view as to what is actually conducive to their best interests. Present attitudes are largely a product of the increased legal protection of children against their parents' cruelty which was initiated in the latter part of the nineteenth century.[2] Prior to that time it was believed that children needed to have their wilfulness tamed and be 'broken in', rather in the manner employed for young animals. Severe floggings and whippings were the standard form of punishment both in the home and at school and the beating of children was regarded as entirely proper among all classes.[3] It was only during the reign of Queen Victoria that pressures for reform really built up to such a pitch that legislation was enacted to afford young people at least some degree of protection.[4]

1 See, e g *Pinchbeck and Hewitt* pp 14-17, 302-4.
2 See, e g the Prevention of Cruelty to Children Acts 1889, 1894 and 1904.
3 L Stone *The Family, Sex and Marriage in England 1500-1800* (Penguin, 1979) pp 116-22.
4 See generally W Clarke Hall *The Queen's Reign for Children* (London, 1897).

English law

6.17 Parents are entitled to inflict moderate and reasonable chastisement upon their children in order to discipline and correct them.[1] What constitutes a reasonable degree of punishment depends upon the surrounding circumstances of the particular case, such as the age and strength of the child, the wrong committed and the nature of the punishment itself.

Once the bounds of reasonableness are exceeded the parent exposes himself to prosecution for a variety of criminal offences, depending on the gravity of the injury inflicted upon the child. These can range from simple assault to murder.[2] The other likely consequence is that the child in question (and perhaps also other children in the same household) will be compulsorily taken into the care of the local authority on grounds of ill-treatment.[3]

1 *Bromley* p 316.
2 See, e g Offences against the Person Act 1861, ss 18, 20, 42, 43; Children and Young Persons Act 1933, s 1; *R v Hopley* (1860) 2 F & F 202; *R v Griffin* (1869) 11 Cox CC 402; H K Bevan *The Law Relating to Children* (Butterworths, 1973) pp 188-201; *Bromley* pp 320-2; Smith and Hogan *Criminal Law* (5th edn, 1983) pp 314, 361.
3 Children and Young Persons Act 1969, s 1(2) (a), (b).

6.18 The question whether a foreign parent who is accused of assault can rely on the standards of punishment accepted as normal in his own native community arose in the case of *R v Derriviere*.[1] A West Indian father was charged with an assault upon his 12-year-old son occasioning him actual bodily harm. In punishing the boy for disobedience and for refusing to apologise to his mother the accused had punched him a number of times in the face causing bruises, swellings and lacerations. The Deputy Chairman of the Inner London Quarter Sessions described the attack as a 'brutal assault' and sentenced the accused to six months' imprisonment. On an appeal against the sentence the Criminal Division of the Court of Appeal upheld the decision reached below and set out the broad principle as follows –

'. . . standards of parental correction are different in the West Indies from those which are acceptable in this country; and the Court fully accepts that immigrants coming to this country may find initially that our ideas are different from those upon which they have been brought up in regard to the methods and manner in which children are to be disciplined. There can be no doubt that once in this country, this country's laws must apply; and there can be no doubt that, according to the law of this country, the chastisement given to this boy was excessive and the assault complained of was proved. Nevertheless had this been a first offence, and had there been some real reason for thinking that the appellant either did not understand what the standards in this country were or was having difficulty in adjusting himself, the Court would no doubt have taken that into account and given it such consideration as it could.'[2]

However, the accused in fact had a previous conviction for assaulting his daughter only about 12 months earlier, for which he had been given a suspended sentence. He had already received a clear warning of the unacceptable nature of this type of behaviour in England.

It would appear from this decision that while the different standards of the accused and his native society may in suitable circumstances lead to a more lenient sentence being imposed, they will not afford any defence to the charge itself. The central question of guilt is decided according to a uniform standard applicable to all members of the community and ignorance of English law can afford no excuse.[3]

1 (1969) 53 Cr App Rep 637.
2 At 638-9.
3 See generally paras 10.03-10.05 below.

6.19 So far as the sanction of making a care order is concerned there does not appear to be any reported decision on exactly what constitutes ill-treatment of a child under the Children and Young Persons Act 1969. No doubt many West Indians whose children are taken into care on this ground are surprised and shocked at such a finding. However, even if the courts were to adopt a restricted interpretation of ill-treatment the relevant section is very widely worded and also authorises the making of a care order where the proper development of the child is being 'avoidably prevented or neglected or his health is being avoidably impaired or neglected'.

In practice it is clearly desirable to strike a balance between the need to remove a child whose welfare is genuinely in danger and the equally important need to buttress and support parents who are endeavouring to maintain discipline among their children for their own good. There is much popular discussion about the lack of discipline among West Indian youth and the prevalence of juvenile crime and delinquency in many inner city areas and it is important not to undermine the authority of their parents to such a degree that any child threatened with parental chastisement can simply run off to a social worker and obtain a care order.[1] Indeed it is worth remembering that it is not so much a parent's 'right' to discipline his child as his 'duty' and that one of the grounds for taking a child into care is that the parent has allowed the child to get beyond his control.[2]

1 See letter by Mrs S Best, a West Indian parent, to *The Times*, 27 July 1981; *Findlay* pp 6, 21.
2 Children and Young Persons Act 1969, s 1(2) (d).

D. TATTOOING AND SCARIFICATION

6.20 The practice of tattooing children occurs in many parts of the world, particularly in many Arab countries, in Melanesia and Polynesia, and in parts of India.[1] The objective is often to protect the recipient from evil or harm. The related custom of scarification is found especially in certain African states. The

process involves making incisions in the faces or bodies of children with a view
to providing them with the distinctive and usually indelible mark of their tribe,
clan or lineage and thereby attempting to ensure their lifelong identification
with and loyalty to their own people. Both practices may also serve other
functions and represent a form of ornamental adornment, an initiation rite or
an ordeal to prove courage.

1 The word 'tattoo' is derived from the Tahitian verb 'tatau' (to strike). On both tattooing and
  scarification see generally, V Ebin *The Body Decorated* (Thames and Hudson, 1979); R Brain *The
  Decorated Body* (Hutchinson, 1979).

Policy considerations

6.21 There would appear to be two principal objections that might be raised
to such scarifications and tattoos being done in this country. The first is that
the practices may occasionally be dangerous when performed by an unqualified
person, possibly resulting in serious injury (e g to the child's eye) or leading to
an infection. The second is that where the marks are designed to be permanent
they may later come to be resented by the child when he has grown up,
particularly if he is living in England and if their original purpose later seems
to him to be misguided or irrelevant.

English law

6.22 So far as the tattooing of children is concerned the matter is now
specifically controlled by statute. Formerly it might have amounted to an
offence where the child did not give a valid consent, but probably not otherwise.
In 1966 in *Burrell v Harmer*[1] the defendant was convicted of causing two boys
of 12 and 13 actual bodily harm by tattooing various devices on their arms.
The marks had subsequently become inflamed. The boys had both consented,
but the Divisional Court held that since they had been unable to appreciate
the nature of the act done to them their apparent consent amounted in law to
no consent at all. The decision has been rightly criticised on the ground that
there was no evidence that the boys had not understood the significance of a
tattoo, though no doubt they had not expected the pain caused by the inflamma-
tion.[2] Had they been held to have in fact done so it seems quite likely that no
offence would have been committed. Much would have depended upon the
court's view of the dictates of public policy in this regard. Assuming that the
degree of bodily harm had been slight the tattoos might well have been held
to be lawful in much the same way as are injuries inflicted in the course of
boxing and other 'manly sports'.[3] In the case of *R v Dilks*[4] in 1964 a recorder
at Nottingham Quarter Sessions had earlier taken the view that the consent of
a 13-year-old boy to a tattoo did afford a defence. Here the boy clearly did
understand the nature of the act since he already possessed an array of no fewer
than 22 previous tattoos.

Fortunately the legislature has intervened to put the matter beyond doubt
and the Tattooing of Minors Act 1969 now makes it an offence to tattoo a person
under the age of 18 except when the tattoo is performed for medical reasons by a
duly qualified medical practitioner or by a person working under his direction.[5]
Tattooing is defined as the insertion into the skin of any colouring material
designed to leave a permanent mark.

During the course of the Parliamentary debates which preceded the Act[6] it
was pointed out that many children who had been tattooed came to resent
it subsequently and suffered considerable psychological distress as adults,

particularly in relationships with members of the opposite sex. Plastic surgery to remove tattoos is both difficult and costly to the National Health Service. Mention was also made of the possible risks of infection where tattooing was performed in unhygienic conditions, although this was not thought in itself to justify the legislation. The broad objective was to protect minors from hasty decisions which, on all the available evidence, it appeared likely many of them would soon come to regret. Their youth and inexperience were seen as proper grounds for what would otherwise have been an unwarranted invasion of personal liberty. It was therefore made an offence for anyone (whether he was a tattoo artist or a parent or friend) to tattoo a minor except on medical grounds, e g to denote the performance of an appendix operation or cover an unsightly birthmark. No offence is, however, committed by the minor who has himself been tattooed.

1 (1966) 116 NLJ 1658.
2 See [1967] Crim LR 169.
3 See Smith and Hogan *Criminal Law* (5th edn, 1983) pp 358-61.
4 (1964) 4 Med Sci Law 209.
5 S 2. It is a defence to show that the person charged had reasonable cause to believe that the person tattooed was over 18 and that he did in fact believe this.
6 776 HC Official Report (5th series) cols 266-70; 780 HC Official Report (5th series) cols 1944-53; 279 HL Official Report (5th series) cols 938-50; 301 HL Official Report (5th series) cols 642-56.

6.23 Turning to the question of scarification it is clear from the case of *R v Adesanya*[1] that a parent or other person who scarifies a child may be convicted of a criminal offence, despite the absence of any legislation on the subject. In that case a Nigerian mother from the Yoruba tribe who had made some small incisions with a razor blade on the faces of her two sons aged 14 and nine was charged at the Old Bailey with assault occasioning actual bodily harm. The fresh marks on the children's faces had been noticed by their English foster-parents on their return from their mother with whom they had been spending the Christmas holidays. The foster-parents has promptly called in the police. However, the boys had clearly been willing parties to the incisions which had been performed in a ceremonial atmosphere at celebrations to mark the coming of the New Year. The eldest son had remarked immediately afterwards 'Now I am a Nigerian'. Mrs Adesanya had worn festive clothes for the occasion and there had been singing and dancing and the burning of incense.

Her main line of defence to the charge was that she had merely been following a Nigerian custom in terms of which marks are made on children's cheeks to identify their tribal origin. In fact the incisions themselves were very small by traditional Nigerian standards, being about half to three-quarters of an inch in length. According to her evidence the cuts had not even drawn blood, but at the time of the trial nearly seven months later the scars were still visible, though they were not considered likely to be permanent in the way in which the authentic tribal marks are. Indeed Judge King Hamilton QC was concerned to emphasise that the injuries caused were really 'comparatively trifling'.

The court held that the existence of the Nigerian custom was no defence to the charge brought. An act which was an offence in terms of the English common law or under a statutory enactment could not be treated as lawful simply because it complied with a foreign custom. A clear distinction could be drawn between the cuts in the present case on the one hand, and the piercing of a girl's ear lobes, the removal of birthmarks and the circumcision of young boys,[2] on the other. These latter operations had been practised in this country for centuries and if done with the consent of the child's parent did not amount to an assault. The judge stressed that it was a highly dangerous practice to make cuts with a razor blade high on a child's cheek as Mrs Adesanya had done. It is worth noting however, that the piercing of girls' ears is very commonly done by jewellers who are apparently only required to take those precautions which may reasonably be expected of members of their trade; they do not fall to be assessed by reference to surgical standards.[3]

The judge held that since the cutting of the skin amounted in law to a wound and since the injury was more than 'merely transient or trifling'[4] he was bound to direct the jury that Mrs Adesanya had occasioned actual bodily harm to her children and that they had no alternative but to convict her.

On the question of sentence the judge took into account the fact that this appeared to be the first case of its kind in England, the evidence given by the Nigerian High Commission that the Nigerian community here did not appreciate that it was against the law to practise this custom and also the emotional strain already placed on Mrs Adesanya (who had a good job and an excellent record) as a result of the charge. In granting her an absolute discharge he proffered this general warning:

'You and others who come to this country must realise that our laws must be obeyed . . . [I]t cannot be stressed too strongly that any further offences of this kind in pursuance of tribal traditions in Nigeria or other parts of Africa . . . can only result in prosecution. Because this is a test case . . . I am prepared to deal with you with the utmost leniency. But let no one else assume that they will be treated with mercy. Others have now been warned.'

1 (1974) Times 16 and 17 July, discussed by Poulter 'Foreign Customs and the English Criminal Law' (1975) 24 ICLQ 136.
2 Circumcision is discussed further at paras 6.25 ff below.
3 See *Philips v Whiteley Ltd* [1938] 1 All ER 566.
4 See *R v Donovan* [1934] 2 KB 498 at 509.

6.24 Although the amount of harm required by the law to be inflicted upon a consenting party in order to constitute a battery still seems far from clear,[1] it is thought that the principle in *R v Adesanya* can be justified on four separate grounds. First, there is obviously a risk of grave injury to the child's eye through a sudden movement, especially if the cuts are made, as they were here, by an unqualified person. Second, the marks may turn out to be permanent (if they are for purposes of tribal identification they will naturally be intended to be so) and although the child may give a de facto consent at the time, he may well come to regret it later when he is more mature. Although the marks in the instant case seemed unlikely to be permanent the fact that charcoal was rubbed into the cuts suggests strongly that permanency may have been the main object of the exercise. Therefore although children who are being brought up in England may express a strong desire (as in this case) to comply with a traditional custom in order to preserve their links with their homes in Africa, considerations of public policy require their special protection in a way which would not apply if they were adults. Third, it seems probable that in Nigeria, and indeed in the rest of Africa, the traditional custom is observed far less today than it was in the past and may soon disappear altogether among those families who live in the urban centres and lead the most sophisticated lives. Modern Africans are naturally more interested in achieving national unity than in fostering customs which might lead to the resurgence of old tribal rivalries. Therefore a child in England is in a very different position from one following a traditional mode of life in an African village. Fourth, the decision is consistent with earlier authorities in applying the same system of criminal law to both natives and foreigners without discrimination and yet taking the full circumstances of the case into account when considering the appropriate sentence to impose.[2] The essence of the criminal law is that it imposes a minimum standard of behaviour upon all who live here save where Parliament has expressly enacted an exception for a particular class of people. This has happened only rarely and in certain very limited fields.[3]

One final point may be raised in connection with the particular facts of *R v Adesanya*. Bearing in mind the very small amount of harm (if any) actually done to the children was this perhaps a case where the police should have used their discretion merely to caution the mother rather than prosecute her?[4] Among the circumstances in which the police may quite properly decide that it is not in the public interest for them to prosecute are occasions where the crime committed amounts only to a trivial contravention or a technical breach of the law or where the law is so complex that the offender could not reasonably be expected to know he was committing an offence.[5] It is possible to argue that all these elements were present to some degree in *R v Adesanya* and that an Old Bailey trial surrounded by considerable publicity caused the mother (and no doubt her children) undue and unnecessary suffering.[6] Wilcox cites an instance where a Portuguese waiter confessed that he had offered money to a Ministry of Transport driving examiner as an inducement to issue him a certificate of competency to drive.[7] His explanation that he was simply following the common practice in Portugal was accepted and he was not prosecuted. On the other hand, *R v Adesanya* did afford an opportunity for a precedent to be established and a public warning to be given for the first time about the criminal nature of the scarification of children in England.[8]

1 See *R v Donovan* [1934] 2 KB 498; Glanville Williams 'Consent and Public Policy' [1962] Crim LR 154; *Smith and Hogan*, pp 360-1.
2 See paras 10.03-10.07 below.
3 See paras 10.08-10.16 below.
4 See the criticism made by Harper (1974) 124 NLJ 708.
5 See Wilcox *The Decision to Prosecute* (Butterworths, 1972) ch 8; Glanville Williams 'Discretion in Prosecuting' [1956] Crim LR 222 at 224.
6 See *Wilcox* p 123.
7 Ibid at p 76.
8 In an unreported case in the Kingston-upon-Thames Crown Court in 1978 Nigerian parents were acquitted of a charge of malicious wounding under the Offences Against the Person Act 1861, s 18 on facts similar to those in *R v Adesanya*. However, it is not clear whether the technical meaning of the word 'maliciously' was fully explained to the jury: see (1978) 142 JP 526; Glanville Williams *Textbook of Criminal Law* (2nd edn) p 576.

E. CIRCUMCISION AND GENITAL MUTILATION

6.25 The circumcision of young boys involves cutting off the prepuce or foreskin of the penis. It has been practised for centuries as a religious rite by Jews and Muslims, for both of whom it represents the fulfilment by man of the covenant made between God and the prophet Abraham that He would protect and multiply His seed for ever.[1] It is also a customary procedure in many other societies in Africa and elsewhere.

The circumcision of young girls involves the removal of the prepuce or hood of the clitoris.[2] This operation is commonly referred to as '*sunna*' circumcision and should be contrasted with the more drastic process of 'excision'. Here the clitoris itself is cut out, as is all or part of the labia minora. Female circumcision and excision are widespread in many parts of Africa and along the southern coast of the Arabian peninsula.[3] In some areas, notably the Sudan (except the south), the Somali Republic, southern Egypt, the Red Sea coast of Ethiopia, northern Kenya and many parts of Mali nearly all the girls are 'infibulated'. This operation (commonly referred to as 'Pharaonic circumcision') involves the cutting out of the clitoris, labia minora and at least the anterior two-thirds and often the whole of the medial part of the labia majora. The two sides of the vulva are then fastened together by silk or catgut stitching or else pinned with thorns. A small opening for the passage of urine and menstrual blood is preserved by the insertion of a tiny piece of wood or reed. The girl's legs are then bound together from hip to ankle for up to six weeks so that scar tissue can form and she is rendered totally immobile for this period. In 1979 one estimate put the number of women and girls affected by all these various customs at around 74 million[4] and the figure is almost certainly even higher today.

A great variety of explanations and justifications for female circumcision, excision and infibulation have been put forward by the peoples who practise them.[5] One is that they are needed in order to reduce the sexual drive of women, to preserve a girl's virginity before marriage and her chastity thereafter. However, these operations in reality serve to reduce female sensitivity rather than desire. Another belief is that they are required by religious principles. It is maintained, for instance, that they are decreed by Islamic doctrine. This is refuted by many leading scholars and there is no clear supporting authority in the Koran. A third explanation is couched in terms of initiation rites, portraying the operations as part of a ceremonial passage from one status to another, e g from childhood into adulthood and readiness for marriage.[6] Nowadays, however, many of the operations are being performed on younger children well before puberty and often in the very early years.[7] A fourth justification is to the effect that many societies believe the female genitals to be 'unclean' and thus their removal is regarded as a process of 'purification'. Infibulation, however, has precisely the opposite effect and is extremely unhealthy. Whatever may be the flaws in the various arguments put forward in favour of these practices there cannot be the slightest doubt that they are deeply rooted in the cultures of many communities and will not easily or speedily disappear.

1 See *Genesis* 17; *The Koran* (Sale trans, London 1801) vol 1, pp 23-25, 73, 185. *Genesis* 17: 12 mentions that circumcision should properly occur when the infant is eight days old.
2 See generally, McLean (ed) *Female Circumcision, Excision and Infibulation* (Minority Rights Group Report No 47, 1980); El Saadawi, *The Hidden Face of Eve* (Zed Press, 1980) ch 6; El Dareer *Woman, Why Do You Weep?* (Zed Press, 1982).
3 Circumcision is also practised by the Muslim population of Indonesia and Malaysia.
4 Hosken 'The Hosken Report – Genital and Sexual Mutilation of Females' (Womens International Network News, 1979).
5 See *McLean* pp 6–8; *El Dareer* pp 66-76.
6 See, e g J Kenyatta *Facing Mount Kenya* (London, 1938) ch VI.
7 The most common age in the Sudan is now between six and eight years – see *El Dareer* pp 12-13.

Policy considerations

6.26 In this country the circumcision of young boys has been a legitimate and accepted surgical operation for very many years. As a routine procedure (as opposed to a religious rite) it has admittedly declined considerably in popularity during the course of this century, from around a third of all boys in the 1930s to only about 6% today. The current view of the medical profession here now generally seems to be that there is no rational justification for mass circumcision since the risks to health and hygiene of not being circumcised are minimal.[1] However, while this view is shared by doctors in Sweden (where the operation is extremely rare) the opposite view is taken in the US where circumcision is regarded as the normal procedure for all male infants regardless of religion or culture. In England ritual circumcision of male infants is usually performed in the case of Jews by *mohelim*, who are primarily religious functionaries albeit highly trained, though the operation may occasionally be done by a doctor in hospital. Provided the proper standards of care are adhered to there is normally no danger of harm to the infant,[2] apart from a short period of pain in cases where no anaesthetic is used. Complications can obviously arise occasionally both from the use of an anaesthetic on a very young child and from intense and prolonged crying followed by vomiting and loss of breathing where it is not used. However, long-term harmful consequences appear to be minimal and there are greater hazards in performing the operation on adult men. Few criticisms of the current situation are ever made.[3]

1 See generally 'The Case against Neonatal Circumcision' (1979) 1 BMJ 1163 and correspondence in (1979) 2 BMJ 554, 933, and 1220, upon which much of the discussion of the medical aspects below is based.
2 The greatest danger appears to arise from instances where the operation is regarded as so straightforward that it is allocated to inadequately trained junior staff who then perform it incompetently. This would be more likely to occur in practice in cases of non-ritual circumcision.
3 Cf Berkovitch 'Let's stop this cutting' *Observer*, 2 September 1984.

6.27 By contrast, there has recently been a considerable outcry in Western circles against female circumcision, excision and infibulation.[1] These practices have been castigated as medically unnecessary, damaging and dangerous and branded as 'mutilations'. There can be little doubt that the risks to physical health are considerable, particularly where the operations are performed in unhygienic conditions by unqualified personnel. All sorts of infections and complications can result involving great pain and, in many instances, death.[2] However, the criticisms go much further than this since many of these hazards could be greatly reduced by transferring the operations to hospitals, as is apparently now happening in some countries. The immediate shock and trauma of the experience itself upon a young girl is considerable – the anxiety beforehand, the terror of being seized by older women and held in position, the dreadful pain in the absence of any anaesthetic and the sense of loss and betrayal by parents. The long-term psychological damage may also be significant though at present little research has been done on this aspect. One must bear in mind that where every other girl in a particular village or community has undergone the operation greater stress may well be suffered by anyone who has managed to avoid the experience, and cultural pressures may lead to a feeling of isolation and ostracism. Finally, of course, a major consequence of the operation is that the sexual enjoyment of the woman concerned is inevitably gravely impaired in an irreversible manner and that she may experience far greater hazards in childbirth.

The suggestion has been made that these practices may often amount to the torture of children and thus constitute a violation of elementary human rights. The UN Declaration of the Rights of the Child, adopted by the General Assembly in 1959, refers to the right of a child to enjoy special protection and be given opportunities to enable him or her to develop physically, mentally, morally, spiritually and socially in a healthy and normal manner and in conditions of freedom and dignity.[3] Moreover, both the International Covenant on Civil and Political Rights and the European Convention on Human Rights outlaw torture and cruel, inhuman or degrading treatment.[4]

1 Eg at the Copenhagen Non-Governmental Organisations Forum held in 1980 parallel to the UN World Conference of the UN Decade for Women.
2 See *El Dareer* ch 2.
3 Principle 2, reprinted in I Brownlie, *Basic Documents on Human Rights* (2nd edn, 1981) p 109.
4 International Covenant, art 7; ECHR, art 3.

English law

6.28 The basic right to bodily integrity which everyone possesses under the English common law means that any unlawful interference with this right amounts to an assault or battery, at the very least, and might in appropriate circumstances entail the statutory offence of unlawful wounding or the causing of grievous bodily harm.[1] The question raised in cases of circumcision, excision or infibulation is whether the operation can be justified as constituting lawful as opposed to unlawful interference with this right. Although there are no precedents in this field to rely on there would appear to be three possible grounds upon which a defence of lawfulness might succeed at common law.[2] The first is that the procedure is therapeutic. If this can be established a parent can validly consent to it on behalf of a child who is too young to understand what is being done.[3] It would appear unlikely that this line of defence could generally succeed other than in comparatively rare instances of physical defect or abnormality.[4] Second, although the matter is not entirely free from doubt, it seems that a parent may equally validly authorise a non-therapeutic operation, provided it is not actively against his child's interests. This would appear to have been the basis upon which the vast majority of male infants have been circumcised in this country with impunity from time immemorial. There is no need under this heading for the parent to establish that the operation is positively beneficial for the child, merely that he was acting reasonably in authorising it.[5] Third, it has been tentatively suggested that a parent may even authorise something that is against his child's interests if it is compensated by sufficient advantage to others and is not seriously detrimental to the child.[6] This exception is particularly apposite for establishing the legitimacy of transplant operations which directly benefit patients in pressing need (eg a brother or sister).[7] It seems extremely unlikely that it could justify the more remote and controversial benefit of satisfying a deeply-felt community attachment to traditional customs. Moreover, to the extent that female circumcision, excision and infibulation are in fact mutilations and hence seriously detrimental to the child, the defence would be ruled out in any event.

It thus appears that, at common law, while the circumcision of infant males here is lawful, provided parental consent has been given, no amount of parental agreement or support can legitimise the circumcision, excision or infibulation of a young girl in this country, unless the operation is for therapeutic purposes.[8] It would be no defence to a charge of assault or battery (or worse) that the operation was performed in a hospital by a qualified doctor (as has recently happened in Sweden) rather than by a traditional practitioner specially brought over for the purpose (as has been reported to have regularly occurred in France).[9]

1 See Offences Against the Person Act 1861, ss 18, 20, 47. If the child is under 16 a prosecution might also be brought under the Children and Young Persons Act 1933, s 1: see Hayter 'Female Circumcision – Is There a Legal Solution' (1984) JSWL 323 at 328-9.

2 See generally Glanville Williams *Textbook of Criminal Law* (2nd edn, 1983) pp 575-6; Skegg 'Consent to Medical Procedures on Minors' (1973) 36 MLR 370.
3 In cases of emergency a doctor may sometimes justify an operation on grounds of necessity and even parental consent would not be required: see Skegg 'Medical Procedures without Consent' (1974) 90 LQR 512; Glanville Williams [1978] Crim LR 132-4.
4 An obvious example in the case of a boy is where he has an unretractable foreskin: see (1979) 1 BMJ 1163.
5 Cf *S v McC; W v W* [1972] AC 24 at 44, 57-8 (blood tests).
6 Glanville Williams p 576 who also expresses the view that in neither of the last two cases would parental authorisation be sufficient if the child was old enough to understand what was involved and was either left uninformed or actually withheld his consent.
7 Cf the American decisions referred to by Skegg (1973) 36 MLR 370 at 377-8.
8 See generally Mackay 'Is Female Circumcision Unlawful?' [1983] Crim LR 717.
9 See *McLean* p 6; Swain 'Curbing "Matrons" from Mali' *Sunday Times* 1 August 1982.

6.29 Although the legal position outlined above seemed to some to offer sufficient protection for girls, the absence of any prosecution in this area could be interpreted by others as evidence that the law on the question was insufficiently clear and that a specific statutory offence needed to be created with all the attendant publicity which such legislation would inevitably entail. Public concern arising from allegations that such operations were being performed in this country eventually led Lord Kennet to introduce a private member's bill on the subject in the House of Lords in 1983. Substantial disagreement over the detailed wording of the legislation contributed, however, to a delay of more than two years before the Prohibition of Female Circumcision Act was finally enacted at the third attempt in 1985.[1]

Section 1(1) of the Act makes it an offence for any person:

'(a) to excise, infibulate or otherwise mutilate the whole or any part of the labia majora or labia minora or clitoris of another person; or
(b) to aid, abet, counsel or procure the performance by another person of any of those acts on that other person's own body'.

This section defines the prohibited operations in the broadest possible terms so that even the mildest form of female circumcision ('*sunna*') is covered. A girl who mutilates herself is not guilty of any offence, but other operators and helpers are, whether or not they possess any medical qualifications, as are parents and relatives who counsel or procure the operation.[2]

A person convicted on indictment of one of the offences listed in s 1(1) is made liable to a fine or to imprisonment for a term not exceeding five years or to both.[3]

1 Of the two earlier bills that were lost, the 1983 Bill fell upon the early dissolution of Parliament occasioned by the general election and the 1984 Bill fell because of government dissatisfaction with certain aspects of the drafting: for the proceedings in Parliament on the three bills see HL Official Reports (6th series): vol 441, cols 673-97; vol 442, cols 439-56, 724-56; vol 444, cols 990-1003; vol 447, cols 72-91, 392-4, 1076-82; vol 450, cols 212-22; vol 463, cols 1223-45; vol 464, cols 570-97; vol. 465 cols 207-24, 1134-48; HC Official Reports (6th series); vol 77, cols 581-5 and *Official Report*, Standing Committee 'C', 3 April 1985.
2 The liability of parents and relatives who 'counsel or procure' arises from s 1(1)(a) and the Accessories and Abettors Act 1861, not from s 1(1)(b) which only covers the counselling and procuring of self-mutilation – see paras 10.24-10.25 below.
3 S 1(2).

6.30 Section 2 sets out the exceptions to the offences and it was in the drafting of these that so much difficulty was experienced in Parliament in obtaining a consensus. Clearly doctors performing legitimate surgical operations were not intended to be affected in the manner in which they dealt with patients whose physical health was endangered by, for example, cancerous or pre-cancerous conditions. Nor were standard incisions (such as episiotomy) performed around the time of childbirth to be interfered with. The same principle applied to operations on girls who were born deformed and needed to have surgery to correct an obvious abnormality, as well as to the manner in which doctors dealt with problems of ambiguous sexual development and secondary virilism. While these three types of exceptions appeared to be sufficient to satisfy a large part of the medical and nursing establishments and were therefore incorporated in the two earlier bills, the Department of Health and Social Security was, in addition, concerned to protect the freedom of surgeons to continue to perform a very limited number of operations (estimated at no more than perhaps 20 a year)[1] where they felt such a procedure was in the interests of a girl's mental health. Some physically healthy girls whose genitals are functionally normal are nevertheless convinced that they are abnormal and consequently suffer from anxiety and depression. Most girls suffering from such delusions can be helped simply by psychiatric treatment and counselling, but a few cannot and good professional practice apparently accepts that surgery known as 'trimming' may be appropriate in these rare instances.[2] However, an exception based too broadly on mental health reasons might have been exploited by practitioners performing excisions or mutilations on the ground that the girls might be depressed because without the operation they would not be conforming with the traditional customs of their community. This led the government to propose an amendment to the mental health exception to the effect that in determining whether an operation was necessary for the mental health of a person 'no account shall be taken of the effect on that person of any belief on the part of that or any other person that the operation is required as a matter of custom or ritual'.[3] This phraseology was criticised by the Chairman of the Commission for Racial Equality in a letter to Lord Kennet in which he stated:[4]

'The Commission shares your concern at the formulation of the amendment. However well-intentioned in seeking to avoid any circumvention of the Bill's purpose, clause 2(2) could be indirectly discriminatory in effect. A doctor, when assessing mental health as justifying the performance of an otherwise prohibited operation, will normally base his judgment on the patient's state of mind as he finds it. To suggest that some reasons for that state of mind may be acceptable and others, broadly confined to those which might affect persons of African origin or descent, are not, is, in our view, discriminatory and therefore to be avoided.

On a more general point, so far as I am aware this is the first time, at least in recent years, that draft legislation has explicitly sought to exclude from consideration the relevance of a custom of an ethnic group settled in the UK. Any such exclusion or precedent would be undesirable on principle.'

In Lord Kennet's view the Government's amendment would have a racist effect in that white mental health would be a good ground for an operation while black mental health would not.[5] Of course, this rather exaggerated the effect of the amendment since under its terms a black West Indian girl, for instance, who was sufficiently distressed by feelings about the size of her genitals would clearly qualify for the 'trimming' operation if there was a sufficient danger to her mental health. On the other hand, a Somali girl whose reason for wanting the operation was based on tradition and custom would be barred, even though her mental anguish might be just as great. Hence the differentiation in the amendment was based on culture rather than colour, on ethnicity rather than race. Indeed, in describing the mental health clause as 'indirectly discriminatory' the Chairman of the CRE no doubt had in mind the provisions of the

Race Relations Act 1976 which render unlawful certain actions which have a disproportionately adverse impact on particular groups defined by their ethnic origin.[6]

The Government's response was given by Lord Glenarthur as follows:

'. . . it seems to me that the essential purpose of the whole Bill . . . is to prevent acts of cruelty or harm from being performed under the cloak of custom or ritual . . . Cruelty or harm is implicit in the custom or ritual in this particular sort of operation. As I said, this custom or ritual is implicit in the title itself, since the term 'female circumcision' has no precise anatomical significance. What it does signify is the customary or ritual character of the acts to which it refers. I submit that interference with that sort of custom or ritual is inherent in the basic purposes of the Bill. What we are saying is that these particular customary practices are not compatible with the culture of this country. I do not see this as attacking any racial group; on the contrary, we are saying that girls and women living here should have the protection of the law against practices which, whatever sanction they may enjoy in other countries, are thoroughly repugnant to our way of life . . .'[7]

Lord Kennet considered the wording of the mental health clause might still cause offence, especially to members of black women's organisations campaigning for the elimination of female circumcision through a process of health education as well as by legal means. He therefore proposed in an amendment that instead of a mental health exemption provision should simply be made for doctors to be free to perform 'minor cosmetic' operations, as well as those required on grounds of physical ill-health.[8] This was rejected by the government on the grounds that the words 'minor' and 'cosmetic' were too vague and, that they might not cover such legitimate surgery as the so called 'sex-change' operations performed on female to male transexuals.[9] Such words, moreover, might bar the rectification of a gross abnormality while possibly leaving a loophole for some of the operations intended to be outlawed.[10] Subsequently Lord Hatch proposed an amendment whereby in place of the reference to 'custom and ritual' it might be made clear that in assessing a person's mental health no account should be taken of the effect upon that person of any 'non-medical factors'.[11] This too was rejected by the government as being insufficiently explicit about mental health reasons and capable of creating a loophole by allowing a person performing the type of operation sought to be prohibited to claim that if he or she had not done so the girl in question would have suffered psychological distress.[12] The final upshot is that s 2 of the 1985 Act provides for exemptions from criminal liability in the following terms:

'(1) Subsection (1)(a) of section 1 shall not render unlawful the performance of a surgical operation if that operation –

    (a) is necessary for the physical or mental health of the person on whom it is performed and is performed by a registered medical practitioner; or

    (b) is performed on a person who is at any stage of labour or has just given birth and is so performed for purposes connected with that labour or birth by –

        (i) a registered medical practitioner or a registered midwife; or

        (ii) a person undergoing a course of training with a view to becoming a registered medical practitioner or a registered midwife.

(2) In determining for the purposes of this section whether an operation is necessary for the mental health of a person, no account shall be taken of

the effect on that person of any belief on the part of that or any other person that the operation is required as a matter of custom or ritual.'

1 See 447 HL Official Report (6th series) col 88 Lord Glenarthur.
2 Ibid cols 74, 87. Strong views were expressed by some members of the House of Lords that such adolescent girls needed psychotherapy rather than surgery: see, eg Lord Kennet (col 77), Baroness Jeger (cols 80-1), Baroness Cox (col 81) and Lord Hatch (col 82). However, a letter from the president of the Royal College of Obstetricians and Gynaecologists to Baroness Masham stated – 'It is in the view of this college very important to have 'mental' and 'physical' included, as mental conditions may require surgical treatment to get rid of the mental problems. The idea that mental problems are all treated by psychiatric means is just not true' (465 HL Official Report (6th series) col 214); see also the speeches of Lords McNair and Richardson, 464 HL Official Report (6th series) cols 579, 581-2.
3 447 HL Official Report (6th series) col 74.
4 Ibid col 78.
5 Idem.
6 For discussion of the Act's provisions on indirect discrimination, see paras 7.24-7.26 and 9.16-9.19 below.
7 447 HL Official Report (6th series) col 86.
8 464 HL Official Report (6th series) cols 571-4.
9 Ibid cols 584-6 (Baroness Trumpington).
10 Ibid cols 577 (Lord Coleraine) and 580 (Lord McNair).
11 464 HL Official Report (6th series) cols 592-3; 465 HL Official Report (6th series) cols 207-9.
12 464 HL Official Report (6th series) cols 594-5; 465 HL Official Report (6th series) cols 212-3 (Baroness Trumpington).

6.31 No doubt when the first prosecution under the Act is undertaken there will be protests from some quarters that the legislation is sexually discriminatory, quite apart from allegations about the ethnic distinction made explicit in s 2(2). The underlying basis for the legality of the custom of male circumcision appears to be that the operation does not involve any real harm to boys, whereas in most forms of female circumcision the harm to girls is incontestable. However, the mildest form of female circumcision, known as *sunna*, is broadly the female equivalent of male circumcision, involving only minor trimming, and if done by a competent person in hygienic conditions it should not cause any greater health risks than male circumcision. Is there, then, a sound justification for distinguishing between the two types of operation? Probably the strongest basis for doing so is by arguing that only by making all variants of the custom of female circumcision unlawful will the more harmful aspects be eliminated. The experience of legislation in the Sudan is illuminating in this regard. In 1946 infibulation (Pharaonic circumcision) was banned there through an amendment to the penal code, while leaving *sunna* circumcision untouched. However, the effect of this was that in practice many parents arranged with midwives for their daughters to undergo an 'intermediate' type of operation, which was far more extensive and damaging than *sunna* circumcision, under the false impression that so long as infibulation was avoided no offence was being committed.[1] If the most injurious operations are to be effectively outlawed in this country, as well as the underlying assumptions about female sexuality and the position of women in society which buttress them, perhaps the Act is right to prohibit even the mildest forms as well.

1 See *El Dareer* pp 3-5.

6.32 So far as the exception to the mental health exemption in s 2(2) is concerned the courts will have to decide upon the meaning to be attributed to the phrase 'required as a matter of custom or ritual.' Although the terms 'custom' and 'ritual' were criticised by Lord Kennet in the House of Lords debates as vague,[1] presumably the intention of Parliament was that reasons based on tradition or religion were to be encompassed by this wording, whether or not the practices were believed to be strictly necessary or not.

Where an operation to circumcise, excise or infibulate a girl has merely been planned here and has not yet taken place the matter could either be reported to the police with a view to a prosecution under s 1(1) (b) of the 1985 Act or steps could be taken to prevent its occurrence by making the child a ward of court. The latter process may be invoked by any interested person who is concerned for the child's welfare[2] and from that moment no operation can take place unless the court holds it to be in the child's best interests. This procedure might well prove useful in an emergency,[3] especially if the police are uncertain about their powers to intervene because, for instance, the plan is to remove the child from the jurisdiction to perform the operation abroad.

1 464 HL Official Report (6th series) col 572.
2 See Lowe and White *Wards of Court* pp 36-8.
3 It was invoked successfully by an educational psychologist to prevent the sterilisation of an 11-year-old girl with a rare congenital handicap in *Re D* [1976] Fam 185, [1976] 1 All ER 326.

6.33 Obviously the impact of any legal proceedings in England would be insignificant in comparison with the enormity of the problem as a whole. That needs to be tackled by the citizens and governments of the countries directly affected, with the backing of international organisations such as WHO and UNICEF, with the moral support of outsiders. The customs are so deep-seated that one should recognise from the outset that the struggle to eliminate them is bound to be a very long one. The 40-year-old legal ban on Pharaonic circumcision in the Sudan, for instance, appears to have had very little practical effect.[1] So far as the English dimension of the question is concerned, it is clearly important that health education programmes should be established quickly to persuade the relatively few members of the ethnic communities concerned who are resident here that they should abandon the practices because of their harmful effects. During the course of the Parliamentary debates on the 1985 Act several pleas were made for government funding to be made available to assist voluntary agencies working in this field and undertakings were given by ministers that applications for support grants would be considered.[2]

1 See *El Dareer* pp 95-6.
2 See e g *HC Official Report*, Standing Committee 'C', 3 April 1985, cols 15-16; 465 HL Official Report: (6th series) cols 1140, 1142.

CHAPTER 7

Education at school

INTRODUCTION

7.01 All cultures depend for their vitality in large part upon the effectiveness of their transmission from one generation to the next through the medium of education. It is, therefore, only natural to expect that the minds of ethnic minority parents should be greatly exercised by what takes place in English schools. They are concerned that their customs and cultures should be afforded proper respect and appreciation, both in the general running and organisation of school activities and in the curriculum itself. In this they have the support of many educationalists who have emphasised the importance for a minority child of the establishment of a strong and positive cultural identity if he is to make the most of his schooling and feel confident and secure in his future contacts and dealings in the wider society.[1]

Superficially, there is perhaps a certain attraction in a philosophy of assimilation in the sphere of formal education, the aim being to improve race relations among the next generation by attempting to ensure that its members all have a uniform cultural background. Such an approach was briefly espoused by educational policy-makers here during the late 1950s and early 1960s,[2] but forced assimilation is likely to meet with a great deal of resistance and it is worth heeding the view of one commentator from the US who is of the opinion that such a venture is misguided and likely to be counterproductive:

'. . . a recognition and appreciation of the culture, heritage and values of disadvantaged minority groups may in fact be essential to the successful integration of these groups. Minority children will be more willing to participate in mainstream America when they are no longer under the threat of having their culture suppressed.'[3]

It seems highly probable that the same is true of ethnic minority children in this country. They will inevitably acquire many of the values and aspirations of their white classmates and grow up to be very different culturally from their parents,[4] but there is nothing to be gained by attempting to impose a wholesale transformation by compulsion.

The range of cultural practices which raise legal issues in the sphere of education is wide, covering such matters as religious instruction, teaching in the mother-tongue, appropriate forms of dress, dietary restrictions and the separation of the sexes. Broad questions relating to the adoption of a multicultural curriculum and the continued desirability of denominational schools also need detailed consideration. First, however, it is necessary to present a brief outline of how the educational system is organised, an indication of the different types of school available and of the general distribution of powers and responsibilities in this sphere.[5]

1 See e g G K Verma and C Bagley *Race, Education and Identity* (Macmillan, 1979); R Jeffcoate *Positive Image: Towards a Multiracial Curriculum* (Writers and Readers Publishing Cooperative, 1979).

2 See 'Education For All': Report of the Committee of Inquiry into the Education of Children from Ethnic Minority Groups (*Swann Committee Report*), Cmnd 9453 of 1985, pp 191-8.
3 Fong 'Cultural Pluralism' (1978) Harvard Civil Rights – Civil Liberties Law Review 133 at 169.
4 See, e g C T Kannan *Cultural Adaptation of Asian Immigrants* (Greenford, 1978).
5 See generally Regan *Local Government and Education* (London, 2nd edn 1979); Liell and Saunders *Law of Education* (Butterworths, 9th edn 1984).

7.02 The foundation stone of the modern system of schooling is the Education Act 1944, a wide-ranging and comprehensive piece of legislation which introduced a number of fundamental reforms.[1] One of the most important of these was the achievement of a new settlement of the long-standing 'religious difficulty' in education, whereby the state gained a greater measure of control over certain schools formerly run by the churches in return for compulsory non-denominational religious education in all state schools and higher government subsidies for schools controlled by voluntary bodies. Up until the latter part of the nineteenth century education had been dominated by church interests with the churches owning, maintaining and running most of the schools.[2] However, as the move towards making education more widely available gathered pace it became clear that substantial financial assistance from the state was required, not only to build more schools but also to bring up to a respectable standard many of those already being run by the churches.[3] The final upshot of the reforms means that the state or 'maintained' sector now includes the following four different categories of school –

(i) 'County schools'. These schools (of which there are about 18,000) are wholly owned, maintained and staffed by a local education authority (LEA). They are somewhat inaptly named since the LEAs are not confined merely to the counties but include the metropolitan districts, the outer London boroughs and the Inner London Education Authority (ILEA). For this reason county schools are more commonly referred to simply as 'LEA schools'. Around 78% of pupils in the maintained sector attend these schools.

(ii) 'Voluntary controlled schools'. Controlled status was a creation of the 1944 Act and was designed to meet the needs of those voluntary bodies who found themselves unable to meet even a small proportion of the cost of upkeep of their schools. It enables a voluntary body to retain a limited influence over the running of the school in return for total relief from any financial burdens. The voluntary body is entitled to nominate only a minority of the governors, while the LEA appoints the majority.[4] Ownership of the school remains with the original foundation, but the LEA bears all the running costs and appoints the teachers. There are about 3,500 controlled schools.

(iii) 'Voluntary aided schools'. No loss of overall control by the voluntary body is involved with these schools, but they benefit from substantial assistance from the state. For this reason they have proved to be acceptable, for instance, to Roman Catholic authorities in a way in which controlled schools are not. Aided status allows the original foundation to appoint the majority of the governors with the minority being appointed by the LEA.[5] It is the governors who are responsible for the appointment of teachers, although the LEA usually has to be satisfied as to their educational suitability. The governors also control admission to the school. The LEA is responsible for the maintenance and repair of the interior of the school buildings as well as for all other educational expenditure such as teachers' salaries. The governors have to pay for the upkeep of the exterior of the school buildings and for improvements generally, but they are entitled to a direct government grant to cover such capital expenditure of up to 85% of the cost. Not surprisingly, in view of these generous terms, the majority of voluntary schools fall into this category and at present there are around 4,800 of them.

(iv) 'Special agreement schools'. This category, which dates back to 1936, occupies an intermediate position between aided and controlled schools. The status arises from a special agreement by the LEA to pay between half and three-quarters of the capital costs of building a new or extending an existing voluntary secondary school. New special agreement schools are rarely established today and only about 100 survive. The arrangements with regard to internal and external upkeep are as for aided schools, as is the right of the foundation to appoint the majority of the governors. However, the teachers are appointed by the LEA.

The vast bulk of schools in the voluntary category are currently owned by the Church of England (about two-thirds) and Roman Catholic foundations (one-third). They are attended by only about 22% of pupils in the maintained sector. Of those pupils undergoing secondary education in this sector 88% are at comprehensive schools. The state sector accounts for the education of around 95% of pupils; the remainder are at private or independent fee-paying schools (many of which are often misleadingly referred to as 'public' schools).[6] These schools (of which there are currently around 2,300) have to be registered with the Department of Education and Science (DES).[7]

1 There have been a number of more recent Education Acts, notably for present purposes that of 1980.
2 See K Evans *The Development and Structure of the English Educational System* (University of London, 1975) p 9.
3 See 'Educational Reconstruction'; Cmd 6458/1943, paras 43-62; *Evans* pp 38-9, 60; M Cruickshank *Church and State in English Education* (London, 1964) p 138; *The Fourth R: Report of the Commission on Religious Education in Schools* ('*Durham Report*') (SPCK, 1970)· p 12.
4 Education Act 1944, ss 18-19; Education Act 1980, s 2.
5 Education Act 1944, ss 18-19; Education Act 1980, s 2.
6 Direct-grant schools are in the process of being phased out, but assisted places schemes at independent schools have been established under the Education Act 1980, s 17 for academically able pupils whose parents cannot afford the full tuition fees.
7 Education Act 1944, s 70.

7.03 Turning next to the structure of authority and responsibility in the educational system, 1 of the 1944 Act provides as follows:

'It shall be the duty of the Secretary of State for Education and Science to promote the education of the people of England and Wales and the progressive development of institutions devoted to that purpose, and to secure the effective execution by local authorities, under his control and direction, of the national policy for providing a varied and comprehensive educational service in every area.'

Since 1944 the relationship between the Minister and the local authority has usually been seen in terms of a partnership of equals for, although in certain circumstances the Minister can impose his will upon a local authority which in his opinion is acting unreasonably,[1] a very large measure of initiative and discretion is conferred upon the LEAs by virtue of the powers and duties specifically allocated to them by the Act.[2] For instance, s 8 provides that it shall be the duty of every LEA to secure the availability in their area of sufficient schools for providing primary and secondary education offering all pupils 'such variety of instruction and training as may be desirable in view of their different ages, abilities and aptitudes'. Section 23 states that LEAs shall broadly control secular instruction in county schools and voluntary schools (other than aided schools). According to the model articles of government of county and controlled secondary schools:

'The local education authority, after consultation with the Governors, shall determine the general educational character of the School and its place in the educational system. Subject thereto, the Governors shall, in consultation with the Head Teacher, have the general direction of the conduct and curriculum of the School . . . the Head Teacher shall control the internal organization, management and discipline of the School . . . .'[3]

In practice in these schools matters relating to the curriculum are devolved to the head teacher and his staff, as indeed they are in aided schools, with the result that they possess a great deal of autonomy.[4] The right and power of the head teacher to prescribe discipline for the school has been specifically confirmed by the courts.[5]

While control by the DES over LEAs and schools generally tends to be confined to the issuing of detailed regulations and the frequent publication of circulars and administrative memoranda rather than any more forceful measures, recent years have witnessed a marked increase in the power of the DES to shape policy in furtherance of central government strategies. LEAs function through education committees established under arrangements approved by the Secretary of State; they are partly elected and normally include teachers and representatives of the main religious denominations.[6] There is a statutory requirement that both teachers and parents be represented on the governing bodies of all schools in the maintained sector.[7]

Information about individual schools has, by law, to be published by LEAs or the governors of aided or special agreement schools in order to assist parents in making an appropriate choice of a school for their children.[8] This information has to cover a number of matters about which ethnic minority parents may be particularly concerned, such as whether the school is co-educational or single-sex, whether it has an affiliation with any religious denomination, particulars relating to religious and sexual education, the policy on rules about dress and uniform and the public examinations for which pupils will commonly be entered.[9]

1 See s 68 of the 1944 Act.
2 See *Regan* pp 31-5.
3 See Alexander and Taylor *County and Voluntary Schools* (London, 1977) pp 89-90.
4 *Regan* p 69.
5 See e g *Spiers v Warrington Corpn* [1954] 1 QB 61 at 68.
6 See Part II of the First Schedule to the 1944 Act; DES Circular 8/73; *Regan* p 24-5.
7 Education Act 1980, s 2.
8 Education Act 1980, s 8(5); Education (School Information) Regulations 1981, reg 4 and Sch 2.
9 See generally Harris 'The Publication of School Information' (1982) 12 Fam Law 156.

A. RELIGIOUS EDUCATION

7.04 Many ethnic minority parents who are adherents to religions other than Christianity naturally feel that the education system should respect and reflect their own faiths and they are therefore opposed to the idea that their children should have to attend classes or assemblies whose aim is confined to the proclamation of Christian doctrine. Instead such parents wish their children to receive at least some religious education at school in their own faiths, as would often happen in their countries of origin.[1] While most see the aim of such teaching as being to promote knowledge and understanding of the significance of religious experience without any attempt being made to inculcate a specific set of beliefs, some ethnic minority parents (notably Muslims) are more concerned that their children should be instructed in the tenets of one particular faith in a doctrinaire fashion.[2] The latter standpoint is sometimes referred to as the 'confessional' or 'dogmatic' approach to religious education, while the former is sometimes described as the 'phenomenological' or 'undogmatic' approach.[3]

1 See *Between Two Cultures* (CRC, 1976) pp 20-2, 60: *The Education of Ethnic Minority Children* (CRC, 1977) pp 35, 41; *Swann Committee Report* pp 473-4.
2 *Swann Committee Report* p 474.
3 Ibid pp 470-1.

Policy considerations

7.05 Many people consider it to be the function of the home and the parents' own religious community to nurture and instruct a child in the beliefs of a particular faith. In their view the proper role of the school is merely to inform pupils about the nature of religion and provide them with the ability to enter into the experience of religion. A claim to religious education of the undogmatic type, involving learning about faiths other than Christianity, would seem to be unexceptionable on liberal democratic grounds. Equally hard to resist on the same grounds would be any request by non-Christian parents to withdraw their children from classes or assemblies involving exclusively Christian teaching of the dogmatic type which the parents felt ran counter to their own religious beliefs. To take any other view on these matters today would amount to bigotry and be contrary to long-established traditions of religious toleration of which the country is justly proud.[1] It would also run counter to art 2 of the First Protocol to the European Convention on Human Rights which provides:

'in the exercise of any functions which it assumes in relation to education and to teaching, the State shall respect the right of parents to ensure such education and teaching in conformity with their own religious and philosophical convictions.'

On the other hand, what would appear to many members of both the majority community and the various minority communities to be a sensible compromise in this age of increasing secularism, agnosticism and ecumenism would be classes and assemblies which gave broadly equal treatment to the whole range of major world religions and thus amounted in essence to a study of a variety of faiths and beliefs and of moral behaviour. At first sight this would seem to be infinitely preferable to the often disruptive, embarrassing and divisive process of withdrawal and separate instruction.[2] Indeed, this 'phenomenological' approach has become increasingly common, especially in schools with large numbers of non-Christian pupils and the doctrinaire style of the past seems to have largely disappeared from many schools.[3] However, it is vital for the success of such a programme that what is taught about any particular religion (whether Christian or otherwise) is neither superficial nor inadequate; otherwise it will neither satisfy the adherents of that faith nor be a worthwhile exercise from an educational point of view. While there are indications that most ethnic minority parents are at present reasonably satisfied with this aspect of their children's schooling,[4] a small number clearly favour the 'confessional' approach and feel that the only way to ensure proper, detailed and rigorous instruction in their religions for their children is through committed instruction given by believers, if necessary in newly established Muslim, Sikh or Hindu schools,[5] as counterparts to those currently run by the various Christian denominations and Jewish organisations. This aspect of the question is explored further below.[6]

1 On the development of religious toleration, see further paras 8.07-8.08 below.
2 See Rolls 'Changes in Religious Education' [1972-73] *New Community* 241 at 242.
3 See H E R Townsend and E M Brittan *Organisation in Multiracial Schools* (NFER, 1972) p 105; *The Education of Ethnic Minority Children* pp 12-13, 36, 44.
4 See *The Education of Ethnic Minority Children* p 36.
5 See, e g Union of Muslim Organisations of UK and Eire *Guidelines and Syllabus on Islam* (1976); Kanitkar 'A school for Hindus?' [1979] New Community 178.
6 See paras 7.40-7.42 below.

English law

7.06 The wishes of parents are accorded considerable legal weight in this sphere of education. Although the Education Act 1944 provides that in all county and voluntary schools the school day must begin with an act of collective worship on the part of all pupils[1] (subject to this being practicable), any parent is entitled to insist that his child be excused from attending.[2] Similarly, a parent may withdraw his child from the classes of religious instruction[3] which are otherwise generally required by the Act.[4] Furthermore, if a parent wishes his child to receive a form of religious instruction which is not available at the school he can demand that the education authority make suitable arrangements for the child to receive it at another school or, if this is not possible, elsewhere during school hours.[5] The only limitation is that the local authority must be satisfied that these outside arrangements do not interfere with his attendance at school except at the beginning or end of the school day. Thus it is perfectly possible for a Muslim child, for instance, to go to his local mosque for religious instruction during the last hour of the school day on Fridays if it is impossible for the *imam* to visit the school to provide regular classes.[6] Children are, in addition, entitled to be absent from school on any day exclusively set apart for religious observance by the religious body to which their parents belong, i e important religious festivals.[7]

1 S 25(1).
2 S 25(4).
3 S 25(4).
4 S 25(2).
5 S 25(5).
6 See *Townsend and Brittan* pp 107-8.
7 Education Act 1944 s 39(2)(b).

7.07 There are certain important distinctions between county, controlled and aided schools in terms of a number of the statutory requirements. In county schools the collective worship is not allowed to be distinctive of any particular 'religious denomination'.[1] Undoubtedly the original idea behind the use of this expression was to outlaw discrimination between the different churches while ensuring that the assembly was devoted to Christian worship.[2] Today, however, it is clear that many schools are organising assemblies which either reflect the variety of faiths of their pupils or else have no specifically religious content[3] and for this reason many ethnic minority parents may well be willing to allow their children to attend such assemblies without demur. It also seems possible to argue that since the primary meaning of 'denomination' is simply a religious body, strictly speaking any assembly devoted exclusively to Christian worship could itself constitute a violation of the existing provision. Obviously this was not the intention of Parliament in 1944 and the matter has never been tested in the courts.

1 Education Act 1944, s 26.
2 See *Swann Committee Report* pp 478-9.
3 See *Swann Committee Report* pp 479-81.

7.08 Similarly, the religious instruction given to the pupils at county schools must be in accordance with an 'agreed syllabus' and must not include any catechism or formulary which is distinctive of any particular religious denomination.[1] The formal mechanism for deciding upon the content of the 'agreed syllabus' is a unanimous decision reached at a conference of four committees appointed by the LEA to represent the teachers' associations, the LEA itself, the Church of England and such other denominations as the LEA consider appropriate.[2] In the case of a small number of LEAs the initial agreed syllabus which was drawn up following the enactment of the 1944 Act has not been revised since that time and many others have not been altered during the past 15 or 20 years.[3] Most of these will, therefore, still prescribe an almost solid diet of biblical study and church history.[4] However, two developments have occurred which are likely to satisfy the large majority of ethnic minority parents. First, even in those areas where no updating of the syllabus has been accomplished in a formal sense many heads of religious education, particularly in secondary schools containing a significant proportion of ethnic minority pupils, have been tacitly allowed to draw up their own broadly-based curricula spanning other faiths, more or less regardless of the wording of the agreed syllabus.[5] Second, a growing number of LEAs have during recent years taken the trouble to convene the necessary statutory conferences and after a great deal of time and effort have revised their syllabuses to incorporate study of other major world religions.[6] In a few areas this process attracted considerable publicity and dissension,[7] but in most parts of the country there has been little public interest or concern. A general pattern has emerged in the revision exercise of separating the formal syllabus (often published as a short pamphlet) from a detailed handbook for the guidance of teachers.[8] In this way the agreed syllabus itself can be limited to a mere outline of the topics to be covered, while leaving the method and the materials to be dealt with more fully in the handbook. The 1978 revised syllabus for Hampshire, for example, which has been adopted by a large number of other authorities,[9] contains chiefly a list of aims and objectives and only specifies content as a way of illustrating how these may be attained.[10] The emphasis is thus placed upon giving teachers as much independence as possible. The principal aim is stated to be to enable pupils to understand the nature of religious beliefs and practices and the importance and influence of these in the lives of believers. Most of the content will be derived from the study of Christianity but there also has to be an introduction to other religious faiths and world views found in contemporary British society. Visible features of religious belief systems are to be examined and an attempt made to evoke sympathetic appreciation of the meanings and values enshrined therein. With older children this involves critical examination as well. Tolerance and empathy are to be encouraged:

'Religious education should foster an attitude of fairminded enquiry towards the whole range of religious and non-religious convictions. It should encourage a willingness to stand imaginatively in other people's shoes. This approach should ensure that pupils allow their own views to be judged against the traditions studied, before they subject those traditions to criticism.'[11]

Details of what might actually take place in the classroom are given in a separate handbook, a far lengthier publication.[12]

1 Education Act 1944, s 26, re-enacting the Elementary Education Act 1870, s 14(2) which embodied the famous 'Cowper-Temple' clause.
2 See the Education Act 1944, ss 26, 29 and Fifth Schedule.
3 For details about the date of the syllabus being used by each LEA in 1981, see B Lealman (ed) *Implementing the Agreed Syllabus* (CEM 1981) pp 15-18.
4 See *The Fourth R* ('*Durham Report*') pp 36, 41; Hull 'Agreed Syllabuses, past present and future' in N Smart and D Horder (eds) *New Movements in Religious Education* (London, 1975) pp 99-101.
5 See *Regan* p 68.
6 The first of these was the ILEA whose syllabus *Learning for Life* was published in 1968.
7 Amidst great controversy Birmingham also included coverage of communism and humanism. For the background to this and the earlier revision of the Bath syllabus, see *Hull* pp 104-112.
8 See Priestley 'A World of Harmonious Confusion: a Study of the Development of Agreed Syllabuses of Religious Education since 1975' in Lealman (ed) pp 7-8.
9 See *Lealman* (ed) pp 17-18.
10 *Religious Education in Hampshire Schools* (Hants LEA, 1978).
11 Ibid p 10.
12 W Laxton (ed) *Paths to Understanding* (Globe Education, 1980).

7.09 Where a parent is not satisfied with the agreed syllabus current in his area but the county secondary school which his child attends is so situated that arrangements cannot conveniently be made for the withdrawal of pupils to receive religious instruction elsewhere then, if the local authority is satisfied that the parent desires his child to receive religious instruction in the school in accordance with the tenets of a particular religious denomination and that satisfactory arrangements have been made for the provision of such instruction at the school and for ensuring that the cost of providing such instruction will not fall upon the authority, then, unless it is satisfied that owing to any special circumstances it would be unreasonable to do so the authority must provide facilities for carrying out those arrangements.[1] The child at secondary school in, for instance, a large city thus stands a good chance of being able to receive separate religious instruction in, for example, Islam at his own school without having to move outside it and the local *imam* can obtain a right of entry there.

So far as controlled schools are concerned religious instruction is also required to be in accordance with the agreed syllabus,[2] but the parents of children attending the school may request that their children receive religious instruction in accordance with the persuasion to which the school adhered before it became a controlled school and unless there are special circumstances making it impracticable to do so the governors must make arrangements for such denominational instruction to be given on the school premises for not more than two periods a week.[3] This right is in addition to the general right of withdrawal and separate denominational instruction outside the school.

1 S 26.
2 S 27(6).
3 S 27(1).

7.10 Aided schools and special agreement schools are given greater flexibility in that religious instruction is under the control of the governors.[1] It can, therefore, be denominational in accordance either with a trust deed or with the practice observed in the school before it became a voluntary school. However, where any parents of children at the school wish them to receive instruction according to the agreed syllabus and the children cannot reasonably attend a school where such instruction is normally given, provision at their own school must be made accordingly, unless owing to special circumstances the LEA is satisfied it would be unreasonable to do so. Again this right is in addition to that of withdrawal and separate instruction outside the school. Exactly the same situation applies with respect to religious instruction at special agreement schools.

There is nothing in the 1944 Act to indicate whether the act of collective worship in controlled, aided and special agreement schools may be denominational or not. Presumably the matter is governed by the trust deed if it contains a provision dealing with the question; otherwise it would appear to be for the governors to decide whether the act of worship should be undenominational or in accordance with the school's former status.[2] In any event the general right of withdrawal exists in all cases.

1 S 28(1).
2 See *Alexander and Taylor* pp 20, 39, 50.

The scope for reform

7.11 The most thoroughgoing reform would, of course, be the total abolition of religious instruction and worship as compulsory ingredients of the school curriculum.[1] It certainly appears anomalous at a time when religious belief is in marked decline among the majority community that this should be the only subject which is a mandatory part of formal education. In the US specific courses in religious education in public (i e state) schools are broadly prohibited by the First Amendment to the Constitution and as Regan has pointed out:

'Given Britain's strong liberal traditions, most overseas visitors are surprised at the heavy public subsidies given to denominational schools and astonished at the compulsory provision of religious worship and instruction in the LEA schools.'[2]

Aside from the fundamental contention of humanists and others that it is not the business of a modern state to teach religion in a largely secular society, the following would seem to be the other principal arguments in favour of abolition.

First, the actual provision requiring religious instruction is so vague as to be virtually meaningless. Section 25(2) of the 1944 Act merely states that '. . . religious instruction shall be given in every county school and in every voluntary school'. The amount of such instruction is not specified and in practice is usually very limited. Moreover, it is clear that by no means all schools regard it as incumbent upon them to provide courses for classes of every year, often dispensing with them completely for older children.[3] One reason for this is that there is a dire shortage of properly qualified teachers in the subject, a situation which seems unlikely to be remedied.[4] If the spirit of the provision is increasingly breached by many schools this may soon bring the law into such general disarray as to warrant drastic action.

Second, the provision relating to the commencement of each school day with an act of collective worship on the part of all pupils is rapidly becoming outmoded.[5] The Church of England Board of Education has acknowledged that 'some schools disregard the law, some perfunctorily observe it, while others have with imagination revolutionised the atmosphere of the assembly'.[6] The Archbishop of Canterbury has called for greater flexibility in terms of worship by smaller groups, while other church leaders have suggested that there should only be one assembly each week.[7] A report from the House of Commons Education, Science and Arts Committee has stated that 'the whole concept and intention behind the school act of worship is in danger of falling into disrepute' and suggested that legislative change might well be needed.[8] Most recently the Swann Committee concluded that the legal requirement for a daily act of collective worship could no longer be justified 'with the multiplicity of beliefs and non-beliefs now present in our society'.[9] Certainly in many schools the assembly, even if it still meets every day, has become almost completely secularised and little purpose would seem to be served by continuing to describe it as an act of worship.

Third, if religious education is regarded as such an important aspect of education to be required by law it seems hard to see why it should be permissible for parents to withdraw their children from it. As the Swann Committee has argued:

'This anomalous position in our view raises serious doubts about the justification for the specific provisions of the Act. Clearly if the provision of religious education (instruction) continues to be required by law, and if there is a likelihood that the provision made may adopt a confessional [i e dogmatic] approach, based on a Christian dominated agreed syllabus, then the right of withdrawal must be retained. If, however, as we wish, religious education is broadened to follow a phenomenological approach which seeks to 'inform' rather than to 'convert' pupils, and if the position of religious education within the curriculum is acknowledged and accepted on *educational* rather than religious grounds, then we feel that the legal requirement for provision to be made, the legal provision for withdrawal and the requirement for agreed syllabuses are no longer justified.'[10]

Fourth, where the requirement that religion be taught means that in practice classes in religious education are given by unqualified and uninterested persons this can often be a worse experience for the pupils than if the subject had not been taught in school at all. Children may become so bored or alienated that they reject religion in later life altogether. The same applies to the act of collective worship. In the case of ethnic minority parents distortion of their faiths by a Christian or agnostic teacher who is attempting to follow a multi-faith agreed syllabus may also give rise to considerable concern. There is certainly a possible argument for saying that both the teaching of religion and the act of worship are best done outside the formal educational system altogether and left in the hands of those with a real conviction.[11]

1 See generally *Regan* pp 67-8.
2 At pp 66-7. For a discussion of religious education in other Western countries, see the *'Durham Report'* ch 6.
3 See the Second Report from the House of Commons Education, Science and Arts Committee, 'The Secondary School Curriculum and Examinations' (1981-82) H C 116-1 para 5.37.
4 *Ibid*; see also 'Initial Government Observations on the Second Report of the Education, Science and Arts Committee' Cmnd 8551 of 1982, p 7.
5 For discussion of some of the pros and cons of making the act of worship compulsory, see the *'Durham Report'* pp 131-9.
6 H C 116-I, para 5.36; H C 116-II, pp 467-8.
7 H C 116-I, para 5.36. The City of Bradford Metropolitan Council has instructed its schools to allow Muslim children to meet for midday prayers, especially on Fridays, in a room set aside for the purpose, and to allow the prayers to be led by an *imam* if the parents so request – see Local Administrative Memorandum No 2 of 1982.
8 H C 116-I, para 5.36
9 *Swann Committee Report* p 497.
10 *Ibid* p 498.
11 See H C 116-II, p 465.

7.12 The two strongest counter-arguments in favour of the retention of compulsory religious education are that it is still strongly supported by the vast majority of parents and that the role of imparting useful information as opposed to inculcating a particular set of beliefs can best be done at school.

There appears to be widespread parental support, even among those who hold no firm religious beliefs, for the idea that children should receive some religious education at school.[1] Some parents may hope that as a result their children will acquire a religious faith or conviction or at least some strong moral values which they find lacking in themselves. Others may simply take the view that there are certain aspects of religion which are worth being well informed about if a child is to grow up with a broad understanding of English political, social and legal history and our existing institutions as well as the context of much of what is occurring in the wider world, including the countries of origin of many of our ethnic minorities. The same applies to the appreciation of literature, art and music. Almost certainly many aspects of the history of the great religions and their impact upon the lives and cultures of their adherents are sufficiently complex to require the expertise of qualified teachers if they are to be convincingly expounded. Neither of these counter-arguments, however, would seem to justify religious education as the only mandatory subject in the curriculum. Both English and mathematics, to take only the most obvious examples, would presumably be insisted upon by parents and equally require professional tuition at school in the vast majority of cases.

1 See *Regan* p. 67; HC 116-1, para 5.35; HC 116-II, p 456; Rae, 'In defence of RE' *Observer*, 6 June 1982.

7.13 Assuming, however, that religious education in state schools is likely to remain compulsory for largely historical reasons,[1] are there any ways in which the existing system could be improved? One possible area lies in the field of separate instruction. Although no statistics for withdrawals are available it is generally thought that the number is extremely small.[2] One reason for this[3] may be that this process is likely to prove embarrassing for the child, who may feel somewhat isolated from his peers if he has regularly to disappear from the school premises for separate tuition at another school or elsewhere. It is surely desirable that wherever possible any separate instruction should be given at his own school. At present the local authority is only bound to arrange this in limited circumstances if the child is attending a county secondary school but not a county primary school or any sort of voluntary school. This seems an anomalous distinction especially in view of the amount of state support given to voluntary schools and should therefore be eliminated. The local authority should be obliged to finance separate tuition in all cases.

To some extent, however, this problem would be greatly alleviated by a guarantee that all local authorities possessed an up-to-date agreed syllabus encompassing all the principal faiths. It surely cannot be satisfactory from a legal point of view that teachers are having to construct new courses in clear contravention of an admittedly outmoded formal syllabus. In 1981 the House of Commons Education, Science and Arts Committee recommended that those authorities which had not already done so should prepare revised syllabuses in consultation with the religious leaders in their communities.[4] This brought forth the following bland response from the government:

'In *'The School Curriculum'*[5] the Secretary of State for Education and Science called on local education authorities to 'reconsider from time to time the appropriateness of the Agreed Syllabus for their area in the light of the needs of particular groups of pupils and changes in the society in which the children are growing up'. A substantial number of revised Agreed Syllabuses have been brought into use: one third of local education authorities in England are using syllabuses adopted since 1970 or are currently revising their syllabuses. The Government hope that this process will continue.'[6]

This hardly seems good enough. If religious education is indeed a proper area in which the law should intervene, its provisions should certainly not be used to permit large numbers of local authorities to perpetuate an anachronistic framework for religious teaching. Either the whole process of having an agreed syllabus should be abolished altogether, with teachers being given in law the same freedom as they possess in other subjects (a solution proposed by a Church of England commission in 1970)[7] or there should be stronger legal control over the revision procedures. At present the Secretary of State's power of intervention is confined to instances where the statutory conference cannot reach unanimity or the local authority fails to adopt the syllabus unanimously recommended by the conference.[8] This should be widened to enable him to compel a suitable revision in appropriate cases.

Finally, the suggestion has been made, by the Archbishop of Canterbury among others, that the 1944 Act should refer specifically to 'religious education' rather than 'religious instruction', on the basis that the latter expression carries connotations of indoctrination which are out of keeping with the current pattern of a broadly-based multi-faith syllabus.[9] However, the relevant sections of the Act are prefaced by a general heading which specifically refers to 'religious education' and there seems to be no pressing need for such a minor amendment.[10]

1 In 1985 the Government ruled out any possibility of change – see 75 HL Official Report (6th series) col 452.
2 See e g Little and Willey *Multi-ethnic Education: The Way Forward* (Schools Council Pamphlet 18, London, 1981) p 25. For the position in the early 1970s see Townsend and Brittan *Organisation in Multiracial Schools* p 169.
3 Parental ignorance of the legal position and general apathy may also be just as significant factors as parental satisfaction with the current arrangements in the particular school.
4 HC 116-I, para 5.38.
5 (DES and Welsh Office, 1981).
6 Cmnd 8551 of 1982, p 7.
7 *The Fourth R ('Durham Report')* pp 104-5.
8 See 1944 Act, Fifth Schedule, paras 10-11.
9 HC 116-I, para 5.35; HC 116-II, p 456.
10 For the negative government response to the suggested change, see Cmnd 8551 of 1982, p 6.

B. BILINGUALISM AND USE OF THE MOTHER TONGUE IN TEACHING

7.14 Many parents whose first language is not English would like their children to acquire or retain a proficiency in their mother tongue or 'home' or 'community' language.[1] Among the Asian communities the support for this is especially strong.[2] It would enable the children to preserve a vital link with their cultural heritage, to maintain greater contact with older members of their families (especially relatives living in their parents' countries of origin) and sometimes to gain access to the scriptures of their religion.[3] It would also enrich the cultural life of this country through increasing the diversity of its linguistic resources and improve Britain's prospects of maintaining valuable links with other nations in commercial, industrial, educational and cultural fields.

Most importantly from the point of view of the children's own early education, mother tongue teaching appears to promote their cognitive and social growth and development and enhance their learning opportunities at the primary school level. Recent research in this area suggests that there are distinct educational advantages in teaching children at this stage through their home languages, at least for part of the school day.[4] This research admittedly runs counter to the traditional suspicions which many educationalists have had in the past about bilingualism. Their view was that the brain only had a finite capacity and that this meant that bilingual children learnt neither language as well as if they had confined themselves to just one language. Bilingualism was thus perceived as something of an intellectual handicap.[5] This perspective has recently been changing and the capacity of bilingualism actually to enhance the learning process is becoming increasingly recognised.[6] Bilingual children become more quickly aware of the structures within a particular language system, they acquire a greater range of verbal expression and they may even be enabled to think better.[7] Competence in one language appears to increase significantly the ability to gain competence in other languages.[8] Studies of bilingual education in Canada, for instance, have shown that young English-speaking children who joined French 'immersion' programmes, involving a large amount of instruction through the medium of French, did at least as well in all aspects of their schooling as their monolingual counterparts.[9] However, one of the keys to their success appears to have been the strong support both at home and in the wider environment for their continued use of their first language, English. The lesson of the Canadian experience would, therefore, seem to be that ethnic minority pupils here are more likely to perform well in English if there is strong support for their mother tongues than if there is not. Continuity in the use of language is vital for a child's educational progress and development and for this reason (amongst others), as the Bullock report aptly put it: 'No child should be expected to cast off the language and culture of the home as he crosses the school threshold'.[10] For a young child to leave its mother tongue at home can produce a damaging dividedness, particularly when the issue is not openly discussed, as Miller has eloquently explained:

'A second language learned and used only in school can feel like a language for passivity, acceptance, attention, listening and . . . obedience. Its use will be constrained by rules and prohibitions, its vitalities and subtleties hidden. Similarly, the home language may be relegated to the terrain of childhood, interesting only as the expression of a vestigial folk culture. The life of action and feeling, of first experiences and what is directly known can become divorced from the world where language has become an instrument for generalisation, organisation and the assimilating of new ideas and knowledge. There is a danger of that happening to any child, but the danger is a much greater one if the two selves, so to speak, talk different languages. Cultural values can be distorted, polarised into what is quaint and half extinguished, on the one hand, and what is practical, modern and remunerated, on the other. Many children are marooned between languages and between cultures, forgetting one more rapidly than they acquire another; and meanwhile they may be regarded by teachers and by other children – ultimately, perhaps, by themselves – as bereft of all the things language stands for: intelligence, humour, daring, inventiveness, enthusiasm, discrimination and curiosity'.[11]

1 See e g *The Education of Ethnic Minority Children* (CRC, 1977) p 37; *Swann Committee Report* pp 404-5, 663, 682-3.

2 See Brown *Black and White Britain* (London, 1984) pp 131, 143.

3 See V Edwards *Language in Multicultural Classrooms* (London, 1983) pp 40-1; *Swann Committee Report* pp 399-401.

4 See D Brown *Mother Tongue to English* (Cambridge, 1979); *Linguistic Diversity and Mother Tongue Teaching* (NUT, 1982); *Ethnic Minority Community Languages: A Statement* pp 8-9.

5 V Edwards *Language in the Multicultural Classroom* p 35.

6 See e g D Houlton and R Willey *Supporting Children's Bilingualism* (Longmans, 1983) pp 14-15.

7 J Miller *Many Voices* (Routledge, 1983) ch 7.

8 See C B Paulston 'Education in a Bi/Multilingual Setting' (1978) 24 International Review of Education 309.

9 M Swain and S Lapkin *Evaluating Bilingual Education: A Canadian Case Study* (Clevedon, 1983).
10 *A Language for Life* (HMSO, 1975) para 20.5.
11 *Miller* pp 9-10.

7.15 So far as the question of what form mother tongue teaching might take the *Swann Committee Report* published in 1985 identified three main categories of provision.[1] The first of these, described as 'bilingual education' would involve a school in using a pupil's mother tongue as a medium of instruction, alongside English, in the same manner as already occurs with the Welsh language in some schools in Wales.[2] At present there appears to be little, if any, demand among ethnic minority parents for part or all of their children's instruction at secondary school level to be through the medium of a language other than English.[3] However, 'bilingual education' at the primary level is felt to be desirable.

The second form, 'mother tongue maintenance' entails the development of a pupil's fluency as an integral part of a primary school's curriculum in order to extend existing language skills by timetabling a set number of hours each week for mother tongue teaching. This appears to be a rather narrower concept with much more limited aims than bilingual primary education.

The third category, described simply as 'mother tongue teaching', would mean the teaching of the home or community languages of ethnic minorities as part of the foreign languages curriculum of secondary schools, alongside subjects such as French and German. It would, of course, enable pupils to sit for public examinations in these subjects and obtain recognised qualifications.

1 At p 399.
2 On education in Welsh, see E G Lewis *Bilingualism and Bilingual Education* (Pergamon, 1981) pp 361-3, 403-7.
3 See *Little and Willey* p 20.

Policy considerations

7.16 The central questions in this area revolve around the compatibility of mother tongue teaching with the attainment of a high degree of competence in the English language and the proper allocation of responsibility for the maintenance of ethnic community languages. A principal concern of educationalists and policy makers (and indeed of parents themselves) is that overriding importance should be attached to ensuring that all children who are being educated in this country should become thoroughly proficient in the English language.[1] Without this most fundamental of skills they will find it extremely hard to flourish here and their employment opportunities are likely to be severely limited. There is a mass of evidence that overall ethnic minority children have not been performing as well as they should in studying English[2] and rectifying this dire state of affairs must be regarded as a matter of top priority if these children are not to be handicapped for the rest of their lives. This immediately raises the question whether it is not asking too much of both these children and their schools to insist on mother tongue tuition or bilingual education as well as a high standard in the English language. To this there are a number of possible rejoinders.

First, much of the evidence about poor performance in English language relates to West Indian children,[3] whereas it is predominantly Asian[4] and European parents who wish their children to receive formal instruction at school in their mother tongue. Second, many of these children are already studying these languages informally in so-called 'supplementary schools' operated at weekends and in the evenings by voluntary associations and local groups.[5] There must, however, surely be clear advantages in transferring a substantial part of this instruction to the ordinary school day and the mainstream curriculum, not only to enhance the status of these languages in the eyes of parents, teachers and children[6] but also to reduce the strain placed on the powers of concentration and learning capacities of the children and ensure a higher standard of expertise on the part of the teachers. As the Bullock Report pointed out in 1975:

'Their bilingualism is of great importance to the children and their families, and also to society as a whole. In a linguistically conscious nation in the modern world we should see it as an asset, as something to be nurtured, and one of the agencies which should nurture it is the school. Certainly the school should adopt a positive attitude to its pupils' bilingualism and wherever possible should help maintain and deepen their knowledge of their mother-tongues.'[7]

Third, if it is accepted as normal practice for secondary schools to offer courses in French, German, Spanish and Italian there can surely be no sound educational justification for not offering courses in modern Greek and Turkish as well as in Urdu, Punjabi and other major Asian languages, where there is a demand for them among the pupils. There is no reason to believe that any of them are of less value academically and they are likely to be of far greater use in later life to Asian members of the community. It is not, therefore, unreasonable to suggest further that CSE, 'O' level and 'A' level courses and examinations complete with up-to-date syllabuses,[8] should be made available in all the main languages of the ethnic minorities.[9] It cannot be a satisfactory state of affairs that some local authorities are at present unwilling to consider offering Asian languages as examination subjects and in 1981 the House of Commons Home Affairs Committee condemned such an attitude and recommended that the Department of Education and Science actively encourage the incorporation of Asian languages into the modern languages curriculum.[10] Standard objections concerning the shortage of teachers and the wide range of languages are no excuse for doing nothing. An appropriate number of teachers could be trained or re-trained as a matter of urgency and the teaching could be rationalised so that, where the demand for a particular language is limited, it is offered only at one or two schools within a given area and adequate publicity is given to this fact so that those parents who wish to apply to send their children there can do so.[11] Nor should it be forgotten that there may be considerable advantages for the country in general in enabling both Asian bilingual and white, monolingual pupils to study these languages. A major recent research report has pointedly remarked that:

'. . . English monolinguals have in general a poor record in learning foreign languages at school, and enormous sums of money are spent annually in language learning for adults in, for example, industry, leisure and the diplomatic services. Yet many of the ethnic minority community languages in England are at present ignored or devalued as an individual and societal resource, when in fact their speakers could with minimal investment have their existing skills developed during their school years, and thus offer the country an educational, economic and political resource of considerable value. And the value of minority languages lies not only in what they offer to the large number of bilingual members of our society. Bilingualism in our society also offers the possibility of changing the narrowly monolingual perspective of many majority institutions and individuals.'[12]

While the 1985 *Swann Committee Report* emphasised the positive value of

Britain's current linguistic diversity it did not favour the introduction of programmes of 'bilingual education' in LEA schools.[13] Similarly it considered that 'mother tongue maintenance' was best achieved within the ethnic minority communities themselves rather than within mainstream schools. On the other hand, it pronounced itself wholeheartedly in favour of 'mother tongue teaching' in the general languages curriculum of maintained secondary schools, with such classes being open to all pupils including those from the white majority community. The Committee opposed the first two categories of tuition because of its concern about the harmful nature of any separate or special teaching which was confined to ethnic minority pupils and which might serve to establish or confirm social divisions. It found the research evidence that the learning of English could be assisted by 'bilingual education' or 'mother tongue maintenance' unconvincing since 'in many instances the most that can be claimed . . . is that the child's learning in English is not impaired and *may* in some respects be enhanced'.[14]

1 See Fifth Report from the Home Affairs Committee on Racial Disadvantage (1980-81) HC 424-1, para 149; Second Report from the Education, Science and Arts Committee (1981-82) HC 116-I, para 7.11; *Swann Committee Report* pp 405, 407.
2 See e g Tomlinson 'The educational performance of ethnic minority children' [1980] *New Community* 213; *The Rampton Committee Report*, 'West Indian Children in our Schools', Cmnd 8273 of 1981, pp 6-7, 19-22; *Swann Committee Report* pp 62-3, 115.
3 See e g *Rampton Committee Report* pp 6-7, 20-22. One of the explanations for the difficulties encountered by West Indians in mastering standard English relates to their use of various Caribbean 'dialects' (sometimes referred to as 'patois' or 'Creole'). There would appear to be a clear need for these dialects to be recognised and respected by teachers as distinctive and different linguistic forms rather than as 'erroneous' usage of the English language: see generally, *Bullock Report* paras 20.6-20.8; V K Edwards *The West Indian Language Issue in British Schools* (London, 1979); *Rampton Committee Report* pp 22-6; Richmond 'Dialect in the Classroom' in James and Jeffcoate (eds) *The School in the Multicultural Society* (London, 1981) pp 88-103 (where the contribution of West African languages in the formation of the dialects is well brought out).
4 For some evidence, albeit not conclusive, that Asian children are doing at least as well as their English counterparts, see J H Taylor *The Half-Way Generation* (NFER, 1976); Driver and Ballard, 'Comparing Performance in Multiracial Schools: South Asian Pupils at 16+' in *James and Jeffcoate* (eds) pp 147-160. *The Swann Committee Report* (at pp 62-3, 115) cites research which shows that in CSE English and GCE 'O' level English Language 15% of West Indians obtained higher grades compared with 21% of Asians and 29% of 'all other school leavers'.
5 See Khan 'Provision by minorities for language maintenance' in *Bilingualism and British Education* (Centre for Information on Language Teaching and Research, 1976) ch 3; Nagra 'Asian Supplementary Schools' [1981-82] *New Community* 431; *Linguistic Minorities in England* (University of London Institute of Education, 1983) ch 4.
6 See Miller 'How Do You Spell Gujerati, Sir' in *James and Jeffcoate* (eds) pp 104-15; *Ethnic Minority Community Languages: A Statement* (CRE, 1982) p 3.
7 *A Language for Life* (HMSO, 1975) para 20.17.
8 Many are currently out-of-date: see e g Russell *Ethnic Minority Languages and the Schools* (Runnymede Trust, 1980).
9 See HC 116-I, paras 7.21-7.22; *Swann Committee Report* p 413.
10 HC 424-I, para 153.
11 See *Ethnic Minority Community Languages: A Statement* pp 7, 13-14; *Swann Committee Report* p 410. Sometimes it may be necessary for individual LEAs to introduce reciprocal pooling arrangements with their neighbours where the numbers are even smaller in any one area.
12 *Linguistic Minorities in England* (University of London Institute of Education, 1983) p 162.
13 At pp 406-11.
14 At p 407.

English law

7.17 Apart from the mandatory provisions concerning religious education, there is no specific legal requirement as to what subjects should be taught in school. Both the availability of particular language courses and any question of offering general tuition through the medium of a language other than English are curricular matters which fall to be decided upon under a school's articles of government by its governors in consultation with the head teacher, under the general supervision of the LEA. The most specific statutory provision bearing upon the issue is the Education Act 1944, s 8 which imposes a duty upon each LEA to secure the provision of such variety of instruction and training as may be desirable in view of the different abilities and aptitudes of pupils. The ability to speak a language other than English would appear to be encompassed by the section, but it is left, at least in the first instance, to the LEA to decide what is 'desirable'. Under s 68 of the Act the Secretary of State can override any LEA which acts unreasonably in this field, but this is by no means an easy charge to substantiate.[1] The LEA might well argue, for instance, that it was in the children's best interests to improve their English rather than be taught further in their mother tongue.

Another pertinent statutory provision is the Race Relations Act 1976, s 71. This provides that it is the duty of every local authority to make appropriate arrangements with a view to securing that its various functions are carried out with due regard to the need to promote equality of opportunity between persons of different racial groups. The availability of mother tongue teaching may be viewed as an essential step in furnishing ethnic minority pupils with equality of opportunity since otherwise they will be denied the chance to build on their existing linguistic skills and develop their abilities in the way in which other children are.[2] However, s 71 falls well short of imposing an enforceable statutory duty upon LEAs to provide mother tongue teaching or bilingual education programmes since it merely requires local authorities to 'have regard' to the need to promote equality of opportunity.

1 See, e g *Secretary of State for Education and Science v Tameside Metropolitan BC* [1977] AC 1014, [1976] 3 All ER 665.
2 See *Swann Committee Report* pp 399-400.

7.18   To date, by far the greatest attention on the part of protagonists of mother tongue teaching has been focused upon the 1977 EEC Directive on the Education of the Children of Migrant Workers.[1] While as a matter of general principle EEC directives are not 'directly applicable' and hence binding in English law in the absence of domestic legislation, it appears that in certain circumstances individuals may be able to rely on their terms before the English courts.[2] The Treaty of Rome Art 189(3) declares:

'A directive shall be binding, as to the result to be achieved, upon each Member State to which it is addressed, but shall leave to the national authorities the choice of forms and methods.'

However, in recent years, the European Court of Justice has felt it necessary to point out that the growing problem of unimplemented or imperfectly implemented directives amounts to a serious breach of community law which has profound and unwelcome consequences for individual rights. In a number of cases the Court has been willing to allow individual citizens direct access to the terms of an unimplemented or inadequately implemented directive on the basis that a member state should not be allowed to plead its own wrong.[3] The crucial precondition is that the language relied upon in the directive satisfies the standard tests of legal certainty, namely unconditionality, clarity and precision. Broadly speaking, the directive's terms can only be relied upon against the state and not against another individual.[4] Hence, in the context of mother tongue teaching a claim could probably only be made against the DES or an LEA and not against the governors or headmaster of a particular school. In view of the House of Lords decision in *Garden Cottage Foods v Milk Marketing Board*[5] that infringements of community law can be actionable in the English courts upon the tortious basis of breach of a statutory duty it has been tentatively suggested that directives which

'remain unimplemented beyond the posited implementation date and whose terms are sufficiently legally certain and which influence the legal relationship between citizen and state can most probably be litigated upon the basis of breach of statutory duty in English tort law.'[6]

1 Council Directive of 25 July 1977 (77/486/EEC).
2 See generally Green 'Directives, Equity and the Protection of Individual Rights' (1984) 9 EL Rev 295.
3 See, eg *Pubblico-Ministero v Tullio Ratti* [1979] ECR 1629; *Becker v Finanzamt-Munster Innenstadt* [1982] ECR 53.
4 See Pescatore 'The Doctrine of "Direct Effect": An Infant Disease of Community Law' (1983) 8 EL Rev 155 at 171.
5 [1984] AC 130, [1983] 2 All ER 770.
6 Green at 324.

7.19   In the light of these possibilities of the individual enforcement of a directive through the English courts it is important to examine very carefully the specific provisions of this particular directive. Article 3 of the Directive deals with mother tongue teaching in the following terms:

'Member States shall, in accordance with their national circumstances and legal systems, and in co-operation with States of origin, take appropriate measures to promote, in co-ordination with normal education, teaching of the mother tongue and culture of the country of origin for the children referred to in Article 1.'

In its turn Art 1 defines the children to whom the Directive applies as those for whom school attendance is compulsory under the laws of the host state:

'. . . who are dependants of any worker who is a national of another Member State, where such children are resident in the territory of the Member State in which that national carries on or has carried on an activity.'

Clearly, therefore, the benefits of the Directive are expressly confined to the children of nationals of the members of the EEC. This is further borne out by the terms of the Directive's preamble which refers to the need to improve the freedom of movement of workers within the EEC and the desirability of a worker's children being taught their mother tongue 'with a view principally to facilitating their possible reintegration into the Member State of origin'. The upshot is that the children of Italian and Greek nationals, for example, are covered by the Directive, while the children of Cypriot, Turkish, Indian, and Pakistani nationals are not.

However, in 1977 the UK government concurred in an agreement reached at the Council of Ministers that the benefits of the Directive should be extended to the children of nationals of non-member states.[1] This agreement, which reflected the spirit of an earlier draft of the Directive, was of a political nature and would not appear to carry any legal obligations. In any event it clearly does not cover mother tongue teaching in this country for the children of UK citizens and thus excludes the majority of ethnic minority children living in Britain today.[2] On the other hand, insofar as any positive action taken by an LEA under the terms of the Directive itself involves discrimination on the basis of a child's race, nationality or ethnic or national origins this could amount to a breach of the Race Relations Act 1976[3] and hence be unlawful. An LEA could not, therefore, promote mother tongue teaching in its schools for the children of Greek nationals while refusing to do the same either for the children of Pakistani nationals or for the children of UK nationals of Pakistani origin. Since, however, it obviously does have a duty to children in the former category it is important to attempt to clarify exactly what is entailed by the words used in Art 3. This article imposes an obligation upon member states to 'take appropriate measures to promote, in co-ordination with normal education, teaching of the mother tongue and culture . . .'.

The DES gave its interpretation of the Article in 1981 in the following guarded terms:[4]

'For local education authorities in this country, this implies that they should explore ways in which mother tongue teaching might be provided, whether during or outside school hours, but not that they are required to give such tuition to all individuals as of right.[5] In some areas provision is already made by the minority communities, either through voluntary self-help schemes or through teachers employed by foreign embassies and, in some instances, such initiatives receive support from local education authorities. There may be further scope for local education authorities to encourage co-operation between mother tongue teachers and the teachers responsible for the same children in ordinary schools, and to provide material help, such as accommodation for classes. For its part, the DES is sponsoring research related to the provision and educational implications of mother tongue teaching, as well as taking a close interest in EEC-sponsored initiatives in this country.'

This limited construction arguably gives too little weight to the word 'promote' and virtually ignores the phrase 'in co-ordination with normal education'. On the other hand, the duties laid upon states appear clearly intended to be less onerous than those set out in Art 2 in relation to the teaching of the language of the 'host State'. This provides in much more direct language that member states 'shall . . . take appropriate measures to ensure that free tuition . . . is offered . . . including, in particular, the teaching . . . of the official language . . . of the host State'. Even so, in view of the small degree of promotion of mother tongue teaching actually undertaken by the Government either within the four-year time-limit set by Art 4 of the Directive or after 1981 it could well be contended that the Directive remains unimplemented.[6] If that could be established, then a dissatisfied Greek parent might be able to bring an action in tort in the English courts if the terms of Art 3 could be shown to possess the necessary attributes of legal certainty. Any LEA which responded to this or other pressures by providing mother tongue teaching would then have to be careful not to discriminate against other ethnic minority children contrary to the Race Relations Act 1976.

1 See *Swann Committee Report* pp 401-2. See also the statement made by Mr Mark Carlisle, then Secretary of State for Education, on 24 March 1980 quoted in *Ethnic Minority Community Languages – A Statement* (CRE, 1982) pp 15-16.
2 *Swann* Committee Report p 402.
3 See ss 1, 3, 17.
4 DES Circular 5/81, paras 7, 8.
5 The same opinion on this point was expressed by the House of Commons Home Affairs Committee in 1981 – see HC 424-I, para 151.
6 For the steps taken, see 'DES Memorandum on Compliance with Directive 77/486/EEC' (1983). However, the EEC Commission's 'Report on the Implementation of Directive 77/486/EEC', Com (84)54 revealed that the UK was doing far less than many other member states.

The scope for reform

7.20 It seems appropriate to begin by examining the limited amount of international human rights law on the subject. The question whether a right to mother tongue tuition is guaranteed under the European Convention on Human Rights was answered in the negative in 1968 in the *Belgian Linguistics* case.[1] Art 2 of the First Protocol to the Convention contains the following provision:

'In the exercise of any functions which it assumes in relation to education and to teaching, the State shall respect the right of parents to ensure such education and teaching in conformity with their own religious and philosophical convictions.'

However, the European Court ruled that this did not require of state parties that they respect the linguistic preferences of parents.[2] To interpret the term 'religious' and 'philosophical' as covering linguistic preferences would, it was held, amount to a distortion of their ordinary and usual meaning. The object of Art 2 was in no way to secure a right for parents to have their children educated in a language other than that of the country in question. On the other hand, it is worth drawing attention to the International Covenant on Civil and Political Rights, Art 27 which declares:

'In those States in which ethnic, religious or linguistic minorities exist, persons belonging to such minorities shall not be denied the right, in community with the other members of their group, to enjoy their own culture, to profess and practise their own religion, or to use their own language.'

No limitation or restriction is placed upon these rights and it would appear that prevention of the use of the mother tongue in school where there is a minority community demand for it might well constitute a violation of the terms of the treaty.[3] It therefore seems desirable that mother tongue teaching in primary schools should be given much greater support. A recent survey shows that in Holland around 80% of ethnic minority primary school pupils receive classes in their mother tongue compared with only a minute proportion in this country.[4] Such a reform could perhaps be implemented by strengthening the Race Relations Act 1976, s 71 to require LEAs actively to promote equality of opportunity between persons of different races.

So far as 'bilingual education' programmes at secondary school level are concerned, there seem to be widespread doubts as to whether these are educationally sensible and in any event few ethnic minority parents appear to want their children taught at this level through any medium other than English. Recent reports from two committees of the House of Commons have expressed concern at the divisiveness which such a system might generate among pupils[5] and have drawn attention to the worries which have surfaced about the wisdom of such programmes in the US.[6]

If it is assumed that much of the teaching of mother tongues is likely to remain the responsibility of the ethnic minority communities themselves, as the Swann Committee recommended, greater state support needs to be given to these activities in the form of free use of school premises and grants for books and equipment and possibly also a contribution towards the remuneration of teachers and help with their training.[7] While some LEAs do grant subsidies for such purposes others continue to charge a rent for the use of school premises. In 1984 this latter practice was criticised in a report of the EEC Commission into the implementation of the 1977 Directive as being clearly incompatible with the duty to promote mother tongue teaching laid down in Art 3.[8] This state of affairs obviously needs to be rectified as soon as possible.

1 (1968) 11 *Yearbook of the European Convention on Human Rights* 832 at 882-4.
2 Ibid at 860-2.

3 See W McKean *Equality and Discrimination in International Law* (OUP, 1983) p 145.
4 See EEC Commission 'A Report on the Implementation of Directive 77/486/EEC', Com (84) 54.
5 Home Affairs Committee, HC 424-I, para 151; Education, Science and Arts Committee, HC 116-I, para 7. 11.
6 For discussion of the problems of determining the success of such programmes in the USA, see Paulston 'Rationales for Bilingual Educational Reforms: A Comparative Assessment' (1978) 22 Comparative Education Review 402. For their legal basis, see the Bilingual Education Acts 1968 and 1974; the Supreme Court decision in *Lau v Nichols* 414 US 563 (1974); Teitelbaum and Hiller 'Bilingual Education: The Legal Mandate' (1977) 47 Harvard Educational Review 138; Fong 'Cultural Pluralism' (1978) 13 Harvard Civil Rights – Civil Liberties Law Review 133 at 146-168; Rosenbaum 'Educating Children of Immigrant Workers: Language Policies in France and the USA' (1981) 29 AJCL 429.
7 See *Swann Committee Report* pp 408-9.
8 Com (84) 54.

C. APPROPRIATE DRESS FOR SCHOOL

7.21 Many Asian parents are concerned that school rules and regulations with regard to uniforms, dress and appearance should not violate their religious and customary norms.[1] In the case of Muslims this particularly relates to the need for girls not to have to bare their legs by wearing skirts as part of the school uniform, nor to be required to wear gym-slips or shorts for games, nor swimming costumes for visits to the public baths.[2] To do so would contravene the injunction in the Koran that they should wear clothes which fully cover their legs and bodies.[3] Traditionally, many girls and women in the Indian subcontinent (including Sikhs) have worn *shalwar*[4] (perhaps best described as trousers which are full in the leg but narrow at the ankle, though styles change), and these are favoured by many Asian parents here as a suitable form of dress for their daughters at school.

Some Sikh parents take the view that their sons should be allowed to wear long hair, beards and bangles to school, if they so wish, since these form part of the well-known 'five symbols' of Sikhism.[5] Strictly speaking, the turban, which many Sikh parents also wish their sons to wear, is not one of the five symbols and a decision not to wear it does not, therefore, breach one of the central injunctions of the Sikh faith. However, there is no doubt that it is a well-known and firmly established Sikh religious custom to wear a turban. Some Sikhs explain it as a functional necessity in order to keep their long hair tidy, although it is arguable that this is achieved by the *kanga* (or small wooden comb) which is one of the five symbols. Others see it as a sign of the religious and social identity and cohesion of the Sikhs as a community.[6] Certainly it is not worn merely as a fashionable or stylish adornment.

1 See *Swann Committee Report* pp 341-2.
2 H E R Townsend and E M Brittan *Organisation in Multiracial Schools* (NFER, 1972) pp 63-5; Hiro *Black British, White British* pp 160-1; *Between Two Cultures* pp 23-5, 60.
3 See M Y McDermott and M M Ahsan *The Muslim Guide* (Islamic Foundation, 1980) pp 47-8.
4 See P Jeffery *Migrants and Refugees* (Cambridge, 1976) pp 26, 111. *Shalwar* is an Urdu word. The trousers are worn with a blouse or shirt *(qemiz)*. The equivalent of *shalwar-qemiz* in Hindi is *churidar-pyjama*.
5 See A G James *Sikh Children in Britain* (OUP, 1974) pp 48-52. Occasionally Sikh schoolboys have additionally claimed the right to wear the *kirpan* (or dagger) which is another of the 'five symbols'. Normally a tiny miniature dagger is sewn securely into the boy's clothing, but in 1983 a pupil in Leicester was suspended from his sixth-form college for insisting on wearing an eight-inch *kirpan* – see *Guardian*, 7 January 1983; *TES*, 11 February 1983.
6 See W O Cole and P S Sambhi (ed) *The Sikhs* (Routledge, 1978) pp 110-12; Singh 'Sikhism' in Iqbal (ed) *East Meets West* pp 102-3.

Policy considerations

7.22 Some school authorities may well object to such parental demands on the basis that every pupil must comply with the regulations concerning uniform, dress and appearance and that to make special exceptions would be disruptive to the organisation and smooth running of the school as a whole. One idea behind the specification of a particular school uniform or a particular style of dress is that pupils should not be ostentatiously differentiated from one another simply because of a disparity in their parents' means and resources. However, while it is indeed socially undesirable that distinctions of wealth should be made strikingly visible at school, since they tend to undermine the concept of equality, this argument does not carry the same conviction in the case of religious or cultural distinctions. These actually require display in order to achieve the desired equality of treatment; hence the rights to withdrawal from religious instruction and separate tuition discussed earlier.[1] Insofar as a school uniform is additionally designed to inculcate a degree of smartness and a sense of loyalty and cohesion among the pupils this can still be achieved through allowing minor variations for ethnic minority pupils. If, for instance, the colour of the uniform is green it is not unreasonable for the school to insist that the girls' *shalwar* or the boys' turbans should be green. Black turbans or white *shalwar* might also be acceptable as neutral alternatives.

There have been at least two much publicised controversies over the wearing of *shalwar*. In 1967 the headmistress of a school in Leicester sent home Asian pupils who came dressed in *shalwar* and insisted they wore the skirts prescribed as part of the school uniform. Only after a protest by their parents and the intervention of the Secondary School Education sub-committee did the school finally give way.[2] Two years later a school in Walsall banned the wearing of *shalwar* and as a result five Muslim girls were kept away from classes by their parents for a considerable period of time.[3] In the past decade or so, however, it would appear that most schools and local education authorities have shown appropriate sensitivity to the requirements of suitable clothing for Asian girls and problems such as those encountered in Leicester and Walsall should in future be extremely rare.[4] White or matching-coloured *shalwar* are not the only acceptable solution to the problem. Many Asian parents may be perfectly satisfied with school rules which authorise the wearing of long skirts, slacks or trouser-suits. A model code in regard to school clothing is to be found in the memorandum which was issued to all its schools by the educational department of the City of Bradford Metropolitan Council in 1982.[5] This provides for the wearing of traditional dress (provided it is in the school colours), the wearing of Sikh bracelets (on the basis that they do not constitute jewellery), the wearing by girls of tracksuits or lightweight trousers for physical education classes, facilities for both sexes to be clothed while showering and the wearing by girls of *churidar-pyjama* for swimming classes.[6]

It also appears that many LEAs and schools are prepared to go even further in the liberalisation of rules relating to dress. There are reports of Rastafarian boys being allowed to wear dreadlocks and knitted 'tam' in red, black, green and gold[7] and many LEAs have issued circulars to their schools forbidding the prescription and enforcement of a particular uniform or style of dress. Policy guidelines issued to its schools by Humberside County Council in 1983, for example, included the following principles:

(a) school uniform is not prohibited; its use may be encouraged but not enforced as a school rule;

(b) where a school adopts a uniform a pupil is nevertheless free to come in any other suitable dress and should not be put under pressure of any kind to do otherwise;

(c) to be suitable, clothing only needs to be clean, tidy and safe;

(d) there is no reason why girls should not wear trousers throughout the year.[8]

In 1985 the Swann Committee, in appealing to schools to act with sensitivity in this area,[9] expressed the clear view that:

'. . . all parents and pupils should be free to act in accordance with their religious beliefs, unless these are seen to be in direct conflict with the essential *educational* function of schools or to place the physical well-being of any child at risk.'[10]

1 See para 7.06 above.
2 See Iqbal 'Education and Islam in Britain – A Muslim View' [1976-77] *New Community* 397; Hiro *Black British, White British* p 160.
3 (1970) Times, 7 January; *Hiro* pp 160-1.
4 See *Townsend and Brittan* pp 58-61; *McDermott and Ahsan* pp 47-8; *Little and Willey* p 25; Iqbal *East Meets West* (CRE, 1981) p 58.
5 Local Administrative Memorandum No 2 of 1982.
6 See also Rochdale's 'Code of Practice for Matters affecting the Muslim Community in Schools'.
7 See Catholic Commission for Racial Justice 'Rastafarians in Jamaica and Britain' (1982) p 10.
8 School Circulars 2/1983 and 9/1983.
9 *Swann Committee Report* pp 342-3, 513.
10 Ibid at p 343.

English law

7.23 The Education Act 1944, s 39 imposes a duty upon parents to ensure that a child who is a registered pupil at a school does in fact attend it regularly. Breach of the duty under s 39 constitutes an offence and the result may also be that the child is taken into care by the local authority.[1] There is clear judicial support for the proposition that it may be an offence under s 39 to send a child to school dressed in such a way as to be in breach of a school rule, so that the child is automatically sent straight home. In *Spiers v Warrington Corpn*[2] it was held that a parent who knew this would happen was guilty of failing to secure the child's regular attendance at school. The case involved a girl who was sent to school wearing slacks in place of the school uniform. Her parents claimed they had dressed her in this manner because she had suffered from bouts of rheumatic fever and, being a delicate child, needed to be warmly clothed in winter. The headmistress refused to admit her without a medical certificate to the effect that such clothing was essential for her health. No such certificate was ever supplied. The Divisional Court held that an offence had been committed under s 39.

Although, as indicated earlier, it would appear that most of the problems in this area relating to the desire of Asian girls to wear *shalwar* (or at least to ensure that their legs are covered) have been ironed out, it is still important to consider the legal consequences of a dispute of this nature.

At the outset it should be borne in mind that s 39 has been held to create an absolute offence[3] and a parent may therefore be convicted even if he or she has taken all reasonable steps to ensure the child's attendance at school.[4] In *Jarman v Mid-Glamorgan Education Authority* the parent had persistently objected to any further corporal punishment being inflicted on her children after one of them had been caned at school. The headmaster had thereupon refused the children further admission to the school because corporal punishment was part of the school's disciplinary code of which the parent had been aware since the first child's entry to the school. The Divisional Court upheld the conviction of the parent under s 39 and ruled that the question of the reasonableness of the school's refusal of admission was immaterial, even though it ran counter to the provisions of the European Convention on Human Rights concerning the need for the state to respect the philosophical convictions of parents.[5] However, whether a conviction under s 39 could still be sustained if the school were itself in breach of the provisions of English law, as opposed to the European Convention, is a rather different question. In *Spiers v Warrington Corpn* the conviction of the parent was only upheld by the Divisional Court because the headmistress was found to have been acting within her rights and hence the refusal to admit the child was justified.[6] Had she been acting unlawfully it seems the parent might well have been acquitted.

There would appear to be two possible lines of argument open to a parent who kept a child away from school because of disagreement over what was appropriate dress. These might be relevant either as a defence to a charge under s 39 or in civil proceedings brought against the school or LEA. The first might be that the school was acting unreasonably in demanding strict compliance with a rule about a prescribed uniform in the face of religious or cultural objections by a parent and was therefore in breach of the Education Act 1944, s 68. However, the courts' powers of review on this ground appear to be severely limited. In two leading cases it has been held by Lord Denning MR that intervention, whether by the courts or by the Minister, can only be justified if the action taken by the local education authority was not only wrong but so unreasonably wrong that no reasonable person could take the view that it has taken.[7] Although a parent might pertinently draw attention to the flexible attitudes now found in most schools and local education authorities on this question, there is clearly considerable difficulty in satisfying a burden of proof as heavy as this.

1 Children and Young Persons Act 1969, ss 1(2)(e) and 2 (8)(b)(ii); *Re S* [1978] QB 120, [1978] 3 WLR 575.
2 [1954] 1 QB 61, [1953] 2 All ER 1052.
3 Certain statutory defences are, however, provided in s 39(2) and (3).
4 *Crump v Gilmore* (1970) 68 LGR 56; *Happe v Lay* (1978) 76 LGR 313; *Jarman v Mid-Glamorgan Education Authority* (1985) Times, 11 February.
5 First Protocol, art 2; *Campbell and Cousans v UK* (1982) EHRR 293 discussed at para 7.35 below.
6 [1954] 1 QB 61 at 69.
7 See *Cumings v Birkenhead Corpn* [1972] Ch 12 at 37-8; *Secretary of State for Education and Science v Tameside Metropolitan BC* [1976] 3 All ER 665 at 671, affirmed by the House of Lords at [1976] 3 All ER 679.

7.24 A second and much easier approach is afforded by the provisions of the Race Relations Act 1976 relating to discrimination in the field of education. Section 17(c) provides that it is unlawful for the body responsible for an educational establishment to discriminate against a pupil:

'in the way it affords him access to any benefits, facilities or services, or by refusing or deliberately omitting to afford him access to them or ... by excluding him from the establishment or subjecting him to any other detriment.'

What amounts to discrimination is defined in s 1. This encompasses the concept of 'indirect discrimination' which occurs when a person applies to another

'a requirement or condition which he applies or would apply equally to persons not of the same racial group as that other but —
(i)   which is such that the proportion of persons of the same racial group as that other who can comply with it is considerably smaller than the proportion of persons not of that racial group who can comply with it; and

(ii) which he cannot show to be justifiable irrespective of the colour, race, nationality, or ethnic or national origins of the person to whom it is applied; and

(iii) which is to the detriment of that other because he cannot comply with it.'

For a school to deny an Asian girl access to its facilities and send her home on the basis, not of overt and direct discrimination, but because of a general and universal requirement that all female pupils must wear skirts might well amount prima facie to unlawful indirect discrimination. The first question to be determined however, would be whether her community constituted a 'racial group' within the meaning of the Act. Section 3(1) states that this expression means 'a group of persons defined by reference to colour, race, nationality or ethnic or national origins'. If that requirement could be satisfied as well as the proportionality test in (i) above, then the school would only have a defence if it could establish that the requirement about the wearing of skirts was 'justifiable' irrespective of the girl's ethnic origins.[1]

1 The requirement of 'detriment' in (iii) above is easy to establish and may take the form of psychological harm as well as material loss – see Lustgarten *Legal Control of Racial Discrimination* (Macmillan, 1981) pp 50-1.

7.25 The leading case on all these questions is *Mandla v Dowell Lee*.[1] This concerned the analogous situation of a Sikh boy who had been denied admission to a private school because both he and his father insisted that he be allowed to wear a turban there and this was ruled out as unacceptable by the school. Proceedings were instituted under s 17(a) of the Act whereby it is made unlawful for an educational body to discriminate against a person in the terms on which it offers to admit him as a pupil or by refusing or deliberately omitting to accept his application to be a pupil.

The first issue which the House of Lords had to decide was whether the Sikhs constituted not merely a religious community (since discrimination on grounds of religion is not prohibited by the Act) but also a racial group within the extended meaning laid down in s 3 of the Act. This in turn depended upon whether they could be described as a group defined by reference to 'ethnic' origins. The Court of Appeal had interpreted the word 'ethnic' narrowly as involving a fixed or inherited racial characteristic and held that on this basis the Sikhs failed to qualify for the protection of the Act since they were biologically indistinguishable from other people living in the Punjab. On appeal, however, the House of Lords adopted a far broader construction of 'ethnic' and one more in keeping with ordinary usage today. In the leading speech Lord Fraser expressed their Lordships' view as follows:

'My Lords, I recognise that "ethnic" conveys a flavour of race but it cannot . . . have been used in the 1976 Act in a strict racial or biological sense. For one thing, it would be absurd to suppose that Parliament can have intended that membership of a particular racial group should depend on scientific proof that a person possessed the relevant distinctive biological characteristics (assuming that such characteristics exist). The practical difficulties of such proof would be prohibitive, and it is clear that Parliament must have used the word in some more popular sense. For another thing, the briefest glance at the evidence in this case is enough to show that, within the human race, there are very few, if any, distinctions which are scientifically recognised as racial.'[2]

Having established that the word 'ethnic' carried wider connotations than merely 'racial' or 'biological', Lord Fraser next proceeded to identify its other ingredients as follows:

'For a group to constitute an ethnic group in the sense of the 1976 Act, it must . . .

regard itself, and be regarded by others, as a distinct community by virtue of certain characteristics. Some of these characteristics are essential; others are not essential but one or more of them will commonly be found and will help to distinguish the group from the surrounding community. The conditions which appear to me to be essential are these: (1) a long shared history, of which the group is conscious as distinguishing it from other groups, and the memory of which keeps it alive; (2) a cultural tradition of its own, including family and social customs and manners, often but not necessarily associated with religious observance. In addition to those two essential characteristics the following characteristics are . . . relevant: (3) either a common geographical origin, or descent from a small number of common ancestors; (4) a common language, not necessarily peculiar to the group; (5) a common literature peculiar to the group; (6) a common religion different from that of neighbouring groups or from the general community surrounding it; (7) being a minority or being an oppressed or a dominant group within a larger community, for example a conquered people . . . and their conquerors might both be ethnic groups.'[3]

On this basis their Lordships had no difficulty in finding that the Sikhs constituted a group identifiable by reference to its ethnic origins and thus entitled to the protection of the 1976 Act. The Sikhs were originally a purely religious community founded around the end of the 15th century in the Punjab by Guru Nanak. They were at one time politically supreme in the Punjab and they still retain aspirations towards a degree of political autonomy in India today. Their members are conscious of being a distinctive community with its own culture and customs. They have a script *(Gurmukhi)* which, while not peculiar to them, can be read by a much higher proportion of Sikhs than non-Sikhs. Most of them come from the Punjab and hence speak a common language *(Punjabi)*, although this language is also shared by other groups living in that region.

The ruling by the House of Lords that Sikhs and their turbans are covered by the 1976 Act corresponds with the intentions of the Government of the day in framing the legislation in such a way as to outlaw indirect discrimination. A White Paper entitled 'Racial Discrimination' published in 1975 specifically declared:

'The provision [about indirect discrimination] will . . . apply to requirements concerning . . . clothing . . . (e g preventing the wearing of turbans or saris) . . . .'[4]

The decision is also a triumph for commonsense in reflecting both the popular understanding of the word 'ethnic' at the present time and the ordinary person's view about the desirability of affording a group like the Sikhs protection from discrimination in English society. It would appear that the Jews would be similarly counted as an ethnic group by reference to Lord Fraser's criteria;[5] indeed even Lord Denning MR in the Court of Appeal was prepared to include the Jews in the light of his narrow concentration upon racial characteristics.[6] Hence were a school to deny a Jewish boy the right to wear a *kippa* or *yarmulka* (skull cap) this would also prima facie amount to unlawful discrimination under the Act.

1 [1983] 2 AC 548, [1983] 1 All ER 1062.
2 At 1066.
3 At 1066-7.
4 Cmnd 6234 of 1975, para 55. The particular reference was to employees rather than schoolchildren but this is of no special significance since the Act outlaws indirect discrimination in the fields of both employment and education. See also the statement of the Government spokesman, Mr Brynmor John MP, during the committee stage of the Bill – *Official Report*, Standing Committee 'A', 4 May 1976, cols 102-3.
5 Jews were expressly held to be an ethnic group by the New Zealand Court of Appeal, applying

a similarly worded provision, in *King-Ansell v Police* [1979] 2 NZLR 531, a case which clearly influenced Lord Fraser's approach in *Mandla v Dowell Lee* (see at 1067-8).
6 [1982] 3 All ER 1108 at 1112, 1113. That Jews were intended to be covered by the original Race Relations Act of 1965 is clear from the statement of the then Home Secretary, Sir Frank Soskice MP in committee – see *Official Report*, Standing Committee 'B', 27 May 1965, cols 82-3.

7.26   We are now in a better position to attempt to answer the question posed at the start of this discussion, namely whether an Asian girl would have the same ground for complaint under the Act if her school insisted that she wear, as an integral part of the school uniform, a skirt which revealed her legs. The first problem is whether she is a member of an ethnic group. If she is a Sikh she clearly qualifies, but do Muslims and Hindus come within this concept or are they merely adherents to a particular religion? The reference to *saris* in the White Paper of 1965 quoted earlier suggests that this type of discrimination was intended to be outlawed, even though religious discrimination per se is not covered by the Act. Perhaps the best way of framing a claim would be for the girl to rely on her membership of a group defined by reference to 'national' rather than ethnic origins, eg Indian, Pakistani or Bangladeshi.

The second question relates to the proportionality test laid down in s 1(1)(b)(i) of the Act. The issue here is whether the rule about skirts is a requirement which is such that the proportion of persons of the particular 'racial' group to which the Asian girl belongs who can comply with it is considerably smaller than the proportion of persons not of that ethnic group who can comply with it. In *Mandla v Dowell Lee* the House of Lords held that the words 'can comply' must not be interpreted literally as meaning 'can physically comply' but as meaning 'can in practice' or 'can consistently with the customs and cultural conditions of the racial group'. Obviously an Asian girl can in physical terms put on a skirt just as any Sikh boy can refrain from wearing a turban, but for the law to adopt this theoretical approach, the House of Lords held, would mean that the protection which Parliament had intended ethnic groups to have would in fact be denied them.[1] Assuming, therefore, that virtually every non-Asian girl can conscientiously wear a skirt and that the percentage of, for example, Indian girls who can do so is considerably smaller (which appears extremely likely) this aspect of the test laid down by the Act will probably be satisfied without any difficulty. In *Price v Civil Service Commission*,[2] a case decided in the same way under the parallel provisions of the Sex Discrimination Act 1975 (and approved by the House of Lords in *Mandla v Dowell Lee*), Phillips J held that it was relevant in determining whether a woman could comply with the condition in question to take into account 'the current usual behaviour of women in this respect, as observed in practice, putting on one side behaviour and responses which are unusual or extreme'.[3]

The third issue that arises is whether the school might be able to justify their requirement about dress under s 1(1)(b)(ii) of the Act. Here the burden of proof is placed firmly upon the school to establish that the condition or rule imposed is justifiable irrespective of the ethnic origin of the person to whom it is applied. In *Mandla v Dowell Lee* the respondent headmaster sought to argue that the rule barring the wearing of turbans was justifiable under two separate heads, namely practical convenience and the Christian nature of the school. The latter justification was dismissed by the House of Lords on the ground that it did not fit within the wording of the subsection. The justification permitted by the subsection has to be irrespective of the child's ethnic origin, yet here the headmaster was objecting to the turban being worn precisely because it would have been a manifestation of a non-Christian faith in what he wished to be a Christian school. This finding effectively proscribed religious discrimination in the circumstances of the particular case, a result which appears to be in conformity with the intentions of the government when the legislation was enacted in 1976.[4] In dealing with a proposed amendment to the Bill which would have also outlawed religious discrimination, Mr Brynmor John MP, Minister of State at the Home Office, made this statement in rejecting the amendment:

'I hope to be able to show . . . that the Bill is a considerable advance in protecting the religions of people in its concept of indirect discrimination . . . . The Bill's new concept, that of indirect discrimination, does a great deal to protect those who are discriminated against by means of their religious observance . . . . Let me give some practical examples of what I mean. Here I must touch upon the Sikh turban problem . . . . It provides a concrete example of how indirect discrimination might be caught.'

The second justification offered by the headmaster in *Mandla v Dowell Lee* was based on practical convenience. He argued that his objectives in prescribing a school uniform were to minimise external differences between races and social classes, to discourage the competitive fashions which tend to exist within a teenage community and to present a Christian image to outsiders (including prospective parents). The rule about the uniform, he claimed, could not be relaxed in favour of a Sikh boy for fear of setting a precedent which could not be satisfactorily explained to other pupils who sought greater diversity of clothing. These attempted justifications were rejected out of hand by the House of Lords, but somewhat surprisingly no reason was given. Presumably they were felt to be too flimsy to qualify, although grounds of general administrative efficiency totally unrelated to ethnicity would presumably be relevant if they were objectively compelling enough in all the circumstances. In *Ojutiku and Oburoni v Manpower Services Commission*[5] the Court of Appeal had earlier held that although the word 'justifiable' in the Race Relations Act did not mean the same thing as 'necessary', it did require reasons which were sound and tolerable to right-thinking people rather than ones which merely related to convenience. However, as has been suggested earlier, a compromise can easily be reached between the conflicting interests involved by permitting turbans or *shalwar* on condition that they are of a particular colour. Any white child who complains about such a dispensation needs to be clearly told the reasons why this is being allowed. As the House of Commons Education, Science and Arts Committee stated recently '. . . tolerance of diversity is in any case one of the values which most people would wish to transmit to the next generation'.[6] While the desire to prevent indirect discrimination must be balanced under the Act against the need for well-run schools and the provision of a good education for all pupils, in the sphere of appropriate dress for school these considerations are far from incompatible and there is a strong argument for saying that no really good educational practice could possibly encompass discrimination outlawed by the 1976 Act.

1 At 1069.
2 [1978] 1 All ER 1228, [1977] 1 WLR 1417.
3 At 1231.
4 See *Official Report*, Standing Committee 'A', 4 May 1976, cols 101 and 102.
5 [1982] IRLR 418.
6 (1981-82) HC 116-I, para 2.4.

D. DIETARY RESTRICTIONS

7.27 Many ethnic minority parents feel that school meals should take into account their various dietary regulations.[1] Strictly, Muslims and Jews should always avoid pork and only eat other meats if the animal or fowl has been slaughtered according to the proper ritual;[2] such meat is generally referred to as *kosher* among Jews and *halal* among Muslims. Strict Hindus and Sikhs should avoid beef, though it has been suggested that the younger generation here do not observe this custom nearly as rigorously as their parents.[3]

1 See *Between Two Cultures* p 20; *The Education of Ethnic Minority Children* p 37; P Jeffery *Migrants and Refugees* p 77.
2 See *McDermott and Ahsan* pp 36, 49-50; Horowitz *The Spirit of Jewish Law* pp 115-7 and see para 10.11 below.
3 See J H Taylor *The Half-Way Generation* (NFER, 1976) pp 91-3; Iqbal *East Meets West* pp 94-5; Kanitkar and Jackson *Hindus in Britain* (London, 1982) p 15.

Policy considerations

7.28 In 1972 a report sponsored by the Department of Education and Science indicated that there had been a significant failure on the part of many schools to pay any attention to the dietary restrictions of their pupils.[1] No doubt it can be argued that to do so might cause a certain amount of inconvenience for the kitchen staff, but this can hardly be regarded as an insuperable barrier to a change of practice. It certainly ought to be feasible to arrange either for a choice of menus or for vegetarian meals or even for a regular supply of ritually slaughtered meat,[2] depending on the circumstances. Not to do so where there is a substantial proportion of ethnic minority children can only lead to an unnecessary wastage of food, and frustrated and possibly hungry ethnic minority pupils. The greater familiarity with the cuisines of other countries which the white majority have (gratefully) acquired during the past 30 years or so surely needs to be matched now by an increased respect for minority dietary restrictions. A significant advance occurred in 1979 when the Inner London Education Authority issued a directive to all its schools requiring them to observe Muslim and Hindu regulations in preparing their meals[3] and there is some evidence to show that this is no longer generally a problem area between schools and ethnic minority parents.[4] In 1982 the City of Bradford Metropolitan Council issued a directive that the dietary restrictions of its school-children should always be respected[5] and in 1983 it successfully made arrangements for the provision of *halal* meat in its schools.[6]

1 See *Townsend and Brittan* pp 61-2, 137-8.
2 For discussion of the alleged cruelty involved in ritual slaughter, see paras 10.12-10.13 below.
3 EO/CS/M74 (July 1979); *Daily Telegraph*, 6 October 1979.
4 See *Little and Willey* p 25.
5 Local Administrative Memorandum No 2 of 1982.
6 See (1983), *Times*, 8 July. By March 1984 about 2,000 out of a total of 14,000 Muslim pupils were receiving *halal* meat – TES, 9 March 1984.

English law

7.29 In terms of the Education Act 1980, s 22 LEAs have a general power to provide pupils in the maintained sector with meals and a duty to provide such facilities as they consider appropriate for the consumption of any meals or refreshments brought to the school by the pupils themselves. They are also obliged to make such provision in the middle of the day for pupils whose parents are in receipt of supplementary benefit or family income supplement as appears to be requisite, without making any charge therefor. Statistics for 1983 revealed that roughly half of all pupils in maintained schools ate school dinners and that of these some 16% were provided free because of limited parental means.[1]

Since the school meals service is entirely a local authority operation[2] the question arises whether any LEA which fails to cater adequately for the special dietary requirements of ethnic minority pupils at its schools is acting in violation of the Race Relations Act 1976. If, for example, pork was served regularly to pupils in a school with a proportion of Jewish or Muslim pupils without any choice of menu this would appear to be indirect discrimination, either in relation to the affording of access to benefits or facilities under s 17 (discussed earlier) or under the more general provisions of s 18(1) which declares:

'It is unlawful for a local education authority, in carrying out such of its functions under the Education Acts 1944 to 1980 as do not fall under s 17, to do any act which constitutes racial discrimination.'

Questions comparable with those discussed earlier in relation to *Mandla v Dowell Lee* would inevitably arise, namely whether Jews or Muslims constitute an ethnic group, whether the proportionality test was satisfied and whether or not the discrimination was justifiable. It is thought that in a suitable case, such as Jews being served pork, the first two of these requirements could easily be met. On the issue of justification, the defence would presumably be raised of the need to operate the school meals system efficiently and economically. This would be a question of fact in each case,[3] but it is thought that the adjustments required to provide an alternative menu would be so small and inexpensive as to negate any plea of justification in most instances.

1 See *DES Annual Report 1983* p 15.
2 See *Regan* p 100.
3 See *Mandla v Dowell Lee* [1983] 1 All ER 1062 at 1070.

The scope for reform

7.30 Even if failure on the part of LEAs to accommodate the dietary require-ments of ethnic minority pupils is at present unlawful, there would seem to be a strong case for a circular to be issued to all LEAs by the DES indicating clearly that the necessary special provision must be made for them.

If, on the other hand, such failure is not unlawful under existing domestic law there would seem to be a strong argument for reform. The First Protocol to the European Convention on Human Rights Art 2 obliges the UK under international law to respect the rights of parents to ensure education and teaching in conformity with their own religious and philosophical convictions.[1] This obligation is expressly stated to relate to the exercise of any functions which the state assumes in relation to education and in the case of *Campbell and Cosans v UK*[2] the European Court of Human Rights held that this referred not only to the content of education but also to questions of school organisation and administration. In view of this it appears likely that since the provision of the school meals service is entirely a local authority operation the UK would be in breach of the Convention if it failed to respect the religious convictions of ethnic minority parents in this regard. Admittedly, the UK only ratified the First Protocol with a reservation that the respect afforded should be compatible with the provision of efficient instruction and training and the avoidance of unreasonable public expenditure,[3] but it is thought this could not provide any defence in the sphere of school meals.

1 The International Covenant on Economic, Social and Cultural Rights, Art 13(3) is in similar vein, obliging state parties to 'have respect for the liberty of parents . . . to ensure the religious and moral education of their children in conformity with their own convictions'.
2 (1982) 4 EHRR 293.

3 See Cmnd 9221 of 1954, echoing the terminology of the Education Act 1944, s 76.

E. SEPARATION OF THE SEXES

7.31 The general pattern of coeducational schools in this country presents a problem for some Asian and Cypriot parents. Many of them wish to follow the traditional practice in their communities of sending their daughters to a single-sex secondary school.[1] In part this is because they are apprehensive about the risks of liaisons being formed at coeducational schools which might prejudice their systems of arranged marriages.[2] However, for Muslim parents there is a further and much more important religious dimension because part of the Islamic doctrine of *purdah* (seclusion) enjoins the separation of the sexes from puberty onwards.[3] Indeed, many Muslims share with orthodox Jews the belief that boys and girls need to be trained for different roles in life, with the girls primarily being educated for marriage, motherhood and domestic activities.[4]

The *Swann Committee Report* revealed that the number of secondary schools for girls in the maintained sector declined from over 1,000 in 1968 to only 415 in 1981, not apparently through any major government policy initiative but largely as a natural consequence of the reorganisation on comprehensive lines which was thought to necessitate fewer and larger schools.[5] The result for those parents who do not feel able to send their daughters to a coeducational school is that they may often be faced with three alternatives none of which is what they really want. The first is to keep their daughters away from school altogether.[6] The second is to send them back to their countries of origin.[7] The third, assuming they can afford the fees, is to send them to private schools; indeed over the past few years there has even been some discussion of new independent single-sex schools for girls in Birmingham and Bradford being specially established with financial assistance from the governments of Saudi Arabia and Pakistan.[8]

1 See *Swann Committee Report* pp 504-7, 678-9.
2 See P Jeffery *Migrants and Refugees* pp 77, 105.
3 See Iqbal 'Education and Islam in Britain – A Muslim View' [1976-77] New Community 397; *McDermott and Ahsan* p 45; *Between Two Cultures* pp 20, 32-3. See also generally Papanek 'Purdah in Pakistan' (1971) Journal of Marriage and the Family 517; P Jeffery *Frogs in a Well: Indian Women in Purdah* (London, 1979).
4 See *Swann Committee Report* pp 505-7.
5 Ibid p 508.
6 In 1983 it was reported that between 500 and 700 Muslim girls were being kept out of school in Bradford – see (1983) *Times*, 18 June.
7 See TES, 11 January 1974; *Birmingham Post*, 5 September 1974.
8 See Rex and Tomlinson *Colonial Immigrants in a British City* (Routledge, 1979) pp 187, 271; Iqbal 'Education and Islam in Britain – A Muslim View' (1976-77) *New Community* 397 at 400.

Policy considerations

7.32 The demand for single-sex schooling to be more widely available in the maintained sector is open to the objection that it runs counter to recent trends in educational thinking here, which explains why the policy of coeducation is favoured by the vast majority of local education authorities. Extensive and influential research by Dale[1] seems to indicate that coeducational schools in England are happier and livelier, have a friendlier atmosphere and are generally more human places than single-sex schools. They also provide educational results that are superior (in the case of boys) or at least as good (in the case of girls) as single-sex schools. One of their major advantages is thought to be their reflection of life in the wider context of English society as a whole, where segregation of the sexes is regarded as wholly artificial. If education is meant to be a training for later life it cannot neglect its role of familiarising the sexes with one another in ordinary, everyday situations of work and outside activities.

Of course, these arguments are by no means equally applicable to patterns of behaviour in traditional Asian families where there is often quite a rigid separation of roles between men and women and the Islamic doctrine of *purdah* so constricts a wife that she will usually neither work outside the home nor mix socially with men other than close relatives. Much depends, therefore, upon what future lifestyle is envisaged for these children in England, a secluded one governed by the doctrines of *purdah* or the more open one which corresponds with the practices and beliefs of the majority community. However, there can certainly be no objection to ethnic minority parents expressing to a local authority their preference for single-sex schooling or sending their children to such schools in the private sector since these are freedoms granted to all parents in this country and many white parents also strongly favour sending their children to these schools.

1 See *Mixed or Single Sex School?* (Routledge, 1969-74), especially Vol III, ch 17. Dale concluded that his researches 'point unmistakeably to coeducation as the preferable system' (at p 273).

English law

7.33 The desire to send children (especially girls) to single-sex schools raises two separate legal issues. The first is the extent to which a parent has the right to demand this type of schooling for his child in the maintained sector.[1]

The Education Act 1944, s 76 provides as follows:

'In the exercise and performance of all powers and duties conferred and imposed upon them by this Act the Secretary of State and local education authorities shall have regard to the general principle that, so far as is compatible with the provision of efficient instruction and training and the avoidance of unreasonable public expenditure, pupils are to be educated in accordance with the wishes of their parents.'

This provision has recently been buttressed by the Education Act 1980, s 6(5) which imposes upon local education authorities a duty to comply with an expressed parental preference unless:
(i) compliance would prejudice the provision of efficient education or the efficient use of resources; or
(ii) if the preferred school is a voluntary aided or special agreement school and compliance would be incompatible with any arrangements between the governors and the local authority in respect of admission; or
(iii) if the preferred school is academically selective and compliance would be incompatible with the operation of the selection process.

The general duty of compliance imposed upon local authorities applies not only to preferences expressed by parents living within a particular authority's area but also to those schools chosen outside the district where the parents reside.

Since there is no question of single-sex schools offending against the Sex Discrimination Act 1975[2] the expressed desire of parents to have their child educated at such an establishment obviously has to be taken into account by any local education authority to whom this preference has been communicated anywhere in the country. However, assuming that the authority to whom application is made does have single-sex school places available, the amount of discretion conferred upon it by the first exception to s 6(5) above is extremely wide and parents are far from being given total freedom of choice in this regard by the 1980 Act. Judicial decisions interpreting s 76 of the 1944 Act have held that authorities are not absolutely bound to give effect to parental wishes and can take account of other considerations, as well as the constraints mentioned in the section itself.[3] It seems probable that the courts will adopt a similar approach under the 1980 Act in view of the broad way in which the duty of the authority is qualified in s 6(5), together with the specific provision of rights of appeal in s 7 to committees whose decisions will be binding on the authority.[4]

Where an education authority has no single-sex schools in its own area it is empowered by statute to arrange for places to be made available at an independent single-sex school in the private sector and to pay the necessary fees there.[5] However, it was held in *Watt v Kesteven CC*[6] that the education authority is not obliged to pay the tuition fees of an independent school which has simply been chosen by a parent but with which they themselves have made no prior arrangements. In such a case the most the parent could expect would be some assistance from the authority with the payment of fees if he would otherwise suffer financial hardship.

From all this one must conclude that a parent has no absolute right either to insist that his daughter be admitted to a single-sex school in the maintained sector or to demand that his local authority pay the fees if he sends her to a school in the private sector.

1 On the general question of parental rights in education, see Masson 'Parental Choice in State Education' (1980) JSWL 193; Meredith 'Executive Discretion and Choice of Secondary School' (1981) Public Law 52.
2 Such schools are exempted under s 26.
3 See *Watt v Kesteven CC* [1955] 1 QB 408, [1955] 1 All ER 473; *Wood v Ealing London BC* [1967] Ch 364, [1966] 3 All ER 514.
4 See Meredith at 72, 75-7, 82.
5 Education (Miscellaneous Provisions) Act 1953, s 6.
6 [1955] 1 QB 408, [1955] 1 All ER 473.

7.34 The second issue is what the legal consequences are if such a parent takes the decision to withdraw his child and refuses to allow her to attend school at all. The basic rule is that parents are under a statutory obligation to educate their children.[1] The Education Act 1944, s 36 provides as follows:

'It shall be the duty of the parent of every child of compulsory school age to cause him to receive efficient full-time education suitable to his age, ability and aptitude, either by regular attendance at school or otherwise.'

The responsibility for ensuring that each child does in fact receive such education lies with the local education authority. If they are not satisfied about this in a particular case they must serve on the defaulting parent a notice requiring him to prove, within 14 days, that the child is being properly educated. If he fails to do this the authority must send him another notice indicating that they intend to serve a 'school attendance order', requiring him to register the child at a particular named school (or an alternative if one is specified by the parent), unless within 14 days he finds another school to accept the child. The parent's choice will then be named in the order unless it is an independent school which the authority considers unsuitable.[2] A parent who then fails to send his child to the school named will be guilty of an offence unless he can show that child is receiving suitable education otherwise than at school, for instance proper tuition from his parents at home.[3] The other possible consequence is that the authority may take the step of bringing the child before a juvenile court under the Children and Young Persons Act 1969.[4] If the court is satisfied both as to the lack of education and that the child is in need of care and control it may proceed to make a 'care order'.[5] No doubt in most cases the threat to the parent of having the child removed and losing parental rights is more potent than the risk of prosecution.[6]

In *Bradford Corpn v Patel*[7] a Muslim father had refused to comply with a school attendance order in terms of which his 15-year-old daughter had been allocated to a coeducational school in Bradford. He had been keeping her at home for the previous two years because the only state schools in the area were coeducational and this offended against his religious beliefs. He put this factor forward as his sole defence to a charge under s 37 of the 1944 Act, but he was duly convicted by the magistrates and only discharged upon the condition that he complied with an attendance order specifying a coeducational school. Clearly, therefore, this line of defence stands little prospect of success in the future. Difficulties in enforcing the law may, however, be anticipated since children who are withdrawn from school may be hard to trace. The parents may sometimes claim that they have sent them back to relatives in their countries of origin, but this may not always be the truth.[8]

1 See generally Bevan *The Law relating to Children* (Butterworths, 1973) pp 432-9.
2 Education Act 1944, s 37 as modified by the Education Act, 1980 s 10.
3 Education Act 1944, s 37(5). Penalties are prescribed in s 40.
4 Ss 1(2)(e) and 2(8)(b)(ii).
5 See *Re S* [1978] QB 120, [1978] 3 WLR 575.
6 Where the child has already been registered as a pupil at a school and then fails to attend it regularly the parent may be convicted of an offence under the Education Act 1944, s 39; see para 7.23 above.
7 Unreported, but discussed in *TES*, 11 January 1974.
8 See, e g *Townsend and Brittan* p 67, who refer to the suspicion that they may be 'hidden behind the curtains'; Lodge 'Muslims "faking evidence to keep girls at home"' *TES*, 6 May 1983.

The scope for reform

7.35 As mentioned earlier,[1] the First Protocol to the European Convention on Human Rights, Art 2 provides as follows:

'... In the exercise of any functions which it assumes in relation to education and to teaching, the State shall respect the right of parents to ensure such education and teaching in conformity with their own religious and philosophical convictions.'[2]

In view of the decision of the European Court of Human Rights in *Campbell and Cosans v UK*[3] that the organisation of education is included within the ambit of this article, there is every reason to believe that the creation and distribution of coeducational and single-sex schools by LEAs can be assessed by reference to its terms.[4] Insofar, therefore, as such arrangements fail to cater adequately for the religious convictions of ethnic minority parents within a particular area the UK may be in breach of the Protocol. In order to comply with international treaty obligations it is thus necessary to ensure that these needs are met by a sufficient number of secondary school places at girls' schools for the children of those parents whose religious convictions demand them. The only limitation upon this duty is provided by the UK reservation to the Protocol, in terms of which the respect for parental convictions only has to be ensured to the extent that this is compatible with the provision of efficient instruction and training and the avoidance of unreasonable public expenditure.[5] Legislative reform giving parents the right to choose single-sex schooling for their children within the maintained sector on religious grounds would therefore seem to be very desirable. However, at least until there is a clear ruling by the European Court of Human Rights on the matter such legislation seems rather unlikely to be introduced and the most that can realistically be expected is a continuation by the DES of its current policy of stressing to LEAs the need to have regard to parental preferences for single-sex schools, on religious or other grounds, when proposals are submitted for reorganisations or closures of schools in the light of falling rolls.[6] Strong support for this line of approach was voiced by the Swann Committee which reported as follows:

'We hope ... that Authorities will be prepared to consider carefully the value of retaining an option of single sex education as part of their secondary school provision and that the Secretary of State will be similarly sensitive to the wider ramifications of any decision which he might need to make on proposals which could lead to the loss of single sex provision in multiracial areas. As Muslim representatives have pointed out to us, they are not alone in favouring single sex education and it must be accepted therefore that single sex schools would not draw their pupils exclusively from the Asian community and could be as multi-racial as their co-educational counterparts.'[7]

The Report continued:

'In cases where LEAs may either no longer provide for single sex education at all, or make only very limited such provision, we would hope that if concern was expressed by parents about the education of, in particular, their daughters, the possibility of establishing or re-establishing single sex schools would be given serious consideration.'[7]

1 Para 7.20 above.
2 The International Covenant on Economic, Social and Cultural Rights, Art 13(3) is couched in similar terms.
3 (1982) 4 EHRR 293.
4 See especially the dissenting judgment of Judge Sir Vincent Evans at 310.
5 See cmnd 9221 of 1954.
6 See DES Circular 4/1982, para 5.
7 *Swann Committee Report* p 512.

F. MULTICULTURAL EDUCATION

7.36 Some ethnic minority parents suspect that one of the reasons why there is so much racism in this country and so many of their children do not achieve their full potential at school is that there is a firmly entrenched cultural bias in many aspects of the teaching, the textbooks, the examinations and indeed the curriculum generally.[1] They are therefore interested in the promotion of a new movement in the direction of 'multicultural', 'multiethnic' or 'multiracial' education, which they hope will redress the balance somewhat in their favour. Ideally, this type of education would accurately reflect not only their own place in modern English society but also the contributions of their cultures, both in world history and in current international affairs. They hope that its incorporation in the formal school curriculum might give their children a pride in their own cultures which would be important for their self-image and sense of identity, as well as being conducive to their academic success.

In seeking such a revision of traditional teaching, not only for their own children but for all pupils in the country, they have the broad support of both educationalists and politicians.[2] The re-orientated curriculum would, of course, have to be carefully planned and would doubtless require a great deal of time, energy, initiative and expertise on the part of both teachers and local authorities.

It cannot be merely a token gesture resulting in an inferior education for all and satisfying no-one.

As a reflection of government policy the 1977 Green Paper, *Education in Schools*, merely stated the obvious when it declared:

'Our society is a multicultural, multiracial one and the curriculum should reflect a sympathetic understanding of the different cultures and races that now make up our society . . . . We also live in a complex, interdependent world, and many of our problems in Britain require international solutions. The curriculum should therefore reflect our need to know about and understand other countries.'[3]

For any school to refuse to attach any value to the cultures, religions and traditions of ethnic minorities living in this country can only contribute to a widespread belief that they are inferior and unworthy of general respect. This in turn may tend to increase the level of prejudice against them and lessen their prospects of integration in the wider community. It is equally important that white children should grow up in an environment in which cultural differences are plainly recognised and appreciated as a normal and natural aspect of English society, rather than something outlandish and strange which they only learn about for themselves by means of half-truths and misleading gossip.

The concept of multicultural education also seems particularly valuable in focusing attention on the need to eliminate any cultural bias in teaching, textbooks and examinations. As Parekh has pointed out:

'Children who grow up reading that Asiatic contribution to man's control over nature is 'negligible' and African contribution 'non-existent' or that these societies, before they were 'civilised' by the Europeans, spent their time killing one another, or that their moral or political achievements are inconsequential can hardly be expected to be other than prejudiced to the non-white community in their midst. By contrast children who are taught to appreciate non-Christian religions, Asian and African music, art, literature and languages, and the great cultural and social achievements of non-European peoples are likely to grow into sensitive, curious and sympathetic adults capable not only of treating all their fellow men with kindness and understanding but also of living a rich and varied life.'[4]

The cultural expression of racist ideas and stereotypes in school textbooks is clearly a serious cause for concern. Not surprisingly the House of Commons Home Affairs Committee recently indicated to local authorities that they should act with vigour to have such books withdrawn as soon as possible.[5]

Little and Willey have also reported that considerable criticism has been voiced by some teachers against certain examining boards on the grounds that they are restricting progressive development of the curriculum to reflect our increasingly multiethnic society.[6] If many public examinations are indeed culturally biased immediate action surely needs to be taken to remedy the situation.

1 See, e g 'West Indian Children in our Schools' *(Rampton Committee Report)* Cmnd 8273 of 1981, pp 35-8.
2 See generally D Milner *Children and Race: Ten Years On* (Ward Lock, 1983); Nixon 'Multiethnic education in Inner London' [1981-2] New Community 381; Fifth Report from the Home Affairs Committee on Racial Disadvantage, HC 424-I, para 155; Second Report from the Education, Science and Arts Committee, HC 116-I, paras 7.18-7.19; *Swann Committee Report* ch 6; 'Better Schools' Cmnd 9469 of 1985, para 206.
3 Cmnd 6869 of 1977, para 10.11.
4 *Colour, Culture and Consciousness* p 237.
5 HC 424-I, para 155. The same plea had been made earlier in the *Bullock Report* (1975) para 20.5.
6 *Multi-ethnic Education: The Way Forward* p 21.

Policy considerations

7.37 The idea of multicultural education has come in for a considerable amount of criticism from a number of quarters, some of it particularly strident. Indeed the degree of passion expressed in the views of its detractors appears almost to match the strength of commitment on the part of its promoters.

Some of the best-reasoned arguments against it have, however, come from a West Indian educationalist, Maureen Stone,[1] who contends that much of its philosophy is based on a complete misapprehension about the self-esteem of West Indian children. During the 1970s serious attention was paid by educationalists to David Milner's research findings[2] that some black children had a poor self-image as a result of bias in the school curriculum and textbooks. He found that they possessed a negative self-concept and showed a tendency to devalue their own group and to have a strong preference for the dominant white group. Some teachers appear to have simplified his conclusions to the point of regarding all black children as psychologically damaged by racism and they therefore saw the role of multicultural education as constituting some form of remedial therapy. Insofar as the goals of a multicultural curriculum were chiefly devoted to increasing the self-respect, fulfilment and happiness of black children, Maureen Stone's principal criticisms were first, that the assumption that black children had low self-esteem was not proven on the available evidence and secondly, that schools should concentrate their efforts on conventional teaching of basic skills, an area in which black children were known to be performing badly, rather than stressing vague psychological goals in pursuance of some romantic vision.[3]

Stone's polemic has undoubtedly had an impact on the debate about multicultural education and has been acknowledged even by David Milner to be an important and timely reminder of the need to clarify the three central values of the concept.[4] These are, first, that every child has a right to have his culture reflected in the school curriculum in order to avoid bias and discrimination and provide equality of educational opportunity; second, that it is important for all children, white as well as black, to be taught both about the present population of this country and indeed about the wider world as it really is; and third, that the principal role of education remains to bring children up to a satisfactory level of achievement to fit them for later life.

A central issue now revolves around Marueen Stone's accusation that multicultural education leads to a lowering of standards in such basic skills as literacy and numeracy. This charge is fiercely resisted by its proponents who argue that this would only come about where a school actually replaced classes in, for example, English and mathematics by, say, steel band sessions, West Indian dialect classes or a 'black studies course'. In practice this does not happen, nor do such activities constitute the core concept of a multicultural curriculum. The kernel of the idea is rather that there should be a wholesale permeation of virtually the entire curriculum with multiracial, multicultural themes, images and materials instead of a piecemeal, segregated approach involving discreet timetable 'slots' for specialised activities of a multicultural nature.[5]

This approach should also help to meet the objection still heard from schools with no ethnic minority pupils that multicultural education has little significance for them.[6] It is just as important for white children in these schools to be taught about the cultures of their fellow citizens if racism is not to be imbued in the majority of the next generation. *The Swann Committee Report* put the matter in the following way:

'We believe it is essential to look ahead to educating *all* children, from whatever ethnic group, to an understanding of the shared values of our society as a whole as well as to an appreciation of the diversity of lifestyles and cultural, religious and linguistic backgrounds which make up this society and the wider world. In so doing, all pupils should be given the knowledge and skills needed not only to contribute positively to shaping the future nature of British society but also to determine their own individual identities . . . . We believe that schools also however have a responsibility, within the tradition of a flexible and child-orientated education system, to meet the individual educational needs of *all* pupils in a positive and supportive manner, and this would include catering for any particular educational needs which an ethnic minority pupil may have, arising for example from his or her linguistic or cultural background.'[7]

Whether the topics of racism, prejudice and discrimination should be tackled explicitly in classroom discussion is a hotly contested issue.[8] One study has even suggested that such teaching may prove counterproductive and actually lead to an increase in prejudice,[9] though another concluded as follows:

'. . . the major finding is that no marked deterioration in the attitudinal or personality characteristics of the pupils was manifested in their test responses after exposure to the teaching programme. The effects of the experiment, although not generally significant, tended to suggest a shift in the direction of inter-ethnic tolerance.'[10]

Significantly, the *Swann Committee Report* advocated the countering of racism by courses in 'political education',[11] but it seems clear that neither teaching about different cultures nor instruction about racism can realistically be expected, on their own, to eliminate prejudice. It is hard in practice to separate discussion of different cultures from an analysis of racism in Britain today and a growing number of teachers appear to be recognising this. The rest, no doubt a majority, would prefer to concentrate on what they perceive as the constructive sharing approach of multiculturalism rather than the overtly political, conflict-ridden and complex issue of racism,[12] though they would no doubt be quick to condemn any racist behaviour which occurred within their own schools.

1 *The Education of the Black Child in Britain: The Myth of Multiracial Education* (Fontana, 1981).
2 'Prejudice and the immigrant child' (1971) 18 New Society 556; 'Racial identification and preference in black British children' (1973) European Journal of Social Psychology 281; *Children and Race* (Penguin, 1975).
3 At pp 253-4.
4 'The education of the black child in Britain: a review and a response' [1981] *New Community* 289 at 291-2. In his *Children and Race: Ten Years On* (1983) Milner explains how the self-esteem of black children has improved markedly since his earlier research: see ch 6.
5 Milner [1981] *New Community* 289 at 290; *Swann Committee Report* pp 323, 327.
6 See e g *Rampton Committee Report* p 5; *Little and Willey* pp 10, 29; Nixon at 392; *Swann Committee Report* pp 232-7, 315.
7 At pp 316-7 (the Committee preferred the phrase 'education for all' to 'multicultural education').
8 See generally R Giles *The West Indian Experience in British Schools* (London, 1977); *Local Authorities and the Education Implications of Section 71 of the Race Relations Act 1976* (CRE, 1981), p 11; Milner *Children and Race: Ten Years On* pp 200-3.
9 See Miller 'The effectiveness of teaching techniques for reducing colour prejudice' (1969) 16 Liberal Education 25.
10 See L Stenhouse *et al Teaching About Race Relations* (Routledge, 1982) p 7.
11 See pp 334-40.
12 For the problems inherent in teaching about race, see Hall 'Teaching Race' (1980) 9 Multiracial Education 3.

English law

7.38 Although the government has shown an increasing desire in recent years to influence the content of the secular curriculum,[1] broadly speaking, English law prescribes neither what subjects shall be taught in schools, nor the particular manner in which the curriculum should be organised and structured, nor the content or standard of examination papers. The provisions which make religious instruction mandatory are, as we have seen, a remarkable exception to this general pattern of legal non-interference in school-life in this country. All the above matters are, therefore, largely left in the hands of local authorities, school governors, head teachers and their staff, and examining boards.

At present it would appear that the only possible legal control over any cultural bias lies in the provisions of the Race Relations Act 1976. It has been suggested by Bindman that the indirect discrimination provisions regarding education may be applicable to cases where ethnic minority pupils are less able to take advantage of the teaching they are given because of cultural bias in the books or materials supplied.[2] So far, no case has yet come to court on this question, but clearly such discrimination would be very hard to establish.

A more important provision in the Act, at least in terms of its symbolic quality, is s 71 which runs as follows:

'Without prejudice to their obligation to comply with any other provision of this Act, it shall be the duty of every local authority to make appropriate arrangements with a view to securing that their various functions are carried out with due regard to the need
(a) to eliminate unlawful racial discrimination; and
(b) to promote equality of opportunity, and good relations, between persons of different racial groups.'

To achieve these objectives it seems vital that every effort should be made by local authorities to eliminate racial bias from the curriculum, school textbooks and other teaching materials as soon as possible and introduce a comprehensive programme of multicultural education.[3] However, the wording of s 71 currently falls short of imposing an enforceable duty on local authorities to ensure that they actually perform their functions with due regard to the needs stated.[4]

Significant pleas for the reform of the existing curriculum, a more sensitive choice of teaching materials and less culturally-biased examinations were made in both the *Rampton Committee Report* in 1981[5] and the *Swann Committee Report* in 1985.[6] Concern about public examinations was also voiced by the House of Commons Education, Science and Arts Committee in 1982 when it stated:

'There is . . . , in our view, a need to review school examinations in so far as they affect ethnic groups. Only one out of 8 GCE and 14 CSE Boards could recently report that it had reviewed its syllabuses to consider their relevance to a multi-ethnic society.[7] We recommend that a greater recognition should be given to the nature of Britain's multi-cultural society by all concerned with examination syllabuses, preparation and administration, and there should be a systematic review of all syllabuses to consider their appropriateness to a multi-cultural society. We further recommend that all examination boards should make a statement of policy on their commitment to equality of opportunity in a multi-racial society.'[8]

The *Swann Committee Report* drew particular attention to the valuable opportunities afforded by the introduction of a new system of examinations at 16-plus in 1988, to be known as the General Certificate of Secondary Education.[9]

Mention may also be made in this connection of Art 3 of the EEC Directive of 1977 on the education of children of migrant workers. This, it will be recalled, obliges member states to take appropriate measures to promote, in co-ordinatifon with normal education, teaching of the cultures of the country of origin of such children, in accordance with national circumstances and legal systems and in cooperation with states of origin.[10] The British government, no doubt mindful of the Race Relations Act 1976, has agreed that the Directive should apply to non-EEC children even though they are not strictly within its terms. Reference to the 'cultures' of these children should be seen as a further justification for affording the development of multicultural education the importance it deserves. The International Covenant on Civil and Political Rights, Art 27 similarly forbids the denial by state parties of the right of ethnic minorities to enjoy their own cultures.

1 See e g 'Better Schools', Cmnd 9469 of 1985, ch 2.
2 'Indirect discrimination and the Race Relations Act' (1979) 129 NLJ 408 at 411.
3 See *Local Authorities and the Education Implications of Section 71 of the Race Relations Act 1976* (CRE, 1981). For an impressive account of the achievements of the Inner London Education Authority in this regard in terms of special projects, the creation of new inspectors, the preparation and dissemination of teaching materials, etc see Nixon 'Multi-ethnic education in inner London' [1981-2] New Community 381.
4 See *Review of the Race Relations Act 1976 – Proposals for Change* (CRE, 1985) pp 35-6.
5 At pp 26-39, 71, 79.
6 At pp 326-34, 350-1.
7 See *Little and Willey* p 21.
8 HC 116-I, para 7.21.
9 At p 351.
10 For developments within the EEC, see L Porcher *The Education of the Children of Migrant Workers in Europe: Interculturalism and Teacher Training* (Council of Europe, Strasbourg, 1981).

The scope for reform

7.39   The movement in favour of multicultural education seems to be slowly gathering pace and a significant number of LEAs have now produced multicultural education policies, with many of these committing themselves unequivocally to take action against racism. One of the most striking sets of guidelines was unveiled by the ILEA in 1983. Its policy document *Race, Sex and Class – A Policy for Equality: Race* marks a shift of perspective away from emphasising cultural diversity (as it had done previously) to a greater concentration on confronting racism in the education system and society at large. While the positive aspects of cultural pluralism are retained they are placed firmly in the wider context of the need to promote racial equality and justice. It is the ILEA's view that as part of their moral, social and political education all pupils should learn to identify, resist and combat racism. This term is defined as referring to the discriminatory policies and practices and the unequal economic relations and power structures in our society ('institutional' racism), as well as the prejudiced beliefs and attitudes of those individuals who regard black people as inferior to white. Courses, syllabuses, textbooks and teaching methods which ignore or deny the validity of black experiences, perspectives and cultures should be removed. Steps will be taken by the ILEA to encourage the recruitment and promotion of black teachers and there will be courses and conferences for all staff on the nature of racism and how to combat it. While each school will be allowed to determine the details of its own policy in this sphere there will be certain elements common to all within the authority. These include a clear statement of opposition to any form of racism or racist behaviour, a firm expression of the right of all pupils to the best possible education, a clear indication of what is not acceptable and the procedures (including sanctions) to deal with any transgressors and finally, an explanation of the way in which the school or college intends to develop practices which both tackle racism and create educational opportunities which make for a cohesive society and a school or college community in which diversity can flourish.[1]

The *Swann Committee Report* strongly urged the Secretary of State to require all LEAs which had not so far done so to prepare clear policy statements along similar lines.[2] In the Committee's view one of the major reasons for the hitherto limited and disappointingly slow rate of progress in responding to this challenge had been the absence of a coherent overall strategy for stimulating developments, co-ordinating initiatives and committing central government resources.[3] However, the best way of ensuring that all LEAs took their responsibilities more seriously in this field would be by imposing a clear legal obligation upon them to do so. One way of achieving this would be to amend the Race Relations Act 1976, s 71 so that LEAs were bound actually to perform their functions with due regard to the need to eliminate racial discrimination and promote equality of opportunity.[4]

1 *Race, Sex and Class – Multi-Ethnic Education in Schools* (ILEA, 1983) p 25.
2 At p 345.
3 At p 344.
4 See *The Race Relations Act 1976 – Time for a Change?* (CRE, 1983) p 41.

G. DENOMINATIONAL SCHOOLS

7.40 There is already a substantial number of denominational schools in this country. Many are independent, but the vast majority are in the maintained sector receiving large subsidies from the state. These schools are predominantly run by the Church of England and by Roman Catholic foundations, but there are also some 70 Jewish day schools in Britain and one boarding school.[1] Of these, only about 20 are 'voluntary aided', the remainder being independent schools.[2] It has been calculated that these Jewish schools cater for around 21% of an estimated 61,500 Jewish children of compulsory school age. The main reason why Jewish parents send their children to these schools appears to be their desire to keep their children's home and school environments in balance with one another and hence avoid any conflicts that might arise through disharmony between them.[3] The parents are particularly concerned about the impact which non-Jewish religious teachers in other schools might have upon their children, either in unwitting Christian proselytising or in setting a poor example by having no religious conviction or belief themselves. Almost certainly these motives are shared by many Christian parents who choose to send their children to denominational schools. Such schools also appear to be valued, even by non-Christian parents, for the carefully structured and disciplined teaching and organisation which often distinguishes them from some LEA schools.[4] They have an ethos which encourages learning and the development of a child's full potential in a rich variety of ways.

In the light of all these considerations there has recently been an upsurge of interest on the part of various newer ethnic minority groups in the possibility of establishing their own schools, preferably in the maintained sector.[5] In his evidence to the House of Commons Education, Science and Arts Committee in 1981 the Deputy Chairman of the Commission for Racial Equality confirmed the interest of Muslims, Sikhs and West Indian Pentecostalists in establishing voluntary aided schools.[6] While not explicitly supporting such an idea, the Committee did in general terms recognise the value of the contribution made by voluntary schools and the choice their presence offers to parents; it therefore recommended that their continued existence in the maintained sector be guaranteed.[7] Although the immediate response of the Government was to indicate its firm commitment to such a guarantee,[8] it did draw attention to the present pattern of a decline in the total numbers of pupils and falling school rolls and it clearly expects the cooperation of voluntary aided school governors with their LEAs in any process of rationalisation that is required.[9] In view of this it is likely that there will be greater difficulties than hitherto in being able to establish a new voluntary aided school or having an existing private school taken into the state system.[10] For example, in 1982 an application to obtain voluntary aided status for three Jewish primary schools in Hackney was rejected by the Secretary of State. Among the reasons given by the DES for his decision was the following:

'He recognises in particular that there is substantial and genuine demand for single sex voluntary aided Jewish school places in the London Borough of Hackney. Nevertheless, while such a demand is an essential pre-requisite for the approval of proposals to establish new voluntary schools, the Secretary of State considers that it does not of itself provide sufficient grounds for approving the proposals. In particular, he has had to have regard to the matters which are set out below.

... in the interest of controlling public expenditure and in the light of his policy on falling rolls, the Secretary of State has to consider the extent to which the existing stock of maintained school places in an area is sufficient to meet the number of children eligible to attend such schools in the period ahead. In the case of the present proposals, he understands that the Inner London Education Authority already has a considerable surplus of primary places in the London Borough of Hackney, and judges that it would be inconsistent with his policy on taking surplus school places out of use to require the Authority to maintain further places in that area at an estimated additional cost of about £500,000 in recurrent expenditure per annum.'[11]

1 Bardi 'Judaism and the pluralist school' in Lynch (ed) *Teaching in the Multi-Cultural School* p 220.

2 The Education Act 1944, s 70 requires all independent schools to be registered with the DES and such registration may be contingent upon the rectification of any deficiencies found by HM inspectors since under s 71 the Secretary of State may serve a notice of complaint upon such a school if, in his view, the premises, accommodation or instruction provided there are 'unsuitable'. In *R v Secretary of State for Education and Science, ex p Talmud Torah Machzikei Hadass School Trust* (1985) Times, 12 April the inspectors had inter alia levelled certain criticisms against the traditional form of education provided by a section of the Orthodox Hasidic community at a school in North London. The instruction there is mainly in Yiddish and concentrates particularly on the study of the Talmud and the Mishnah. Upon an application for judical review of a notice of complaint the High Court held that education would be 'suitable' within s 71 if it primarily equipped a child for life within the community of which he was a member rather than that of the community as a whole so long as it did not foreclose the child's option in later years to adopt some other form of life if he wished to do so. Although the Secretary of State was entitled to lay down a minimum standard for all schools, the Court stressed the need for him to be sensitive to the traditions of a minority sect and to take account of the wishes and religious convictions of parents as required by s 76 of the 1944 Act and the First Protocol to the European Convention on Human Rights.

3 Bardi ibid.

4 A Dummett and J McNeal *Race and Church Schools* (Runnymede Trust, 1981) pp 16, 52.

5 See *Swann Committee Report* pp 498-517.

6 HC 116-I, para 7.16. See also Lodge 'Putting their money where their faith is' *TES* 25 February 1983, in relation to applications for Muslim schools in Bradford.

7 HC 116-I, para 5.41.

8 CMND 8551 of 1982, p 7.

9 Ibid p 8; see also DES Circular 2/1981.

10 In 1983 there were only 35 new voluntary schools established, whereas 156 were discontinued – see *DES Annual Report 1983* p 7. For the procedure involved in establishing a voluntary school, see Education Act 1980, s 13.

11 See DES Press Notice 64/1982.

7.41 Bearing in mind the important and established place of voluntary schools within the existing system and some of the practical problems of extending such status to new schools at the present time, what are the advantages and disadvantages of permitting Muslims, Hindus, Sikhs, Pentecostalists and other minority groups to operate their own schools within the maintained sector?[1]

One of the most important considerations must surely be the need for the state to emphasise publicly the principle of non-discrimination. If, for example, a Muslim foundation can satisfy the required standards it surely cannot be refused voluntary status while Jewish schools continue to possess such status, assuming, of course, that the necessary demand exists and that there are insufficient schools in the particular area. All denominations must be clearly seen to be treated equally. A positive response by the Secretary of State to such applications would have the added merit of giving the newer ethnic minorities greater confidence in their future stake in this country.

A particular benefit which many of the minorities feel their own voluntary aided schools could provide would be specialised instruction in their own religion and culture. They might fairly argue that truly multicultural education has not yet been developed far enough in LEA schools and currently offers their children insufficient detailed information about their own cultures. Greater significance would almost certainly be attached in their own schools to mother tongue teaching and religion, the latter being taught by a person with a real conviction in the faith. Single sex schooling at secondary level for girls could also be made more widely available.

Among the possible disadvantages of allowing such schools to be established the following deserve careful scrutiny. First, their creation might be socially divisive and lead to racially segregated schooling. If, as seems quite possible, the only pupils attending such schools were in practice to come from specific ethnic minority groups there might be a feeling of resentment on the part of the majority that these were, for example, exclusively 'black' schools or 'Muslim' schools.[2] Racial tension might be fermented through a lack of contact between young people from different communities at school. Even so, fears of a general pattern of segregated education (such as exists in Northern Ireland)[3] are almost certainly groundless, since probably only a small proportion of ethnic minority parents and children would wish to make use of such exclusive schools.[4] Many of the children see themselves as part of a multiracial and multicultural Britain and would want to mix in with members of other communities. Even those from Muslim families would by no means all want to undergo a strict, formal Islamic education.[5] The girls, in particular, might well have their horizons considerably narrowed and their potential restricted under such a regime. On the other hand, community pressures upon parents to send their children to such schools might be hard to resist in some cases.

The second problem could be that the majority community might be hostile towards the idea of having to finance the teaching of certain minority religions. A significant portion of religious education in Islam involves learning the Koran by heart. Less importance is attached to comprehension of what is learnt and any critical appraisal is strictly prohibited. This is unattractive to non-Muslims. Reports that at present Muslim and Sikh children are being given false information about one another's faiths in mosques and temples in this country are similarly disquieting.[6] One way of attempting to solve this problem would be to provide by law that denominational religious education in all voluntary aided schools should be open to inspection by the state in the same fashion as the 'agreed syllabus' is currently inspected.[7] If this were to be done then many majority fears might well be dispelled. On the other hand, no strong objection is presently taken to religious instruction in Jewish schools proclaiming that Jesus was not the son of God and the strong tide of resistance which existed at the turn of the century against financing the teaching of 'Rome on the rates'[8] appears somewhat bizarre in today's world. The same degree of tolerance must therefore be extended to other faiths.

1 See generally *A Future in Partnership* (National Society for Promoting Religious Education, 1984) pp 87-91; *Swann Committee Report* pp 498-517 (the committee was divided on this issue).
2 This seems to have been one of the principal reasons why an independent Sikh school was not set up in Gravesend in 1971 – see A Helweg *Sikhs in England* (OUP, 1979) ch VII.
3 It was such fears which prompted Lord Scarman to voice concern about the creation of Muslim and Hindu schools: see *TES*, 29 January 1982.
4 There was recently little support among London's Hindus for a denominational school to be established there even after the idea had been properly canvassed – see Kanitkar and Jackson *Hindus in Britain* (London, 1982) p 30.
5 The campaign in 1983 for Muslim voluntary aided schools in Bradford eventually foundered for lack of support among local Muslims – see *TES*, 9 September 1983.
6 See Cole 'World Religions in the Multi-Faith School' in *James and Jeffcoate* p 189.
7 Education Act 1944, s 77(5). A proposal to this effect was made in the 'Durham Report' p 266.
8 This cry was raised by Dr Clifford, the Baptist leader, as part of the opposition of the Free Churches to the 1902 Education Act in terms of which voluntary aided schools (including Roman Catholic Foundations) were to receive assistance out of the rates.

7.42   The inevitable conclusion would seem to be that if there is the slightest cause for concern about the establishment of new voluntary aided schools to cater specifically for ethnic minority pupils, the best general way of reducing the growing pressure for their creation is through a greater concentration on genuinely multicultural education in existing schools.[1] An imaginative alternative which might be viable, albeit on a far more limited scale, and necessitating considerable local initiative and enterprise, has been proposed by Ann Dummett:

'One possibility might be to have "multi-faith schools" in some areas. Many parents, whether Christian, Sikh, Muslim or Hindu, take the attitude that a school which has *some* religious character is better than a completely secular school. They value the respect which such an institution gives to religious belief as such; they think that teachers who believe in God will approach moral questions seriously and with some confidence and will understand the importance of religious ritual, dietary requirements, and special observances, even if their own beliefs and ceremonies differ from those of the parents. There are great differences between religions, but none of these is so great as the gulf between people who practise a religion and those with no religion at all.'[2]

   In such a school secular instruction, as well as all matters relating to general management, finance and admissions would be a joint operation. Religious education and prayers would be organised separately and run in parallel among the various faiths, but the opportunities of learning about other religions would be enhanced. The merits of the scheme are that it would guarantee not only a variety of faiths among the pupils but also a racially mixed community. It could also, as Ann Dummett points out:

'. . . enable Church Schools that were seriously undersubscribed by Christian children to remain open, and to accept the Christian children whose parents wanted a church school, while at the same time offering a service to children of one or more other faiths and, incidentally, to the community at large by setting an example of inter-faith cooperation and racial equality.'

   To sum up, it is thought that in general terms the values of increased choice for parents and diversity of approach offered by the existence of voluntary aided schools clearly outweighs any potential risks of divisiveness and they should therefore be retained as an integral part of the state sector of education.

1 See *Swann Committee Report* pp 508-10.
2 *Race and Church Schools* p 23.

CHAPTER 8

Religious observances

INTRODUCTION

8.01 There are no official government statistics concerning religious affiliation or church membership in this country. No doubt one reason for this is scepticism as to the value of the figures which might be produced. As one writer has been concerned to explain:

'Religious statistics must . . . be viewed with caution. They tell us how many people belong to the Churches, but they do not tell us how many of them go to church. Still less are they able to point to the 'strength of religion', or the place held by religious belief in people's hearts and minds.'[1]

However, the assessments of the individual religious bodies and denominations themselves can at least be presented as a very rough guide to religious adherence here today. Exact numbers are not, after all, crucial in the context of the present work so long as the overall impression is reasonably accurate. The following estimates of adherents to minority religions germane to this study can be given for persons aged 14 or over who were resident in the UK in 1985 on the basis of figures originally provided by the denominations themselves[2] –

Muslims	912,000
Jews	222,000
Sikhs	175,000
Hindus	140,000
Orthodox Churches	125,000
Pentecostal and Holiness Churches	95,000
African and West Indian Churches	79,000
Buddhists	20,000
Seventh Day Adventists	16,000

There are also significant numbers of Rastafarians, perhaps running into several thousands, but in the absence of any central organisation keeping records of adherents to that faith it is impossible to give even an approximate figure.[3]

Claims are often made that the Muslim population of England and Wales already far exceeds one million[4] and this seems realistic on the basis of the figures presented above if children under the age of 14 are included. Indeed, on the assumption that most young children of believers should be regarded as adherents to their parents' faith (and bearing in mind the predominantly youthful age profile of the 'black' and Asian ethnic communities),[5] several of the figures given above should probably be very substantially increased, perhaps almost doubled.[6]

1 A F Sillitoe *Britain in Figures* (Penguin, 1973) p 13.
2 Figures extracted from P Brierley (ed) *UK Christian Handbook, 1985-86 Edition* (Bible Society, 1984) pp 106-18. For the popularity of the Pentecostal and Seventh Day Adventist Churches among West Indians, see Hiro *White British, Black British* (Penguin, 1973) pp 31-2.
3 See *Rastafarianism in Greater London* (GLC 1984) p 15.

4 See, e g McDermott and Ahsan *The Muslim Guide* (Islamic Foundation, 1980) p 11 where a figure of 1.5 million is given.
5 See Runnymede Trust *Britain's Black Population* (London, 1980) p 9.
6 The total Jewish population is given as 385,000 in the *Jewish Yearbook* (1985) p 172.

8.02 In this chapter it is proposed to explore the extent to which English law regulates or controls certain aspects of religious observance practised by one or more of the ethnic minority communities. The principal areas of interest here are freedom of worship (including matters connected with the ownership and registration of religious buildings, the recognition of religious festivals and the rights of prisoners), the swearing of oaths in judicial proceedings and questions relating to burial and cremation. A variety of other aspects of religious observance have already been discussed in earlier chapters, for example those which relate to the solemnisation[1] or dissolution[2] of marriage and the religious upbringing and education of children,[3] including their diet and dress at school. Observances which principally affect a person in relation to his work or employment are considered in ch 9 below, while those which are liable to attract the attention of the criminal law are mainly dealt with in ch 10 below.

1 See ch 2 above.
2 See ch 5 above.
3 See chs 6 and 7 above.

A. FREEDOM OF WORSHIP

8.03 Members of all religions naturally wish to be free to adhere to their convictions and beliefs without state interference or coercion. Religious beliefs are, in their view, a matter for the conscience of the individual and are accordingly entitled to proper respect as part of the fundamental dignity of man. Furthermore, for the right to freedom of religion to be meaningful in practice adherents to a faith usually require, in addition, the freedom to manifest their religious beliefs in worship, either alone or in community with others, both privately and in public. This involves not only the right to private prayer but also the right to hold assemblies, meetings and processions and the capacity to establish, hold and maintain buildings as places of public worship. Hence Christians need to have their churches, Muslims their mosques, Jews their synagogues, Sikhs their *gurdwaras* and Hindus and Buddhists their temples. They wish to be able to assemble there regularly for worship and in particular to hold services or gatherings on specific days of the week or the year in order to celebrate or mark significant events or occasions, including festivals and holy days. Public recognition of their distinctive annual festival days is also important. Just as Christians celebrate Easter and Christmas so do Jews celebrate the feasts of *Shavuot* (Pentecost) and the Passover, *Rosh Hashana* (New Year) and *Yom Kippur* (the Day of Atonement); Muslims celebrate *Id-al-Fitr* (marking the end of fasting during the month of Ramadan) and *Id-al-Adha* (the Sacrifice of the Pilgrimage), while Hindus and Sikhs celebrate *Baisakhi* (New Year) and *Diwali*, and so on. In their countries of origin such days would often be regarded as public holidays, but in this country the only public holidays with any religious significance are those linked to the Christian faith.

Quite apart from being allowed to worship freely, either privately at home or in public congregations in the normal way, religious minorities would also like their members to be permitted to continue with their worship and other religious practices if for any reason they happen to be detained in a prison or other penal institution in this country.

Policy considerations

8.04 In an enlightened and sceptical age it is hardly possible to object on any rational grounds to the exercise of freedom of worship by minorities unless either some higher moral value is thereby jeopardised or the particular mode of worship demanded raises practical problems of such magnitude that the freedom has of necessity to be curtailed.

In former times (as will be shown) religious orthodoxy was insisted upon under threat of legal sanction because it was felt that to permit diversity might gravely imperil the very existence of the state. The gradual development of a more tolerant attitude on the part of the general public during the past four centuries owes much to the fact that religious passions have waned and the survival of the state is no longer felt to be threatened by religious non-conformity. As Lord Sumner explained in 1917:

'The words, as well as the acts, which tend to endanger society differ from time to time in proportion as society is stable or insecure in fact, or is believed by its reasonable members to be open to assault. In the present day meetings or processions are held lawful which a hundred and fifty years ago would have been deemed seditious, and this is not because the law is weaker or has changed, but because the times have changed, society is stronger than before. In the present day reasonable men do not apprehend the dissolution or the downfall of society because [the Christian] religion is publicly assailed by methods not scandalous.'[1]

Some idea of the value attached to freedom of worship in modern Britain can be deduced from the adherence by the UK to the European Convention on Human Rights and the International Covenant on Civil and Political Rights, both of which require contracting states to guarantee 'freedom of thought, conscience and religion', including the freedom to change religion or belief, as well as a person's freedom 'either alone or in community with others and in public or private, to manifest his religion or belief, in worship, teaching, practice or observance'.[2] However, under the terms of each treaty a contracting state is empowered to impose legal limitations upon the manifestation of religion to the extent that these are necessary in the interests of public safety, for the protection of public order, health or morals, or for the protection of the rights and freedoms of others.

So far as freedom of worship is concerned the principal justification for any interference is likely to rest upon the last-named ground. Insofar as, for example, a Jewish examination candidate seeks to sit a paper on a different day from other candidates because the date already fixed clashes with a Jewish holy day, this may sometimes have to be disallowed if it would be unfair to the other candidates. Certain forms of worship may on occasion be so noisy as to cause disturbance to neighbours and other people in the vicinity and may therefore have to be restrained. Public safety or order may also be relevant in deciding what freedom, for example, a prisoner may be afforded in this sphere.

1 *Bowman v Secular Society Ltd.* [1917] AC 406 at 466-7.
2 ECHR, Art 9; International Covenant, Art 18.

English law

1 Historical development[1]

8.05 General freedom of worship has only been legally guaranteed in England to members of all faiths and denominations since the middle years of the nineteenth century. During the Middle Ages non-conformity with the Catholic faith was penalised as an offence under ecclesiastical (or canon) law. The canon law of Rome was accorded the fullest recognition in this field by the English common law and where necessary the state would afford the ecclesiastical authorities assistance in enforcing their decrees, as for example in the issuing of writs by the common law courts for the burning of heretics.[2] Following the Reformation of the English Church in the sixteenth century non-conformity with the Anglican faith became punishable as a direct contravention of the law of the state under two separate headings. On the one hand, there were the laws of heresy and blasphemy which proscribed the proclamation, teaching or propagation of doctrines at variance or inconsistent with the tenets of the Established Church. On the other, there were the 'laws of uniformity' rendering criminal any failure by a person to attend services of the Church of England, as well as any attendance at services of any other faith or denomination. The role which such laws were expected to play in the maintenance of civil society has been admirably summarised by Holdsworth:

'During the Tudor period, as in the Mediaeval period, Church and State were regarded, from many points of view, as a single society which had many common objects; and the two members of that single society were still regarded as bound to give one another assistance in carrying out those common objects. The church must help the state to maintain its authority, and the state must help the church to punish non-conformists and infidels. The church was the church of the state, and membership of it was therefore a condition precedent for full rights in the state; the King was the supreme governor of the church; and the law of the church was the King's ecclesiastical law. But if the church is thus regarded as an integral part of the state, if the church's law is as much the King's law as the law of the state, a fortiori Christianity must be regarded as part of the law of England. In fact, not only Christianity, but also that particular variety of Christianity taught by the Anglican church, was part of that law.'[3]

Many people were severely punished for heresy during the sixteenth century.[4] Indeed the crime remained legally punishable by death until 1679,[5] although the last executions for the offence took place in 1612.[6] Prosecutions for heresy appear to have died out after 1640,[7] but successful indictments at common law for blasphemy or blasphemous libel (though they carried less severe penalties) were soon capable of covering almost identical ground.[8] In *Taylor's Case*[9] in 1676 the Court of King's Bench held that the utterance of blasphemous words was criminal, both as an offence against religion and as an offence against the government and the state. It was in this case that Sir Matthew Hale CJ pronounced his famous dictum that 'Christianity is part and parcel of the laws of England; and therefore to reproach the Christian religion is to speak in subversion of the law'.[9] The principal concern apparent in his judgment was to protect the civil order and fabric of society. At this period it was a crime not only to revile or ridicule the fundamental doctrines of Christianity in a scurrilous or contemptuous fashion (which is the essence of the crime of blasphemous libel today),[10] but also to deny their truth in a sober and serious manner.[11] This continued to be the legal position well into the nineteenth century[12] and it was not until the case of *R v Hetherington*[13] in 1841 that sober and temperate discussion of the correctness of Christianity was ruled by Lord Denman CJ to fall outside the scope of the criminal law. Indeed the question was not really put beyond doubt until 1883 when in the two cases of *R v Bradlaugh*[14] and *R v Ramsay and Foote*[15] the old approach was decisively rejected.

1 A masterly treatment of the period from 1530 to 1660 is to be found in W K Jordan *The Development of Religious Toleration in England* (4 vols, London 1932-40).
2 Holdsworth *A History of English Law* vol XIII, p 402.
3 Ibid p 403.
4 See *Jordan* vol I, p 172; vol II, pp 43-4.
5 See 29 Car 2, c 9.
6 See *Jordan* vol II, pp 43-52; HSQ Henriques *The Jews and the English Law* (Oxford, 1908) p 70.
7 *Henriques* pp 72-3.
8 See generally GD Nokes *A History of the Crime of Blasphemy* (Sweet and Maxwell, 1928).
9 (1676) 1 Vent 293.
10 See *Bowman v Secular Society Ltd.* [1917] AC 406; *R v Lemon* [1979] AC 617, [1979] 1 All ER 898.
11 Holdsworth *A History of English Law*, vol XIII, p 410.
12 See Law Com Working Paper No 79: 'Offences Against Religion and Public Worship' (1981) para 2.4.
13 (1841) 4 State Tr NS 563.
14 (1883) 15 Cox CC 217.
15 (1883) 15 Cox CC 231.

8.06   The other penal weapons available to combat non-conformity after the Reformation were the series of 'Acts of Uniformity'. The first of these in 1548[1] entitled 'An Act for Uniformity of Service and Administration of the Sacraments throughout the Realm' prescribed that only the Book of Common Prayer according to the use of the Church of England should be employed in church services. The second Act in 1551 enacted that henceforth:

'. . . every person . . . shall diligently and faithfully (having no lawful or reasonable excuse to be absent) endeavour themselves to resort to their Parish Church or Chapel accustomed . . . upon every Sunday and other days ordained and used to be kept as Holy days . . . , upon pain of punishment by the censures of the Church, . . .'[2]

Any person who was willingly present at any other manner or form of common prayer or administration of the sacraments committed a crime punishable, in the case of a first offence, by six months' imprisonment.[3]

The penalties for non-conformity were increased in subsequent Acts.[4] Under the terms of an Act in 1592 anyone who obstinately refused to come to church without lawful cause and in addition either
(i)   persuaded any other person to abstain from going to church or receiving communion or to be present at any unlawful assemblies, or
(ii)   willingly joined in or was present at any such assemblies under colour or pretence of any exercise of religion contrary to that prescribed by law
was to be committed to prison until he should conform and openly submit and declare his conformity. If he did not do so within three months he was to abjure the realm and the Queen's dominions for ever. If he refused to abjure or following his abjuration did not leave the realm, he was to be adjudged a felon and suffer death and forfeiture of his lands and goods.[5]

Non-conformists who refused to attend services of the Anglican church were known as 'Recusants'. If they were Roman Catholics they were known as 'Papists' or 'Popish Recusants', and were subjected to different statutes involving even greater disabilities, particularly after the discovery of the Gunpowder Plot in 1605.[6]

1 2 & 3 Edw 6 c 1.
2 5 & 6 Edw 6, c 1, s 2.
3 S 6.
4 See, e g 23 Eliz 1, c 1, s 5.
5 35 Eliz 1, c 1, s 1.
6 See, e g 3 Jac 1, c 4 and c 5; *Jordan* vol II, pp 72-6.

8.07   During the reign of Charles II the law against dissenters was strengthened by the passing, in 1664 and 1670, of two Conventicle Acts[1] designed to prevent clandestine meetings of non-conformists. However, Charles II seems himself to have been an advocate of religious tolerance in an intolerant age, though he was invariably out-manoeuvred in this sphere by an over-zealous Parliament. His attitude towards the Jews is particularly instructive.[2] All Jews had been banished from England in 1290 by Edward I. They began to return in small numbers during the early years of the reign of Charles I, but for a long time had to maintain their faith in secret for fear of persecution. However, under Charles II they boldly took the initiative, openly defied the legislation against recusants, organised themselves as a community and established a synagogue for public worship. When in 1664 they were molested and threatened with prosecution the wardens of the synagogue directly petitioned the Crown. The King responded by declaring that he had given no orders for their molestation and that they could expect the same favour as they had formerly enjoyed so long as they conducted themselves peaceably and quietly and without scandal. This royal dispensation afforded the Jewish religion valuable protection, but it needed further reinforcement in 1673. In that year the leaders of the Jewish community in London were indicted on a charge of riot for joining together in an act of public worship. A true bill was found against them by a grand jury. Again they petitioned the Crown. This time the King in Council responded with an order that the Attorney General should stop all proceedings against them by entering a *nolle prosequi*. This was duly done.

When James II came to the throne in 1685 he was determined to do what he could to remove all religious disabilities, especially those affecting his fellow Catholics.[3] In relation to the Jews he merely followed the practice of his brother in issuing an order in council dispensing a group of them from suffering the penalties imposed by the recusancy laws. However, with regard to Catholics and Protestant dissenters he acted precipitately and imprudently. He abused the royal prerogative both in the wholesale granting of dispensations and subsequently in the issue of a general indemnity which allowed the free exercise of every form of religion in flagrant contradiction of the wishes and enactments of Parliament. As a result the nation united against him and he was quickly driven from the throne. Toleration on such a wide scale could only have been introduced in an acceptable manner through an Act of Parliament and this was appreciated by the Protestant dissenters themselves as well as by the members of the Established Church. Indeed when the Glorious Revolution of 1688 brought William and Mary to the throne the loyalty which those Protestant dissenters had displayed to the constitution was promptly rewarded by the enactment of the Toleration Act 1688.[4] This piece of legislation with its fine sounding title is usually hailed as marking a major advance in religious tolerance, which indeed it was, but its actual terms were somewhat limited. They were confined to removing the penalties for recusancy from Protestant non-conformists and they offered no respite either to Roman Catholic dissenters or to those who denied the doctrine of the Trinity. Nor did the Act extend to Jews. As a result of the Revolution Roman Catholicism had come to be associated more than ever with treasonable intentions and the laws against 'Papists' were in fact strengthened.[5]

1 16 Car 2, c 4 and 22 Car 2, c 1.
2 See *Henriques* pp 125-52. Charles II also displayed a very tolerant approach towards the French Protestant refugees: see R Gwynn *Huguenot Heritage* (Routledge, 1985) pp 129-30.
3 See *Henriques* pp 152-6; Holdsworth *A History of English Law* vol VI pp 192-3.
4 William and Mary, c 18.

5 See Holdsworth *A History of English Law* vol VI, pp 201-2.

8.08 The benefits afforded to the Protestant non-conformists were that their meetings for worship were henceforth legalised, so long as they were not held behind locked doors[1] and provided their places of worship had first been certified to the bishop or archdeacon or to a justice of the peace and duly registered.[2] Anyone who disturbed their services became liable to a penalty.[3] In return for these favours non-conformists merely had to take the oath of allegiance and swear that they renounced the deposing power of the Pope and the belief that he possessed any jurisdiction in England.[4]

More than a century was to elapse before the growing spirit of toleration could be translated into legal protection for other denominations. Unitarians were not afforded the same privileges of freedom of worship until 1813,[5] Roman Catholics had to wait until 1832[6] (and some penalties were retained for Jesuits even then) and the de facto tolerance already extended to the Jewish religion since the latter half of the seventeenth century was not formally embodied in statute law until 1846.[7] Finally, in 1855 the Liberty of Religious Worship Act[8] removed some of the criminal penalties which had been laid down by an Act of 1812[9] for holding services of religious worship with more than 20 people present in a building not duly certified for the purpose. As a result congregations and assemblies in such buildings are now perfectly lawful provided they are conducted or authorised by the incumbent or curate of the parish or are held in a private dwelling house or on premises belonging to the congregation in question or are merely occasional meetings in a building not usually appropriated to purposes of religious worship.[10] Other assemblies in unregistered premises remain unlawful and render the occupier liable to a fine if the building is used for such purposes with his consent.

One particular historical anomaly does, however, remain. It seems clear that only the Christian religion in general, together with the particular rituals and doctrines of the Church of England, are protected by the laws of blasphemy and blasphemous libel.[11] Unless intended or likely to occasion a breach of the peace,[12] scurrilous and outrageous attacks on other faiths do not amount to an offence under English law, even though they may arouse feelings of deep shock and resentment among their followers.

1 S 5.
2 S 19.
3 S 18.
4 S 1.
5 Unitarians Relief Act 1813 (53 Geo 3, c 160).
6 Roman Catholic Charities Act 1832 (2 & 3 Will IV c 115). Some remission from penalties and a wider freedom of worship had earlier been afforded by the Roman Catholic Relief Act 1791 (31 Geo 3, c 32) and the Roman Catholic Emancipation Act 1829 (10 Geo 4, c 7).
7 Religious Disabilities Act 1846 (9 & 10 Vict, c 59); see generally *Henriques* pp 171-6.
8 18 & 19 Vict, c 86.
9 52 Geo 3, c 155.
10 Liberty of Religious Worship Act, s 2.
11 See Law Com Working Paper No 79: 'Offences against Religion and Public Worship' (1981) paras 3.2 and 6.9; *R v Gathercole* (1838) 2 Lew CC 237 at 254; *R v Lemon* [1979] 1 All ER 898 at 921 (per Lord Scarman).
12 As to which, see Public Order Act 1936, s 5.

BLASPHEMY — THE SCOPE FOR REFORM

8.09 In *R v Lemon*,[1] the only modern authority on the subject, Lord Scarman criticised the common law offence of blasphemy for being 'shackled by the chains of history' and 'not sufficiently comprehensive'.[2] He considered there was a case for extending the ambit of the crime by legislation so that it also protected the religious beliefs and feelings of non-Christians, adding:

'The offence belongs to a group of criminal offences designed to safeguard the internal tranquillity of the Kingdom. In an increasingly plural society such as that of modern Britain it is necessary not only to respect the differing religious beliefs, feelings and practices of all but to protect them from scurrility, vilification, ridicule and contempt.'[3]

The strongest justification for retaining an offence which many believe should be abolished[4] would appear to be the need to protect the religious feelings of individuals from being hurt by outrageous and offensive publications.[5] If the criminal law is felt to be an appropriate vehicle for such protection then non-Christian faiths must surely be included. A reasonably suitable foreign precedent exists in the Indian Penal Code, s 298, originally drafted by the first Indian Law Commission, of which Lord Macaulay was President, in 1837. This provides as follows:

'Whoever, with the deliberate intention of wounding the religious feelings of any person, utters any word or makes any sound in the hearing of that person or makes any gesture in the sight of that person, or places any object in the sight of that person, shall be punished . . .'

Similar provisions are to be found in a number of African penal codes.[6] In its Working Paper on the subject published in 1979 the Law Commission's provisional view was that since it was impossible to define the word 'religious' satisfactorily and since the arguments about the desirability of creating such a statutory offence were finely balanced in any event, it might be better to abolish the existing common law offence and put nothing new in its place.[7] However, in its final report in 1985 the Law Commission was divided on the issue. While three Commissioners adhered to the view expressed in the Working Paper, two Commissioners felt that a new statutory offence should be created and that its scope should be wide enough to cover non-Christian faiths as well as Christianity itself.[8]

1 [1979] 1 All ER 898.
2 At 922.
3 At 921.
4 See, e g Smith [1979] Crim LR 313-4; Spencer [1981] Crim LR 810.
5 See Law Com Working Paper No 79, para 7.12.
6 See J Collingwood *Criminal Law of East and Central Africa* (Sweet and Maxwell, 1967) pp 117-8.
7 See para 9.2.
8 Law Com Report No 145: Offences Against Religion and Public Worship (1985).

20 Places of worship and their registration

8.10   Under the Places of Worship Registration Act 1855 future registration of such premises was made optional, but there remain a number of important advantages to be derived from the process of certification and registration at the present time.

First, as we have seen, in certain circumstances the occupier of a building used for religious worship which has not been certified may be liable to a fine. An example would be where regular services are held in a hall which does not belong to the denomination in question. Second, there is statutory protection against a disturbance occurring on premises which have been certified. The Ecclesiastical Courts Jurisdiction Act 1860, s 2 penalises any person guilty of 'riotous, violent or indecent behaviour' not only in any church or chapel of the Church of England but also in any certified place of religious worship, 'whether during the celebration of divine service or at any other time'.[1] Third, a registered building together with any connected land and ancilliary buildings is excepted from the need for registration under the Charities Act 1960.[2] It is thus freed from the regime of supervision and control exercised by the Charities Commission. Fourth, a building registered under the 1855 Act may be registered again under the Marriage Act 1949, s 41 for the purpose of having marriages lawfully solemnised there. It needs to be a 'separate' building for this purpose[3] and registration under the latter Act requires a certificate signed by at least 20 householders stating that the building is being used by them as their usual place of public worship and that they desire registration for the purpose of having weddings celebrated there.[4]

1 For discussion of whether this offence is in need of modernisation, as well as its overlap with the Offences against the Person Act 1861, s 36, see Law Com Working Paper No 79 'Offences against Religion and Public Worship' (1981) paras 12.1-12.23; Law Com Report No 145, paras 3.14-3.22. Where a breach of the peace is likely to be occasioned by abuse or insulting behaviour in a public place (whether it is a certified place of worship or not) the Public Order Act 1936, s 5 may be used, as it was in 1980 when two people were fined for depositing the head of a pig in a mosque while a group of Muslims were present – see Law Com Working Paper No 79 'Offences against Religion and Public Worship' (1981), para 12.16.
2 S 4(4) (d).
3 S 41(1). For the problems caused by this requirement, see para 2.31 above.
4 S 41(2).

8.11 Finally, premises which are 'for the time being certified as required by law as places of religious worship' are exempt from liability to pay local rates, provided they are places of 'public' religious worship.[1] In *Broxtowe BC v Birch*,[2] it was held by the Court of Appeal that private premises used by a community for religious worship could only qualify as a place of public worship for this purpose if either the public at large were invited to worship there by some outward and visible indication that the premises were used for religious worship and members of the public were not regarded as trespassers, or there was evidence that the public at large did in fact attend the premises to worship. In that case it was clear that two meeting halls used for worship by groups of a Christian sect known as the Exclusive Brethren were not places of public worship in this sense.

In the earlier case of *Church of Jesus Christ of Latter-Day Saints v Henning*[3] the House of Lords similarly declined to recognise as a place of public worship a Mormon temple to which were admitted only a select class of the sect, namely 'Mormons of good standing'. This meant persons considered by a local 'bishop' and a 'president' to be worthy, on the ground of their spiritual and secular qualities, to receive a written authorisation which was valid for only one year at a time. The decision naturally raises the question whether any restrictions imposed upon the admission of members of the public can be introduced without forfeiting the claim. to be a place of public worship and hence the exemption from liability for rates. In the leading speech Lord Pearce expressed the following view:

'For this purpose the admission of the public means, I think, the admission of those members of the public who are reasonably suitable, who come in reverence, not mockery, and who are prepared to behave in a reasonable conformity with the requirements of the religion which they are visiting, e g by covering their heads where that is required or by removing their shoes on entering a mosque.'[4]

Lord Morris expressed more or less the same idea when he stated that to be open to the public meant 'open to all properly disposed persons who wished to be present'.[5]

The test was not, as the appellants had contended, related to the standpoint of the individual who comes to worship. Seen from his vantage-point attendance at the temple clearly was 'public' in the sense of 'congregational' rather than mere private or family devotion. However, the House of Lords held that the meaning of 'public' had to be objectively determined by reference to the nature and quality of the meeting itself. In reaching this conclusion Lord Pearce took comfort from the fact that it accorded with the view of an Australian judge, Lowe J, in the case of *Association of the Franciscan Order of Friars Minor v City of Kew*[6] in which he stated that to be public, worship had to be 'open without discrimination to the relevant public'. However, as Lord Pearce pointed out:

'By the word 'relevant' he left open the question of how universal and discriminating must be the admission of the public. The question is one of fact and there might clearly be difficult questions whether some discrimination might be insufficient to deprive the worship of its public character.'[7]

This issue may well possess some relevance for Asian minority groups in this country. One commentator has pointed to the exclusive nature of some aspects of worship here in the following terms:

'Among the first generation, untouchability is practised and believed in Britain as much as it is in India (where it is officially outlawed)[8]. The Hindus of Southall have a separate temple for their untouchables. The Sikhs of Birmingham have two *gurdwaras* for their two types of untouchables (*Valmik* and *Ravidasa*). The Muslims of Bradford have exclusive mosques for their *'Khandari'* (socially accepted) castes.'[9]

There are also Hindu temples for 'untouchables' in Coventry.[10] If a proportion of adherents to a particular faith are excluded from such places of worship in a discriminatory manner the rating authority might well be entitled to levy rates in the usual way on the grounds that the buildings in question were not in law places of public worship. Exemption from the payment of rates is often a significant benefit in financial terms and any aggrieved 'untouchable' would thus possess a formidable weapon if he sought to challenge traditional caste divisions. Under the European Convention on Human Rights freedom of religion has to be guaranteed without discrimination on the basis of social origin, birth or other status[11] and this might well incline an English court on grounds of public policy, to uphold a rating authority's decision to levy rates in such circumstances.

1 General Rate Act 1967, s 39(2).
2 [1983] 1 All ER 641.
3 [1964] AC 420, [1963] 2 All ER 733.
4 At 437.
5 At 435.
6 [1944] VLR 199.
7 At 440.
8 See Constitution of India 1949, art 17; see also art 25(2) (b) which declares that any law providing for the throwing open of Hindu religious institutions of a public character to all classes and sections of Hindus shall not be regarded as a violation of the constitutional guarantee of religious freedom. For discussion of this question, see H M Servai *Constitutional Law of India* (Bombay, 2nd edn, 1975) vol I, pp 581-7.
9 Karan Thapar 'No such thing as an Asian "community"' *The Times*, 24 June 1982.
10 D G Bowen (ed) *Hinduism in England* (Bradford, 1981) pp 61-3.
11 See art 14.

8.12 Under the General Rate Act 1967, s 39(2) the exemption from liability for rates extends not only to places of public religious worship as such, but also to 'any church hall, gospel hall or similar building used in connection with any such place of public religious worship and so used for the purposes of the organisation responsible for the conduct of public religious worship in that place'. In *Gillett v North West London Communal Mikvah*[1] it was held that a Jewish *mikvah* or ritual bath-house did not qualify as a 'similar building' within the meaning of the section and was therefore not exempt from rates. However, providing the building does qualify under s 39(2) there is no need for the activities carried out there to be of a religious nature; they may be of a social or welfare character so long as the connection laid down by the section can be shown to exist.[2] However, where a church hall or other similar building is let out and the income so derived exceeds the outgoings it becomes subject to assessment for rating purposes for the following year based on the amount of the excess.[3]

1 (1982) 264 Estates Gazette 541.
2 *Swansea City Council v Edwards* (1976) 239 Estates Gazette 731; Morgan and Morgan 'Rating and places of public religious worship' (1983) 147 LGR 631.
3 General Rate Act 1967, s 39(3).

8.13 Turning to the actual process of registration, the first step is for the place of meeting to be certified in writing in the form set out in the 1855 Act. This merely involves someone certifying that a specific building is intended to be used as a place of meeting for religious worship by a congregation or assembly of persons, together with a reference to the name of their denomination if mention of this is desired.[1] Any person who has a connection with the meeting place may sign the form, for example the owner or occupier of the building, a minister or even someone who has merely been attending meetings there.[2] The certificate has to be delivered in duplicate to the superintendent registrar of births, deaths and marriages in the district in which the meeting place is situated[3] and must then be forwarded by him to the Registrar General.[3] Before issuing a certificate of registration the Registrar General is entitled to inquire whether the place mentioned is indeed a place of meeting for religious worship. *In R v Registrar General, ex p Segerdal*[4] it was held by the Court of Appeal that his functions in this regard are not merely ministerial and he does not therefore necessarily have to accept the view of the certifier. As Lord Denning MR pointed out:

'I cannot believe that a mere "attendant" or "occupier" can certify a place, when he may have little or no ground for his certification, and yet call upon the registrar to record it straight away without inquiry. That would lead to many abuses. No, that cannot be. I think that the registrar has only jurisdiction to register a place so long as it is truly a place of meeting for religious worship.'[5]

The Court defined religious worship as connoting some form of reverence towards or veneration of a god or deity or supreme being. On the facts of the case this effectively excluded meetings of Scientologists at a chapel they had sought to have registered because these were chiefly devoted to instruction in the tenets of a philosophy which placed man at the centre of their beliefs. However, strictly applied, this definition would also exclude Buddhist temples from registration as places of religious worship and it must therefore admit of some exceptions, as Lord Denning himself recognised.[6] Mainstream Buddhists do not revere a deity but rather seek to attain lofty moral and social standards without the help of an external agency, yet their faith has long been regarded as one of the world's great religions and their temples have been registered under the 1855 Act over a period of many years.

It appears that the Registrar General also has to be satisfied that the place certified is principally used for purposes of religious worship (though it may also be used for other purposes)[7] and that the congregation is an identifiable, settled body.[8] There is no reason why part of a building should not be registered such as, for instance, a room in a private dwellinghouse.

Once the Registrar General has decided to approve the registration and has recorded the place of worship in a book kept for this purpose he returns one copy of the certificate through the superintendent registrar to the original certifying person. Upon it is noted the date on which it was registered. The other copy is retained by the Registrar General as part of the records of his office.[9]

1 See Sch A.
2 See marginal notes to Sch A.
3 S 2.
4 [1970] 2 QB 697, [1970] 3 All ER 886.
5 At 705.
6 At 707. See also *Barralet v AG* [1980] 3 All ER 918 at 925.
7 *R v Registrar General, ex p Segerdal* at 707. While Sikh *gurdwaras*, for example, are mainly used for worship they are also community centres in which a variety of social activities are pursued: see *East Meets West* pp 92-4.
8 See Law Com Working Paper No 79 'Offences against Religion and Public Worship' (1981) para 12.7; Law Com Report No 145, para 3.7.
9 S 2.

8.14 The Registrar General's records of certified places of worship in England and Wales for 1984 included the following figures for buildings used by non-Christian faiths[1] –

Jews	351
Muslims	290
Sikhs	126
Hindus	53
Buddhists	18

However, since registration is entirely voluntary these statistics by no means account for all the places of worship owned or occupied by each of these faiths. It has been estimated, for example, that there are now as many as 2,000 mosques in the UK as well as about 130 Hindu temples.[2] A dramatic illustration of the rich diversity of religious buildings in modern English cities is apparent from the following description of Coventry:

'If you stand at a particular spot called Fiveways in the Foleshill district of Coventry, and slowly rotate yourself in an anti-clockwise direction, you can see in turn a purpose-built mosque, a Ukrainian hall where Ukrainian Orthodox and Catholic Christians meet for social and cultural events, a Spiritualist church, a Sikh *gurdwara* in the foreground with the spires of Holy Trinity church and the ruin of the old Coventry cathedral in the distance, an Evangelical gospel hall, a Hindu temple and a late nineteenth century Methodist church. Not far out of view are the Polish and Ukrainian Catholic churches, the West Indian First United Church of Jesus Christ (Apostolic), two Hindu temples (with a third in Hillfields, just outside Foleshill), three *gurdwaras* and a second mosque'.[3]

1 See OPCS *Marriage and Divorce Statistics 1984* (series FM2). (The figures for Hindus and Buddhists are included in 'other bodies' in the tables).
2 See P Brierley (ed) *UK Christian Handbook: 1985-6 Edition* (Bible Society, 1984) p 118. A more realistic estimate of the number of mosques is about 700.

3 D G Bowen (ed) *Hinduism in England* (Bradford, 1981) p 61.

3 Acquisition of places of worship

8.15 The legal problems facing minorities in acquiring places of worship are very different today from those encountered in the past. Before the modern era of religious toleration one of the principal hindrances lay in the fact that trusts or bequests for the advancement of any denomination other than the Established Church, through the construction or maintenance of religious buildings, were legally unenforceable. Such endowments were automatically held invalid on the ground that they were contrary to public policy. Hence, prior to the Toleration Act 1688 gifts in favour of the places of worship of Protestant dissenters were declared void,[1] as were such gifts in favour of Roman Catholic chapels until 1832[2] and those in favour of Jewish synagogues until 1846.[3] In *Da Costa v De Paz*,[4] for instance, decided in 1743, a legacy providing for the maintenance of a *yeshiva* (or assembly) for the daily reading of Jewish law and the advancement and propagation of the Jewish religion was held to be bad in law and the money was therefore placed at the disposal of the Crown. Part of it was subsequently allocated to finance the instruction of children in the Christian religion at the Foundling Hospital,[5] a clear indication of the public policy of the period.

Today any religious body is fully protected in the enjoyment of its endowments with respect to places of worship and the ordinary law relating to charitable trusts applies.[6] A trust will be recognised as a valid charitable trust, with considerable advantages in terms of fiscal privileges,[7] provided it can be categorised as being for the advancement of religion.[8] This includes the erection, maintenance and repair of churches and other places of worship and so long as there is some form of worship of a god or gods (rather than mere adherence to high ethical principles[9]) the law no longer discriminates in any way against non-Christian religions.[10] There must be some tangible benefit to the public, but it appears that this condition can be fulfilled even if the trust is in favour of a small religious community provided its members have some contact with the public at large.[11] In *Neville Estates Ltd v Madden*[12] a trust in favour of the members for the time being of a particular synagogue was held by Cross J to be a charitable trust because he considered that the general public derived a genuine benefit from the fact that the members of the synagogue went out after worshipping there and made contact with their fellow citizens.[13]

1 *AG v Baxter* (1684) 1 Vern 248; reversed (1689) 2 Vern 105.
2 Roman Catholic Charities Act 1832, s. It was held, however, in *West v Shuttleworth* (1835) 2 My & K 684 that this Act did not operate to validate trusts for the maintenance of 'superstitious uses' such as masses for the dead. This remained the law until the decision of the House of Lords in *Bourne v Keane* [1919] AC 815.
3 Religious Disabilities Act 1846, s 2.
4 (1754) Amb 228.
5 See *Henriques* pp 19-22.
6 See 14 Halsbury's Laws of England (4th edn) paras 343-4.
7 These include exemptions from liability for income tax, corporation tax, capital gains tax and capital transfer tax and relief from local rates, as well as the exemptions and reliefs granted to donors and testators.
8 See *Comrs for Special Purposes of Income Tax v Pemsel* [1891] AC 531 at 583 (per Lord Macnaghten).
9 See *Barralet v AG* [1980] 3 All ER 918, [1980] 1 WLR 1565.
10 See M Chesterman *Charities, Trusts and Social Welfare* (Weidenfeld and Nicolson, 1979) pp 157-9. As to Buddhism, see para 8.13 above.
11 *Chesterman* pp 160-3.
12 [1962] Ch 832, [1961] 3 All ER 769.

13 Cf *Gilmour v Coates* [1949] AC 426, [1949] 1 All ER 848 in which a trust in favour of the nuns of a Carmelite priory, an enclosed community, was held not to be charitable.

8.16 At the present time the chief practical problem facing many minority faiths is the difficulty posed by the planning laws of establishing purpose-built places of religious worship in areas in which they have not been located before. The necessary planning permission has to be obtained under the Town and Country Planning Act 1971 and opposition may be encountered not only from planning departments but also from local residents of other faiths, as it was, for example, in relation to the siting of the Central London mosque in Regents Park. In exercising their discretion whether or not to grant planning permission in respect of a particular site the local planning authority has to bear in mind a wide range of factors, including its own development plan and other material considerations such as the physical appearance of the proposed building, its likely impact on the neighbourhood, noise levels, traffic flows, and car parking facilities, as well as local issues of social and economic policy including racial integration.[1]

Converting an existing building such as a private dwelling-house, a school or business premises may prove easier and cheaper, but any change into a place of public worship represents in law a 'material change of use' and hence also requires the prior permission of the planning authorities.[2] This practice or the conversion of two adjoining properties to provide space for congregations to worship, albeit often in rather cramped conditions appears quite common among the Muslim, Sikh and Hindu communities.[3] Planning permission in such cases may well only be granted subject to conditions. In order to keep the noise level within reasonable bounds the size of the congregation may be restricted to a specified number, the holding of weddings there may be prohibited and the installation of a system of sound-proofing may be required. The conditions imposed must not be manifestly unreasonable,[4] as they would be if they were imposed in a discriminatory fashion. Planners have sometimes been criticised for insisting on the rigid application of accepted car parking standards in refusing permission for a change of use to one of religious worship despite the fact that many adherents will walk to the building rather than drive there.[5] Greater flexibility appears to be required in this regard. If the necessary planning permission is not obtained or any conditions imposed are not complied with, the local planning authority may as a last resort, issue an enforcement notice, if it appears expedient to do so, to try to remedy the situation.[6] Eventually if the owner does not comply with the notice requiring him to return the property to its former use he may be liable to a fine.[7]

A procedure which does not require planning consent (because it does not represent a material change of use[8]) and may well therefore be preferable for that reason, is the purchase of a building already designated for religious worship which is no longer required for this purpose by its existing owners. It is clear, for example, that the Church of England possesses a number of redundant churches which might be sold and put to other uses rather than being demolished. In 1983 the question arose whether it should for the first time sell one of these churches for use by a non-Christian denomination as a place of worship. The issue of policy was debated at the General Synod of the Church in February 1983, ending with a motion in favour of such sales being narrowly defeated. The Houses of Bishops and Clergy voted in favour by 35 votes to 3 and 101 to 92 respectively, but the House of Laity voted against by 96 votes to 90. However, when later in the same month the specific case of a church in Southampton being sold for use as a Sikh *gurdwara* came before the Board of Governors of the Church Commissioners (a body independent of the Synod) the sale was authorised because of the strength of local opinion, both church and secular, in support of the idea.[9] A precedent was thus established which may prove useful in the future where the local conditions are right.[10] Sales of church buildings by Christian denominations other than the Church of England for use by non-Christian faiths have been occurring for a number of years.

1 See Town and Country Planning Act 1971, s 29(1); M Grant *Urban Planning Law* (Sweet and Maxwell, 1982) ch 7.
2 1971 Act, s 22(1); Town and Country Planning (Use Classes) Order 1972, Sch, class XIII.
3 See, e g *East Meets West* p 72; Rex and Tomlinson *Colonial Immigrants in a British City* (London, 1979) p 272; *James* p 36; Kanitkar and Jackson *Hindus in Britain* (London, 1982) pp 4, 8.
4 See generally *Grant* pp 342-51.
5 See *Planning for a Multi-Racial Britain* (CRE, 1983) p 47. See also D G Bowen (ed), *Hinduism in England* pp 66-7.
6 1971 Act, s 87(1).
7 Ibid s 89.
8 Ibid s 22(2).
9 See 38 HC Official Report (6th series) written answers col *558*; *Sunday Times*, 20 February 1983; *The Times*, 25 February 1983.
10 Provision for the sale of redundant Anglican church buildings is made by the Pastoral Measure 1968. It is unlawful to sell such buildings without the authority of an Act of Parliament or a Measure of the Church Assembly or General Synod.

8.17 In Muslim countries a mosque will almost invariably have attached to it a minaret or tower from which the call to prayer is issued to the faithful at the appropriate times each day. Traditionally the call was made by the *muezzin* in person, but the normal practice today is for the summons to prayer to be recorded and proclaimed to the public through loudspeakers. Bearing in mind the likely reactions of the majority of non-Muslim residents in England to hearing such recordings issuing forth at regular intervals throughout the day, local planning authorities here usually impose a condition, if they grant consent to the construction of a minaret, that no amplification system be used in it.[1] If the noise level were such as to interfere substantially with the ordinary comfort of neighbouring inhabitants it would in any event constitute in law the tort of nuisance and could be restrained by the grant of an injunction.[2] On the other hand if a call to prayer were made only once a week, at midday on Fridays, and the sound was not particularly loud this might well fall short of what is required for the creation of a nuisance.[3]

1 Such conditions have been imposed in Birmingham (in respect of the Balsall Heath Mosque) and in Halifax.
2 See 34 Halsbury's Laws of England (4th edn) paras 323-4. Proceedings might also be taken by the local authority pursuant to the Control of Pollution Act 1974, Part III.
3 An injunction to restrain the tolling of church bells and the chiming of a church clock was refused in *Hardman v Holberton* [1866] WN 379 on the ground that the noise was insufficient.

4 Religious processions

8.18 Of particular interest under this heading are the processions of members of the International Society for Krishna Consciousness (ISKCON), more commonly known as the Hare Krishna movement.[1] Wearing their saffron robes, shaven heads and top-knots and chanting their transcendental *mantras* to the accompaniment of tambourines and other musical instruments, they are often to be seen marching up and down Oxford Street and on other beats in Central

London. They also hold festivals near their temple at Letchmore Heath and elsewhere. Although the movement was only founded as recently as 1965 and initially appealed mainly to Western devotees, its message is a traditional Hindu one and ISKCON is now increasingly attracting as adherents in England Hindus who migrated here from East Africa. The full-time membership remains very small, amounting to no more than a few hundred, but there is a growing number of those who join in the movement's activities on an occasional basis.[2]

Participation in a procession in a public place such as a highway may render a person guilty of a large number of possible offences. Some of these fall under local Acts and byelaws, while others have been created by Parliament. Such a procession may, for instance, constitute a wilful obstruction of the highway under the Highways Act 1980, s 137 or else it may amount to the creation of a public nuisance at common law. In *R v Clarke* (No 2)[3] it was held that for the obstruction of a highway to constitute an offence of public nuisance there must have been an unreasonable use of the highway. This might be established by showing that there had been an undue encroachment upon the rights of others through, for example, the creation of excessive noise or conduct which rendered ordinary passage for vehicles or pedestrians either impossible or extremely hazardous.

Members of the Hare Krishna sect have usually been prosecuted in London either under the Highways Act 1980, s 137 or under the Metropolitan Police Act 1839, s 54(13) which covers instances of threatening or insulting behaviour which might cause a breach of the peace.[4] The defence of religious freedom does not appear to have been raised, but even if it were it seems unlikely that it would succeed. In the Canadian case of *R v Harrold*[5] the accused was charged with violating a byelaw of the City of Vancouver which made it an offence to create a loud and objectionable noise in a public place in such a manner as to disturb the comfort and convenience of the public. He and his fellow members of ISKCON had marched up and down the main streets of the City chanting to the accompaniment of drums and cymbals and attempting to project their message to the public at large. The accused's defence that the byelaw was inapplicable to him because he was engaged in good faith in the practice of his religion was rejected by the British Columbia Court of Appeal on the ground that the right to freedom of religion did not permit anyone to violate the law of the land under the umbrella of his religious teachings or practice. The same principle would appear to be applicable in this country in relation to criminal offences.[6] No contravention of the European Convention on Human Rights would be involved because of the exception in Art 9 for legal limitations placed on the manifestation of religion in the interests of public safety, for the protection of public order and for the protection of the rights and freedoms of others.

1 See generally, Carey 'The Hare Krishna movement and Hindus in Britain' [1983] *New Community* 477.
2 This may be as high as 50,000: see *Brierley* p 118.
3 [1964] 2 QB 315.
4 Personal communication from the Chief Clerk to the Justices, Marlborough Street Magistrates Court, London.
5 (1971) 19 DLR (3d) 471.
6 See generally paras 10.03-10.05 below.

5 Annual holy days and festivals

8.19 Problems can arise when a date fixed by a public body for a person to attend for the performance of some function or activity clashes with one of the holy days or festivals recognised by that person's religion.

A leading instance of a case in which such an issue arose was *Prais v EC Council.*[1] The applicant, who was Jewish, had applied to be considered for a post with the Council. She was notified that a written examination would be held on Friday 16 May 1975. This happened to be the first day of the feast of *Shavuot* (Pentecost). She then informed the Council that her faith precluded her from travelling or writing the examination on that day and requested the fixing of an alternative date. However, the Council refused either to change the date or to allow her to sit on a different day from the other candidates. The first procedure, it alleged, would have involved practical difficulties because the other candidates had already been told of the date and the examination was only three weeks away; the second procedure might have involved a risk of unequal treatment to the various candidates. The applicant claimed that the Council's failure to allow her to sit the examination on another day breached both Art 9 of the European Convention and a provision of the Council's staff regulations which barred religious discrimination in the selection of its employees.

In giving his opinion to the European Court of Justice the Advocate General pointed out that it appeared to be the invariable practice of professional and academic bodies in the UK to make, when requested, alternative arrangements for 'observant Jewish candidates' whose examinations fell on Jewish holy days. He referred to a letter from the Education officer of the Board of Deputies of British Jews which elaborated as follows:

'Alternative arrangements are generally either that
– an alternative paper is set to be taken by the candidates at an agreed date. Some professional bodies always have a second paper available for candidates who may have been ill or otherwise indisposed, and Jewish candidates are normally allowed to sit this paper; or
– the Jewish candidate remains under the invigilation of an approved third party (for example in the cases of Oxford and Cambridge an MA of the university, or in the case of the ICA a member of the Institute of Chartered Accountants) from the time that the examination is due to begin until he is escorted after Shabbat/Yom Tov to his own examination by the invigilator. If, for example, the examination was set on Shabbat and the student was given permission to sit the examination before, then he is invigilated from the time his examination finishes until all candidates have completed their examinations.
In all cases it is generally accepted that candidates seeking alternative arrangements on religious grounds will defray any expenses occasioned by the examining board.'[2]

The period of the summer GCE examinations commonly covers the Jewish feast of Pentecost and it is the normal practice of the various GCE Boards to schedule only minor examinations with a small number of candidates on that particular day. Where Jewish candidates are due to sit a paper on this day the Boards make special arrangements either by setting an alternative paper to be taken on a different day or by allowing them to sit the same paper on the following day, subject to overnight parental supervision.[3]

On the other hand, as the Advocate General explained in the *Prais* case, the practice of the English Civil Service Commission is quite different. While it has a list of Jewish festival dates and tries, so far as possible, to avoid holding examinations on those dates which would cause most difficulty, no special arrangements are ever made for those who cannot sit on a particular day once that day has been fixed. No separate or deferred sittings are allowed. A possible reason for this dichotomy of approach suggested by the Advocate General was that whereas the academic and professional examinations are designed to test the attainment of a certain standard, Civil Service examinations are competitive and intended for the recruitment of staff. Bearing this in mind the European Court of Justice ultimately decided to reject the application by Mrs Prais and commented as follows:

'If a candidate informs the appointing authority that religious reasons make certain dates impossible for him the appointing authority should take this into account in fixing the date for written tests, and endeavour to avoid such dates. On the other hand, if the candidate does not inform the appointing authority in good time of his difficulties, the appointing authority would be justified in refusing to afford an alternative date, particularly if there are other candidates who have been convoked for the test.'[4]

The Court went on to hold that even if it was desirable that an appointing authority should inform itself in a general way of dates which might be unsuitable for religious reasons and seek to avoid them, neither the staff regulations nor the Convention could be regarded as imposing a duty to avoid a conflict of which the authority had not been informed in good time. The same result would surely be reached under English law in relation to civil service entry examinations.

1 [1976] 2 CMLR 708, [1977] ICR 284.
2 [1976] 2 CMLR 708 at 714.
3 Personal communications from the various GCE Boards.
4 [1977] ICR at 293.

8.20 A similar type of problem was encountered by the Queen's Bench Division in *Ostreicher v Secretary of State for the Environment*.[1] The applicant claimed she had not been afforded an opportunity to be heard at an inquiry held under the Housing Act 1957 in relation to a compulsory purchase order. She was unable to attend the inquiry because it had been fixed for the seventh day of the Passover, one of the holy days recognised by the Chasidim congregation of Jews of which she was a devout member. However, the deputy High Court judge held that neither the rules of natural justice nor the European Convention had been breached by the decision to hold the inquiry without her because she had not notified the Secretary of State in good time of her religious difficulty in attending. Other interested parties had already been informed of the date of the inquiry, her surveyor's written objections had been taken fully into account and her presence there would have been otiose in any event since the matters to be canvassed were of a technical nature. Furthermore, although it appeared at the trial that she was precluded by her faith from employing anyone to work on her behalf on the holy day in question, she had not notified the Secretary of State of this earlier and he had therefore had every reason to assume that her surveyor might appear on the day to represent her objections. Her appeal was dismissed by the Court of Appeal[2] on the grounds that there had been no breach of the rules of natural justice. While an adjournment of judicial proceedings might be appropriate to accommodate such religious beliefs,[3] an administrative inquiry was of a different order because of the large number of other parties involved whose interests also had to be considered. Having been notified of the date of the inquiry some ten weeks beforehand the applicant's problem only came to light three weeks before the date of the inquiry. If she had objected to the date from the moment when she was told of it the case might well have been decided differently.[4]

1 [1978] 1 All ER 591.
2 [1978] 3 All ER 82.

3 For illustrations of such adjournments in the course of litigation, see *Barker v Warren* (1677) 2 Mod Rep 271 and the unreported cases referred to by *Henriques* pp 183-4.
4 See per Waller LJ at 88.

THE SCOPE FOR REFORM

8.21 One method of alleviating the difficulties experienced by persons in the position of the applicants in these last two cases is by extending the number of public holidays to include some of the annual festivals recognised by the principal non-Christian religions practised in England today. This question raises important issues in the field of employment and is therefore considered further in ch 9 below.[1]

1 See para 9.26 below.

6 Prisoners' rights

8.22 Under English law a convicted prisoner basically retains all his civil rights except those which are taken away expressly or by necessary implication.[1] Specific provisions are to be found in the Prison Act 1952 and in rules made by the Secretary of State pursuant to s 47 of that Act which deal with matters of treatment, employment, discipline and control, whether the prisoner is in a prison, youth custody centre, detention centre or remand centre. The Prison Rules themselves are, however, merely directory and do not confer upon a prisoner any right of action if they are broken.[2] In such a case the prisoner's remedy is to complain to the governor or the Secretary of State.

Under the Prison Act 1952, s 10(1), where in any prison the number of prisoners who belong to a religious denomination other than the Church of England is sufficiently large, in the opinion of the Secretary of State, as to require the appointment of a minister of that denomination, the Secretary of State may appoint such a minister to that prison. Under s 10(3) where such an appointment is not warranted, the Prison Commissioners may nevertheless allow such a minister to visit prisoners of his denomination and in terms of the Prison Rules 1964, r 12(3) the prison governor must do what he reasonably can, if so requested by a prisoner, to arrange for regular visits by a minister of such a denomination. Rule 13(2) provides for services to be conducted for denominations other than the Church of England 'at such times as may be arranged' and there are reports of prison services being held for Jews, Muslims, Hindus, Sikhs, Buddhists, members of the Greek Orthodox Church and Pentecostalists.[3]

Where there are only a very few prisoners of a particular denomination the holding of regular services may simply not be feasible. In one case a Jewish prisoner only received visits from a Jewish lay-visitor (rather than a rabbi) who was assisted by the prison chaplain. His complaint to the European Commission that his freedom of religion was being violated by the failure to hold services was rejected by the Commission.[4] The limited numbers and availability of ministers of minority faiths to visit prisoners are obviously controlling factors in this regard.

Under the Prison Rules 1964, r 15 arrangements must be made so as not to require Christian prisoners to do any unnecessary work on Sundays, Christmas Day or Good Friday. The same principle applies to prisoners of other religions in relation to their recognised days of religious observance. Rule 16 provides that, so far as reasonably practicable, every prisoner shall have made available to him such religious books recognised by his denomination as are approved by the Secretary of State.[5] Similar rules about each of these matters apply in the case of youth custody centres and detention centres.[6]

Neither the Prison Act nor the rules applicable to prisons, youth custody centres or detention centres make express provision concerning matters of diet or dress. Instructions on the subject are issued periodically to prison governors in the form of Home Office circulars and in general a serious attempt seems to be made to accommodate the requirements of different religions insofar as it is reasonably practicable to do so.[7] Thus Sikhs are allowed to keep their hair uncut and to wear beards and turbans,[8] Jews may be permitted to have special food brought in for the Passover,[8] Muslims are given similar privileges to mark the end of Ramadan[9] and pork-free or vegetarian diets are available at all times.[9] Various prisons have also made arrangements for *halal* meat for Muslims to be brought in from outside.[10] In one case taken before the European Commission for Human Rights by a Jewish applicant it was found that despite his allegations that the prison was failing to respect his dietary rules he had in fact been offered *kosher* food.[11]

1 *Raymond v Honey* [1982] 1 All ER 756 at 759, 762, HL.
2 See *Arbon v Anderson* [1943] KB 252, [1943] 1 All ER 154; *Williams v Home Office* [1981] 1 All ER 1211 at 1242.
3 See Robilliard 'Religion in Prison' (1980) 130 NLJ 800.
4 *X v UK* (1976) 5 Decisions and Reports of the European Commission of Human Rights 8. A similar approach was adopted by the US Supreme Court in *Cruz v Beto* 405 US 319 at 322 (1972).
5 In *X v UK* (1976) 5 Decisions and Reports of the European Commission of Human Rights 100 the Commission held a prison governor was entitled to withhold a religious book from a prisoner on the ground that it contained a chapter on martial arts. Such interference with religious freedom was held to be justified as a necessary protection of the rights and freedoms of others.
6 See Youth Custody Centre Rules 1983, rr 27-33; Detention Centre Rules 1952, rr 48-55.
7 See *Robilliard* at p 801; *Prisons and the Prisoner* (HMSO, 1977) p 40; Circular Instruction No 56/1983.
8 *Robilliard* ibid.
9 See Minister of State, Home Office, 3 HC Official Report (6th series) col 475.
10 See McDermott and Ahsan, *The Muslim Guide* p. 68.
11 *X v UK* (1976) 5 Decisions and Reports 8.

8.23 Rastafarians in prison have been at the centre of an important controversy. A Home Office circular issued in 1976 stated that Rastafarians did not qualify as members of a religious denomination for the purposes of the Prison Act and therefore no special religious facilities should be provided for them.[1] In practice it seems that they were encouraged by the prison authorities to register their religion as 'Ethiopian Orthodox'.[2] However, this is something very different and the wearing of dreadlocks is certainly not one of the religious requirements or customs of this church, as it is with Rastafarians.[3] Hence the circular declared that governors were perfectly justified in arranging for Rastafarians to have their dreadlocks cut if this seemed appropriate.

The principal reason given to Parliament by the Home Office Minister in April 1981 for not recognising the Rastafarians as members of a religious denomination was that they had no central organising authority. However, by January 1982, following pressure from a number of quarters[4] and discussions with the Commission for Racial Equality, it was announced that the prison department was reviewing its policy towards Rastafarians.[5] Instructions had already been issued to wardens of detention centres, where the general practice is to require all inmates to have their hair cut short, to give Rastafarians the opportunity to retain their dreadlocks.

Rastafarians believe in the divinity of Emperor Haile Selassie of Ethiopia and are generally considered to be members of a religious faith by those outsiders who have carefully investigated their convictions.[6] They certainly appear to satisfy the test laid down by the Court of Appeal in *R v Registrar-General, exp Segerdal*[7] that religious worship connotes reverence of a god or deity or supreme being. In their perspective, since God inhabits each man and his body thus becomes a temple, there is no necessity for churches or formal worship.[8] However, they pray regularly and do hold meetings at which chanting, singing, praying and preaching occur.[9] Their uncut hair is part of their philosophy of natural living, though it may have been stimulated in part by a desire for identification with African warriors; it is also justified by Rastafarians as in conformity with Old Testament teaching.[10]

1 Home Office Circular 60/1976, quoted by Mr T Cox MP 3 HC Official Report (6th series) col 473.
2 *Robilliard* at p 801.
3 See E Cashmore, *Rastaman* (Unwin, 2nd edn, 1983) p 156.
4 See, eg the report of the Catholic Commission for Racial Justice, 'Rastafarians in Jamaica and Britain' (January, 1982) advocating legal recognition.
5 See 16 HC Official Report (6th series) written answers col 220.
6 See, eg K M Williams *The Rastafarians* (Ward Lock, 1981) p 12; *Cashmore* pp 6-7 (who prefers to describe them as a 'millenarian movement'); Catholic Commission for Racial Justice 'Rastafarians in Jamaica and Britain' (1982) p 11.
7 [1970] 2 QB 697, [1970] 3 All ER 886.
8 *Williams* p 13.
9 Ibid p 18.
10 See *Cashmore* p 156 where reference is made to Lev 21:5 and Numbers 6:5.

THE SCOPE FOR REFORM

8.24 The International Covenant on Civil and Political Rights, Art 10(1) provides that all persons deprived of their liberty shall be 'treated with humanity and with respect for the inherent dignity of the human person'. While it is thought that in practice this standard is generally maintained in English prisons, the fact that prisoners clearly do not have legally enforceable rights in relation to such matters as worship, dress, appearance and diet is a matter of some concern. Even so, despite the lack of any constitutional protection of freedom of religion in English law, the treatment of prisoners' religious needs appears to compare favourably with that accorded in the US where such protection is enshrined in the First and Fourteenth Amendments to the American Constitution. In the absence of a US Supreme Court ruling on the rights of prisoners to wear beards or follow special diets for religious reasons there have been a number of conflicting lower court decisions on these issues. Some courts appear to have been rather too easily inclined to accept the arguments of prison officials about the financial costs and administrative inconvenience of adherence to special dietary norms and the security, identification and hygiene problems posed by allowing prisoners to grow beards. Fortunately, others have been more robust in their protection of religious freedom.[1]

In the only case decided by the European Commission of Human Rights concerning a prisoner's appearance it was held that the Austrian prison authorities were entitled to prevent a Buddhist prisoner from growing a beard because of the problems involved in identifying bearded prisoners.[2] The limitation was felt to be justified within Art 9(2) of the Convention as one that was necessary for the protection of public order. The decision has been criticised[3] and it is submitted that it should not be followed in the future.[4] The problem of identification only really arises, as it did in that case, where the prisoner in question arrives without a beard and subsequently seeks to grow one. If the religious ground is a genuine one, e g upon conversion to a different faith or a case of spiritual regeneration, there will normally only be a single alteration in appearance which the prison authorities should easily be able to accommodate through the daily routine of contact with prison officers and rephotographing where necessary. The Prison Rules already very properly allow a prisoner to register a change of religion from the one registered at entry, provided the prison governor consents,[5] and no doubt the governor would always do so in practice unless there was some evidence that the request for a change in registration was not made in good faith.[6] On the other hand, this is yet a further illustration of a situation in which a prisoner should arguably be given a legal right, enforceable through the ordinary courts, if necessary.[7]

1 See generally 'The Religious Rights of the Incarcerated' (1977) 125 Univ of Pennsylvania LR 812.
2 *X v Austria* (1965) 8 Yearbook of the European Convention on Human Rights 174 at 184.
3 See F Jacobs *The European Convention on Human Rights* p 150.
4 The Council of Europe's *Standard Minimum Rules for the Treatment of Prisoners* contains a clear implication in r 15 that beards should be allowed in prison.
5 R 10(2).
6 *Robilliard* p 800.
7 Support for the idea of spelling out clearly exactly what rights a prisoner has and, in the case of the more important ones, giving him access to an independent tribunal is to be found in *Justice in Prison* (Report by 'Justice' 1983).

B. OATHS IN JUDICIAL PROCEEDINGS

8.25 Adherents to faiths other than Christianity sometimes have their own distinctive customs and practices regarding the swearing of an oath to tell the truth in judicial proceedings. Mindful of the eighth of God's commandments to Moses not to bear false witness,[1] Jews naturally wish to be sworn in a manner binding on their consciences, which means taking the oath upon the Pentateuch or the Old Testament, rather than upon the New Testament.[2] Most Jews swear with their heads covered, but some may leave their heads uncovered.[3] Muslims are sworn on the Koran,[4] provided they believe in its authority as holy scripture.[5] On the other hand, Hinduism encompasses such a large number of sects, each of which attaches different importance to a variety of holy books and objects, that it is impossible to state that one particular method of taking the oath is the norm. Indeed there is good authority for the proposition that Hinduism does not provide for the taking of such oaths at all.[6] The *Bhagavad Gita* is the best known book of Hindu scriptures in the West, but there are many others (including the *Vedas*) and it is necessary to inquire of each individual Hindu witness which book, if any, he regards as suitable for use in taking an oath,[7] assuming that he is prepared to swear in any event.

The Sikhs possess their own distinctive holy book, the *Guru Granth Sahib*, but according to some commentators its holiness depends upon its location in a *gurdwara* where it is under the control of temple officials and the same spiritual significance is not attached to it when it is stored in a court of law under the supervision of a clerk or usher.[8] Hence, it is argued, an oath taken upon it by a Sikh witness in such circumstances would not be regarded as binding on his conscience. For this reason the rules of many Indian and Pakistani High Courts apparently provide that a copy of the *Guru Granth Sahib* should on no account be brought into court.[9] Instead, courts in India and parts of East Africa have used a *Gutka* (or prayer book).[10] On the other hand, in a number of English cases[11] Sikh witnesses have expressed a willingness to be sworn on the *Guru Granth Sahib*, seemingly regarding such an oath as binding upon them. Certainly there are strict rules governing the respect which must be accorded the *Guru Granth Sahib*; the congregation must sit below it in the *gurdwara*[12] and if a copy is kept in a private house a special room must be set aside for it and it must be placed in a position where no one is likely to walk over it, for example on the floor above.[13] It also appears that it should not be handled by anyone who is not a Sikh.[14] No doubt this is a sphere in which there are different schools of orthodoxy, but each of them can be accommodated since it is the conscience of the individual witness which is of central importance. Some Sikhs may regard an oath sworn in court on the *Guru Granth Sahib* or a *Gutka* as binding, others not, just as some Hindus may regard an oath on the *Bhagavad Gita* as binding while others would not.

Parsees are sworn on their holy book, the *Zendavesta*.[15]

1 See Exodus 20:16.
2 *Henriques* p 178.
3 *Stringer on Oaths and Affirmations* (4th edn, 1929) p 161.
4 Both *Stringer* (at p 166) and *Phipson on Evidence* (13th edn, 1982, para 31-38) are surely wrong in stating that it is very doubtful whether Muslims should be sworn. *Stringer* appears to distinguish, without explanation, between Indian Muslims and Arabs in this regard.
5 Some Ismailis, followers of the Aga Khan, may not do so: see Schofield and Channan 'Oaths of Hindu, Sikh and Muslim witnesses' (1972) 136 Justice of the Peace 831, reprinted in [1974] New Community 409.
6 See Anstey. 'On Judicial Oaths as Administered to Heathen Witnesses' (1868) 3 Juridical Society Papers 371 at 375-8.
7 *Schofield and Channan* at 832, 410.
8 Idem.
9 Idem.
10 Preetam Singh 'Oath or Affirmation for the Sikhs' Sikh Courier, June 1963, p 9.
11 See, e g *R v Moore* (1892) 66 LT 125; *R v Pritam Singh* [1958] 1 All ER 199, discussed at para 8.30 below.
12 *East Meets West* p 93.
13 James *Sikh Children in Britain* p 32.
14 See [1958] Crim LR 325.
15 See *Stringer* p 167.

Policy considerations

8.26 The taking of an oath in the context of judicial proceedings performs two rather separate functions. The first is to bind the conscience of the person concerned, usually through fear of divine or supernatural retribution if the oath is broken. On this basis it is clear that whenever possible non-Christian witnesses should be allowed to swear according to whatever mode will bind their consciences. To require them to subscribe to a Christian oath on the New Testament would be both illogical and pointless. The only problem likely to arise in this area concerns the identification of the appropriate method in each individual case and the practicality of having the required holy books readily available. Neither of these should prove insurmountable, though a number of difficulties have been experienced in the past and on occasion an adjournment of the proceedings may be necessary or resort had to the alternative of a solemn affirmation. In 1958, for example, there were said to be only three copies of the *Guru Granth Sahib* in the the whole of Britain and clearly not all the courts in the country can realistically expect to be stocked with works which may never be required.

The second function performed by an oath is to lay the foundation for legal sanctions if the oath is broken and the witness does not speak the truth. However, this function can be equally well served by any procedure which makes it clear to a witness that he is obliged by law to answer questions truthfully and that criminal sanctions may follow if he does not.

Insofar as it is thought that fear of spiritual or moral sanctions is a more compelling force for certain sections of the population than the prospect of a prosecution, it seems only right and proper that there should be no discrimination, on grounds of religion, in the opportunity to take an oath. It would be both wrong and imprudent either to insist that non-Christians should subscribe to a Christian oath or to deny them the opportunity of swearing an oath altogether, while still retaining the oath for Christians. Moreover, while there is a danger that a person may declare a particularly exotic form of oath binding upon his conscience when in reality he does not believe in it, the problem of disbelief arises even with those members of the predominantly secular majority community who subscribe to the normal Christian oath out of habit or a desire to conform rather than from any religious conviction.

English law

8.27 The law relating to the swearing of oaths in the context of judicial proceedings has had a chequered history, full of disputes, anomalies and misconceptions.[1] Writing in 1628 Lord Coke declared that no 'infidel' could be a witness in an English court[2] and by an infidel it is clear that he meant all those who did not believe in the Christian religion; Jews were thus included as well as heathens.[3] The principal reason he gave was that he did not think them creditworthy.[4] If Coke was right the legal position, according to Professor Cross, was that:

'. . . evidence had to be given on oath and that oath had to be taken on the Gospel. If it could be shown that the proposed witness did not accept the authority of the Gospel, he would be held incompetent to give evidence.'[5]

In his *History of the Pleas of the Crown*[6] published in 1676 Sir Matthew Hale strongly opposed Coke, arguing the necessity of accepting the oaths of Jewish brokers upon the Old Testament in cases involving foreign mercantile contracts, drawing attention to the practices of other nations and pointing out the illogicality of allowing a Turk or a Jew to subscribe to the normal Christian oath when he might well not regard it as imposing any obligation upon him.

1 See generally, Anstey 'On Judicial Oaths as Administered to Heathen Witnesses' (1868) 3 Juridical Society Papers 371.
2 Co Lit 6 b.
3 See, e g 2 Inst 507.
4 In *Calvin's case* (1608) 7 Co Rep 1(a) he had earlier expressed the view that all 'infidels' were, in the eyes of English law, 'perpetual enemies'.
5 *Cross on Evidence* (6th edn, 1985) p 188.
6 Vol 2, p 279.

8.28 Although there are reports of a Jew being sworn on the Pentateuch in 1668[1] and of a Muslim being sworn on the Koran in 1738[2] the first occasion upon which the issue was fully argued by counsel and in which the question was authoritatively determined for the future was the landmark case of *Omychund v Barker*[3] in 1744. A Hindu merchant had brought proceedings against an English debtor in the Court of Chancery in connection with some dealings transacted in Calcutta. The Court had sent a commission to Calcutta to take evidence on oath from various witnesses there and had instructed the commission to administer the oath to Hindu witnesses[4] with the word 'solemnly' being substituted for the phrase 'on the Holy Evangelists'. The commission had returned with the depositions, which had apparently been taken in accordance with current Hindu practice by touching the brahmin's hand or foot, and the question then arose whether they could properly be read in evidence. Considering the issue to be one of considerable importance the Lord Chancellor, Lord Hardwicke, sought the assistance of Lord Chief Justice Lee, Lord Chief Justice Willes and Lord Chief Baron Parker. After hearing full argument they were unanimously of the opinion that the depositions should be received as evidence. In the leading judgment Willes LCJ rejected the views of Coke as

'. . . contrary not only to the scripture but to common sense and common humanity. And I think that even the devils themselves, whose subjects he says the heathens are, cannot have worse principles; and besides the irreligion of it, it is a most impolitic notion and would at once destroy all that trade and commerce from which this nation reaps such great benefits . . . It is a little, mean, narrow notion to suppose that no one but a Christian can be an honest man'.[5]

In his support Willes LCJ was able to cite not only Hale but also the practice of the English courts in relation to Jewish witnesses both before their expulsion by Edward I and after their return in the seventeenth century.[6] Taking an oath the learned judge declared, was no more a part of Christianity than of any other religion and so long as the person concerned believed in a deity who would punish him if he swore falsely, he could be admitted as a witness to testify here. It did not matter whether the divine retribution would be meted out in this world or the next.[7] The ceremonial details accompanying the taking of the oath were not the important aspect:

'The kissing of the book here, and the touching of the Bramin's hand and foot at Calcutta, and many other different forms which are made use of in different countries, are no part of the oath, but are only ceremonies invented to add the greater solemnity to the taking of it, and to express the assent of the party to the oath when he does not repeat the oath itself . . .'[8]

As to the credit which should be attached by the court to the testimony of non-Christian witnesses, Willes LCJ had this to say, although it no longer represents the legal position on the issue today:

'. . . I do not think that the same credit ought to be given either by a Court or a jury to an infidel witness as to a Christian, who is under much stronger obligations to swear nothing but the truth . . . To come nearer to the present case; supposing an infidel who believes [in] a god and that he will reward and punish him in this world, but does not believe [in] a future state, be examined on his oath, . . . and on the other side to contradict him a Christian is examined, who believes [in] a future state and that he shall be punished in the next world as well as in this, if he does not swear the truth, I think that the same credit ought not to be given to an infidel as to a Christian, because he is plainly not under so strong an obligation.'[9]

The final question in the case was whether infidel witnesses could be indicted for perjury if they swore falsely. The precedents revealed that they could and that the words relating to the Holy Evangelists could be omitted from such a charge without invalidating it.

1 *Robeley v Langston* (1668) 2 Keb 314.
2 *Fachina v Sabine* (1738) 2 Stra 1104.
3 (1744) 1 Atk 21; Willes 538.
4 They are referred to in the reports as 'Gentoos'.
5 (1744) Willes 538 at 542.
6 See, e g *Robeley v Langston* (1668) 2 Keb 314; *Henriques* pp. 179-80.

7 See also *A-G v Bradlaugh* (1885) 14 QBD 667 at 697.
8 (1744) Willes 538 at 548.
9 At 550-1.

8.29 Twenty years later, in 1764, it was given as the unanimous view of 12 Old Bailey judges in *R v Morgan*[1] that an oath sworn by a Muslim upon the Koran was permissible in the prosecution of a capital charge for theft. Subsequently, however, more difficult questions occasionally arose as to the proper mode of swearing witnesses[2] and in 1838 an Act was passed 'to remove doubts as to the validity of certain oaths'.[3] It provided that:

'. . . in all cases in which an oath may lawfully be and shall have been administered to any person, either as a juryman or a witness or a deponent in any proceeding, civil or criminal, in any court of law or equity in the United Kingdom, . . . such person is bound by the oath administered, provided the same shall have been administered in such form and with such ceremonies as such person may declare to be binding; and every such person in case of wilful false swearing may be convicted of the crime of perjury in the same manner as if the oath had been administered in the form and with the ceremonies most commonly adopted.'

1 (1764) 1 Leach 54.
2 See, e g *R v Gilham* (1795) 1 Esp 284.
3 1 & 2 Vict c 105.

8.30 The right of Quaker witnesses solemnly to affirm rather than take an oath had been recognised at the end of the seventeenth century[1] and when this dispensation was extended to other persons by the Oaths Act 1888 it was still confined to two carefully circumscribed sets of circumstances. The witness had of his own initiative to object to being sworn and then state, as his grounds for objection, either that he possessed no religious belief whatsoever or that the taking of an oath was contrary to his religious belief.[2] In 1892 in *R v Moore*[3] a conviction had to be quashed on appeal because two of the witnesses, who were Sikhs, had affirmed despite the fact that their beliefs did not fit within either of these two categories. All that had happened prior to the affirmation was that one of the Sikhs had informed the court usher that he did not wish to be sworn on either the Bible or the Koran. Similarly in 1958 in *R v Pritam Singh*[4] it was held that no charge of perjury could succeed against a Sikh who had affirmed rather than given evidence on oath in previous proceedings at a magistrates court. He had expressed no religious objection to taking an oath and had only affirmed because of the practical difficulty of locating a copy of the *Guru Granth Sahib*. The problem identified in the latter case, which was of a purely administrative nature, was eventually solved by the enactment of the Oaths Act 1961 which authorised an affirmation to be made by a person to whom it was not reasonably practicable, without inconvenience or delay, to administer an oath in the manner appropriate to his religious belief.[5]

1 See 7 and 8 Will 3 c 34 (1695).
2 S 1.
3 (1892) 66 LT 125. See also *Nash v Ali Khan* (1892) 8 TLR 444.
4 [1958] 1 All ER 199, [1958] 1 WLR 143.
5 S 1.

8.31 The various Oaths Acts passed between 1838 and 1961 have been consolidated in the Oaths Act 1978. Section 1 now provides as follows:

'(1) Any oath may be administered and taken in England, Wales or Northern Ireland in the following form and manner:-

The person taking the oath shall hold the New Testament, or, in the case of a Jew, the Old Testament, in his uplifted hand, and shall say or repeat after the officer administering the oath the words 'I swear by Almighty God that . . .' followed by the words of the oath prescribed by law.

(2) The officer shall (unless the person about to take the oath voluntarily objects thereto, or is physically incapable of so taking the oath) administer the oath in the form and manner aforesaid without question.

(3) In the case of a person who is neither a Christian nor a Jew, the oath shall be administered in any lawful manner.'

This leaves the position flexible enough to accommodate both Christians who wish to incorporate some special ceremonial into the taking of an oath[1] and non-Christians who wish to follow their own forms. One problem such liberality may well have given rise to, however, is the recognition of certain exotic practices as authentic religious customs when in reality they are nothing of the kind. In 1842 in *R v Entrehman*,[2] a private prosecution for assault arising from a fracas on board ship, an oath was purportedly administered according to Chinese usage along the lines suggested by a Chinese interpreter who claimed to have seen it administered in this form. It involved the witness in kneeling down and breaking a China saucer by dashing it against the rail of the witness box and the officer of the court enjoining the witness: 'you shall tell the truth and the whole truth; the saucer is cracked, and if you do not tell the truth, your soul will be cracked like the saucer'.[3]

This now appears to be the standard form of oath for Chinese witnesses,[4] yet there seems to be little if anything in Chinese tradition or religious belief to support it.[5] Indeed one commentator reported as long ago as 1868 that Chinese witnesses here usually grinned at the bizarre ceremony in which they participated.[6] Such an oath had no real significance for them, it was never used in courts in China and was merely invented so as to provide an impression that the Chinese had some recognisable equivalent to the English procedure for giving sworn evidence.[7]

The Oaths Act 1978, s 3 permits anyone who wishes to do so to swear the oath with uplifted hand (but without a book) in the form and manner in which an oath is administered in Scotland, regardless of whether the oath is being taken there or not. In *Shrinagesh v Kaushal*[8] Hindu witnesses were sworn in this manner in the absence of a copy of their sacred book since it was clear that they believed in a single God.

In *Sibunruang v Sibunruang*[9] a Buddhist from Thailand was allowed to subscribe to the following oath:

'I declare, as in the presence of Buddha, that I am un-prejudiced, and if what I shall speak shall prove false, or if by colouring truth others may be led astray, then may the three Holy Existences, Buddha, Dhamma and Pro-Sangha, in whose sight I now stand, together with the Devotees of the 22 Firmaments, punish me and my migrating soul.'

Mr Commissioner Latey, sitting in the Divorce Court, commented that in the course of a fairly long judicial career he had never come across this type of oath before.[10]

However, the Act does at least provide some very necessary safeguards against a witness later seeking to deny the validity of an oath to which he has subscribed. Section 4 provides as follows:

(1) 'In any case in which an oath may lawfully be and has been administered to any person, if it has been administered in a form and manner other than that prescribed by law, he is bound by it if it has been administered in such form and with such ceremonies as he may have declared to be binding.

(2) Where an oath has been duly administered and taken, the fact that the person to whom it was administered had, at the time of taking it, no religious belief, shall not for any purpose affect the validity of the oath.'

Moreover, it has been held that even in relation to the normal type of oath described in s 1 the words of the statute are merely directive and failure to comply with them does not necessarily invalidate the oath.[11] Hence if a Jew were to take the oath upon the New Testament in error this would not render his evidence invalid.

A solemn affirmation in place of an oath may be made today by anyone who objects to being sworn, regardless of the reason for his refusal, as well as in those instances where the swearing of an oath is not reasonably practicable without inconvenience and delay.[12]

1 See, eg the instance described in *The Times*, 26 January 1918, p 3 of a member of the Greek Orthodox Church who pointed two fingers to heaven.
2 (1842) Car & M 248.
3 A similar imprecation was made by a Japanese witness in a case in 1910 after he had extinguished a lighted candle 'with much ceremony': see (1910) 129 LT 432.
4 It was administered in *The Orianada* (1907) 122 LT Jo 531.
5 Anstey 'On Judicial Oaths as Administered to Heathen Witnesses' (1868) 3 Jur Soc Pap 371 at 374, 379-80. Anstey suggests (at 384-5) that this form of oath originated in the Old Bailey trial of *R v Alsey* in 1804. However, in that case it was the body of the witness which was to be cracked like a saucer if he failed to tell the truth, not his soul, i e it was not really an oath of testimony at all but an oath of 'ordeal'.
6 Anstey at 388.
7 Wigmore suggests that this form of oath may be derived from certain Chinese secret societies – see *Wigmore on Evidence* (3rd edn, 1940) vol vi, para 1818.
8 (1956) *Times*, 3 October.
9 (1964) *Times*, 25 January.
10 An identical version of this oath is to be found in *Stringer* at p. 165, but no authority is given for its use.
11 *R v Chapman* [1980] Crim LR 42
12 Oaths Act 1978, s 5.

The scope for reform

8.32 Abolition of the oath and its replacement by a solemn declaration to tell the truth has been advocated by number of individuals and groups over a period of many years.[1] Some of the most cogent reasons in favour of abolition are to be found in the Eleventh Report of the Criminal Law Revision Committee in 1972. The Committee was in fact divided on the issue and in any event declined to recommend any change in the law because it considered that it would be undesirable to create different rules for criminal and civil proceedings, but the six arguments put forward by the majority in favour of abolition may be summarised as follows:

(i) The oath is a primitive institution whose origin dates back to a period when people believed in magic and in the efficacy of curses. It is anomalous that those who believe in a deity should subscribe to an oath since it amounts, in effect, to a request for vengeance from heaven rather than divine mercy.

(ii) Even if it is appropriate to call in aid divine displeasure as a penalty for lying there is something inconsistent about confining this invocation to a limited range of official proceedings.

(iii) By allowing persons to affirm rather than take an oath, even where they do possess religious beliefs, Parliament has undermined the importance of the oath to such an extent that there seems no reason why everyone should not be required to affirm.

(iv) Many witnesses probably take the oath despite the fact that they have no religious beliefs. They do so because they do not wish to call attention to themselves by objecting and affirming or because they fear the impact of their evidence will be weakened if they depart from the customary oath. In practice, however, little attention is paid in evaluating evidence to the fact that it was given on oath.

(v) It is particularly incongruous to require an accused, as opposed to any ordinary witness, to take the oath because he is under an obvious temptation to lie.

(vi) There is no reason to believe that retaining the oath increases the amount of truth told. Perjury is widespread and the rare individual who feels that an oath might hamper his ability to lie can simply opt to affirm instead.

The minority of the Committee, who were strongly opposed to the replacement of the oath by declaration, did not find these arguments convincing. They felt that there were still many people to whom the oath, administered properly and in complete silence, served to bring home most strongly the solemnity of their obligation to tell the truth and to be careful in giving their evidence.[2]

It is thought that the majority's reasoning generally carries greater conviction, but in the absence of hard facts it seems to be very much a matter of surmise what impact the oath has on people's decisions about telling the truth. If even a small proportion are saved from perjuring themselves the oath seems worth retaining.[3] From the point of view of the ethnic minorities the important aspect is to ensure that their own oaths are afforded proper recognition on the basis of equality and that they are administered and taken in an authentic fashion. The law has taken a long time to adjust its provisions in this regard to the needs of non-Christians, but it now appears to be in a reasonably satisfactory state. Only in the case of Chinese witnesses does there appear to be a clear need for a change of practice. In future they should be encouraged by clerks and ushers to affirm rather than unnecessarily deplete the court's stock of saucers.

Finally, every person called to give evidence should be given an entirely free choice as to whether to take an oath or affirm and should be informed in advance of his right to choose to affirm. It should no longer be necessary for a person to have to register an objection to taking an oath before he is given the opportunity to affirm.

1 See, e g Anstey 'On Judicial Oaths as Administered to Heathen Witnesses' (1868) 3 Jur Soc Pap 371; Eleventh Report of the Criminal Law Revision Committee, Cmnd 4991 of 1972, paras 279-80; Radevsky 'Is the Oath Out of Date?' (1980) 130 NLJ 397.

2 Para 281.

3 The number might be increased if greater solemnity were injected into the occasion, e g by following the Scottish practice of having the oath administered by the presiding judge or magistrate, rather than a minor court official. For many who swear it at present it appears to be no more than a meaningless ritual.

C. BURIAL AND CREMATION

8.33 Although the desire to ensure a decent departure from worldly life for one's relatives and friends is a deep-rooted and universal one among all sections of mankind, the forms and ceremonies adopted by different groups of people to accomplish this are extremely varied. In a wide-ranging study Haberstein and Lamers summarise the position by stating:

'Men dispose of their dead in many ways: by burying them in the earth or beneath mounds of stones or bricks, by burying them in caves, or rock ledges, by exposing them in trees or on platforms, by feeding them to birds, by burning them, by exposing them to scavenging animals, by roasting them, by sinking them in water or allowing them to drift to seas or down rivers.'[1]

If attention is focused upon the principal ethnic minority practices found in

England at the present time the chief differences appear to be the following. Hindus generally cremate their dead. For them death is just another stage in the endless cycle of rebirth and a new life, with the result that ceremonial formalities are kept to a minimum.[2] In India the ashes would commonly be deposited in the river Ganges, and in this country a similar practice of scattering them in the waters of a river or in the sea is often followed. Cremation is also the normal method of disposal used by Sikhs, Buddhists and Parsees.[3]

Orthodox Jews and Muslims bury their dead, preferably in separate plots set aside for members of their respective faiths.[4] In both these religions emphasis is placed upon the need for the burial to take place as soon as possible after the death occurs and some Muslims consider that ideally it should be completed within 24 hours.[5] This is not, however, a rule admitting of no exceptions.[6] It is obviously a sensible practice to adopt in hot countries for sanitary reasons, but the problem is not such a pressing one here and burials can usually be arranged quite easily within three or four days at the most.[7] In any event arrangements have to be made by Muslims for the ceremonial washing and shrouding of the corpse,[8] as well as for the digging of the grave. Neither Jews nor Muslims approve of autopsies which are perceived as a desecration of the deceased's body,[9] but they recognise that post-mortem examinations may have to be carried out when there exist compelling legal or medical reasons to do so, for instance where the death has occurred in suspicious circumstances.

Muslims have special rules about the alignment of a grave and the positioning of the body within it. The best opinion appears to be that the grave should run from north-east to south-west, i e at right angles to the direction of Mecca which lies to the south-east. The head of the corpse should be at the south-west end of the grave, with the head turned to the right so that it faces towards Mecca.[10] Muslims also believe that graves should be raised a few inches from the ground so that they are clearly visible and will not be desecrated unwittingly by people walking, standing or sitting on them.[11] For the same reason they are opposed to any practice of subsequently levelling graves flat with the ground. In hot, dry countries they do not generally use a coffin and merely wrap the corpse in one or two sheets of white cloth.[12] In England they appear willing to use coffins because of the dampness of the soil but would prefer these not to be permanently sealed until after the funeral prayer which occurs shortly before burial. This gives relatives and friends a final opportunity to see the face of the deceased, as well as affording an opportunity to ensure that the body is positioned so that the deceased's face is properly turned towards Mecca.

1 *Funeral Customs The World Over* (Milwaukee, 1963) p 760.
2 P Sookdhe, *Asians in Britain* (Exeter, 1977) p 18.
3 Traditionally Parsees in Persia and India practised the rite of exposing their dead in remote and barren places (e g the so-called 'towers of silence') to await depredation by birds and animals, but today that custom appears to have virtually disappeared: see M Boyce *Zoroastrians; Their Religious Beliefs and Practices* (Routledge, 1979) pp 221-2.
4 M Anwar *Muslim Burials* (CRC 1975) p 4. Jews who are members of the Reform and Liberal Synagogues have no religious objection to being cremated.
5 *Anwar* p 6; *Haberstein and Lamers* p 195.
6 McDermott and Ahsan *The Muslim Guide* p 63.
7 Many burial authorities require at least 48 hours' notice (excluding weekends and public holidays) and do not allow interments at weekends or on public holidays.
8 *McDermott and Ahsan* p 63; *Anwar* pp 6-7.
9 *McDermott and Ahsan* p 63.
10 *Anwar* p 5; *East Meets West* p 60.
11 *Anwar* pp 4-5.
12 *Anwar* pp 5-6.

Policy considerations

8.34 Respect for the customs and observances of non-Christians with regard to the disposal of their dead would appear to be an integral part of religious toleration and thus a matter of considerable importance. The practices of the majority community are themselves no longer uniform. Today nearly 70% are cremated compared with only about 30% who are accorded the traditional burial in a churchyard or cemetery.[1] The first steps towards the introduction of cremation to this country were taken during the last quarter of the nineteenth century when the scarcity of land available for cemeteries (particularly in urban areas) and the dangers to health posed by overcrowded graveyards had become a public scandal and a campaign had to be mounted by social reformers to obtain some amelioration of the position. In 1874 Queen Victoria's distinguished surgeon, Sir Henry Thompson, published an article on the subject,[2] in which he explained how he had become attracted to the idea of the sanitary disposal of the dead through the use of furnaces designed by Italian scientists in the 1860s. He joined with other notable men of his day such as Trollope, Millais and Tenniel in forming the Cremation Society in order to propagate these ideas and, despite the considerable opposition and prejudice which the Society initially encountered, the practice is now followed by the large bulk of the population. Although the ashes of the dead are usually scattered on the ground in gardens of remembrance or else buried in graves or consigned directly to the sea, there seems no reason why they should not be deposited in a river. No pollution or silting is likely to result from the deposit of such small quantities.

The desire of Jews and Muslims for speedy burial without an autopsy should normally be easy to accommodate, but where the death has occurred in suspicious circumstances which suggest that it may have been due to unnatural causes a delay may be necessary to enable either a post-mortem examination or an inquest to be held.

The special rules governing the alignment of Muslim graves may very occasionally present practical problems for cemetery authorities, but most of these are capable of resolution without undue difficulty. Where a cemetery has been organised on the basis that all graves face in one particular direction and a request is made for a Muslim to be buried facing in a different direction this can obviously result in a small loss of space to the burial authority. If, on the other hand, a separate plot is set aside for Muslims, no such wastage would occur since all the graves in that section would follow the same alignment.[3] Many burial authorities have already adopted the practice of setting aside separate plots and it is hoped others with significant Muslim populations will adopt the same course.[4] Even where this is not done it is thought that it would be reasonable to expect a burial authority to follow the Muslim rules despite the small loss of space involved.

Burial without a coffin poses two principal difficulties. First, there is the offence to public decency and the possible health hazards which might be involved in the transport of the corpse to the cemetery clad merely in a sheet. These problems could easily be overcome if the body were to be conveyed in an unsealed coffin and only removed at the graveside. Second, a corpse buried without a coffin decays more quickly than one buried inside a coffin and this would tend to limit the time available for a useful exhumation if one were later to be needed. Bearing in mind the fact that such exhumations are rendered totally impossible once a body has been cremated, this does not appear to be a sufficiently cogent objection.

Following a burial it is normal practice for the gravediggers to build a small mound of earth over the grave. This subsides as rain falls and eventually leaves a reasonably level piece of ground which can then be maintained in a tidy fashion by mowing the grass which is sown on top of it. Ease of maintenance is also the reason why many burial authorities no longer allow any monument other than a headstone to be erected in their cemeteries.

1 See (1984) 50 Pharos International 44. The Pope removed the ban on the cremation of Roman Catholics in 1963.
2 The article first appeared in the *Contemporary Review* and was re-issued later the same year with other material in a pamphlet entitled *Cremation: The Treatment of the Body after Death* (London, 1874).
3 *Anwar* p 5.
4 *Anwar* pp 4, 8, 10.

English law

1 Historical background

8.35 Following the Reformation all burials involving a religious ceremony had by law to take place according to the rites of the Church of England. Although there was no general prohibition on burials taking place without religious ceremony on private land, Roman Catholics were singled out for discriminatory treatment and an Act of 1605 provided for penalties to be imposed in any case where a 'Popish recusant' was buried other than in an Anglican church or churchyard or otherwise than according to the ecclesiastical law of the realm.[1]

In 1657 a lease of land for the first Jewish cemetery of the resettlement period was obtained over what is now part of the Old Burial Ground at Mile End in East London.[2] In its earliest years it must have been used in a clandestine manner in view of the prohibition placed on all forms of religious service other than those of the Established Church by the Acts of Uniformity.[3] However, as we have seen,[4] Charles II openly afforded the Jewish community his protection in 1664 and 1673 and its members must soon have felt a reasonable degree of confidence that they could hold burial services for their dead more openly at Mile End with impunity. At all events sufficient burials had taken place there by 1724 to make it necessary for them then to acquire a further plot of land and this was accomplished through the execution of a 999-year lease of what is now known as the New Burial Ground there.[5]

1 (1605) 3 Jac 1, c 5, s 15. This provision was not repealed until 1844 by 7 & 8 Vict c 102.
2 See *Henriques* pp 109-14; Diamond 'The Cemetery of the Resettlement' (1955-9) 19 Trans Jewish Hist Soc of England 163.
3 See para 8.06 above.
4 See para 8.07 above.
5 Diamond at 190.

8.36 As explained earlier, the origins of cremation in England lie in the work of Sir Henry Thompson and the Cremation Society which he founded with others in 1874. Although the Society eventually found a suitable site for a crematorium in Woking and built one there in 1878, it was unable to proceed with this venture because of opposition from the Church of England and the Home Secretary. The legality of cremation was a matter of considerable doubt and, somewhat ironically, the issue ultimately fell to be determined not in any test case brought by the Society itself, but in proceedings brought in *R v Price*[1] against a Welsh farmer, aged 84, who had attempted to incinerate the corpse of his five-month-old child in a cask of petrol in one of his fields. He was charged with wrongfully attempting to burn his child's body instead of burying it. In his direction to the jury, Stephen J reviewed the history of the matter. Cremation had been practised by the Romans, as indeed it had been by the Hindus, but it appeared to have been discontinued in Europe with the establishment of Christianity.[2] The destruction of a corpse by fire was considered contrary to the Christian belief in the resurrection of the physical body and the substitution of burial for burning had become so complete in England that the burning of the dead received no mention whatsoever in the law. On the other hand, it was not formally or expressly forbidden. English law simply presumed that everyone would wish to be buried. The learned judge concluded:

'After full consideration, I am of opinion that a person who burns instead of burying a dead body does not commit a criminal act, unless he does it in such a manner as to amount to a public nuisance at common law. My reason for this opinion is that upon the fullest examination of the authorities . . . I have been unable to discover any authority for the proposition that it is a misdemeanour to burn a dead body, and in the absence of such authority I feel that I have no right to declare it to be one.'[3]

If, however the child's body had been burnt with the intention of preventing a lawful coroner's inquest into the death it was clear that a common law offence would have been committed.[4] The jury brought in a verdict of 'not guilty' and Price was acquitted.

Following the ruling in *R v Price* the Cremation Society began to advertise the availability of cremation at its Woking Crematorium, but it was not until 1902 that an Act of Parliament was finally introduced to regulate the process.

1 (1884) 12 QBD 247.
2 See also per Lord Stowell in *Gilbert v Buzzard* (1821) 2 Hag Con 333 at 341.
3 At 254-5.
4 At 248. See also *R v Stephenson* (1884) 13 QBD 331.

2 The modern law[1]

(i) CREMATION

8.37 The place, manner and conditions of cremation are governed by the Cremation Acts 1902 and 1952 together with regulations made by the Secretary of State for the Environment. It is an offence to effect any cremation in contravention of the Acts and regulations.[2] Nothing in the legislation authorises a burial or cremation authority or any other person to commit a nuisance.[3]

Crematoria may be provided and run either privately or by local authorities,[4] but no cremation may take place unless an application for it has been made in the prescribed form, usually by an executor or the nearest relative of the deceased.[5] The express wishes of the deceased, whether in favour of cremation or opposed to it, are not strictly binding upon the executors or relatives and even though they would normally be honoured there have been instances where Orthodox Jewish executors have been urged by the Chief Rabbi to override the deceased's expressed desire to be cremated on the grounds that this amounts to a serious violation of Jewish law.[6] Where the local authority has itself a duty to dispose of a body because no suitable arrangements appear likely to be made otherwise (eg in the absence of executors or relatives), it may not cause the body to be cremated where it has reason to believe cremation would be contrary to the wishes of the deceased.[7] After the cremation has taken place the ashes must be delivered to the person who applied for the cremation, if he so desires, and he is then free to retain them or dispose of them as he sees fit. Otherwise they must be retained by the cremation authority and disposed of by interment or scattering.[8]

No cremation is allowed to take place in the absence either of two medical certificates given by different practitioners as to the cause of death or of a post-mortem examination or a coroner's inquest.[9]

1 See generally Russell Davies *The Law of Burial, Cremation and Exhumation* (Shaw, 5th edn, 1982); 10 Halsbury's Laws of England (4th edn) paras 1001-1239.
2 Cremation Act 1902, s 8.
3 Ibid s 10.
4 Local Government Act 1972, s 214.
5 Cremation Regulations 1930, reg 7(2), as substituted by Cremation Regulations 1952, reg 1(1).
6 See *Jewish Chronicle*, 13 July 1984.
7 National Assistance Act 1948, s 50(1), (6). For a similar provision regarding children in local authority care, see Child Care Act 1980, s 25(1).
8 Cremation Regulations 1930, reg 16.
9 Ibid reg 8.

(ii) BURIAL

8.38 Burial in a churchyard is primarily regulated by ecclesiastical law. Local authorities have powers to provide and maintain public cemeteries pursuant to the Local Government Act 1972 and these may be located either within or outside their own areas.[1] Burial places may also be established by any person without statutory authority in private ground, provided no nuisance is caused,[2] and a cemetery may be maintained as a commercial enterprise.

A local burial authority may apply to the bishop of the diocese in which a cemetery is situated to have part of it consecrated. Before it does so, however, it has by law to be satisfied that there will remain after consecration a sufficient part of the cemetery which will neither be consecrated nor set apart for the use of any particular denomination.[3] Similarly, before it uses its powers to set aside a part of the cemetery for a particular denomination it must be satisfied that a sufficient part remains both unconsecrated and unreserved in this manner.[3] At the request of the particular denomination the burial authority has power to prohibit the interring or scattering of cremated human remains in or over that part of the cemetery so reserved.[4] No right to prevent the burial there of a person of a different denomination is, however, vested in any private individual; only the Attorney General may institute proceedings to restrain such a burial.[5]

Local authorities have power to provide both denominational and non-denominational chapels at their cemeteries for the holding of funeral services.[6] However, the provision of a denominational chapel can only be made at the request of the religious body in question and out of funds made available by someone other than the local authority itself.[7] There is no requirement that burial in a cemetery be accompanied by any religious service.[8]

Local authorities are given extensive powers by delegated legislation to level the surface of graves in certain circumstances, particularly those consisting wholly or substantially of earth or grass, to the same level as the adjoining ground.[9] Moreover, no burial may occur in a local authority cemetery, nor may any headstone or other memorial be placed there, nor any additional inscription be made on it without the permission of the officer appointed for the purpose by the burial authority in question.[10] In recent years, in pursuance of policies of more efficient management, many local authorities have drawn up regulations which not only prohibit any fencing or railings bordering graves but also ban the planting of any flowers or shrubs on graves and the placing of any vase or container which does not meet with the authority's requirements.

The aim is usually to grass over large parts of the cemetery in the interests of greater tidiness. In *North Bedfordshire BC v Foresterio*[11] the validity of such regulations was upheld by the High Court and the defendants, who were Italians, were held to be in contempt of court in transgressing them contrary to the terms of an earlier injunction. The defendants, who had merely followed the Italian custom of adorning the graves of their deceased relatives with floral decorations, were ordered to contribute to the plaintiff's costs and were threatened with more forceful sanctions by the court if they persisted in their breaches of the regulations.

There is no express statutory prohibition on uncoffined burials and the matter is left to the discretion of individual burial authorities.[12] However, it is an offence for any person wilfully to create any disturbance in a cemetery, to commit any nuisance there or to interfere with any burial taking place there or with any grave, headstone or other memorial or with any flowers placed thereon or to play any sport or game in a cemetery.[13]

1 Local Government Act 1972, s 214(2).
2 *Clegg v Metcalfe* [1914] 1 Ch 808.
3 Local Authorities Cemeteries Order 1977, SI 1977/204, art 5(1), (2).
4 Ibid art 5(6).
5 *Preston Corpn v Pyke* [1929] 2 Ch 338.
6 Local Authorities Cemeteries Order 1977, art 6(1).
7 Ibid art 6(3).
8 Ibid art 5(5).
9 Ibid art 16.
10 Ibid art 10(1), Sch 2, Part 1, para 1.
11 (1984) *Times*, 22 August.
12 Local Authorities Cemeteries Order, Sch 2, Part 1, para 8.
13 Ibid art 18(1). Riotous, violent or indecent behaviour in a churchyard or burial ground is also an offence under the Ecclesiastical Courts Jurisdiction Act 1860, s 2 and the Burial Laws Amendment Act 1880, s 7. See also the Cemeteries Clauses Act 1847, s 59.

(iii) INQUESTS AND POST-MORTEM EXAMINATIONS

8.39 Coroners are empowered by law to hold inquests, summon medical witnesses and direct post-mortem examinations. The Coroners Act 1887, s 3 provides for the holding of an inquest where, for example, there is reasonable cause to suspect that a person has died either a violent or an unnatural death or has died a sudden death of which the cause is unknown. As part of the proceedings of the inquest the coroner may direct the performance of a post-mortem examination.[1] Where a coroner is informed that the dead body of a person is lying within his jurisdiction and there is reasonable cause to suspect that the person has died a sudden death of which the cause is unknown, if the coroner is of opinion that a post-mortem examination may prove an inquest to be unnecessary he may also arrange for such post-mortem examination to be performed.[2] In either instance he is empowered to order the removal of the body from the place where it is lying so that the examination may take place.[3]

Coroners also have power to order the exhumation of a body where this appears to be necessary for the purpose of holding an inquest or for reasons connected with the institution of criminal proceedings in respect of a death.[4]

1 Coroners Act 1887, s 21(2).
2 Coroners (Amendment) Act 1926, s 21.
3 Ibid s 24.
4 Coroners Act 1980, s 4.

The scope for reform

8.40 It would appear that there is a reasonably strong argument in favour of placing a legal obligation upon burial authorities to respect Muslim customs both in the alignment of graves and in authorising graves to be raised permanently a few inches from the ground. While there seems to be little resistance in practice to the demand for graves to be aligned with Mecca, there are many authorities whose regulations prohibit raised mounds or memorials other than headstones in the interests of easier maintenance. When it is borne in mind that memorials other than headstones have always been allowed in the past and remain a characteristic feature of English cemeteries and that modern machinery now enables grass to be cut quickly and easily, both in confined spaces between memorials and on the top of raised mounds, this attitude seems hard to justify. If there really are greater costs involved and if it is felt that the additional expenditure should not be borne by the local ratepayers as a whole, there still seems no reason why those who are arranging for a burial could not be charged at a higher rate for any memorial or raised mound which they desired. If this plan were to be adopted no distinction would need be made on religious grounds and any person, whether Muslim or not, could be commemorated by a flat memorial stone or a raised mound, provided the higher charges were paid. Certainly as matters stand at present there would appear to be a real danger of the regulations of some local authorities amounting to a violation by the UK of the guarantees of freedom of religious observance enshrined in the European Convention on Human Rights and the International Covenant on Civil and Political Rights.

CHAPTER 9

Employment

INTRODUCTION

9.01 At a time of high unemployment ethnic minority communities are naturally particularly concerned that their members should not suffer discrimination
in the job market. Unfortunately all the evidence suggests that racial discrimination is widespread in this area,[1] despite two legislative attempts to prohibit it.[2]
However, the main focus of this chapter is not upon discrimination on the basis
of the colour of a person's skin but rather upon those religious and customary
practices found among the ethnic minority communities which impinge directly
upon a person's prospects of obtaining work and remaining in employment.
This principally involves an examination of two central issues. The first is how
far the law is prepared to accommodate the absence of an employee from work
in order to allow him to attend to religious worship and devotion. The second
is the extent to which the law protects employees and applicants for jobs from
discrimination on the basis of their dress or appearance. Since, however, both
matters involve questions of religious discrimination it is desirable to begin by
tracing very briefly the development of English legal principles relating to the
religious affiliations of employees from the sixteenth century to the present
time.

1 See, e g D J Smith *Racial Disadvantage in Britain* (Penguin, 1977) ch 5; C Brown *Black and White
  Britain* (London, 1984) pp 170-3; CRE Annual Report (1983) pp 15-17.
2 See the Race Relations Acts 1968 and 1976.

9.02 Before the modern era of religious toleration it seemed natural for the
state automatically to exclude by law from many important jobs those who did
not subscribe to the doctrines and beliefs of the Established Church. Under the
Act of Supremacy 1558, for example, it was necessary for all judges, magistrates
and mayors to take an oath of allegiance to the Crown which no Roman
Catholic could conscientiously swear because it denied the spiritual power of
the Pope.[1] Four years later the obligation to take this oath was extended to
schoolmasters and legal practitioners.[2] A more specific oath designed against
'papist recusants' was introduced after the Gunpowder Plot in 1605, but its
repercussions were more far-reaching. Its concluding words '. . . and I do make
this recognition and acknowledgement heartily willingly and truly, upon the
true faith of a Christian' were, of course, quite incapable of being subscribed to
by any self-respecting member of the Jewish faith.[3]

The fact that Jews could not conscientiously take oaths of this type, coupled
with the fact that certain other oaths could only be sworn upon the New
Testament and not the Old, meant that Jews were effectively barred from many
trades and professions. They could not become freemen of the City of London

and were thus excluded from exercising any retail trade there.[4] In theory at least, they were barred from the professions of the law, medicine and teaching, although in practice they were eventually enabled to circumvent the ban by annual Indemnity Acts which from 1728 onwards indemnified and recapacitated those who had neglected to qualify themselves for any office or employment during the previous year by omitting to take the necessary oath.[5] The right to hold office in a municipal corporation and that of holding an office or place of trust under the Crown were further restricted by the requirement, in addition to the normal oath, that the holder should take the sacrament of Holy Communion according to the rites of the Church of England.[6]

These statutory disabilities imposed on Jews and Roman Catholics were gradually removed during the course of the nineteenth century by measures such as the Roman Catholic Relief Act 1829, the Oaths Act 1838, the Jewish Disabilities Removal Act 1845, the Oaths Act 1858, the Jews Relief Act 1858, the Qualification for Offices Abolition Act 1866 and the Promissory Oaths Act 1868,[7] though doubts as to whether, as a result of these enactments, a Roman Catholic could lawfully be appointed Lord Chancellor were not finally dispelled until Parliament resolved the matter in 1974.[8] The position today is that there are hardly any significant religious restrictions imposed by statute upon the holding of offices or employments other than those necessitated by the nature of the job itself.[9] However, this does not mean that such restrictions may not be lawfully imposed by a particular employer, for the legality of such discrimination on an individual basis is an entirely separate question.

Religious discrimination in employment is not outlawed per se by the Race Relations Act 1976.[10] Only racial discrimination is unlawful and this is defined to mean discrimination on grounds of colour, race, nationality or ethnic or national origins.[11] Some forms of indirect discrimination on the ground of ethnic origin may, as will be seen, encompass religious differences, but if an employer decides not to employ a person simply because he is a Jew, a Muslim or a Sikh no breach of the Act's provisions will have occurred.[12] This leaves the matter to be governed by the common law which has long taken the view that an employer is perfectly entitled to refuse to hire a workman for any reason whatever, however capricious his decision may be or however morally reprehensible his motives.[13]

1 1 Eliz 1, c 1.
2 5 Eliz 1, c 1.
3 See 3 Jac, c, 4, s 15.
4 See Henriques *The Jews and the English Law* pp 198-200.
5 Ibid pp 202-8.
6 See the Corporation Act 1661 and the Test Act 1672.
7 See generally *Henriques* ch IX.
8 Lord Chancellor (Tenure of Office and Discharge of Ecclesiastical Functions) Act 1974, s 1. As to whether a Jew may become Lord Chancellor, see *Henriques* pp 262-3; 8 Halsbury's Laws of England (4th edn), para 1171, note 5.
9 For example, since the monarch is the head of the Established Church no Roman Catholic may occupy the throne and anyone who marries a Roman Catholic is excluded from the succession – see Bill of Rights 1688, Act of Settlement 1700, s 2.
10 *Mandla v Dowell Lee* [1983] 1 All ER 1062 at 1066, 1071; cf the express protection of religion in Northern Ireland by virtue of the Fair Employment (Northern Ireland) Act 1976.
11 S 3(1).
12 See Lustgarten *Legal Control of Racial Discrimination* pp 78-9. For discussion of problems where the religious discrimination is essentially based on race, see Robilliard 'Discrimination and indirect discrimination: the religious dimension' [1980] New Community 261.
13 See *Allen v Flood* (1898) AC1 at 172-3 (per Lord Davey).

A. ABSENCES FROM WORK FOR PURPOSES OF RELIGIOUS WORSHIP

9.03 As one would expect, different religions impose different requirements upon their adherents in relation to matters of worship. For present purposes it is convenient to analyse separately the various practices and precepts of certain non-Christian faiths in terms of daily, weekly and annual devotions.

First, so far as daily religious devotion is concerned, Muslims are enjoined to pray at five specified times during each day.[1] The five obligatory prayers are scheduled, roughly speaking, at dawn *(fajr)*, early afternoon *(zuhr)*, late afternoon *(asr)*, sunset *(maghrib)* and late evening *(isha)*, but the exact times are reasonably flexible. Where a suitable meeting place is available, congregational prayers are preferable to an individual Muslim praying on his own, but these are by no means compulsory though, as will be seen, the *zuhr* prayers on Fridays ought to be congregational whenever this is practicable. All prayers should be preceded by ritual ablutions without which the prayers would be counted as void and worthless. Such ablutions may take as long as five minutes, while the prayers themselves may last for between ten and 20 minutes. The congregational *zuhr* prayers on Fridays (known as *jumua*) may well last for between 45 minutes and one hour.

When considering the nature of the obligation placed upon Muslims to pray five times each day it is vital to bear in mind the fact that in claiming to be a universal religion applicable to all conditions of men, Islam has of necessity to be realistic and flexible in its requirements. As *The Muslim Guide* explains:

'Misdirected zeal, exhibitionism and fanaticism are alien to Islamic teaching, but Muslims are not allowed to miss prayers so long as it is possible not to do so. Although the prayers are compulsory and should be performed within specified periods, there is still sufficient flexibility to prevent real inconvenience. Prayers missed due to reasons beyond one's control can be made up later . . . There should certainly be no need for a Muslim bus driver (as was reported) to stop and park his bus, full of passengers, on the roadside while he prayed on the pavement . . .'[2]

Turning, secondly, to the question of weekly devotional worship the obvious point to make at the outset is that, although only about 16% of the adult population of the UK are members of Christian churches,[3] it is still thought of by most residents as a predominantly Christian country and both the running of the economy and the organisation of family life are premised upon the assumption that Sunday is the principal day of rest from ordinary work. There is thus nothing to prevent those Christians who wish to do so from going to church on that day. Nor does this designation of Sunday as a non-working day present any problems for Sikhs and Hindus. In these faiths no specific time or day has to be kept apart for worship and Sunday is often used in this country merely as the most convenient day for holding public gatherings in *gurdwaras* and temples.[4] For Jews and Seventh Day Adventists, on the other hand, the Sabbath or day set aside for rest and worship is Saturday. Indeed for Jews the Sabbath begins at dusk on Friday and lasts through until after nightfall on Saturday. The most important day of worship for Muslims is Friday when the *zuhr* congregational prayers take place at the mosque and everyone who can attend should do so. The practicality of attendance obviously depends for most workers on the proximity of their place of employment to the nearest mosque and if the mosque is too far away the prayers can quite properly be held elsewhere provided a clean and quiet room can be made available.[5] Any Muslim of good moral character who is well versed in the Koran can act as *imam* and lead the congregational prayers. It is important to note that there is nothing in Islamic doctrine which requires Muslims to cease work for the whole day on Fridays when they are living in a non-Muslim country. Friday is not, therefore, a day of rest comparable to the Jewish Sabbath or Christian Sunday. It is only the break for early afternoon (congregational) prayers which is a vital requirement.

Third, the same sorts of variations between religions arise with regard to annual festivals and holy days. Jews celebrate the feasts of the Passover and Pentecost, New Year *(Rosh Hashana)* and the Day of Atonement *(Yom Kippur)*; Muslims celebrate *Id-al-Fitr* (marking the end of fasting during the month of Ramadan) and *Id-al-Adha* (the Sacrifice of the Pilgrimage); and Hindus and Sikhs celebrate *Baisakhi* (New Year) and *Diwali*. In their countries of origin such days would often be regarded as public holidays, but in this country the only public holidays with any religious significance are those linked to the Christian faith. Naturally, members of religious minorities would like, if possible, to be able to take at least their own respective holy days off work in order to participate in the congregational worship and festivities involved.[6] Otherwise these activities will have to be fitted in hurriedly during the evening or else postponed to the following weekend, if they are not to be dispensed with altogether. In the case of Muslims a further practical problem is presented by the fact that the annual fasting during the month of Ramadan involves abstaining from food and drink from sunrise to sunset, a period lasting as long as 16 to 18 hours each day when Ramadan falls during an English summer.[7]

1 See generally McDermott and Ahsan *The Muslim Guide* pp 24-5; *Religious Observance by Muslim Employees – a framework for discussion* (CRE 1980) pp 3-4.
2 *McDermott and Ahsan* p 25.
3 P Brierley (ed), *UK Christian Handbook: 1985-86 Edition* (Bible Society, 1984) p 5.
4 *East Meets West: a background to some Asian faiths* pp 12, 92-3; James *Sikh Children in Britain* p 36; Bowen (ed) *Hinduism in England* p 44.
5 *McDermott and Ahsan* pp 24, 39-40; *Religious Observance by Muslim Employees* p 4.
6 See, e g *The Muslim Guide* pp 32-3, 57.
7 Ibid p 56.

Policy considerations

9.04   As indicated in the previous chapter,[1] in modern Britain no rational objection can be made to the extension of the principle of freedom of worship to minority faiths, particularly in the light of the adherence by the UK to the European Convention on Human Rights and the International Covenant on Civil and Political Rights. However, under the terms of each treaty a contracting state is entitled to impose legal limitations upon the manifestation of religion to the extent that these are necessary in the interests of public safety, for the protection of public order, health or morals, or for the protection of the rights and freedoms of others. As will be seen, certain forms of worship by an employee might be thought to operate in such a disruptive manner that they had to be curtailed in order to protect not only the rights and freedoms of the employer but also those of fellow employees.

1 See para 8.04 above.

English law

9.05   The three principal problems in this field are related first, to the requirements of Islam that Muslims should if possible pray five times each day and attend congregational prayers at a mosque in the early afternoon on

Fridays; second, to the fact that for Jews and Seventh Day Adventists the Sabbath falls on a Saturday rather than a Sunday (and in the case of the Jews commences just before sunset on Fridays); and third, to the diversity of annual festivals among the different religions. These issues will be discussed *seriatim*, but the same general common law principles operate as a starting point in each instance. In the absence of any controlling statutory provision the terms of a person's employment, including his hours and days of work, are to be found in his contract of employment. If this contract does not deal with these matters expressly suitable terms and conditions may nevertheless be implied by the courts to give the contract business efficacy and fulfil the common expectations and intentions of the parties. If an employee is absent without authorisation he will be in breach of his contract and if there are repeated recurrences of the breach the employer may eventually be justified in summarily dismissing him from his employment on the basis of a repudiation of the contract.[1] Alternatively the employer may dismiss the employee by giving him the appropriate period of notice.[2] On the other hand, where the employee is acting within his legal rights in absenting himself any dismissal will be wrongful and render the employer liable for damages for breach of contract.

Superimposed upon these common law principles there are statutory provisions relating to 'unfair dismissal'. Even if an employee has been properly dismissed for a breach of contract his dismissal may still be unfair and hence unlawful under the Employment Protection (Consolidation) Act 1978 (EP(C)A) if his employer has acted unreasonably in treating the breach as a sufficient reason for dismissal.[3] A fortiori an employee who has been wrongfully dismissed in breach of his contract will normally find that he is entitled to sue his employer for unfair dismissal as well as claim damages for breach of contract. In practice it is usually the claim for compensation for unfair dismissal which is the more valuable of the two rights.

1 See generally Smith and Wood *Industrial Law* (2nd edn, 1983) pp 172-5.
2 Ibid at pp 169-71.
3 See EP(C)A 1980, s 57, as amended by Employment Act 1980, s 6.

9.06 In 1984 a Code of Practice for the elimination of racial discrimination and the promotion of equal opportunity in employment came into force.[1] One of its recommendations was that employers should consider whether it was reasonably practicable for them to vary their normal requirements to enable ethnic minority employees to observe prayer times and religious holidays.[2] Failure to adhere to the provisions of the Code does not, of itself, render an employer liable to any proceedings, but the Code is admissible in evidence in any case before an industrial tribunal.[3]

Clearly where a business employs a substantial number of Muslim employees it would be sensible for negotiations to take place (through a trade union if that was the appropriate channel) with a view to reaching an agreement acceptable to both employer and employees. Non-Muslim employees also need to be involved in the process in order to dispel any feeling on their part that preferential treatment is being afforded to the Muslim employees at their expense. Contractual arrangements might be made, for example, so that Muslims were able to take their teabreaks and lunch hours at times which coincided with those appropriate for prayers. The provision on the site of a suitable room for congregational prayers, together with separate ablution facilities, might be in everyone's interest in saving travelling time to a mosque or other building outside the premises. Time off to visit a mosque in the early afternoon on

Fridays might be granted as unpaid leave or have to be made up at another time. Paid holiday leave entitlement might be synchronised with the major Muslim festivals. If Muslim employees agreed to work through the teabreaks and lunch hours during Ramadan they ought to be able to negotiate in return for some leave at other times. Many Muslims may be agreeable to working night-shifts so as to be able to fulfil their religious duties more easily. How far any individual employer will be able to go in accommodating the religious needs of his Muslim employees will clearly depend on the nature of his business, whether there is a need for continuous production, the number of Muslim employees, the flexibility of work patterns and so on.[4] However, the essential point is that the legal rights and duties of employer and employee in this area rest largely on what has been negotiated and incorporated into the contract between them in the form of express or implied terms.

1 (CRE, 1983), discussed at para 9.16 below.
2 Para 1.24.
3 Race Relations Act 1976, s 47(10).
4 The various suggestions given above are to be found in *Religious Observance by Muslim Employees – a framework for discussion* (CRE, 1980).

1 Absences by Muslims for prayers

9.07　The only reported case relating to a Muslim's absence from work for purposes of Friday prayers is the important one of *Ahmad v Inner London Education Authority*.[1] Ahmad, a devout Muslim was employed as a full-time school teacher by the ILEA in 1968. His hours of attendance at school were not specified in his letter of appointment, but his employment was subject to the rules and regulations of the ILEA which provided for standard school hours of 9.30 am to 12.30 pm and 2 pm to 4.30 pm, subject to variations allowed by school governors to suit the particular circumstances of the individual school.[2] During the years 1968 to 1974 he was employed at schools too far distant (in his view) from a mosque for him to be able to attend, but in 1974 he was transferred to a series of schools which were only 15-20 minutes away from the nearest mosque. As a result he attended the mosque regularly for early afternoon prayers on Fridays, but this meant that since at one of these schools the lunch break allowed by the governors ran only from 12.30 pm to 1.30 pm and since the prayers lasted from 1 pm to 2 pm he returned to the school some 40-45 minutes late. Some of the schools were able to accommodate his absences without too much difficulty but at least one school could not, in consequence of which he had no teaching duties at all on Friday afternoons, while still remaining a full-time employee on full pay. This caused some resentment among other teachers and eventually the ILEA informed him that if he wished to continue going to the mosque on Fridays he must relinquish his full-time appointment and accept a part-time contract, covering only four and a half days a week with a consequent reduction in salary. Rather than accept this he resigned and then applied to an industrial tribunal for compensation and reinstatement in full-time employment on the ground that the ILEA's conduct had forced him to resign and thus amounted to unfair dismissal. His complaint was rejected by the industrial tribunal and his appeals to the Employment Appeal Tribunal and the Court of Appeal were both unsuccessful. Finally, he petitioned the European Commission of Human Rights, but his application was held to be manifestly ill-founded and hence was declared inadmissible under Art 27(2) of the Convention.

1 [1978] QB36, [1978] 1 All ER 574.

2 These details are not given in the English report but can be found in the report of *X v United Kingdom* (1981) 22 Decisions and Reports of the European Commission 27 at 28.

9.08 So far as English Law is concerned the crucial statutory provision affecting the outcome of the case was the Education Act 1944, s 30. This provides as follows:

'. . . no person shall be disqualified by reason of his religious opinions, or of his attending or omitting to attend religious worship, from being a teacher in a county school or in any voluntary school . . .; and *no teacher in any such school shall* be required to give religious instruction or *receive any less emolument* or be deprived of, or disqualified for, any promotion or other advantage by reason of the fact that he does or does not give religious instruction or *by reason of* his religious opinions or of *his attending* or omitting to attend *religious worship* . . .' (Italics added).

Although it was accepted that the provisions of s 30 had to be incorporated into Ahmad's contract and would override any other conditions, the individual members of the Court of Appeal were by no means agreed as to its interpretation or significance. Ahmad claimed that the section's reference to lower emoluments had been satisfied by ILEA's insistence that he only be paid for a four-and-a-half-day week.

Orr LJ's principal reason for finding against Ahmad was that in his view the section could not be construed as authorising a breach of contract by a teacher in absenting himself during school hours for the purpose of attending religious worship. He considered that the latter part of the section dealing with emoluments was probably enacted because there was thought to be a danger that a teacher might be offered a lower rate of remuneration either because he did or because he did not give religious instruction or attend religious worship *within* the school. Historically, this seems very likely to have been the true explanation for the provision. Orr LJ was also concerned about the practicalities involved. Although in some cases the brief absence of a Muslim teacher on Fridays might result in only minor inconvenience, the disadvantage of allowing it as a matter of principle was that it would involve detailed investigation about the degree of difficulty caused in each case as well as authorising what was technically a breach of contract. If there was difficulty in maintaining the Friday afternoon programme this might lead to resentment among non-Muslim staff about having to undertake additional burdens and ultimately it might have made education authorities reluctant to employ Muslim teachers in the future.

Lord Denning MR accepted that if the words of s 30 were read literally and without qualification Ahmad would be entitled to succeed. However, he too could not accept that this was what the statute intended. In his view the section had to be read subject to the implied qualification 'if the school time-table so permits'.

His Lordship continued:

'So read, it means that he is to be entitled to attend for religious worship during the working week if it can be arranged consistently with performing his teaching duties under his contract of employment. It has been so interpreted by the great majority of Muslim teachers in our schools. They do not take time off for their prayers. Nor should Mr Ahmad if he wants to get his full pay for a five-day week. The tribunal said that 'none of the other education authorities has ever received such a request from Muslim staff . . .'. I have no doubt that all headmasters will try and arrange their time-table so as to accommodate devout Muslims like Mr Ahmad; but I do not think they should be compelled to do so, if it means disrupting the work of the school and the well-being of the pupils.'[1]

At first sight this appears to be a sensible compromise between the right to freedom of worship and the legitimate requirements of other persons directly affected, notably the rights of fellow teachers and the education authority, and the needs of the school children. The essence of this approach is that if the rights of others are jeopardised then freedom of worship has to be restricted, but that an effort should be made by an employer to accommodate the religious needs of his employees in this regard if it is possible to do so.

However, Scarman LJ in a vigorous dissenting judgment approached s 30 in a quite different way. In his view it had to be interpreted not against the background of 1944 (when it was enacted) but in the context of a greatly changed society in which many new religions were now being·practised. A policy of understanding was needed if adherents to these new faiths were not to suffer discrimination contrary to the spirit of s 30. He continued:

'The change in legal background is no less momentous. Since 1944 the United Kingdom has accepted international obligations designed to protect human rights and freedoms, and has enacted a series of statutes designed for the same purpose . . . Today, therefore we have to construe and apply s 30 not against the background and law of 1944 but in a multi-racial society which has accepted international obligations and enacted statutes designed to eliminate discrimination on grounds of race, religion, colour or sex.'[2]

Scarman LJ rejected the argument that the section was only dealing with the attendance of a teacher at religious worship taking place within his school. This would mean that a Muslim who took his religious duty seriously could never accept employment as a full-time teacher but must always be content with the lesser emoluments of part-time service. This would be unacceptable in modern English society and, in his view, 'almost certainly' a breach of the European Convention on Human Rights. He went on:

'No doubt, Parliament in 1944 never addressed its mind to the problems in this case. But if the section lends itself, as successful human rights or constitutional legislation must lend itself to judicial interpretation in accordance with the spirit of the age, there is nothing in this point, save for the comment that Parliament by refusing to be too specific was wiser than some of us have subsequently realised.'[3]

Next Scarman LJ tackled the practicalities of the problem. Could a teacher in Ahmad's position take time off work and still comply with the terms of a full-time contract? In his Lordship's view in order to give business efficacy to such a proposition it would be necessary to imply a limitation that the period of absence be 'no longer than is reasonably necessary, nor so frequent or of such duration as to make it impossible for the teacher to offer full-time service'.[3] In his opinion 45 minutes off once a week was clearly small enough to be acceptable, especially since the contract expressly provided for whole days to be taken off on full pay on religious holidays.[4]

Second, Scarman LJ dealt with the question of whether the interests of others would be adversely affected by such an arrangement. In his view all that was required to solve the problem was that the education authority should make suitable administrative arrangements to ensure that the children were taught, that Muslim teachers attended their mosques and that their colleagues were not unfairly burdened.

'It may mean employing a few more teachers either part-time or full-time; but, when that cost is compared with the heavy expenditure already committed to the cause of non-discrimination in our society, expense would not in this context appear to be a sound reason for requiring a narrow meaning to be given to the words of the statute.'[5]

His Lordship therefore concluded that Ahmad's absences did not amount to a breach of contract and he had been unfairly dismissed.

1 *Ahmad v ILEA* [1978] 1 All ER 574 at 577.
2 At 583. This statement is perhaps rather misleading in suggesting that discrimination on grounds of religion has been outlawed by English domestic law; such discrimination is not specifically covered by the Race Relations Act 1976: see para 9.02 above.
3 At 585.
4 This matter is discussed further at para 9.12 below.
5 At 585.

9.09 Since Ahmad subsequently invoked the provisions of the European Convention on Human Rights and since all the members of the Court of Appeal specifically considered its applicability to the facts of the case its detailed wording merits careful examination. Article 9 guarantees freedom of worship

'subject only to such limitations as are prescribed by law and are necessary in a democratic society in the interests of public safety, for the protection of public order, health or morals, or for the protection of the rights and freedoms of others.'

In the Court of Appeal, as we have seen, Scarman LJ was strongly influenced in giving his dissenting judgment by its requirements. To interpret s 30 narrowly and restrictively against Ahmad would be, in his words, 'almost certainly a breach of our international obligations'.[1]

As to the relevance of the Convention in English law he declared:

'. . . it is no longer possible to assume that because the international treaty obligations of the United Kingdom do not become law unless enacted by Parliament our courts pay no regard to our international obligations. They pay very serious regard to them; in particular, they will interpret statutory language and apply common law principles, wherever possible, so as to reach a conclusion consistent with our international obligations . . .'[2]

Orr LJ reached the conclusion that the Convention's terms did not assist Ahmad because of the exceptions allowed for 'the protection of the rights and freedoms of others'. This meant that an employee was not entitled to absent himself from work in breach of his contract of employment.

Lord Denning MR took the same view, stressing the rights of the education authority under the contract and the interests of the children at the school. He commented:

'The Convention is not part of our English law but, as I have often said, we will always have regard to it. We will do our best to see that our decisions are in conformity with it. But it is drawn in such vague terms that it can be used for all sorts of unreasonable claims and provoke all sorts of litigation. As so often happens with high-sounding principles, they have to be brought down to earth . . . I venture to suggest that it would do the Muslim community no good, or any other minority group no good, if they were to be given preferential treatment over the great majority of the people. If it should happen that, in the.name of religious freedom, they were given special privileges or advantages, it would provoke discontent, or even resentment among those with whom they work. As indeed, it has done in this very case . . . So whilst upholding religious freedom to the full, I would suggest that it should be applied with caution, especially having regard to the setting in which it is sought.'[3]

When the case came before the European Commission of Human Rights[4] three central issues fell to be resolved. The first was whether in guaranteeing freedom of worship 'either alone or in community with others' Art 9 of the Convention obliged a state to grant both of these modes of worship or whether it could choose between them and claim that the individual's right had been satisfied if only one had been afforded. The Commission had little difficulty in deciding that the UK had not complied with its obligations merely by affording Ahmad a right to worship alone and that worship in community with others had always been regarded as an essential part of freedom of religion.

The second issue concerned the ambit and scope of the Islamic injunction to worship in a mosque on Fridays. Clearly the rule is subject to some exceptions since, for example, Ahmad (who was certainly devout) had not insisted on visiting a mosque on Fridays during the period 1968 to 1974, when he was a teacher at schools further away from a mosque. The exception is, as already indicated earlier,[5] related to what is practically feasible. This is often expressed in terms of distance between a person's workplace and the nearest mosque, but proximity of itself is unhelpful as a measurement. If a man is unemployed or on holiday he may realistically be expected to travel for a far longer time to reach a mosque because what is practically feasible depends upon what other commitments a man has. Clearly the reason why Ahmad made no attempt to visit the mosque on Fridays between 1968 and 1974 was that it was not a realistic possibility bearing in mind the conditions of his employment. The European Commission concluded on this aspect of the case that it did not consider that Ahmad had:

'. . . convincingly shown that, following his transfer in 1974 to a school 'nearer to mosques', he was required by Islam to disregard his continuing contractual commitments vis-a-vis the ILEA, entered into six years earlier in 1968 and accepted throughout the years, and to attend the mosque during school time.'[6]

However, the Commission held that even if Islamic doctrine did require such attendance it did not justify Ahmad's claim. This raised the third issue concerning the limitations placed upon the right to freedom of worship.

Having held that the right was certainly not an absolute one, the Commission concentrated not so much upon the exceptions listed in Art 9 but rather upon the fact that 'it may, as regards the modality of a particular religious manifestation be influenced by the situation of the person claiming that freedom'.[6] The Commission felt that in principle the ILEA was entitled to rely upon its contract being fulfilled and that it had given due consideration to Ahmad's religious position by offering him a part-time post for four and a half days a week (which he had eventually accepted). Regard had to be had to the educational system as a whole and the ILEA had not arbitrarily disregarded Ahmad's freedom of religion. The upshot seemed to be that Ahmad's exercise of his freedom of worship had to be subordinated to the contractual rights of the local authority which were entitled to protection under the exceptions to Art 9.

1 *Ahmad v ILEA* [1978] 1 All ER 574 at 585.
2 At 583.
3 At 577-8.
4 Sub nom *X v United Kingdom* (1981) 22 Decisions and Reports of the European Commission 27.
5 See para 9.03 above.
6 At 35.

9.10 What principle, then, finally emerges from *Ahmad v ILEA*? It would seem that an employee cannot justify an absence from work in breach of his contract of employment by reference to his need to worship. No such defence is recognised either in English law or under the provisions of the European Convention. This would appear to be a principle of general application not confined merely to teachers employed by local authorities governed by the

Education Act 1944, s 30. On the other hand, if such absences can be satisfactorily accommodated by an employer through a flexible adjustment of individual duties by reference to schedules, timetables and so on, no breach of contract will, of course, have occurred and the employer will have accorded due respect to the employee's freedom of religion. However, it is clear that an employer is under no legal duty to allow freedom of worship in circumstances where this would conflict with the terms of the contract he has already entered into with an employee. Exactly the same principles would apply to an orthodox Jew who left work early on a Friday afternoon as to a Muslim who absented himself for *zuhr* prayers.

These principles have been applied and extended on a number of occasions by industrial tribunals in cases where a Muslim employee has been held to have been fairly and lawfully dismissed for insisting upon saying his daily prayers when he should have been working.[1] In *Hussain v London Country Bus Services Ltd*[2] for example, the applicant, who was employed to clean buses and coaches, insisted on praying regularly at sunset even when this coincided with his early evening shift. Although he was otherwise acknowledged to be a good and productive worker his absences at a time of the day when there was often pressure to clean buses quickly and return them to service caused problems both for his employers and for his workmates. Unlike Ahmad in the previous case he did not claim or receive any payment for his periods of absence for prayer despite the fact that the amount of work he did overall during his hours of duty appeared to be as great as his colleagues. However, the tribunal, after finding on all the evidence that the requirement to pray at sunset was not an inflexible one, held that if he was going to insist on an exact observance of sunset prayers regardless of the pressures of work he should have made this clear from the beginning. His employers had stated that they had no objection to him praying silently while he was working or praying during his 30-minute meal break or the ten-minute tea break but that they could not accept his right to pray at sunset regardless of the flow of work in their garage and the effects of his absence on his fellow employees. The tribunal's decision that he had not been unfairly dismissed was upheld by the Employment Appeal Tribunal.

1 See, e g *Rashid v Metallifacture Ltd* (Nottingham Industrial Tribunal, 14 April 1976, unreported).
2 *IDS Brief 283* p 5.

2 Saturday absences for Sabbatarians

9.11 The question whether an employee who regards Saturday as the Sabbath is entitled to take the whole of that day off work arose in the case of *Esson v United Transport Executive*.[1] The applicant was employed by the respondents as a bus conductor under a contract which contained a rule that there were no guaranteed rest days on Saturdays. The days an employee spent on duty depended upon the employers' roster. After he had rejoined the Seventh Day Adventists and subsequently taken unauthorised leave on a number of Saturdays because of his religious beliefs, the applicant was dismissed for breach of contract. The industrial tribunal ruled that his dismissal was not unfair and commented:

'For Mr Esson to have had his way it would have been necessary for other members of the respondents' staff, if such could have been found, to work on Saturdays instead of having that day as a rest day. This would in our opinion have been wholly unreasonable unless it could have been achieved by mutual agreement and there was no evidence that it could.'[2]

The same general principles thus apply to total absences for religious reasons on Saturdays as govern shorter absences on Fridays. Nevertheless, it is worth noting that a person whose religion treats Saturday as the Sabbath will not be precluded from obtaining unemployment benefit or supplementary benefits simply because he is unavailable for work on that day.[3]

1 [1975] IRLR 48.
2 At 49.
3 See Social Security Act 1975, s 17; Social Security (Unemployment, Sickness and Invalidity Benefit) Regulations 1975, regs 4, 7; Supplementary Benefits (Conditions of Entitlement) Regulations 1980, reg 7. Cf *Variacha v Department of Health and Social Security* (1982) unreported but noted in (1982) 4 CRE Employment Report 12, in which it was held that inability to speak or write English did not preclude entitlement to benefit, on the basis that a person might be available for work even though the language barrier meant that employment would be harder to obtain.

3 Annual festivals and holidays

9.12 Annual religious festivals and holy days are not legally recognised as public holidays in England and Wales unless they fall at Easter or Christmas. Christmas Day and Good Friday are public holidays at common law, while Easter Monday is one of six bank holidays given legislative force by the Banking and Financial Dealings Act 1971. Even so, apart from certain statutory exceptions,[1] an employer is not legally bound to recognise these public and bank holidays and the availability of an employee's days off work is left to be regulated by the terms of the contract between them.[2] Since this is the strict legal position even with regard to Christian holy days and festivals it is hardly surprising that the same rule should apply in the case of the special days recognised by other religions. In practice, of course, most contracts provide for Good Friday, Easter Monday and Christmas Day to be paid holidays.

An example of an express contractual provision dealing with non-Christian holidays is to be found in the ILEA staff code for teachers which was discussed in passing by the Court of Appeal in *Ahmad's case.*
One of the code's clauses provided as follows:

'Religious observance: teachers (other than supply teachers) in any establishment aided and maintained by the Authority, who for reasons of conscience have objections to working on a particular day in term time, it being a day of special obligation in their religion, shall be allowed leave with pay, on the understanding that such leave shall be restricted to days which are generally recognised in their religion as days when no work may be done.'

In the absence of such a provision there would appear to be no such entitlement and any day which an employee wished to take off on religious grounds has to be the subject of negotiation and agreement and would commonly have to be counted as part of the employee's annual paid leave entitlement. Otherwise an employer would be entitled to deduct a day's pay in respect of each day of absence from work.[3] Interestingly, in dismissing Ahmad's petition as inadmissible under the European Convention on Human Rights the European Commission added the following rider at the end of their judgment:

'The Commission further observes in respect of the general question of religious and public holidays, discussed in the parties' submissions, that, in most countries, only the religious holidays of the majority of the population are celebrated as public holidays. Thus Protestant holidays are not always public holidays in Catholic countries and vice versa.'[4]

The implication of this comment appears to be that no violation of the freedom of religion guaranteed by the Convention is occasioned by this pattern of legal holidays.[5]

1 See eg Factories Act 1961, s 94; Holidays with Pay Act 1938.
2 Hepple and O'Higgins *Encyclopaedia of Labour Relations Law* vol 1, para 1-234.
3 For an example of Muslims having such deductions made after absences to celebrate the festival of *Id-al Fitr* at the end of Ramadan, see *The Times*, 7 January 1970.
4 At 38.
5 See also the European Social Charter 1961, Art 2.

B. FREEDOM FROM DISCRIMINATION ON THE BASIS OF DRESS OR APPEARANCE

9.13 The major concerns of ethnic minorities in this sphere have revolved around claims that at work Sikh men should be entitled to wear long hair, a beard, a steel bracelet and a turban, and that Asian women should be permitted to wear clothes which fully cover their legs.

The distinctive appearance of devout Sikhs has its origins in the actions of the tenth and last guru, Guru Gobind Singh at the end of the seventeenth century.[1] At a time when, although the Sikh religion was some 200 years old, its adherents were under threat of extermination by Muslims, he baptised five men to form the nucleus of a brotherhood of dedicated followers, henceforth known as the *Khalsa*. He simultaneously instituted the five symbols which all initiated Sikhs should wear in future, namely *kesh* (long hair), *kanga* (a comb), *kara* (a steel bangle), *kirpan* (a dagger or short sword) and *kaccha* (long underpants). The Guru did not himself give any explanation for the form of these symbols, but one interpretation often given subsequently is that by making his followers easily identifiable it would be virtually impossible for them to deny their faith when challenged and this would in turn breed in them a quality of defiant courage. The fact that he gave the name of *singh* (lion) to his followers suggests that he saw them as having to be a strong and militant force.

The effect of Guru Gobind Singh's new initiative was to establish a distinction between two classes of Sikh, the baptised *('keshdharis')* and the uninitiated *('sahijdharis')*. In modern times the difference lies not so much in the fact of baptism as in the fact that the first group wear beards, long hair and turbans as a reflection of their commitment to the discipline of the *Khalsa*, while the second group do not. Although the turban was not one of the Guru's 'five symbols' it has, over the years, taken on the quality of a distinctive religious and cultural symbol quite separate from its functional ability to keep long hair clean and tidy. Sikhs have always been wary of being reabsorbed into the enveloping folds of Hinduism and the retention of some striking outward manifestations of their distinctiveness is seen as a prudent response to this ever-present danger.

In modern Britain the challenge to Sikh religion and culture has come not from Hinduism but from secular materialism and pressures to abandon the five symbols have been fuelled by the need for Sikhs to present an acceptable image to prospective employers in the search for jobs. This has involved many *keshdharis* in cutting their hair, often with a considerable feeling of shame.[2] As Beetham has reported:

'Those who migrated here in the 1950s found that they could only secure a job if they were clean shaven. This was rarely openly demanded by an employer, but Sikhs soon learnt that they might present themselves one day wearing a turban and be refused, only to be accepted the next day if they applied clean shaven. The message was quickly passed on to relatives who followed.'[3]

However, this erosion of Sikhism was naturally viewed with alarm by the more devout members of the community here and the tide slowly began to turn, as James has explained:

'As the numbers of Sikhs in various towns increased, with wives and families, *gurdwaras* were founded and self-contained communities developed, the wearing of *kesh* became more common – new arrivals did not shave, and some who had shaved felt shamed into growing their hair again.'[4]

The leaders of the new trend were principally drawn from amongst those who had arrived from East Africa. These Sikhs were Ramgarhias who were not only generally better educated than the Jats who came to Britain directly from India but were also particularly concerned to improve their status in the community through a strict conformity with religious orthodoxy. They were confident of their ability to survive as a distinctive ethnic minority in this country because of their long experience of doing so in East Africa.[5]

From 1959 onwards a few individual Sikhs were prepared to make a stand over the issue and in two highly publicised and long drawn-out campaigns in the field of public transport set out to demonstrate not only the significance of the wearing of turbans to English employers but also the value of maintaining Sikh culture intact for the benefit of other members of their own community.[6]

In 1959 Mr G S S Sagar applied to the Manchester Transport Department to be taken on as a bus conductor, wearing his beard and turban. He was rejected on the grounds that his turban did not conform with the current conditions of service in the department, despite the fact that the rule about busmen's caps was rarely adhered to or enforced[7] and that Mr Sagar was prepared to wear a navy-blue turban with the Council's badge on it.[8] This seemingly trivial matter took Manchester seven years to resolve, including four full council debates on the issue, and was said afterwards to have occupied more of the Transport Committee's time than any other single question.[9] The end result was that by the time the Council finally reversed its ruling against turbans in 1966 Mr Sagar had passed the maximum age for the recruitment of busmen and so was denied the fruits of his victory in terms of a job for himself. The way had, however, been opened for other turbanned Sikhs.

The other campaign was in Wolverhampton. Mr T S Sandhu was a Sikh employee of the Transport Department who had obtained his job there when clean-shaven. In 1967 after three weeks' illness he returned to work wearing a beard and claiming to have had a spiritual revival. He was told by his employers to go home and not to return until he had shaved. He was also informed that he would not be allowed to wear a turban. This dispute only lasted for two years, but it required a mass march to the British High Commission in New Delhi, pressure from the Indian government, a threat of suicide and a visit from a Government minister before a decision was finally reached to authorise the wearing of beards and turbans by Sikh busmen.[10]

The Wolverhampton controversy was more acrimonious and caused more widespread soul-searching among Sikhs in general than the episode in Manchester. Thousands of them who had learnt to live with shorn hair with a certain air of resignation now had to rethink their positions.[11] Many no doubt reverted to being *keshdharis*, but it would appear that while disputes of this nature may have triggered off a revival in enthusiasm for *kesh*, the overall pattern in the country today is one in which perhaps only a minority of all Sikh men, whether young or old, wear long hair, beards and turbans.[12] On the other hand, in an unreported case heard in the Birmingham County Court in 1980[13] expert testimony was given that the proportion of Sikh men in this country who adhere to the practice of wearing a turban is somewhere between two-thirds and three-quarters and this appeared to be accepted by the judge.[14] One commentator has suggested that the practice is mainly confined to the elites of the Sikh community such as teachers, bus-drivers, shop-keepers and older heads of families.[15] However, whatever the exact proportions may be, the fact remains that for orthodox Sikhs the wearing of long hair, a beard and a turban has deep religious and cultural significance and represents a badge of their communal identity.

1 See generally, Khushwant Singh *The Sikhs* (London, 1953) p 31; D Beetham *Transport and Turbans* (OUP 1970) pp 9-11; A James *Sikh Children in Britain* (OUP, 1974) pp 47-52.
2 See *Beetham* p 11; Hiro *Black British, White British* p 126.
3 At p 11. See also R Desai *Indian Immigrants to Britain* (OUP, 1963) p 77.
4 At p 49. See also A Helweg *Sikhs in England* (OUP, 1979) pp 46, 84.
5 Watson *Between Two Cultures* pp 37-8.
6 For full details of the two campaigns, see *Beetham* chs 2 and 3.
7 *Beetham* p 3.
8 Ibid p 18.
9 Ibid p 1.
10 *Hiro* pp 129-30.
11 *Hiro* pp 128-9, 163.
12 J H Taylor *The Half-Way Generation* (NFER, 1976) pp 75, 93; *Hiro* p 163; *James* p 49.
13 *Commission for Racial Equality v Genture Restaurants Ltd* (Birmingham County Court, 1980, unreported).
14 See also Watson *Between Two Cultures* p 47.
15 *James* p 49.

9.14 So far as Asian women are concerned, in many of the societies from which they have come it has long been the practice for women to wear clothes which fully cover their legs. Some wear saris, but for most the traditional dress has been an over-shirt or tunic worn with baggy trousers.[1] This combination is called *qemiz-shalwar* in Urdu and *churidar-pyjama* in Hindi. For Muslim women the requirement that their legs and bodies be fully covered is strengthened by the fact that it is derived from verses of the Koran,[2] but there is nothing in the Hindu or Sikh religions which specifically imposes a similar obligation,[3] though modesty in women is certainly enjoined.[4]

1 *James* p 50, and see para 7.21 above.
2 McDermott and Ahsan *The Muslim Guide* pp 47-8.
3 H Kanitkar and R Jackson *Hindus in Britain* (London, 1982) p 15.
4 *Guidance Note on Sikh Men and Women in Employment* (CRE, 1981) para 1.1.

Policy considerations

9.15 There are a variety of possible reasons which an employer might put forward to explain a refusal to allow his employees to adopt the types of dress just described.

First, it might be argued that where there is a rule prescribing a particular uniform for employees which is designed to maintain the image of the establishment this rule must be upheld and kept to, both for purposes of easy identification by members of the public and to maintain internal morale within the workforce. Usually, however, these functions can be perfectly adequately fulfilled by allowing religious and cultural variations on the condition that they conform to the colours of the prescribed uniform. For example, blue turbans are now permitted in the police force, blue and yellow ones are worn by traffic wardens, and white turbans are worn by judges and barristers in place of wigs.

Second, it might be contended that once an exception from the rule is made for one group it will have to be extended to numerous other groups if the employer is not to be accused of unfair discrimination. One of the arguments put forward by the transport departments in Manchester and Wolverhampton was that if they authorised the wearing of turbans they would find it hard to deny Scots the right to wear kilts or a Turk the right to come dressed in a fez.[1] Such 'bogeys' can all too easily be raised by those seeking to resist change, but they serve the valuable purpose of identifying the principle upon which exceptions are to be allowed. The more important the rule's purpose the more limited the range of exceptions likely to be permissible. One can probably expect exceptions to be allowed more easily on religious grounds than purely cultural ones, but on occasion it will be equally appropriate to respect cultural as well as religious traditions.

A third argument is of a more philosophical nature, to the effect that to allow any departure from the norm for minorities is to afford them preferential treatment and hence to undermine the principle of equal treatment for all, regardless of colour or creed. The answer to this is that in circumstances where religious or cultural differences are involved genuine equality can often only be achieved by giving effect to these differences. Denial of them through an insistence upon uniformity under the slogan of equality can only in fact result in discrimination.

Fourth, some conservative employers may fall back on the contention that since a rule about uniforms has existed for a long time without creating problems it should remain as it is. Such a lack of openness to change needs to be contrasted with the significant developments that have occurred in many enterprises and institutions here during the past 20 years or so. Turbans are now widely allowed in the private sector as well as in such spheres as public transport, the armed forces and the police.[2] Moreover, Parliament has specifically exempted Sikhs wearing turbans from the law requiring motorcyclists to wear crash-helmets.[3] If Sikhs wearing turbans were an acceptable part of the British army in two World Wars (in which 82,000 of them were killed and numerous VCs won) a very good reason surely has to be given in explaining why they cannot wear turbans at work in this country today.[4]

Finally, there are some important practical reasons why in a particular job restrictions may be neccessary. Steel bangles may get caught up in fast-moving machinery,[5] a beard may make it harder for an ambulance driver to give mouth-to-mouth resuscitation[6] or pose a health hazard in the food manufacturing industry,[7] and a turban may not afford sufficient protection in certain dangerous industrial and mining operations. On the other hand, it may sometimes be possible to accommodate the cultural practice in question while maintaining proper standards. Turbans may be covered by specially manufactured helmets or 'hard hats.' Beards can be netted in a 'scoop' and the respiratory equipment required in certain jobs involving dust[8] may be capable of being fitted over a beard.[9] Surgical operations are, after all, being carried out every day by surgeons with beards and girls with long hair are often involved in the manufacture, sale, preparation and cooking of food.

1 *Beetham* pp 19, 46.
2 *Beetham* p 31.
3 Motor-Cycle Crash Helmets (Religious Exemption) Act 1976, discussed at para 10.15 below.

4 *Beetham* p 21.
5 *James* p 51.
6 See *The Times*, 7 January 1970 reporting an instance where a job was denied to a Sikh on this ground.
7 See paras 9.17 and 9.21 below.
8 See, eg the Asbestos Regulations 1969, SI 1969/690, reg 8(3).
9 See generally the *Guidance Note on Sikh Men and Women and Employment* (CRE, 1981) pp 4-5.

English law

1 Race relations legislation

9.16 Under the Race Relations Act 1976, s 4, it is unlawful for an employer to discriminate either against an applicant for a job or against one of his employees, whether in relation to his treatment during the currency of his employment or in his dismissal.[1]

Section 4(1) provides as follows:

'It is unlawful for a person, in relation to employment by him at an establishment in Great Britain,[2] to discriminate against another –
(a) in the arrangements he makes for the purpose of determining who should be offered that employment;
or
(b) in the terms on which he offers him that employment;
or
(c) by refusing or deliberately omitting to offer him that employment.'

This covers the process of engaging persons as employees.

Section 4(2) deals with the situation of those who have already been taken on for work and runs:

'It is unlawful for a person, in the case of a person employed by him at an establishment in Great Britain, to discriminate against that employee –
(a) in the terms of employment which he affords him;
or
(b) in the way he affords him access to opportunities for promotion, transfer or training, or to any other benefits, facilities or services, or by refusing or deliberately omitting to afford him access to them;
or
(c) by dismissing him, or subjecting him to any other detriment.'

It will be recalled from ch 7 above[3] that the Act defines racial discrimination as including discrimination on the ground of a person's 'ethnic or national origins'[4] and that it encompasses the concept of 'indirect discrimination' which occurs when one person applies to another:

'a requirement or condition which he applies or would apply equally to persons not of the same racial group as that other but:
(i) which is such that the proportion of persons of the same racial group as that other who can comply with it is considerably smaller than the proportion of persons not of that racial group who can comply with it; and
(ii) which he cannot show to be justifiable irrespective of the colour, race, nationality or ethnic or national origins of the person to whom it is applied; and
(iii) which is to the detriment of that other because he cannot comply with it.'[5]

Where discrimination is alleged to have occurred in the field of employment a complaint may be made to an industrial tribunal.[6] If in its view the complaint is well-founded the tribunal is empowered to declare the rights of the complainant and respondent, to make a compensation order in favour of the complainant and to recommend action on the part of the respondent to obviate or reduce the adverse effect upon the complainant of any act of discrimination.[7] Any damages awarded may include compensation for injury to feelings in addition to compensation under any other head, but no award of damages in respect of indirect discrimination can be made at all if the respondent proves that the requirement or condition in question was not applied with the intention of treating the claimant unfavourably on racial grounds.[8] The total amount of compensation is, in any event, limited to that available for the time being for unfair dismissal under the Employment Protection (Consolidation) Act 1980 s 75.[9]

Section 47 of the 1976 Act empowers the Commission for Racial Equality to issue 'codes of practice' for the elimination of discrimination in the field of employment and for the promotion of equality of opportunity in that sphere between persons of different racial groups. Such a code was issued in July 1983, was duly laid before Parliament by the Secretary of State for 40 days in terms of section 47 and came into force on 1st April 1984. It includes the following provision:

'Where employees have particular cultural and religious needs which conflict with existing work requirements, it is recommended that employers should consider whether it is reasonably practicable to vary or adapt these requirements to enable such needs to be met. For example, it is recommended that they should not refuse employment to a turbanned Sikh because he could not comply with unjustifiable uniform requirements. Other examples of such needs are –
(a) observance of prayer times and religious holidays;
(b) wearing of dress such as sarees and the trousers worn by Asian women.'[10]

The legal significance of a provision in a code of practice is that while a failure to observe it does not of itself render a person liable to any proceedings, it is admissible in evidence and can be taken into account in a case before an industrial tribunal.[11] Prior to April 1984 the cultural and religious needs of minorities in relation to dress and appearance had been raised before tribunals on a number of occasions and, as will be seen, it is unlikely that the Code adds anything new to the criteria upon which decisions have to be made.[12]

1 Various exceptions exist, eg for employment in private households and where being of a particular racial group is a genuine occupational qualification for the job: see generally ss 4(3), 4(4), 5, 6 and 9; *Lustgarten* ch 7.
2 The expression 'an establishment in Great Britain' is defined in s 8 of the Act.
3 See para 7.24 above.
4 S 3(1).
5 S 1(1).
6 S 54. For the possibilities of settling disputes by conciliation, see s 55.
7 S 56(1).
8 S 57(3), (4); *Orphanos v Queen Mary College* [1985] 2 All ER 233 at 241-2; *Gurmit Singh Kambo v Vaulkhard* (1984) Times, 7 December. For criticism of this rule, see *Review of the Race Relations Act 1976 – Proposals for Change* (CRE, 1985) p 28.
9 S 56(2).
10 *Code of Practice* for the elimination of racial discrimination and the promotion of equal opportunity in employment (CRE, 1983) para 1.24.
11 S 47(10).
12 The wording of the Code is in any event extremely generous to the employer in merely requiring him to 'consider' a possible variation of his normal requirements. An earlier consultative draft stated, more directly, that employers should actually change these requirements wherever it was practicable and reasonable to do so: see *Code of Practice: Consultative Draft* (CRE, 1980) para 2.5.1.

9.17 The first two of these cases brought under the 1976 Act, *Singh v Rowntree Mackintosh Ltd*[1] and *Panesar v Nestlé Co Ltd*,[2] concerned Sikh men who had applied for jobs at confectionery factories. They were both orthodox Sikhs who insisted upon retaining their beards and both were refused employment because the companies in question had rules prohibiting the wearing of beards by employees at these particular factories. In both cases it was assumed, rather than decided, that Sikhs, as a group, were protected by the indirect discrimination provisions of the Act, a question ultimately resolved in their favour, as described in ch 7 above,[3] by the ruling of the House of Lords in *Mandla v Dowell Lee*,[4] in 1983. In both cases it was equally taken for granted that the provisions of s 1(1) (b) (i) were satisfied in the sense that the proportion of Sikhs who could comply with the 'no beards' rule was considerably smaller than the proportion of non-Sikhs who could comply with it. In view of the decision in *Mandla v Dowell Lee* that the words 'can comply' mean 'can in practice' or 'can consistently with the cultural conditions of the racial group comply', rather than can comply by simply shaving off their beards, this was undoubtedly the correct approach. The issue in the two cases therefore revolved around the question whether the employers could establish that the 'no beards' rule was justifiable under the Act. In *Singh v Rowntree Mackintosh Ltd* the Employment Appeal Tribunal held that the rule was justified on grounds of hygiene. However, the employers had to surmount the difficulty that while they enforced the rule rigidly in their factories at Edinburgh (where the complainant had applied) and Newcastle, they did not do so at their six other factories in the UK and even at Edinburgh they allowed employees to have moustaches and side-whiskers. Perhaps somewhat surprisingly, the Tribunal's attitude towards the disparity between the various factories was to see it as reflecting credit upon the higher standard of hygiene maintained at the Edinburgh factory rather than undermining the logical consistency of the employers' case. Lord MacDonald concluded:

'. . . in this industry at least an employer must be allowed some independence of judgement as to what he deems commercially expedient in the conduct of his business. Standards of hygiene may vary between manufacturers and indeed between sections of the consuming public. We do not consider that an employer can be said to have acted unjustifiably if he adopts a standard in one of his factories which is supported by medical advice and which has the approval of a local food and drugs officer. He cannot reasonably be said to have adopted such a standard as a matter of convenience. It could more properly be described as a commercial necessity for the purposes of his business.'[5]

As to the question whether there was a reasonable alternative method of achieving the level of hygiene demanded by the employers, such as by requiring bearded employees to wear face masks, this had clearly been considered by the industrial tribunal at first instance and rejected. It did not, therefore, warrant any further investigation on appeal.

In *Panesar v Nestlé Co Ltd* a similar overall conclusion was reached by the industrial tribunal and its ruling was upheld by the Employment Appeal Tribunal and the Court of Appeal. The industrial tribunal found first that all the evidence pointed to the need for improving the standards of hygiene applied within the food production industry; second, that while beards were not the only potential cause or even a major potential cause of bacterial infection or contamination the company was entitled to maintain a regulation against a well-recognised risk and third, that the interests of the public and consumers of their products were best served by taking all reasonable precautions to maintain the quality of their products.

In the Court of Appeal counsel for the complainant drew attention to the guarantee of freedom of religion in Art 9 of the European Convention on Human Rights but, as Lord Denning pointed out, there is an express reservation placed upon that freedom for laws which are 'necessary in a democratic society' for the protection of public health.[6] On the other hand, it should be borne in mind that in determining in what circumstances an otherwise discriminatory practice is legally authorised by the Act, the question is not whether it is absolutely necessary or essential but merely whether it is 'justifiable'. As Kerr LJ explained in *Ojutiku v Manpower Services Commission*[7] 'justifiable' clearly applies a lower standard for the employer than 'necessary', though it is not as low as mere convenience which would certainly fail to satisfy the test.[8] In *Singh v Rowntree Mackintosh Ltd* the test accepted by the Employment Appeal Tribunal was whether the rule was necessary 'provided that term is applied reasonably and with common sense',[9] while in *Ojutiku's case* Eveleigh LJ stated that:

'. . . if a person produces reasons for doing something, which would be acceptable to right-thinking people as sound and tolerable reasons for so doing, then he has justified his conduct.'[10]

This shows that the standard is an objective one and does not depend upon the whim, preconception or mere custom of the person discriminating, even if he is acting in good faith.[11] To complete the test, however, there needs to be added, in the field of employment, first a requirement that the condition laid down be imposed for reasons closely related to the actual job which the applicant is seeking or being called upon to perform[12] and second, some clear indication that the employer's objectives cannot be achieved satisfactorily by other reasonable non-discriminatory means.[13] Some form of balancing act is called for. The fact that a given condition is in itself discriminatory and hence thoroughly undesirable has to be outweighed by the positive benefits to the business (and indirectly to society at large) which are to accrue from its retention.

1 [1979] IRLR 199.
2 [1980] ICR 144.
3 See para 7.25 above.
4 [1983] 2AC 548 [1983] 1 All ER 1062.
5 [1979] IRLR 199 at 201.
6 [1980] ICR 144 at 147.
7 [1982] IRLR 418 at 422.
8 See *Steel v Union of Post Office Workers* [1977] IRLR 288 at 291; *Ojutiku v Manpower Services Commission* [1982] IRLR 418 at 423; *Mandla v Dowell Lee* [1983] 1 All ER 1062 at 1069-70.
9 At 200.
10 At 421.
11 Nor, it seems, would a general custom of etiquette suffice as a justification. In *Commission for Racial Equality v Genture Restaurants Ltd* (Birmingham County Court, 1980, unreported) it was held that the social custom that as a matter of good manners men should remove their headgear in a restaurant could not justify a ban on Sikhs wearing turbans there.
12 Cf the unlawfulness of English language tests which require a standard higher than that needed for the particular job or rules which require job applicants to complete a form unassisted in English in their own handwriting where such an ability is not required for the job itself: see *Mohammed Isa v British Leyland* (1981) unreported but noted in (1981) 2 CRE Employment Report 10; *Lustgarten* pp 44, 56-7.
13 See *Steel v Union of Post Office Workers*, above at 291; *Lustgarten* pp 52-61.

9.18 Apart from public health the most likely justification related to dress or appearance would seem to be public safety. Rules prohibiting the wearing of bangles in proximity to fast-moving machinery or the wearing of turbans in hazardous occupations where headgear of a more protective nature is desirable would both appear to be capable of being justifiable on such a basis. Indeed, a very small number of industrial operations are governed by specific safety regulations contained in statutory instruments which go so far as to prescribe that the wearing of helmets is compulsory.[1] If in such a case it was physically impossible for a helmet to be worn safely over a turban an employer who refused to recruit a Sikh employee who wished to retain his turban would in any event be protected under the 1976 Act because s 41(1) excludes from being unlawful any act of discrimination done in pursuance of any enactment or any instrument made under any enactment by a minister of the Crown. Whether s 41 affords protection where the statutory rule applies more indirectly seems far from clear. For instance, a general duty is imposed upon employers by the Health and Safety at Work etc Act 1974[2] to ensure the health, safety and welfare of their employees so far as reasonably practicable. This would on many occasions involve the requirement that a helmet or a 'hard hat' be worn. Similarly the Food Hygiene (General) Regulations 1970 provide that a person who engages in the handling of food shall keep as clean as may be reasonably practicable all parts of his person which are liable to come into contact with the food.[3] In neither instance, however, do these statutory provisions specifically ban the wearing of turbans or beards in the interests of public health or safety.

In *Kuldip Singh v British Rail Engineering Ltd*[4] a Sikh employed in one of British Rail's engineering workshops brought an action against his employers alleging unlawful discrimination, on the ground that he had been demoted for failure to wear a 'bump cap'. This form of protective headgear had been introduced, on a voluntary basis, for employees working in the applicant's section of 'scotchers' long after he himself had started work there. No steps had actually been taken to enforce the wearing of these bump caps because the employers hoped that by a process of education and persuasion the workforce would gradually be willing to wear them, but the applicant had made it clear from the start of discussions that he would not do so in any circumstances.

In rejecting the applicant's complaint the Southampton Industrial Tribunal held that the requirement to wear a bump cap was justifiable within the Race Relations Act 1976, s 1 for the following reasons. First, although the risk of injury was admittedly very small and no reportable accident had occurred during the 12-year period the applicant had worked in the section, the wearing of protective headgear could reduce the risk of injury still further and a reasonable and responsible management was entitled to make up for past neglect in not introducing such measures earlier. Second, in the absence of such a requirement it was possible that the employers would be in breach of their duties under the Health and Safety at Work etc. Act and might leave themselves open to a claim for damages by an injured employee. Third, a special exception could not be made for the applicant because this would be resented by the other (non-Sikh) members of his section, who would themselves then be likely to refuse to wear bump caps. The internal discipline of the rest of the workforce would thus probably decline as a result. Exceptions made by the Army and the Police for turbanned Sikhs, as well as the statutory exemption for Sikh motorcyclists, were regarded as irrelevant by the Tribunal to the specific issue in this dispute. The upshot of the case was, therefore, that while the Tribunal clearly felt the employers had behaved unreasonably in demoting the applicant rather than finding him a post in an equivalent grade,[5] no unlawful discrimination was held to have occurred. The decision was upheld by the Employment Appeal Tribunal.

1 For an example, see the Blasting (Castings and other Articles) Special Regulations 1949, SI 49/2225, reg 12(1).
2 S 2.
3 SI 1970/1172, reg 10(a).
4 (1985) Times, 6 August.

5 Had the action been brought for 'unfair dismissal' (as to which see further at para 9.20 below), the Tribunal stated that it would have ruled in favour of the applicant since his demotion really amounted to the termination of one contract and the beginning of another.

9.19 A case in which a similar form of justification was put forward by the employer was *Kingston and Richmond Area Health Authority v Kaur*[1]. The applicant was a Sikh woman who wished to train as a nurse and who had been accepted by the respondent health authority for a two-year course. When she subsequently intimated that she intended to continue wearing *shalwar* (trousers) upon her qualification as a nurse the authority withdrew their offer of a training place on the ground that all nurses had to wear a standard uniform consisting of a dress or frock. The industrial tribunal before which she brought her claim of indirect discrimination against the Health Authority accepted evidence to the following effect about the wearing of *shalwar* by Indian women. They found that 60-70% of Sikh women living in the UK wore *shalwar* and that this was both a requirement of the Sikh religion (which may perhaps be doubted) and, more accurately, that it was a Sikh custom. They therefore concluded that the proportion of Sikh, Punjabi or Indian women who could comply with the rule about nurses' uniforms was considerably smaller than the proportion of other persons who could comply with it. Their ultimate decision was that the uniform rule was not justifiable. This ruling was, however, overturned on appeal by the Employment Appeal Tribunal. The Enrolled Nurses Rules Approval Instrument 1969, made by the General Nursing Council under the Nurses Act 1957, s 10 provided that the uniform for nurses should be a frock and, although it was not compulsory for nurses to wear it,[2] if they did so it had to be strictly adhered to in all its detail without alteration or embellishment. The Employment Appeal Tribunal held that it was justifiable for the health authority to require a uniform of some sort to be worn by nurses and that since the form it should take was laid down in the statutory instrument the health authority could not lawfully allow a variation in the uniform. The applicant's claim to wear *shalwar* as a part of it was therefore dismissed. However, the Tribunal did express a feeling of regret that:

'. . . the requirements as to uniform are so inflexible, and so inflexibly operated, that they do not permit of any variation to meet the genuine and deeply felt convictions as to dress of minority groups . . .'[3]

Leave to appeal to the Court of Appeal was refused by the Tribunal but was later granted by the Court of Appeal itself. This fact, coupled with pressure from the Department of Health and Social Security and other bodies, as well as the knowledge that the General Nursing Council was about to revise the uniform rules anyway, eventually led the Health Authority to change its mind. The applicant was once again offered a training place, this time on the understanding that when she worked as a nurse she would wear grey trousers and a white tunic top.[4] Soon afterwards, in October 1981, the General Nursing Council issued a revision of its rules and these now confine themselves to simply stating that in future a nurse (whether registered or enrolled) 'shall while working wear any uniform required by the person or authority by whom she is employed.'[5] Thus no statutory instrument can now be used to defend an act of indirect discrimination in relation to nurses' dress and any rule preventing Asian nurses from wearing trousers would be extremely hard to justify under the Act in the light of the final outcome in the *Kingston and Richmond* case.

In the case of *Malik v British Home Stores*,[6] decided by the Manchester Industrial Tribunal a year earlier, it was held that the respondent store could not justify a rule that all their female sales staff had to wear skirts, with an overall on top. The applicant, an 18 year old schoolgirl of Muslim faith and Pakistani origin, had been refused employment in the respondent's Blackburn store because her religious beliefs demanded that she wear clothing which fully covered her legs. The purported justification put forward by the respondent was that commercial necessity required that all their shop assistants should wear a uniform and that it was for the benefit of the image of their shops that the uniform rules should be adhered to nationally. The Tribunal, however, on learning that other stores in Blackburn allowed Muslim women employees to wear trousers under their skirts as an integral part of their uniforms, held that the respondent's requirement was not justifiable. The store's argument based on commercial necessity had to be balanced against the severe detriment to Muslim women of being denied jobs there when Muslims as a group might well form about 14% of the store's customers. In this case the detriment clearly outweighed the alleged commercial necessity since it was comparatively simple for the store to modify its regulations to allow a Muslim woman to wear a neat pair of slacks under her overall. Using its powers under s 56(1) of the Act the Tribunal declared that the applicant had been indirectly discriminated against and it recommended that within 28 days of the decision the store should revise its rules about uniform so that women of Pakistani descent and Muslim religion were able to wear a uniform which included trousers.[7]

In April 1984 Woolworths changed their 'skirts only' rule to accommodate those women whose culture and customs require their legs to be covered.[8] This followed the settlement out of court of a case involving a woman of Bangladeshi origin who had been refused employment in Northampton on the ground that she would not agree to wear a skirt as her uniform.

1 [1981] IRLR 337.
2 Presumably some nuns, for example, did not do so.
3 At 339.
4 *Guardian*, 26 June 1981.
5 Nurses and Enrolled Nurses (Amendment) Rules Approval Instrument 1981, SI 1981/1532.
6 COIT 987/12 (unreported), discussed in *CRE Annual Report 1980* pp 78-9; *IDS Brief 179* p 15.
7 It appears that no breach of the Sex Discrimination Act 1975 is occasioned by a rule that female employees may not wear trousers, at any rate if there is some restriction upon the clothing male employees may wear: see *Schmidt v Austicks Bookshops Ltd* [1977] IRLR 360.
8 See (1984) 6 CRE Employment Report 14.

2 Unfair dismissal legislation

9.20 At the beginning of this discussion it was pointed out that the Race Relations Act 1976, s 4(2) covers discrimination in the dismissal of an employee. This creates something of an overlap with the provisions concerning unfair dismissal contained in the Employment Protection (Consolidation) Act 1978. A discriminatory dismissal is almost certainly 'unfair' within the terms of the 1978 Act and it may well be to an employee's advantage to claim under the latter Act since the remedies it provides are both more broadly based and more generous.[1] On the other hand, the 1978 Act imposes certain qualifying conditions upon claimants, such as a minimum length of employment and an upper age limit,[2] which are not found in the 1976 Act. Detailed treatment of this complex branch of the law is outside the scope of the present work,[3] but briefly stated the basic position is as follows. Leaving aside certain special cases, a dismissal will be unfair unless the employer can prove first, that it occurred wholly or mainly because of the employee's incapacity, misconduct, breach of statutory duty, redundancy or 'other substantial reason' and second, that in all the circumstances (including the size and administrative resources of his undertaking) the employer acted reasonably in treating it as a sufficient reason for dismissal; the question then falls to be determined in accordance with equity and the substantial merits of the case.[4]

1 See *Lustgarten* pp 126-30.
2 S 64.
3 See generally, S Anderman *The Law of Unfair Dismissal* (2nd edn, 1984).
4 1978 Act, s 57 as amended by the Employment Act 1980, s 6.

9.21 It seems clear that where there are no express rules governing the dress and appearance of employees it is reasonable to imply a contractual term that they will wear suitable and acceptable attire and will not wear articles of personal adornment calculated to cause danger to themselves or others or to outrage commonly accepted standards.[1] Hence in *Turnock v Golders Green Crematorium*[2] a female employee at a crematorium, whose duties included contact with elderly bereaved people, was held to have been fairly dismissed after she had ignored repeated instructions not to wear a trouser suit. However, if an employer suddenly attempts to introduce a new and arbitrary rule about dress or appearance and then dismisses those existing employees who refuse to comply with it, such dismissals will be held to be unfair.[3] An example of this would be where a Muslim employer decided that in future all his female employees should cover their heads and arms and not wear skirts, a rule which the City of London branch of the Bank Melli Iran threatened to apply in 1984.[4]

In *O'Connor v MacPherson Bros (Wales) Ltd*[5] decided under earlier legislation[6] framed in broadly similar terms, the claimant had been employed as a supermarket manager by the respondent. He returned from his holiday sporting a beard and having allowed his hair to grow below collar length. He was ordered by the managing director to cut his hair and shave off his beard but he refused to comply and was promptly dismissed. The respondent argued that the claimant's long hair and beard endangered the hygiene standards of the store, but the Industrial Tribunal found this unconvincing. In the words of the Chairman:

'Girls were employed, girls whose hair, we have no doubt at all was far longer than that of [the claimant]. It is a matter of common knowledge that many people concerned with the manufacture, preparation and sale of foodstuffs have beards . . . leading chefs whose names are household words have beards: and it is never suggested that if those beards were kept in proper order and the hair, if long, is kept clean that that is any danger to hygiene.'[7]

The Tribunal held the dismissal to be unfair. The employer's objection was evidently merely an aesthetic one and could not be justified as reasonable on grounds of either safety or hygiene or in terms of good public relations.

The decision in *O'Connor's* case needs to be contrasted with that in *Singh v Lyons Maid Ltd*.[8] The claimant, a Sikh, was engaged in the manufacture of ice-cream at the respondent's factory. When he was first recruited he was clean-shaven. The company had a rule, of which he was well aware, that beards were not allowed to be worn by staff on the production floor for reasons of hygiene. However, when he returned from a holiday, after working for six years in the same company, he was sporting a beard and declared that he had undergone a spiritual revival. When on religious grounds he refused to shave the beard off, despite repeated requests to do so, he was dismissed because no other suitable work could be found for him in any other section of the company. His claim for unfair dismissal was rejected by the Industrial Tribunal on the ground that the rule about beards was a condition of his contract and was not an unreasonable one:

'We accept that the process of manufacturing ice cream requires high standards of hygiene and that the company in imposing the condition as it did, was endeavouring to maintain such standards.'[9]

It would seem that these two decisions are capable of being reconciled in the following way. As we have seen from cases such as *Panesar*,[10] while hygiene is an important consideration in the manufacture, sale and preparation of food, the threat to public health from beards is a comparatively minor one. Food inspectors from environmental health departments would be concerned if they discovered employees engaged in these occupations wearing untidy and dirty beards, but not otherwise. On the other hand, individual enterprises seriously concerned to maintain the highest standards of hygiene may very properly institute methods of working which endeavour to eliminate even the remotest risks of infection or contamination from their products. In this they will have the full support of food inspectors and if by some mischance they are prosecuted under the food and drugs legislation they will be able to point to their system of work in mitigation of any offence which they may have committed. However, since any decision to restrict hair-length or prohibit beards on the part of employees amounts to a major interference with individual liberty, while only effecting a minor improvement in standards of hygiene, any such rule must either be notified to an employee from the start or be introduced subsequently with his consent. This, it is submitted, is the heart of the distinction which emerges from a comparison between the two cases under review. Admittedly the jobs of the individuals concerned were of a different nature but the analogy drawn in *O'Connor's* case with the bearded chef indicates that the frequency and directness of the contact between an employee and food was not the decisive issue.

1 For a case where a nurse was held to have been fairly dismissed for a refusal to wear the uniform provided by her employers and appropriate to her grade, see *Atkin v Enfield Group Hospital Management Committee* [1975] IRLR 217.
2 COIT 9071/83/LC (1983, unreported).
3 See *Fowler v Fraser* COIT 950/232 (1979 unreported), but noted in *IDS Brief 174*, pp 6-7.
4 See The Times, 8 March 1984.
5 [1974] IRLR 306.
6 Industrial Relations Act 1971, s 24(2).
7 At 307.
8 [1975] IRLR 328.
9 At 329-30.
10 Discussed at para 9.17 above.

9.22 Where an employee is dismissed for failure to comply with an express term of his contract concerning dress or appearance he may still, on occasion, have a claim for compensation for unfair dismissal if his employer has previously condoned his non-compliance. This principle can be illustrated by reference to a case concerning dismissals made on very different grounds. In *Patel v Mansfield Hosiery Mills Ltd*[1] four Hindu machine cleaners had refused to clean men's toilets because of their belief that this was a task which should be done by 'untouchables'. Although they were warned by the manager that if they maintained their refusal the company would have to consider replacing them, no further action was taken for a period of nearly two years. Then they were again asked to clean the toilets and when they refused they were dismissed. The Industrial Tribunal held that although Hindus were not entitled to concessions of this nature which did not apply to other members of the workforce, their dismissal in this case was unfair because the employer had condoned their disobedience for nearly two years and was estopped from asserting the right to enforce the rules strictly against them. Even if the obligation to clean the toilets was part of their duties (which itself seemed far from clear on the facts) the company had agreed to a variation of it which exempted the Hindus from the need to carry out this task.

Much, however, depends upon the facts of each individual case and in certain circumstances it may only be necessary for the employer to give adequate warning to the employee that he intends to enforce the contract rules to the letter before being entitled to dismiss him fairly.[2]

1 COIT 485/179 (1976, unreported but noted in *IDS Brief 94* p 6).
2 See *Wilcox v Humphreys and Glasgow Ltd* [1975] IRLR 211 at 212.

The scope for reform

9.23   Although discussion of general improvements to the enforcement procedures and remedies available under the Race Relations Act 1976 are beyond the ambit of this book,[1] a few suggestions may be made with regard to some of the issues specifically dealt with in the preceding pages.

The impression left by many of the employment cases analysed above is that the law usually tends to be interpreted in favour of the employer. Great weight almost always seems to be attached both by industrial tribunals and by the courts to the commercial interests and business preferences of management, often to the severe detriment of those employees who seek respect for their religion and cultural practices and traditions. Clearly this is a field in which a compromise has to be struck between competing values, but the exact point at which the balance should be set may well be in need of review at the present time. To make concessions to minority practices can be expensive, not merely in terms of, for example, additional wages for replacement workers to fill absences for religious worship on Fridays or Saturdays, but also in administrative time spent in taking pains to accommodate turbans and *shalwar*, design new uniforms, order beard masks and so on. On the other hand, the expense involved in some forms of accommodation to the needs of ethnic minority customs may be regarded as so small in comparison with the social and moral values at stake that a greater effort to do so simply has to be demanded of employers.

If the rights of ethnic minority employees to adhere to their cultural and religious practices were felt to need strengthening this could be accomplished in a variety of ways. First, the use of the word 'justifiable' in the indirect discrimination provision of the Race Relations Act may have afforded employers too much leeway and may therefore need to be replaced by a more stringent test. In their proposals for reform of the Act the Commission for Racial Equality have recommended that the formula should be altered to 'necessary'.[2] In the cases of *Singh v Rowntree Mackintosh*,[3] *Panesar v Nestlé Co Ltd*[4] and *Singh v Lyons Maid Ltd*[5] it seemed very doubtful whether the employers had given enough thought to issuing bearded Sikhs with 'snoods' or face masks to net their beards.[6] This might have proved just as hygienic as their strict 'no-beards' rule. Similarly, in *Kuldip Singh v British Rail Engineering Ltd*,[7] although some discussions had been held between the applicant and his employers as to the possibility of some alternative form of protective headgear being available, no consideration seemed to have been given by the employers to the idea of having a suitable bump cap specially made for the applicant which he could wear over his turban. That this may be a feasible and an acceptable solution to problems of this nature is clear from the case of the Sikh jockey Daljeet Kalirai. Finding that the normal jockey's skull cap required by the Jockey Club's 'Rules of Racing' would not fit over Daljeet's turban, the trainer for whom he rides, Toby Balding of Fyfield in Hampshire, commissioned a specially manufactured helmet which could be worn over a lightweight turban and which would still satisfy the Jockey Club rules.[8]

In *Steel v Union of Post Office Workers*[9] stress was placed on the need to see whether the employer's objectives could be satisfactorily achieved in a manner that did not indirectly discriminate and perhaps this consideration should be incorporated in any new statutory formula. This would come very close to a test of objective necessity which might well be the most appropriate.[10] It would correspond closely with Art 9 of the European Convention on Human Rights which permits only such limitations upon the manifestation of religion as are 'necessary in a democratic society'.

1 For detailed examination of these aspects, see *Lustgarten* Part III; *Review of the Race Relations Act 1976 – Proposals for Change* (CRE, 1985).
2 *Review of the Race Relations Act 1976* pp 4-6.
3 [1979] IRLR 199.
4 [1980] ICR 144.
5 [1975] IRLR 328.
6 See Pearl [1980] New Community 148; *Guidance Note on Sikh Men and Women and Employment* (CRE 1981) paras 1.5 and 3.4.
7 (1985) Times, 6 August discussed at para 9.18 above.
8 Private communication from Baldings (Racing) Ltd.
9 [1977] IRLR 288 at 291.
10 For discussion of the differences in meaning between 'necessary' and 'justifiable', see *Lustgarten* pp 52-9.

9.24 An alternative approach to the whole issue of discrimination in employment is to frame a more general statutory provision which requires employers to respect the religious and cultural practices of their employees save where this would be excessively burdensome. The difficulty here is again to find a formula which strikes what is felt to be the right balance between competing values and once Parliament has decided where to draw the line to ensure that the courts and tribunals give proper effect to it. The American experience in this regard is far from salutary.[1] In 1964 the US Congress enacted Title VII of the Civil Rights Act thereby outlawing discrimination in employment practices on grounds of race, colour, religion, sex or national origin. Exceptions were, however, made to allow account to be taken by an employer of the accrued seniority rights of his employees, but the provision designed to achieve this objective proved to be so difficult to interpret that in 1972 Congress had to pass amending legislation to clarify the position and provide greater protection against discrimination. The amendment declares that the employer's obligation not to discriminate on grounds of religion includes reasonable accommodation to the religious observances or practices of an employee or prospective employee unless this would result in 'undue hardship' to the conduct of the employer's business. In a number of cases, however, of which *TWA v Hardison*[2] is the most notable, the US courts have interpreted the amendment in such a restrictive manner that very little protection is given to the religious practices and beliefs of employees. In *TWA v Hardison* the Supreme Court ruled that any accommodation required of an employer under the legislation should not burden him with more than minimal cost.[3] On the facts of the case this meant that the dismissal of a Sabbatarian for refusal to work on Saturdays was upheld as justified because his lack of seniority made it impossible for him to so arrange work assignments that he was never required to work on a Saturday. The cost of replacing him with another worker on Saturdays was felt by the Court to be excessive. The decision attracted a powerful dissent from Justices Brennan and Marshall in which they pointed out the relative ease with which the work schedules could have been adjusted to accommodate Hardison's religious needs. In their view the decision dealt a fatal blow at efforts made by Congress under Title VII to accommodate religious practices. They added:

'As a question of social policy, this result is deeply troubling, for a society that truly values religious pluralism cannot compel adherents of minority religions to make the cruel choice of surrendering their religion or their job. And as a matter of law today's result is intolerable, for the Court adopts the very position that Congress expressly rejected in 1972, as if we were free to disregard congressional choices that a majority of this Court thinks unwise.'[4]

1 See generally, Retter 'The Rise and Fall of Title VII's Requirement of Reasonable Accommodation for Religious Employees' (1979) 11 Columbia HR Law Review 63.
2 432 US 63 (1977).
3 At 84.
4 At 87.

9.25   Third, the omission of religious discrimination per se from the provisions of the Race Relations Act 1976 appears increasingly anomalous.[1] Such discrimination is covered by comparable American and Canadian legislation and freedom of religion is guaranteed under the European Convention on Human Rights as well as the International Covenant on Civil and Political Rights. The practical repercussions of the anomaly can be illustrated by the following example. An employer who refused to employ an orthodox Jew because he operated a rule that all his employees should be available for work on Saturdays would probably be in breach of the indirect discrimination provisions of the 1976 Act unless he could show the rule to be justifiable. This is because Jews appear to be regarded as an ethnic group under the Act. If, on the other hand, he refused to recruit a Muslim because of his dislike of certain Islamic beliefs and practices (including the need to pray five times each day) no action would seem to lie against him because his discrimination would have been based upon purely religious grounds.

1 See generally, Robilliard 'Should Parliament Enact a Religious Discrimination Act?' (1978) PL 379; *Review of the Race Relations Act 1976* (CRE, 1985) pp 6-7.

9.26   A rather different question is whether there is any scope for giving greater legal recognition to non–Christian festivals. Possibly some consideration might be given to the idea of according the status of bank or public holidays to three of the major annual festivals recognised by the principal non-Christian faiths practiced in England today.[1] These might perhaps be *Diwali* (celebrated by both Sikhs and Hindus and falling at a suitable time in late October or early November when there is no other public holiday), the Jewish *Pentecost* (which would simultaneously restore a holiday at Whitsuntide and could replace the present spring bank holiday at the end of May) and the Muslim festival of *Id-al-Fitr* (which moves forward by roughly 11 or 12 days each year). The grant of official recognition to these holidays would not only provide the general public with an important and statutory reminder of the religious diversity of the country's different communities but should also mean in practice that most employees would be able to take paid leave on these days as part of their contractual entitlement.[2]

Three objections to this proposal can easily be anticipated. First, that an increase in the number of public holidays is not conducive to the achievement of greater productivity, which the economy of the country badly requires. The present suggestion, however, only involves an extra two public holidays, raising the total number from eight to ten, whereas most countries in Western Europe already possess more than ten. The French have as many as 13 and the West Germans 11.[3] Indirectly a few thousand extra jobs might be created as a result of establishing one or two more public holidays, surely a worthwhile goal at the present time. In the Parliamentary debates preceding the enactment of the Banking and Financial Dealings Act 1971 the attitude of the Government was that any increase in holidays was a matter for negotiation between individual employers and their employees. Apart from the illogicality of applying this argument only to the issue of additional holidays, this approach overlooks the need for the holidays of all family members to be synchronised (especially with the increase in the number of working wives and mothers) and the economics of organising forms of mass entertainment.[4]

A second line of objection might be that if one minority religion is to have a festival recognised officially in this way, the principle of non-discrimination requires that all religious denominations and faiths (even those with very few adherents) should receive similar treatment. This would clearly be impracticable, but it seems reasonable to draw the line at those faiths with, say, at least 250,000 adherents or roughly 0.5% of the total population of the country. Certainly such a scheme could no more be in breach of the European Convention on Human Rights than the present system.

Third, the exact date of *Id-al-Fitr* each year is not usually fixed until quite close to the festival itself.[5] The Islamic calendar is linked to the lunar system and the start of Ramadan depends upon the sighting of the new moon. Practical considerations would clearly indicate that if *Id-al-Fitr* were to become a public holiday the date of its official celebration in England should be settled at least a year in advance.

1 Diverse religious festivals are accorded the status of public holidays in a number of Commonwealth countries: see, e g the Singapore Holidays Act (cap 307), the Kenyan Public Holidays Act (cap 110) and the Sri Lankan Holidays Act (cap 177).
2 It would also remove clashes between Pentecost and GCE examinations for Jewish candidates: see para 8.19 above.
3 Canada and the USA each have nine.
4 825 HC Official Report (5th series) col 1455; 827 HC Official Report (5th series) col 395.
5 *The Muslim Guide* p 57.

CHAPTER 10

The criminal law

INTRODUCTION

10.01 In previous chapters ethnic minority customs have been considered chiefly in the context of the civil law. Their significance in terms of the criminal law has been touched upon only incidentally, for example in brief discussions of bigamy, incest, sexual relations with girls under 16, the ill-treatment of children and so on. The purpose of the present chapter is to draw together these and other offences in which such a custom may be relevant, with a view to presenting a coherent analysis of the special problems raised in this field.

Prima facie, the notion of a universal minimum standard applicable to each and every member of the community appears to be a sensible and logical one in the criminal law sphere. However, the position is by no means as straightforward as it might seem. As will be shown, it cannot simply be asserted that ethnic minority customs provide no defence or excuse whatever in the administration of the criminal law and that members of these minorities are invariably treated in exactly the same way as members of the majority community.

A. THE AMBIT OF ENGLISH CRIMINAL JURISDICTION

10.02 A preliminary question to consider is the extent of the jurisdiction possessed by the English courts in criminal matters. Broadly speaking, such jurisdiction is exercised upon the 'territorial principle', which means that a prosecution can only be instituted if the offence was committed in England and Wales. Hence if the allegation is, for example, that a girl has been forcibly circumcised in Ethiopia or that a half-brother and half-sister have had sexual intercourse in Sweden or that a parent has overzealously punished his child in the West Indies, there in no question of the matter coming to trial in this country. The most important exception to the territorial principle arises where jurisdiction is based upon nationality. English courts do claim jurisdiction over a limited number of crimes committed abroad by British subjects, for example in cases of treason, murder and bigamy.

B. THE GENERAL APPROACH OF THE COURTS

10.03 Where the English courts possess the requisite jurisdiction to hear criminal proceedings they have tended, for well over a century, to follow a consistent pattern in their handling of cases involving foreign or immigrant customs. They have generally decided that the question of guilt must be determined according to a uniform standard applicable to all-comers, regardless of their origins.[1] For example, in *R v Barronet and Allain*[2] in 1852 the accused, who were both Frenchmen, faced a charge of murder in consequence of having acted as seconds in a duel in England in which one of the participants was killed.[3] They sought to argue that as the duel was a fair one and not punishable as a crime in France they should receive special treatment before the English courts.

Lord Campbell CJ reacted to this suggestion with the following brusque statement:

'Persons who fly to this country as an asylum must obey the laws of the country, and be content to place themselves in the same situation as native born subjects.'[4]

Coleridge J remarked:

'We are told to lay down a different rule to what we should apply to native born subjects, because these persons are foreigners and ignorant of our law relating to duelling. But I agree with the Lord Chief Justice that foreigners who come to England must in this respect be dealt with in the same way as native subjects. Ignorance of the law cannot, in the case of a native, be received as an excuse for a crime, nor can it any more be urged in favour of a foreigner.'[5]

Erle J added:

'To make a difference in the case of foreigners would be a most dangerous practice. It is of great importance that the administration of the law should be uniform. It must be administered without respect to persons, and it would be dangerous and unjust to introduce into a general rule an exception in favour of foreigners.'[6]

Some 16 years earlier the same approach had been adopted in the case of a sailor from Baghdad who was charged with having committed an 'unnatural offence' on board a ship in the London docks.[7] The judges of the Central Criminal Court indicated that it would be no defence for the accused to show that such conduct was not a crime in the country he came from and that he believed it to be totally innocent.

In the light of these and other judicial decisions, it would appear that foreign customs such as the killing of twins,[8] kidnapping and false imprisonment pursuant to a family feud,[9] assault and battery in the excessive punishment of a child,[10] the circumcision of a young girl[11] or the tattooing or scarification[12] of children will afford no defence to an appropriate charge brought in this country relating to an offence against the person. Presumably the same stance would be adopted by the courts in a suitable case if a Sikh were to carry a *kirpan* (a short sword or dagger recognised as one of the five distinctive symbols of Sikhism) with the intention of using it to cause personal injury and was charged with possession of an 'offensive weapon' in a public place under the Prevention of Crime Act 1953, s 1. No offence would, however, seem to be committed if the *kirpan* was being carried or worn merely for religious reasons since the section allows a defence of 'reasonable excuse'. In *R v Graham John*,[13] which involved the same defence to a different charge (failure to supply a specimen of blood under the Road Safety Act 1967) Roskill LJ commented:

'For a man to be punished for an offence which is committed by reason only of his adherence to his own religion or belief can only be justified if the court is satisfied that the clear intention of the statute creating the offence was in the interests of the community as a whole to override the privileges otherwise attaching to freedom of conscience and belief, which it must always be the duty of the courts to protect and defend.'[14]

The carrying of *kirpans* is expressly recognised as included in the profession of the Sikh religion in the Indian constitution[15] and the privilege of carrying them here would probably be respected by the English courts. In practice Sikhs living in this country generally carry a miniature replica or a substitute rather than the *kirpan* itself.[16]

1 For an excellent introduction to the relevant cases, see Shyllon 'Immigration and the Criminal Courts' (1971) 34 MLR 135.
2 (1852) Dears CC 51.
3 For the background to the English law forbidding duelling, see Glanville Williams 'Consent and Public Policy' [1962] Crim LR 74 at 77-8; C Woodham-Smith *The Reason Why* (Penguin, 1978) ch 5.
4 At 58.
5 At 59.
6 At 60.
7 *R v Esop* (1836) 7 C & P 456.
8 For details see the Nigerian case of *R v Ugo Chima* (1944) 10 WACA 223; Seidman *A Sourcebook of the Criminal Law of Africa* (Sweet and Maxwell, 1966) pp 17, 525-6.
9 *R v Dad and Shafi* [1968] Crim LR 46.
10 *R v Derriviere* (1969) 53 Cr App Rep 637, discussed at para 6.18 above.
11 See paras 6.25-6.33 above.
12 *R v Adesanya* (1974), discussed at paras 6.23-6.24 above.
13 [1974] 2 All ER 561, [1974] 1 WLR 624.
14 At 564.
15 Art 25.
16 James *Sikh Children in Britain* p 51; Sookde *Asians in Britain* (Exeter, 1977) p 40.

10.04 In general terms a uniform standard must equally be applicable with regard to sexual offences.[1] However, it seems probable that it would be a defence for an accused to establish that the particular act of intercourse with which he was charged was not only sanctioned by a custom but also occurred within a foreign marriage recognised as valid in this country. It will be recalled that in the case of *Alhaji Mohamed v Knott*[2] one of the parties to an Islamic marriage contracted in Nigeria was a 13 year old girl. The marriage was held to be entitled to full recognition here and Lord Parker CJ took the commonsense view that intercourse between the couple could hardly be said to fall within the Sexual Offences Act 1956 s 6(1) which provides:

'It is an offence . . . for a man to have unlawful sexual intercourse with a girl . . . under the age of 16'.

The intercourse could not be said to be 'unlawful' where the parties were man and wife.

The position is by no means so clear in the case of incest since the relevant sections of the 1956 Act[3] do not specify that the intercourse must be unlawful. However, it is submitted that if a foreign marriage between, for example, a half-brother and half-sister were to be afforded recognition here no offence would be committed. Clearly the existence of the incest prohibition would itself be one of the factors to be considered by the courts in deciding whether or not the marriage should be recognised.[4]

Bigamy presents greater problems. It has already been pointed out in ch 3 above that where a person who has married abroad (and whose marriage is recognised as valid here) subsequently contracts a second marriage in this country this ought to constitute the crime of bigamy regardless of whether, in terms of any foreign law, the first marriage was potentially or actually polygamous. The two cases which purport to establish that no offence is committed unless the first marriage was of a monogamous nature are based on thoroughly unsound reasoning.[5] What is the position where the sequence of marriages is the other way round? Is it bigamy to marry abroad under a polygamous system having entered a prior monogamous marriage in this country? As explained earlier, a British subject can be convicted by an English court of bigamy even if the offence occurs abroad, but the central question is whether the second marriage would be void in English law if it was regarded as valid by the *lex domicilii* or personal law of the person concerned. The matter is controversial and no clear answer can be given.[6]

1 See *R v Bailey* [1964] Crim LR 671; *R v Byfield* [1967] Crim LR 378 (intercourse with girls under 16).
2 [1969] 1 QB1, discussed at para 2.17 above.
3 Ss 10(2) and 11(2).
4 See para 2.10 above.
5 *R v Sarwan Singh* [1962] 3 All ER 612; *R v Sagoo* [1975] QB 885, [1975] 2 All ER 926 criticised at para 3.16 above.
6 See paras 3.03 and 3.07 above.

10.05 The general approach of applying a uniform standard to the question of guilt, together with the maxim that ignorance of the law is no defence, would seem to be appropriate for offences involving bribery and corruption,[1] a notoriously widespread custom in many parts of the world. It also seems right for offences involving controlled drugs covered by the Misuse of Drugs Act 1971. There appears to be quite a widespread use of cannabis by Rastafarians, for whom *marijuana* (or *'ganja'* as they call it) is important not only as a form of natural living but also as a religious practice.[2] They regard it as bringing wisdom, assisting meditation and prayer and facilitating communication among fellow adherents to the sect, as well as possessing valuable medicinal properties. The approach of the English courts to date has been to refuse to treat Rastafarians differently from other drug users, while naturally adhering to the general principle that a less serious offence is committed by someone whose intention is merely to use the drug himself and supply it in small quantities to friends than one who imports it on a large scale as a professional smuggler.[3]

1 For details of the various offences, see Archbold *Pleading, Evidence and Practice in Criminal Cases* (41st edn, 1982) pp 1864, 2007-29.
2 See K Pryce *Endless Pressure* (Penguin, 1979) p 147; K M Williams *The Rastafarians* (Ward Lock, 1981) p 20; *The Scarman Report on the Brixton Disorders*, Cmnd 8427 of 1981 (Penguin, 1982) pp 76-7; E Cashmore *Rastaman* (Unwin, 2nd edn, 1983) p 178.
3 See, eg *R v Williams* (1979) 1 Cr App Rep (S) 5; *R v Daudi and Daniels* (1982) 4 Cr App Rep (S) 306; *R v Aramah* [1983] Crim LR 271; *R v Dallaway* (1983) 148 JPN 31.

C. THE USE OF DISCRETION IN THE CRIMINAL PROCESS

10.06 While the question whether an accused is guilty or not guilty of the offence with which he is charged falls to be determined by a strict application of the law, there are other areas of the criminal process in which greater flexibility is afforded through the use of discretion. This may enable the rigours of the law to be tempered by the need to strive for a just outcome in each individual case.

The first occasion for the application of discretion arises before any trial even commences. It is for the prosecuting authorities to decide whether or not charges should be preferred and the likelihood of obtaining a conviction is only one of many considerations that may properly be taken into account.[1] Where the offence is of a trivial nature or amounts merely to a technical breach of the law the police may legitimately conclude that it is not in the public interest to mount a prosecution and that a caution will be sufficient response on their part to the illegality that has occurred.[2] One example of this is the widespread practice of many police authorities merely to caution those found in possession of very small quantities of cannabis and to concentrate their main energies in this field on prosecuting those who are the suppliers of controlled drugs.[3]

Wilcox cites an instance where a Portuguese waiter confessed to the police that he had corruptly offered money to a Ministry of Transport driving examiner as an inducement to issue him a certificate of competency to drive.[4] His explanation that he was simply following the common practice in Portugal was accepted and no prosecution was brought against him.[5]

It appears that the battery of laws which are available to control unauthorised gypsy encampments are often not applied with their full force and vigour. As one leading authority on the subject has put it:

'The dominant concern of local authorities to remove [gypsies] from their boundaries has influenced police action. The objective has become not to prosecute Gypsies, as housedwellers committing offences would be prosecuted, but to persuade them to move on by explaining that they can be charged with one offence or another. In many areas a tacit suspension of the due process of law has been allowed to develop.'[6]

There is also evidence to suggest that greater leniency is sometimes shown to gypsies who are suspected by the police of certain motoring offences than to other members of the public. Many gypsies fail to comply with the laws relating to driving licences, road tax and vehicle insurance, yet a blind eye is occasionally turned.[7]

1 See generally, Royal Commission on Criminal Procedure, *Report* (Cmnd 8092 of 1981) pp 173-5; *The Investigation and Prosecution of Criminal Offences in England and Wales: The Law and Procedure* (Cmnd 8092-I of 1981) pp 53-4, 210-17.
2 See Wilcox *The Decision to Prosecute* (Butterworths, 1972) ch 8; Glanville Williams 'Discretion in Prosecuting' [1956] Crim LR 222 at 224.
3 See, e g Farrier *Drugs and Intoxication* (Sweet and Maxwell, 1980) p 57.
4 At p 76.
5 See also the tolerant attitude of the stipendiary magistrate for Liverpool with regard to prosecutions of Chinese for illicit gambling in 1906, described in Holmes (ed) *Immigrants and Minorities in British Society* (London, 1978) p 118. A similar approach seems to be adopted today: see *Chinese Community in Britain* Second Report of the House of Commons Home Affairs Committee (1984-5) HC 102-I, vol 1, paras 185-191.
6 Adams, B and others, *Gypsies and Government Policy in England* (London, 1975), pp 159-60.
7 *Adams* pp 161-2. In the case of many minor motoring offences, of course, a caution is very often the normal police response with respect to all members of the community.

10.07 The second occasion for the application of discretion arises when a court has convicted the accused of an offence and has to determine the appropriate sentence. At this stage of the proceedings the fact that the defendant is of foreign origin, that his offence would not be regarded as a crime in the country he comes from, that he quite reasonably did not appreciate that his act was contrary to English law and that he was having difficulties in adjusting to English standards of behaviour are all relevant factors to be taken into account.[1] Often they will be accepted as mitigating circumstances and a lighter sentence than usual will be imposed, particularly in the case of a first offender.

The courts appear to be willing to consider cultural patterns of behaviour when deciding whether or not to impose a sentence of imprisonment and, if so, for how long. In *R v Bibi*[2] the defendant, a Kenyan Asian widow aged 48, was found guilty on two counts of being concerned in the fraudulent evasion of the prohibition of the importation of cannabis under the Misuse of Drugs Act 1971. The social inquiry report revealed that she spoke no English and had been totally dependent for her support and welfare on her brother-in-law. It was he who had organised the illegal importation of the drugs and he had been duly convicted and sentenced to a period of three and a half years' imprisonment. She had merely unpacked the parcels of cannabis when they arrived at her home from Kenya and was clearly only on the fringes of the whole enterprise. She was so well socialised into the Muslim traditions of seclusion and male dominance that it seemed unlikely that she really appreciated the significance of what she had done. She had had no contact with wider English society and her involvement in the offence appeared to arise out of a normal response of acceptance of the decisions made by her male relatives. She clearly enjoyed far less independence of mind and action than the average white Englishwoman. The sentence of three years' imprisonment imposed upon her by the Crown Court was therefore reduced by the Court of Appeal to one of six months. This was felt to be far more appropriate both to the offence and to the offender and it meant her immediate release from the gaol where she had already been serving her sentence.

1 See e g *R v Esop* (1836) 7 C & P 456; *R v Rapier* [1963] Crim LR 212; *R v Bailey* [1964] Crim LR 671; *R v Byfield* [1967] Crim LR 378; *R v Dad and Shafi* [1968] Crim LR 46; *R v Derriviere* (1969) 53 Cr App R 637.
2 [1980] 1 WLR 1193.

D. SPECIFIC RELIGIOUS EXEMPTIONS

10.08   In the case of a very small number of statutory offences Parliament has been prepared to provide specific exemptions from criminal liability in order to accommodate the religious beliefs of ethnic minorities. These will be briefly described in turn.

1 Opening hours for shops

10.09   The Shops Act 1950, s 47[1] provides, subject to numerous exceptions for various classes of goods,[2] that every shop shall be closed for the serving of customers on Sundays. Contravention of this provision renders the occupier of the shop liable to a fine not exceeding £50 in the case of a first offence and £200 in the case of subsequent offences.[3] Historically, the principal justification for this was the need to observe the Lord's Day, Sunday being the day set aside by Christians for worship and rest.[4] However, such a law, if unmodified, was bound to have adverse consequences for members of those faiths which prescribed the setting aside of other days of the week for religious observance. They might reasonably claim that the elimination of both these days from the ordinary conduct of their businesses (one for religious reasons and the second as a matter of legal obligation) was unduly burdensome.

Principal concern was expressed for the position of Jewish traders. In early Jewish law it was a capital offence to labour on the Jewish Sabbath[5] and orthodox Jewish shopkeepers in this country follow the traditional practice of not trading on Saturdays, while having no objection to working normally on Sundays. To meet these requirements the Shops Act 1950, s 53(1) provides as follows:

'... the occupier of any shop who is a person of the Jewish religion shall be entitled, upon making to the local authority an application in accordance with the provisions of this section, to have the shop registered under this section by the local authority, and so long as the shop is so registered then–

(a) the shop shall be closed for all purposes connected with trade or business on Saturday; and
(b) the provisions of this Part of this Act requiring the shop to be closed for the serving of customers on Sunday shall not apply until two o'clock in the afternoon; and
(c) there shall be kept conspicuously placed in the shop a notice stating that it will be closed on Saturday and, if the shop will be open for the serving of customers on Sunday after two o'clock in the afternoon for the purposes of any transaction for which it is permitted under this Part of this Act to be so open, specifying the hours during which, and the purposes for which, it will be so open.'[6]

Applications for registration of shops under this section have to be accompanied by a statutory declaration made by the occupier of the shop declaring that he conscientiously objects on religious grounds to carrying on trade or business on the Jewish Sabbath, together with a certificate signed by a panel appointed by the Board of Deputies stating that the conscientious objection is genuine.[7]

So long as a shop is registered under the section no other shop occupied by the same person can be kept open for Saturday trading and no-one by whom the statutory declaration was made can be employed or engaged on Saturdays about the business of any shop.[8]

1 Replacing the Shops (Sunday Trading Restriction) Act 1936, s 7.
2 The exceptions are specified in Part IV of the Act and the Fifth Schedule.
3 S 59, as amended by the Criminal Justice Act 1972, s 31.
4 For early legislation, see the Sunday Observance Acts 1677, 1780 and 1833; see also para 8.06 above for laws relating to religious worship.
5 Horowitz *The Spirit of Jewish Law* pp 185-8.
6 Similar provisions specifically exempting Jewish retail dealers in meat from the ban on Sunday trading are found in s 62 of the Act.
7 S 53(2); Shops Regulations 1979, SI 1979/1294.
8 S 53(5).

10.10 The basic idea behind all these provisions was summarised by Walton J in *Thanet DC v Ninedrive Ltd*[1] as being that:

'. . . as a devout Jew will be prevented by the tenets of his faith from opening his shop on Saturday, it is hard on him that he should in fact be forced to close his shop for two days a week whilst his Christian neighbour is only forced to close it for one.'[2]

His Lordship drew attention to the fact that the 1950 Act also contained an exception for other faiths. However, the wording of the statute is such that this dispensation only applies to members of a religious body 'regularly observing the Jewish Sabbath'.[3] It would, therefore, cover Sabbatarians such as the Seventh Day Adventists, but not Muslims whose special day of prayer is Friday. However, there is nothing in the Koran or Islamic doctrine generally which actually requires a total cessation of all business activity on a particular day of the week. There is no Sabbath day as such and Friday for Muslims in a non-Islamic country is not a full day's holiday. Rather Muslims are expected, where practicable, to leave their work for congregational prayer in a mosque lasting for only about one hour and then return to their normal activities.[4]

No public resentment seems to be occasioned by the religious exemption in the Shops Act, but in an increasingly secular society there is a growing demand for trading to be allowed on seven days a week if shopkeepers are willing to remain open this long. Many classes of goods may be sold on Sundays in any event and the anomaly of allowing, for example, the sale of 'soft' pornography, while prohibiting the sale of bibles (except at a railway or bus station)[5] has led to numerous attempts in Parliament over recent years to reform the law.[6]

1 [1978] 1 All ER 703.
2 At 705.
3 S 53(12).
4 McDermott and Ahsan *The Muslim Guide* p 40.
5 See 427 HL Official Report (6th series) col 141.
6 See, eg, the Shops Bills 1981 and 1985.

2 The slaughtering of animals and poultry

10.11 The Slaughterhouses Act 1974 lays down that as a standard practice no animal in a slaughterhouse or a knacker's yard shall be slaughtered otherwise than instantaneously by means of a mechanically operated instrument in proper repair, unless it is instantaneously rendered insensible to pain until death supervenes by a process of stunning or such other means as are prescribed by regulations under the Act.[1] Similar provisions in the Slaughter of Poultry Act 1967 apply to the slaughter, for purposes of preparation for sale for human consumption, of turkeys kept in captivity and domestic fowl.[2] The objective is, of course, in both instances to ensure a humane method of slaughter. A person who slaughters a bird or animal in contravention of these provisions commits an offence.[3]

Both Acts contain an express exemption for the slaughter, without the infliction of unnecessary suffering, of a bird or an animal 'by the Jewish method for the food of Jews and by a Jew duly licensed for the purpose' by a specially appointed Rabbinical Commission and 'by the Mohammedan method for the food of Mohammedans and by a Mohammedan.'[4]

The justification for these exemptions is that according to both Jewish law and Muslim custom animals and poultry have to be slaughtered in a specified ritual manner involving loss of blood while they are still conscious, if their meat is to be acceptable for human consumption.[5] Jews refer to this method of slaughter as *shechita* and to such meat as *kosher*, while Muslims describe it as *halal*.

1 S 36(1). The provision refers to horses, cattle, sheep, swine and goats: see s 36(5).
2 S 1(1).
3 Slaughter of Poultry Act, s 1(3); Slaughterhouses Act, s 36(4).
4 Slaughter of Poultry Act, s 1(2); Slaughterhouses Act, s 36(3). In the case of animals this exemption dates back to the original English legislation on the subject, namely the Slaughter of Animals Act 1933, s 1. This, in turn, was based on earlier Scottish legislation, namely the Slaughter of Animals (Scotland) Act 1928.
5 See generally *Horowitz* pp 115-7; Homa *Shechita* (Board of Deputies of British Jews, 1967); Lawrence *Some Aspects of Shechita* (Council of Christians and Jews, 1971); McDermott and Ahsan *The Muslim Guide* p 36.

10.12 Over the period of more than 50 years since these statutory dispensations were first granted by English law to Jews and Muslims there has been a steady stream of criticism of their methods from the RSPCA and others.[1] However, whether or not *shechita* and *halal* in fact involve greater cruelty than the pre-stunning system seems to have been extremely hard to establish. In the case of *shechita* the animal or fowl is killed by means of a single rapid transverse cut to the neck (involving an uninterrupted backwards and forwards motion) which severs the carotid arteries and jugular veins. The knife is honed to a surgical sharpness, with a perfect edge free from even the most minute notch or flaw. It takes many months of training before the *shochet* (the official who performs the slaughter) is skilled enough to undertake the task. He has to be licensed by a Rabbinical commission and is often himself a local minister and teacher of religion. He is also imbued with the knowledge that kindness to animals is one of the ideals of Judaism. The speed of the incision produces a very sudden and substantial drop in blood pressure and Jewish authorities (with the support of expert scientists)[2] have long claimed that this results in virtually instant unconsciousness, almost certainly within a couple of seconds.[3] Thereafter death quickly supervenes. No pain is caused at the immediate moment of the cutting since the animal is motionless in a 'casting pen' and there is no tearing. Subsequent convulsions are caused by a lack of oxygen to the brain and are in themselves a proof of unconsciousness. A similar procedure is followed by Muslims in the case of *halal*.

The standard statutory pre-stunning technique is not acceptable to orthodox Jews (though it is acceptable to some Muslims) because it is an essential requirement of Jewish law that the animal must, immediately before slaughter, be completely sound and well and must not have suffered injury.[4] Indeed, when one considers in practical terms the humaneness of the normal system of pre-stunning it seems clear that there is no guarantee that the methods prescribed will eliminate all unnecessary suffering on the part of the animal. Mistakes are not uncommon, including failures through 'missed shots' with the 'captive bolt pistol' technique or 'missed shock' in the case of electrical stunning, both of which cause undoubted pain to the animal and necessitate a fresh attempt to stun it.[5]

In the early 1980s interest in the controversy, having lain dormant for a time, revived with the discovery that the number of animals being slaughtered in Britain by *halal* was rising rapidly not only as a result of the increase in the Muslim population in this country, but also because a lucrative export trade was being developed with states in North Africa and the Middle East.[6] This had led to a growing number of abattoirs being licensed by local authorities with the export market in *halal* meat specifically in mind. Protests in various parts of the country where these abattoirs were sited prompted the introduction of a bill in the House of Lords to amend the Slaughterhouses Act by confining the religious exemptions to meat that was for consumption either within the UK and its dependent territories or on a British ship or aircraft.[7] This appeared to be, in substance, a fresh attempt to designate *shechita* and *halal* as inhumane and the bill predictably failed to gain a second reading.[8] Not only did it seem hard to justify a double standard as between what was acceptable for home consumption and what was suitable for export, but it was also clear that any ban on the export trade would almost certainly be worse for the animals themselves in that they would then have been shipped abroad alive, often in unsatisfactory conditions. In any event it appeared that in a growing number of abattoirs licensed for *halal* the pre-stunning method was in fact being used with the agreement of the local *imam* who justified his permission on the basis that there is no clear injunction against it in Islamic doctrine.

1 See, e g M D Ward *Jewish kosher – should it be permitted to survive in a new Britain?* (Ilfracombe, 1943); *Legalised Cruelty* (RSPCA, 1948); *Humane Slaughter* (RSPCA, 1981); *Ritual Slaughter* (RSPCA, 1984).
2 Contrary findings have, however, been produced by the Farm Animal Welfare Council: see para 10.13 below.
3 See *Homa* pp 6-7; Sassoon *A Critical Study of Electrical Stunning and the Jewish Method of Slaughter* (Letchworth, 1955) pp 7-11.
4 The process of stunning, apart from itself constituting an injury to the animal, might produce other injuries (or even death): see *Sassoon* pp 23-7. On the other hand, it appears that certain types of injury such as bruising sustained in the transport and penning of animals do not prevent the meat being accepted as *kosher* – see, e g Farm Animal Welfare Council *Report on the Welfare of Livestock When Slaughtered by Religious Methods* (HMSO, 1985) p 16.

5 See, e g Farm Animal Welfare Council *Report on the Welfare of Livestock (Red Meat Animals) at the Time of Slaughter* (HMSO, 1984) pp 31-8; *Sassoon* pp 11-18.
6 For details of the substantial numbers of animals involved, see Farm Animal Welfare Council *Report on the Welfare of Livestock When Slaughtered by Religious Methods* (HMSO, 1985) pp 8, 37.
7 Slaughter of Animals (Amendment) Bill 1981.
8 See 425 HL Official Report (6th series) cols. 1215-39.

10.13 In 1985 the whole issue of the acceptability of religious methods of slaughter was re-examined in a report prepared by the Farm Animal Welfare Council at the request of the Ministry of Agriculture, Fisheries and Food.[1] The Report's principal conclusion was that, although there was a dearth of scientific evidence to indicate at precisely what stage in the process of losing consciousness the ability of animals to feel pain ceases, loss of consciousness following severance of the major blood vessels in the neck is certainly not immediate and animals may experience pain for as long as 10-17 seconds after their throats have been cut, even in the best conditions.[2] The Council's ultimate assessments were that this period was 'unacceptably long' and that 'humane slaughter can best be achieved by effective stunning'.[3] Addressing itself to the religious dimension of the question, the Report declared:

'We believe that such a conclusion does not carry with it inherently anti-Jewish or anti-Muslim views, or restrict religious freedom. Our terms of reference have been to consider the welfare of birds or animals at the time of slaughter and in this we have become aware of the common ground shared between ourselves and the formally expressed views of Jewish and Muslim bodies concerning the need for kindness to and humane treatment of animals. Difficulties and disagreements arise, in the matter of religious slaughter, almost entirely over the question of stunning and other matters are subsidiary to it. We have already referred to the minimal scriptural antecedents and note that Jewish law and practice are considerably governed by continuing Rabbinical oral tradition, while Muslim [practice] is less consistent. Practices that almost certainly had practical and necessary beginnings many centuries ago, relating to kindness to animals, food hygiene and a repugnance at the possibility of eating blood, thought of as the life substance, are now part of religious practice, with much greater symbolic rather than practical significance.

We recognise the minefield to be crossed in trying to deal with such a combination of religious symbolism and ceremonial, ethnic and religious identity and practical issues concerning the humane treatment of animals. We believe, however, that members of the Jewish and Muslim faiths should once again be encouraged to adapt their methods of slaughter in ways which still meet the needs of dietary habit and religious identity, whilst accepting modern methods to ensure that the bird's or animal's welfare benefits from sound contemporary practice.'[4]

The Council's principal recommendation was that the government should require the Jewish and Muslim communities to review their methods of slaughter so as to develop alternatives which permit effective stunning. Their findings should then be presented to the government so that the statutory provisions exempting Jews and Muslims from the stunning requirements could be repealed 'within the next three years'.[5]

The Jewish and Muslim communities have, of course, always maintained that their practices do not involve any unnecessary suffering and indeed are the most humane method known to man. Moreover, there has been considerable scientific support for this point of view. It was, therefore, entirely predictable that the scientific evidence relied upon by the Council would be strongly challenged by Jewish and Muslim authorities as selective, partial and inconclusive.[6] If the true scientific facts are still in genuine dispute then there seems no justification whatever for depriving Jews and Muslims of their time-honoured exemptions. Their traditional concern for animal welfare should not be belittled and their freedom to practise their religions under international human rights conventions should be respected. If the scientific evidence were eventually to become overwhelming in its conclusiveness that such methods of slaughter involved unnecessary suffering to animals then Parliament could justifiably restrict religious freedom on the ground that the practice needed to be curbed in the interest of the protection of public morality, an exception recognised in both the European Convention and the International Covenant on Civil and Political Rights.[7] Other aspects of animal husbandry (such as intensive rearing) practised by the majority community, might, however, also have to be scrutinised at the same time in order to ensure that they did not offend against current values of public morality with regard to the ill-treatment of animals.

It is noteworthy that in other Western countries there is a substantial degree of accord that religious exemptions from stunning should be allowed. There is legislation to this effect in all the countries of the EEC.[8] It is true that in Norway and Switzerland there is no such religious exception, but ancient legislation in these countries banning *shechita* seems to have been the product of anti-semitism as much as concern for the welfare of animals. In the USA and Canada religious methods of slaughter are expressly recognised by legislation as 'humane'.

The Farm Animal Welfare Council also expressed concern in their Report over a number of subsidiary issues. Under the Slaughter of Animals (Prevention of Cruelty) Regulations 1958 no adult bovine may be slaughtered by the Jewish or Muslim method without the use of a casting pen of the Weinberg, Dyne or North British Rotary type or such other type as may be approved by the Minister of Agriculture. These rotary pens were originally introduced in the interests of humane slaughter, but the Council considered their continued use to be unsatisfactory on welfare grounds because it involves the unnatural inversion of the animals so that they are lying on their backs with their necks extended, which is likely to cause them both terror and discomfort.[9] The Council therefore recommended that the use of rotary pens be prohibited within a period of two years and that in their place there should be introduced pens which restrained the animals in a standing position, such as the 'Cincinnati pen' which is widely used in the USA and approved by the American Society for the Prevention of Cruelty to Animals and is also currently in use by Muslims in Northern Ireland.[10] Second, the Council found that animals are sometimes shackled and hoisted onto the bleeding rail before they have fully lost consciousness.[11] It recommended that animals should not be moved in these circumstances and that at least 20 seconds should elapse in the case of the slaughter of sheep and goats and at least 30 seconds in the case of calves and adult bovines.[12] Third, the Council discovered that while there was close supervision of Jewish slaughter practices by the Jewish authorities there was a noticeable lack of direction and supervision of slaughter operations within the Muslim community. Concern was expressed at the lack of formal training of Muslim slaughtermen in comparison with the Jewish *shochetim*.[13] Fourth, the Council found that a substantial proportion of meat produced by means of religious slaughter is marketed to the general public without any indication of its origins. The Council felt the consumer was entitled to be aware of the method of slaughter employed and it therefore recommended that all meat from carcasses slaughtered by religious methods and offered for sale should be clearly labelled accordingly.[14] Apparently the proportion of *kosher* meat which is made available on the general market may be as high as two-thirds[15] and those members of the public who wish to avoid purchasing it or *halal* meat obviously require information on this point. Their freedom of choice surely merits adequate legal protection.

1 *Report on the Welfare of Livestock when Slaughtered by Religious Methods* (HMSO, 1985).
2 Ibid pp 19-20.
3 At p 19.
4 At p 21.
5 At p 25.
6 See e g 'Comments by the Jewish Community on the FAWC Report' (1985).
7 ECHR Art 9(2); International Covenant, Art 18(3).
8 See *FAWC Report* (1985) pp 38-40; 'Comments by the Jewish Community on the FAWC Report' pp 18-19.
9 FAWC Report pp 15-16.
10 At p 25.
11 At p 19.
12 At p 26.
13 At p 21.
14 At p 27.
15 At p 9. The hindquarters are invariably treated as non-*kosher* in England.

10.14 Turning next to the slaughter of animals outside a slaughterhouse, an offence may be committed under the Protection of Animals Act 1911 if the slaughter involves cruelty. This is defined to include unreasonably doing any act by which unnecessary suffering is caused to an animal.[1] There is an exception for acts done in the course of the destruction of an animal 'as food for mankind', but this does not apply where the destruction is accompanied by the infliction of unnecessary suffering upon the animal.[2]

In 1984 an Iranian diplomat ritually slaughtered a sheep in his front garden by slitting its throat, to the horror of those of his neighbours who witnessed the incident.[3] Had diplomatic immunity not been claimed a court might have been faced with the difficult question whether or not an offence had been committed under the foregoing provisions of the 1911 Act.[4] Assuming that it could have been established as a fact that unnecessary suffering had been caused to the animal the court would then have had to decide whether this had been done 'unreasonably'. The comments of Roskill LJ in *R v Graham John*[5] referred to earlier[6] would appear to be pertinent to this type of issue and the clear intention of Parliament in enacting the statute would have to be sought. The interests of the community as a whole in reducing cruelty to animals might well be given precedence over the religious beliefs of the defendant. However, an alternative charge, which appears easier to substantiate in such circumstances, is available under s 1(1) (e) of the 1911 Act which makes it an offence to subject an animal to any 'operation' which is performed 'without due care and humanity'. In the unreported case of *R v Efstathiou* a Greek Cypriot was fined £200 by the Avon North Magistrates' Court in 1984 upon conviction of an offence under this subsection after he had slaughtered three goats at his home by cutting their throats.

1 S 1(1) (a).
2 S 1(3) (a).
3 See (1984) Times, 24 and 26 September; *Guardian*, 25 September 1984.
4 A charge might also have been brought in relation to a breach of the peace.
5 [1974] 2 All ER 561 [1974] 1 WLR 624.
6 See para 10.03 above.

3 The wearing of crash helmets by motor-cyclists

10.15 The Road Traffic Act 1972, s 32 empowers the Minister of Transport to make regulations requiring persons driving or riding on motor-cycles to wear protective headgear of such description as he may specify. By s 32(3) any person who drives or rides on a motor-cycle in contravention of such regulations is guilty of an offence. The current regulations require the wearing of helmets complying with particularly high safety standards.[1]

Following a vigorous public campaign by Sikhs and their supporters, an amending Act was passed in 1976 designed to take proper account of the religious custom practised by devout Sikhs of invariably wearing turbans in public places.[2] The Motor-Cycle Crash Helmets (Religious Exemption) Act 1976, s 1 provides that any requirement imposed by regulations under the 1972 Act shall not, whenever made, apply to any follower of the Sikh religion while he is wearing a turban. Although the amending legislation, which was the result of a private member's bill, did not arouse much controversy in Parliament,[3] it is worth drawing attention to the issues which were raised.[4]

The first question was whether the wearing of turbans was really a central feature of the Sikh religion or merely a religious custom. During the course of the campaign which preceded the legislation Sir Herbert Thompson, the last British Resident for the Punjab States during the days of Empire, had written to *The Times*[5] to refute the claim that the wearing of a turban was a specific religious requirement and his views were referred to in the debate in the House of Lords.[6] Despite this, many speakers seemed prepared to accept that if the vast majority of Sikhs in this country felt strongly enough about the religious aspect involved then the central issue involved was indeed one of religious toleration and freedom. Parallels were drawn with the special religious exemptions available in respect of Sunday trading and the slaughter of animals discussed earlier. Mention was also made of comparable road traffic legislation in Singapore, Malaysia, Western Australia and Saskatchewan in terms of which special exemptions were granted to Sikhs.[7]

Second, it was pointed out that to insist upon crash helmets for Sikhs on the roads would tend to undermine the progress made in persuading employers in government and industry to dispense them from the normal requirements of caps, uniforms, hard-hats, etc provided they wore turbans. Such dispensations had already been given in the armed forces (a continuation of the military tradition of British India), the police, bus transport and posts and telecommunications. It would mean, for instance, that each time a Sikh soldier or policeman or post office engineer needed to ride a motor-cycle in pursuance of his duties he would have to break the law or his conscience in the process, even though this was not required when he was engaged in other equally hazardous operations.

Third, concern was briefly expressed at possible abuse by people masquerading as Sikhs. The broad feeling, however, seemed to be that the police would have little difficulty in determining the bona fides of those claiming the exemption. Each of them would, of course, have to be wearing a turban.

The final issue, and probably the most important, was whether the right to religious freedom should triumph over the enforcement of equal treatment under the criminal law where the matter concerned safety on the roads. In fields such as this the imposition of statutory requirements is not purely an act of paternalism on the part of government, for the treatment of injuries is a burden which falls upon the state through the National Health Service. Although even before helmets were made compulsory in 1973 a large majority of motor-cyclists wore them voluntarily, many non-Sikhs did not do so because they regarded them as too irksome and irritating to justify the bother. No doubt these people felt that if Parliament was going to insist upon a regime of compulsion there should be no exemption for special groups.[8] Moreover, the evidence appeared to show quite a significant saving of nearly 120 fatal and 80 serious casualties in the year following the introduction of compulsion.[9]

1 Motor Cycles (Protective Helmets) Regulations 1980, SI 1980/1279.
2 See para 9.13 above.
3 The bill passed through its second and third readings in the House of Commons without a debate: – see 906 HC Official Report (5th series) col 874, 915 HC Official Report (5th series) cols 1142, 1295-6.
4 See HC Standing Committee F, 23 June 1976; 374 HL Official Report (5th series) cols 1055-69, 376 HL Official Report (5th series) cols 1163-75.
5 *The Times*, 11 November 1975.
6 376 HL Official Report (5th series) col 1165.
7 374 HL Official Report (5th series) col 1057.
8 See the poll in the magazine *Motorcycle Rider* referred to in 376 HL Official Report (5th series) col 1168. 69% of respondents to a questionnaire objected to any exemption being granted exclusively to Sikhs.
9 951 HC Official Report (5th series) written answers col 156.

10.16 Although there have been criticisms of the 1976 Act for elevating religious practice above the interests of safety,[1] as well as some protest demonstrations on the streets,[2] it is thought that Parliament was right to grant the exemption. No absolute values are involved in the imposition of health and safety standards upon members of the public principally for their own self-interest, otherwise there would be laws banning smoking, glue-sniffing and boxing. A balance of convenience has to be maintained and deep-seated religious customs are entitled to proper recognition in this sphere. On the other hand, it must be admitted that the 1976 Act appears to go beyond what is required under the European Convention on Human Rights. Art 9(2) of the Convention entitles a state party to impose limitations upon a person's freedom to manifest his religion or beliefs, provided these limitations are prescribed by law and are necessary in a democratic society in the interests of public safety, health or the protection of the rights and freedoms of others.

In *R v Crown Court at Aylesbury, exp Chahal*[3] a Sikh motor-cyclist, who had been convicted under the 1973 regulations before the 1976 Act came into force, had sought an order of mandamus directing the Crown Court to state a case on appeal for the opinion of the High Court. In his grounds of application he sought to pray in aid the provisions of the European Convention, but the Divisional Court dismissed his application as wholly without substance, pointing out simply that no one was bound to ride a motor-cycle. More importantly, a subsequent application to the European Commission of Human Rights by a Sikh who had been prosecuted, convicted and fined 20 times between 1973 and 1976 for failure to wear a crash helmet was declared inadmissible in 1978.[4] The Commission decided that there was no violation of Art 9 because the compulsory wearing of crash helmets was considered to be a necessary safety measure. Any interference with the applicant's freedom of religion was thus justified on the ground of protection of health within Art 9(2) of the Convention.

1 See Samuels 'Legal Recognition and Protection of Minority Customs in a Plural Society in England' (1981) Anglo-American Law Review 241 at 244.
2 See, e g *The Times*, 7 December 1981.
3 [1976] RTR 489.
4 *X v United Kingdom* (1978) 14 Decisions and Reports of the European Commission 234.

4 The scope for further exemptions

10.17 In the light of these three exemptions it may be possible to propose, albeit rather tentatively, certain criteria by which other candidates for special dispensation might be assessed in the future. It would appear that the following conditions would need to be satisfied:

(i)   The offence should not come within the category of really serious crimes and the maximum sentence should be comparatively light. In the case of two of the exemptions just discussed the conduct penalised is probably regarded by many members of the public as scarcely warranting its treatment as an offence at all. On the other hand, perhaps if there is a really strong tide of popular opposition to the statutory enactment of the offence itself, a specific exemption for one minority or religious group should not be created because it may breed so much resentment among the majority that it would ultimately prove to be unacceptable.

(ii)   There should be a firmly established and proven religious basis for the exemption. However, it should not matter whether the religious practice in question is explicitly required by Holy Writ or whether it is the product of long-standing custom so long as it is of an obligatory nature.

(iii)   There should be some reasonably simple method of external verification of the bona fides of anyone claiming the exemption, rather than merely the assertion of the individual concerned. This can be achieved through a requirement for prior registration or by a process of licensing and inspection or by insisting on some form of quid pro quo from members of the exempt group. In the case of crash helmets, for example, Sikhs actually have to wear their turbans and cannot ride motorcycles bareheaded.

In the light of these criteria is there any case for arguing that Rastafarians should be given a special exemption from the cannabis laws on the grounds of their religious beliefs? The first issue involves an assessment of the gravity of the offence. While the possession of *marijuana* by the defendant for his own use is not regarded as a particularly serious offence the closely related crimes of importing, supplying and possession with intention to supply the drug clearly fall within this category. An important question would be whether it is practicable to authorise the official supply of cannabis to Rastafarians while banning any distribution to non-Rastafarians. Under the existing law a doctor may prescribe a controlled drug to his patients and a pharmacist may supply such a drug in the course of his business[1] and a variant of this scheme might possibly prove feasible. On the other hand, a substantial section of the general public believe that the use of cannabis is relatively harmless and should be legalised for everyone and their likely resentment at the creation of any special exemption for Rastafarians is clearly an important factor to be borne in mind, especially since so much of the medical evidence on the subject appears to be inconclusive.[2]

The second question which would need to be answered is whether the use of *marijuana* is an obligatory requirement of the Rastafarian religion comparable, for example, with the consumption of bread and wine at the Christian sacrament of holy communion.

Third, if an exemption were to be introduced there would need to be some system whereby Rastafarians could be distinguished from non-Rastafarians. In the absence of any central organising body for the faith which might regulate any scheme of licensed distribution this would obviously present a further practical difficulty.

It is perhaps worthy of note that courts in the US have experienced considerable problems in handling cases in which American Indians have relied upon the defence of religious freedom in relation to charges under the narcotics laws in respect of their use of *'peyote'*, a hallucinogen containing mescaline derived from a cactus. In some states the defence has succeeded while in others it has failed.[3] Significantly, in the leading case in which the defence was upheld the

California Supreme Court expressly found as a fact that the use of *peyote* by Indians neither resulted in any permanent deleterious effects upon them nor rendered them more likely to become addicted to other drugs.[4] However, in 1982 the Report of the Expert Group on the Effects of the Use of Cannabis (a committee set up by the Advisory Council on the Misuse of Drugs) informed the Home Secretary that there was insufficient evidence to enable the group to reach any incontestable conclusions as to the effects on the human body of the use of cannabis.[5] Although much of the research undertaken had failed to demonstrate positive and significant harmful effects in man, there was evidence to suggest that deleterious effects might result in certain circumstances.

1 Misuse of Drugs Act 1971, s 7(3).
2 See generally, *Report of the Advisory Committee on Drug Dependence: Cannabis* (HMSO, 1968); *Report of the Expert Group on the Effects of Cannabis Use* (Home Office, 1982); J Young *The Drugtakers* (Paladin, 1971); Farrier *Drugs and Intoxication* (Sweet and Maxwell, 1980).
3 See Doyle 'Constitutional Law: Dubious Intrusions – Peyote, Drug Laws and Religious Freedom' (1980) 8 American Indian LR 79.
4 *People v Woody* (1964) 40 Cal Rptr 69 at 74.
5 At para 20.

E. TWO AREAS OF SPECIAL INTEREST

10.18 In two particular fields the details of some of the relevant provisions of the criminal law are felt to warrant separate treatment. These are medical practice and female circumcision.

1 The practice of medicine

10.19 In all societies the practice of medicine is to a large degree shaped and directed by cultural forces; it is far from being limited to the mere application of the exact sciences.[1] The basic patterns and values of particular cultures determine to a significant extent how people view the causes of illnesses and diseases as well as how to prevent, contain and cure them. Religious beliefs and social structures have an important influence on community attitudes and behaviour in relation to what is, as often as not, perceived as 'the art of healing' rather than the science of medicine.

While 'modern' or 'Western' medicine has spread to most parts of the world many societies still find that there remains a substantial role for the application of 'traditional' or 'popular' medicine. In some places this may be based on a belief in magic and witchcraft,[2] in others on the healing properties of various herbs and plants and so on. Among the most notable of the 'traditional' systems are the Ayurvedic (based upon the Vedas or sacred books of Hinduism and involving, for instance, the use of herbs and minerals such as iron and mercury), the Unanic (based on Greek medicine but overlaid with Islamic principles and employing similar remedies) and the Chinese (with its particular concentration on acupuncture).[3] In many instances it is possible to draw a distinction between a traditional 'homeopathic' approach in which diseases are treated by the administration (in very small doses) of drugs which would produce symptoms of the disease in healthy persons and the modern 'allopathic' approach of curing illnesses by remedies which produce effects opposite to that of the ailment. In homeopathic medicine diseases are often seen as manifestations of an imbalance of bodily 'humours' such as bile, phlegm and wind.[4] Diet is commonly regarded as particularly important.

One reason, of course, for the continuing popularity of traditional healers is that they are far more accessible to the bulk of the population in most Third World countries than their Western-trained counterparts, who are found mainly in the urban centres and may well charge substantial fees.

Bearing in mind the inability of 'Western' medicine to cure or even greatly alleviate a substantial number of illnesses and diseases, as well as the strength of many immigrants' beliefs in the efficacy of their own traditional systems of medicine, one can expect these systems to continue to be used in this country. Indeed it would appear that within the various Asian communities here traditional practitioners (known as *'hakims'* in respect of Unanic medicine and *'vaids'* in the case of Ayurvedic medicine) function in much the same way as they do in the Indian subcontinent.[5] Moreover, many members of the white majority are now turning to these and similar forms of 'alternative medicine' in the hope that they may prove more efficacious than the conventional treatment they are offered by their own general practitioner or specialist.[6]

1 See generally FNL Poynter (ed) *Medicine and Culture* (London, 1969).
2 Belief in witchcraft remains widespread in many parts of Africa. See generally E E Evans-Pritchard *Witchcraft, Oracles and Magic among the Azande* (Oxford, 1937).
3 See generally C Leslie (ed) *Asian Medical Systems* (Berkeley, 1977) who makes the valuable point (at pp 6-7) that the terms 'Western' and 'traditional' are liable to be misleading. 'Traditional' medicine is constantly evolving and 'Western' medicine has become truly cosmopolitan.
4 See *Leslie* p 4.
5 Davis and Aslam 'Eastern treatment and eastern health' (1979) Journal of Community Nursing 16.
6 See generally A Stanway *Alternative Medicine* (Penguin, 1982).

Policy considerations

10.20 There are two possible grounds upon which objection might be taken to allowing 'traditional' systems of medicine to be adminstered in this country. The first is that since many of their methods do not stand up to the rigours of Western scientific analysis and their remedies cannot be proved to be effective in controlled clinical trials they should either be outlawed altogether as quackery or in the case of those techniques which can provide some scientific justification for their claims, at least regulated by a proper system of licensing and training. However, although 'Western' medicine is held in very high esteem in this country it is thought that to confer upon it a virtual monopoly in place of the pre-eminence it currently possesses would be too narrow-minded an outlook. While some restrictions may be needed in order to prevent false claims being made by practitioners, the public has a right to the freedom to seek alternative cures in case these prove more efficacious than those offered by 'Western' medicine.

The second area of concern is in the comparatively rare case where it can be scientifically established that a particular 'traditional' remedy constitutes a grave danger to the health of patients, rather than merely not living up to expectations. Here the state is called upon to intervene in the public interest.

Recent research has, for instance, revealed a disturbing association between the use of the Asian medicine and cosmetic known as *'surma'* and dangerously high blood-lead concentrations in those using it here.[1] *Surma* is a fine powder which looks rather like mascara, but instead of being applied to the outside of the eyelids it is painted on to the conjunctival surfaces of the eye. From there it is washed by tears from the eyes, swallowed through the back of the throat and hence absorbed into the blood. Asian parents appear to be applying it here to their children's eyes not only for cosmetic purposes but also to relieve eyestrain and soreness, as well as to ward off evil spirits. The name *surma* is derived from the Urdu word for antimony and the substance has been used in the East for centuries, both for medical and for cosmetic purposes. However, due to the current scarcity of antimony sulphide, *surma* now often contains lead sulphide instead. It would appear that this new form of *surma* is continuing to be used by Asian families here despite government health warnings[2] and in one case it was considered to have contributed to the death of a four-year-old boy in Oldham. Numerous children are being admitted to hospital every year suffering from lead poisoning as a result of using it.

Lead poisoning has also been shown to have been caused by certain other Asian medicines such as the baby herbal tonic 'Bal Jivan Chamcho' (which is distributed with a lead-contaminated spoon) and the aphrodisiac and tonic 'Kushtay' (which may also contain mercury and arsenic).

1 Ali, Smales and Aslam 'Surma and lead poisoning' (1978) 2 BMJ 915; Aslam, Davis and Healy 'Heavy Metals in Some Asian Medicines and Cosmetics' (1979) 93 Public Health (London) 274; Lobo *Children of Immigrants to Britain* (London, 1978) pp 33-4.
2 See Home Office press notice 'Lead Poison Warning' dated 20 September 1968.

English law

(i) QUALIFICATIONS FOR MEDICAL PRACTICE

10.21 Unlike the position in North America and many European countries where the practice of any form of 'traditional' or 'alternative' medicine is illegal unless legislation·specifically permits it (as for example in the case of chiropractic and osteopathy),[1] the English common law takes the more liberal approach of countenancing all forms of such therapy upon one vital condition. This is that the practitioner does not describe himself as a medical doctor.[2]

The Medical Act 1983 (which makes provision for the registration of properly qualified medical practitioners) provides in s 49(1):

'. . . any person who wilfully and falsely pretends to be or takes or uses the name or title of physician, doctor of medicine, licentiate in medicine and surgery, bachelor of medicine, surgeon, general practitioner or apothecary, or any name, title, addition or description implying that he is registered under any provision of this Act or that he is recognised by law as a physician or surgeon or licentiate in medicine and surgery or a practitioner in medicine or an apothecary, shall be liable on summary conviction to a fine . . .'[3]

The precedents establish that it is no defence for someone not registered as a medical practitioner under the Act to show that one of the taboo words that he used was qualified by an explanatory adjective as in expressions such as 'manipulative surgeon'[4] or 'osteopathic physician'.[5]

It is clear from the decision of the Divisional Court in *Wilson v Inyang*[6] that the requirement of 'wilfulness' in the section means that it would be a defence for a 'traditional' therapist to show that he genuinely did not realise that he was not entitled to use one of the medical titles therein designated. The defendant Inyang, an African who had been living in England for about two years, had published an advertisement in a West London newspaper in the following terms: 'Naturopath Physician, ND, MRDP. Patients visited; also evening surgery for chiropody'.

He was prosecuted under the Medical Act 1858. He had never been a registered medical practitioner but he had obtained a diploma in drugless therapy after following a correspondence course, six months' practical training and taking some written examinations. After being awarded the diploma he had obtained a certificate of membership of the British Guild of Drugless Practitioners. He believed that by reason of his course of instruction he was qualified to diagnose diseases within his course of study and to relieve some of these in their early stages by minor manipulation and by prescribing exercises and diet.

The magistrate held that it was a defence for Inyang to show that he genuinely believed he was entitled to call himself a physician and although no-one brought up in England could reasonably hold such a belief in these circumstances it was perfectly reasonable for an African brought up in Africa to do so. On appeal the Divisional Court stressed that the issue was not whether Inyang was acting reasonably in believing in his entitlement to designate himself a physician but whether he honestly held such a belief. Since the magistrate had found as a fact that he did there was no ground for upsetting Inyang's acquittal.

1 See *Stanway* pp 37-9.
2 Cf the wider form of protection afforded to other professional persons such as solicitors and veterinary surgeons who are granted a virtual monopoly: see Glanville Williams *Textbook of Criminal Law* (2nd edn) p 461.
3 This section replaced identical provisions in the Medical Act 1956, s 31, which in turn replaced a provision in the Medical Act 1858.
4 *Jutson v Barrow* [1936] 1 KB 236.
5 *Whitwell v Shakesby* (1932) 147 LT 157.
6 [1951] 2 KB 799, [1951] 2 All ER 237.

(ii) DANGEROUS MEDICINES AND COSMETICS

10.22 In terms of the Medicines Act 1968 the manufacture, sale, supply or import of a medicinal product in the course of a business is prohibited except under a licence from the Department of Health and Social Security. Moreover, where it appears to the Department to be necessary in the interests of safety to prohibit altogether the sale, supply or importation of any medicinal product the Department is empowered to do this by means of a statutory instrument.[1] An order banning 'Bal Jivan Chamcho' indefinitely came into operation in May 1977[2] following the making of an earlier temporary order.

So far as cosmetics are concerned the Consumer Protection Act 1961 authorises the Secretary of State to impose safety requirements with respect to any class of goods available commercially[3] and in 1978, pursuant to the exercise of that power, the Cosmetic Products Regulations came into force.[4] These impose a ban on the incorporation of a large number of substances in cosmetics,[5] including lead, arsenic and mercury.[6] It is now an offence in the course of a business to sell or have in one's possession for the purpose of sale any cosmetic product containing any of the prohibited ingredients.[7] Moreover, there is a general prohibition on sales of any cosmetic product which causes damage to human health when applied under normal conditions of use.[8] This also amounts to an offence, although prosecutions may only be brought upon the consent of the Secretary of State or by or with the consent of the Director of Public Prosecutions.[9]

1 Ss 62 and 129(2).
2 Medicines (Bal Jivan Chamcho Prohibition) (No 2) Order 1977, SI 1977/670.
3 Ss 1 and 2.
4 SI 1978 1354.
5 Reg 4.
6 Sch 1, col 1, nos 57, 380 and 395.
7 Consumer Protection Act 1961, ss 2, 3.
8 The Cosmetic Products Regulations 1978, reg 3.

9 Reg 6(2).

The scope for reform

10.23 There would appear to be at least an arguable case in favour of some form of licensing and registration of 'traditional' and 'alternative' therapists in order to protect the public from 'quacks' and charlatans. Such a system of screening operates in West Germany and it is worth remembering that in India and Pakistan the 'traditional' physicians have to undergo a course of training at university medical school on the same footing as those intending to practise 'Western' medicine and that they are both registered under the same statute.[1] Under the Local Government (Miscellaneous Provisions) Act 1982 local authorities here are now empowered to institute a system of registration for acupuncturists and tattooists and their premises if they so wish,[2] but the main purport of this process of licensing seems to be to ensure the cleanliness of the premises, instruments and persons involved in this form of treatment, rather than the competence of the acupuncturist or tattooist himself. In any event registration is not to be required where acupuncture or tattooing is performed by or under the supervision of a registered medical practitioner.[3]

There also seem to be grounds for banning the importation of *surma* and 'Kushtay' since the prohibition on their commercial sale in this country does not appear to be preventing them from being sent directly here by friends and relatives in the Indian subcontinent.[4] However, the greatest need is for effective communication and education to make members of the Asian communities aware of the dangers to health involved in using these substances.

1 See *Stanway* pp 37-8; Davis and Aslam at 17.
2 Ss 13-17.
3 Ss 14(8), 15(8).
4 See Aslam, Davis and Healy at 279.

2 Female circumcision

10.24 The operations of female circumcision, excision and infibulation carried out in various parts of Africa and Arabia have already been fully described in ch 6 above where the legal implications are analysed in some detail.[1] Allocation of the subject principally to that chapter was felt to be most appropriate since female circumcision mainly relates in practice to the manner in which parents bring up their children. The operations are almost invariably performed at the instigation of the parents before the onset of their daughter's puberty and it is increasingly common for the girls to be less than seven or eight years of age.[2] Performance of such an operation on an adult woman appears to be very rare. However, allegations in 1983 that one or two operations of this type had recently occurred in England[3] led to the criminal offences defined in the Prohibition of Female Circumcision Act 1985 being framed so widely that they cover operations on adult women as well as girls.

1 See paras 6.25-6.33 above.
2 See S McLean *Female Circumcision, Excision and Infibulation* (Minority Rights Group Report No 47) pp 3, 7; A El Dareer *Woman, Why Do You Weep?* (London, 1982) pp 12-13.
3 See 441 HL Official Report (6th series) col 674.

English law

10.25 The Prohibition of Female Circumcision Act 1985, s1(1) provides that it is an offence for any person:

(a) 'to excise, infibulate or otherwise mutilate the whole or any part of the labia majora or labia minora or clitoris of another person; or

(b) to aid, abet, counsel or procure the performance by another person of any of those acts on that other person's own body.'

Section 2 preserves the legality of surgical operations which are necessary for the patient's physical or mental health and are performed by a registered medical practitioner, but in the case of the mental health exemption no account can be taken of the effect on the patient of any belief by herself or any other person that the operation is required as a matter of custom or ritual. There is also an exception for operations performed around the time of childbirth by doctors and midwives and persons training for these professions.

A woman who performs an operation on her own body or who arranges for another person to do so does not herself commit an offence under s 1(1). The wording of s 1(1) (b) is modelled on the Suicide Act 1961, s 2 and reflects the intention of the promoters of the legislation that no liability should attach to the woman in these circumstances.[1]

1 HC Official Report, Standing Committee 'C', 3 April 1985, col 14.

The scope for reform

10.26 Glanville Williams has questioned

'whether the criminal law has any acceptable place in controlling operations performed by qualified practitioners upon adults of sound mind with their consent, whether for reasons of therapy, charity or experiment. Controls exercised by the medical profession itself should be accepted as sufficient. If any particularly serious problems arise they should be left for the consideration of Parliament.'[1]

Was Parliament wise, therefore, to draft the 1985 Act so widely, especially in view of the uncertainty of the previous position at common law?[2] In 1983 the General Medical Council had issued a statement on the subject which concluded:

'In the opinion of the Council, there must be strong and incontrovertible medical indications before the performance of such an operation in the UK can be justified. The Council regards performance of such an operation in the UK on other than medical grounds as unethical.'

On the other hand, a few months earlier it had seemed unwilling to go as far as this,[3] no doubt because of a natural reluctance to undermine the autonomy of the profession to minister to the needs of those patients who sought purely cosmetic surgery for reasons which were closer to the gratification of personal wishes than the product of medical necessity.[4] The difficulty of drawing a valid distinction between the two types of operation has been well brought out by Hayter:

'Purely elective cosmetic surgery is an obvious case where the right of the individual to consent is not seriously questioned. Breast reduction, for example, is an unnecessary and mutilating operation involving considerable pain and scarring to the patient. If justification for its performance were called for, medical evidence of anxiety and depression brought on by the woman's dissatisfaction with her body would undoubtedly be sufficient to outweigh the injury inherent in the treatment . . . Precisely the same justification would be pleaded in support of the legality of female circumcision and should, by analogy, in the absence of further justification for its prohibition, be sufficient. In both cases the women's perception of themselves reflects the demands of the social group to which they belong. The justification is the greater in the case of female circumcision where its necessity extends beyond mere aesthetic appeal, being crucial to the women's status within the group.'[5]

Hayter goes on to argue rather tentatively, however, that there may perhaps be a case for criminalising the circumcision of female adults in order to free women in the communities affected from the pressures to conform which they might otherwise be powerless to resist. Legal paternalism might be justified here because their cloistered lifestyle and state of acute economic dependence deny them any opportunity to form a balanced and informed judgment of the merits and demerits of the practice.[6] This approach, as he admits, still amounts to a slight on their intelligence as well as a denial of the right to self-determination accorded to other women in this sphere.

1 *Textbook of Criminal Law* (2nd edn, 1983) p 590.
2 For doubts as to whether there was criminal liability before the Act, see 450 HL Official Report (6th series) col 220; Hayter 'Female Circumcision – Is There a Legal Solution?' (1984) JSWL 323 at 327.
3 See Mackay 'Is Female Circumcision Unlawful?' [1983] Crim LR 717 at 722.
4 See Hayter at 331.
5 Ibid at 325.
6 Ibid at 326.

Index

Note: references in this index are to paragraph numbers